Community Organizing in a Diverse Society

Third Edition

Community Organizing in a Diverse Society

Felix G. Rivera
San Francisco State University

John L. Erlich
California State University, Sacramento

Allyn and Bacon
Boston • London • Toronto • Sydney • Tokyo • Singapore

Editor-in-Chief, Social Sciences: Karen Hanson
Series Editor, Social Work and Family Therapy: Judy Fifer
Editorial Assistant: Jennifer Muroff
Marketing Manager: Susan E. Brown
Sr. Editorial Production Administrator: Susan McIntyre
Editorial Production Service: Ruttle, Shaw & Wetherill, Inc.
Composition Buyer: Linda Cox
Manufacturing Buyer: Suzanne Lareau
Cover Administrator: Jenny Hart

Library of Congress Cataloging-in-Publication Data

Community organizing in a diverse society / [edited by] Felix G.
   Rivera, John L. Erlich. — 3rd ed.
      p. cm.
   Includes bibliographical references and index.
   ISBN 0-205-26834-X
   1. Community development—United States.   2. Minorities—Housing—
United States.   3. Community organization—United States.
4. Neighborhood—United States.   I. Rivera, Felix G.   II. Erlich,
John.
HN90.C6C6633   1997
307.1'0973—dc21   97-18437
                                                                    CIP

Printed in the United States of America

10 9 8 7 6   RRD-VA   04   03

In Tribute
To our colleague Antonia Pantoja
who received the Presidential Medal of Freedom in 1996
for her continued commitment to poor communities

In Memoriam: Cesar Chavez, 1927–1993

For 41 years, Cesar Chavez taught the poorest people in America to stand up for their rights—and to do it without violence. Against tremendous odds, he organized the first successful farm workers union in U.S. history. He turned compliant and submissive people into courageous champions of their families and communities.

Later, critics would sometimes say Cesar was out of fashion, that people in the 1990s are tired of social causes. But at a time when so few Americans seem willing to risk their careers—much less their lives—on behalf of a principle in which they believe, the life of Cesar Chavez shines through ever more brightly.

His formal education ended after the eighth grade. He never owned a home or earned more than $6,000 a year. He chose a life of self-imposed poverty, grueling hours, and the frequent threat of physical violence and death. Yet his deeds live on in the millions of people he inspired with an unshakable conviction that society can be transformed from within. "You have to convert one person at a time, time after time," he once said. "Progress only comes when people just plow ahead and do it. It takes patience. The concept is so simple that most of us miss it."

Arturo S. Rodrigues, President
United Farm Workers of America, AFL-CIO

Contents

Contributors

Carlos B. Córdova, Ed.D., is professor of La Raza Studies and director of the "Ignacio Martín-Baró" Central American Research Institute at San Francisco State University. A native of El Salvador, Professor Córdova has been actively involved in Central American issues in the San Francisco Bay Area since 1965. He has conducted extensive research on Central Americans in eight different Central American communities in the United States. At the present time, he is conducting research on the transnational cultural experiences of Guatemalans and Salvadorans in California and Central America. This particular project has been funded by the Ford Foundation.

Wynetta Devore, Ph.D., is professor at the School of Social Work, Syracuse University, New York, where she teaches practice. Dr. Devore is coauthor of *Ethnic-Sensitive Social Work Practice.*

E. Daniel Edwards, D.S.W., is associate professor at the Graduate School of Social Work, University of Utah. He is a member of the Yurok tribe and a longtime director of the American Indian Social Work Program at the university. His varied publications reflect his broad concern for Native American cultures.

Margie Egbert-Edwards, Ph.D., is a retired professor of social work at the Graduate School of Social Work, University of Utah; she is the former codirector of the American Indian Social Work Career Training Program.

John L. Erlich, A.B.D., is a professor in the Division of Social Work at California State University, Sacramento, where he has chaired the child and family services concentration and taught a variety of foundation and advanced practice courses. He has worked as an organizer in New York City, Michigan, and Northern California. Professor Erlich has served as a planning and organizing consultant to numerous community-based organizations. He has published extensively in the areas of community organization and planning, social change, emerging minority communities, generalist practice, and burnout. Among the books he has coauthored or edited are *Taking Action in Organizations and Communities, Tactics and Techniques of Community Intervention,* and *Strategies of Community Intervention.*

Lorraine M. Gutiérrez, Ph.D., is an associate professor at the School of Social Work, University of Michigan. She teaches courses in community and organizational services and in the concentration on women and minorities. Her publications have added to the theories about empowerment and women of color. Dr. Gutiérrez has extensive experience organizing against violence against women, particularly within urban, multiethnic communities.

Peter C. Y. Lee, Ph.D., was a professor at the College of Social Work at San Jose State University and director of the Center for Human Service. He is currently working in the administration of the university. He has worked with numerous community organizations such as Asian Americans for Community Involvement, as vice president of the American Cancer Society, as president of Chinese American Economic and Technology Development Association, and currently serves as president of South Bay Charity Cultural Service Center. Dr. Lee has written or edited several books, including *Social Policy Analysis: Theory and Practice* (1994) and *Dimensions of Social Welfare Transition* (1988). He is also on the editorial board of the *Journal of Social Development Issues* and now serves as secretary-general of the Inter-University Consortium for International Social Development.

Edith A. Lewis, Ph.D., is an assistant professor at the School of Social Work, University of Michigan, where she teaches practice. She has done research on social support systems and low-income mothers, and role strain in African American women. Her publications cover such diverse topics as students of color, socialization, and social supports as a prevention strategy.

Miguel Montiel, Ph.D., is a professor in the School of Public Affairs at Arizona State University. He taught at the School of Social Welfare at the University of California, Berkeley, and at Arizona State University's School of Social Work where he also served as assistant vice president for academic affairs. In 1995 Dr. Montiel and a colleague conducted a policy analysis of youth programs for the city of Phoenix, which has led to several publications. He has just coauthored a book (under review) on higher education entitled *No Fair Play.*

Julio Morales, Ph.D., is a professor at the School of Social Work, University of Connecticut. A longtime activist, he has been instrumental in founding Puerto Rican Studies Projects and numerous social service agencies and programs in New York, Massachusetts, and Connecticut.

Royal F. Morales, M.S.W., is a longtime community activist in the Los Angeles Pilipino community. He teaches field work at UCLA and a course in the Pilipino experience in the Asian American studies program. He has been the past director of NASW's Region I, as well as NASW's representative to the Committee to Rebuild Los Angeles. His organizing work has emphasized alcohol-related services for Pilipino and Tongan youth. Mr. Morales builds and demonstrates the art of Pilipino kites. His kites have been represented at cultural fairs, on television, and in museums.

Kenji Murase, D.S.W., is a retired professor from the Department of Social Work Education, San Francisco State University. His areas of teaching and community involvement are minority issues, research, and program planning and development, to mention a few. He is noted for his teaching, research, and grantsmanship skills and many publications pertaining to Asian American communities.

Felipe Ortego y Gasca, Ph.D., is professor of English at Arizona State University. He has taught English and Chicano literature at various universities. He is a long-time activist.

Antonia Pantoja, Ph.D., has taught at the schools of social work at Columbia University and the University of Puerto Rico. She has also taught at the New School for Social Research, New York. She has been responsible for the development of such organizations as the Puerto Rican Association for Community Affairs, The Puerto Rican Forum, Aspira, and Boricua College. In 1984 she began to work with residents to organize Producir, Inc., a community economic development corporation in Canovanas, Puerto Rico. Dr. Pantoja's publications reflect a broad-based commitment to multicultural approaches to social change and community development. She is also a consulting editor to the *Journal of Progressive Human Services.* Dr. Pantoja's acceptance of the highest civilian award, the president's Medal of Freedom, is an eloquent affirmation of an accomplished career that is still going strong.

Wilhelmina Perry, Ph.D., was a faculty member at the School of Social Work, Stony Brook, N.Y. Dr. Perry has been adjunct faculty for students in alternative educational programs, such as the Union Graduate School, Rural Development Leadership Network, and the Western Institute for Social Research. She resigned her tenured faculty position at the School of Social Work, San Diego State University, to organize, administer, and teach with Dr. Pantoja at the Graduate School for Community Development, a private alternative educational institution working with low-income and people of color learners from communities around the United States. She helped establish Producir, Inc. She is a consulting editor to the *Journal of Progressive Human Services.*

Felix G. Rivera, Ph.D., is a professor in the Department of Social Work Education, San Francisco State University, where he has chaired the social development concentration and teaches social and evaluative research. Dr. Rivera has been a grassroots organizer in East Los Angeles and northern California and has worked with numerous community-based organizations as a planner, program developer, and evaluator. He has worked as a consultant with HUD, NIMH, the YMCA, and ASBA to mention a few organizations. His research and numerous publications range in subject from emerging and changing communities of color and social change to the application of Bushido (martial arts) strategies to community organizing and decision making. He is on the editorial boards of the *Journal of Community Practice, Journal of Progressive Human Services,* and the *Humboldt Journal of Social Relations.*

Vu-Duc Vuong, M.A., M.S.W., J.D., has been the executive director and economic development specialist with the Southeast Asian Refugee Resettlement Center. He was born in Nam Dinh, Vietnam, and came to the United States in 1968. Mr. Vuong is highly visible throughout the refugee communities in the San Francisco Bay Area both as an economic developer and as a social activist. He was the first Vietnamese American to run for political office in San Francisco, California. Mr. Vuong is the president of the Southeast Asian Chamber of Commerce, another vehicle to promote trade and understanding between the United States and Southeast Asia.

Preface

Yeah, it was the smells. Even more than the sights and sounds, the neighborhoods where we grew up had rhythms defined by smells. Aromas of frying pork and plantains, simmering pasta and sausage, boiling cabbage and chicken greeted a homecoming as we returned to our apartments after school or a gutter game of stickball.

The city streets were alive with people and action—talking, walking, playing, bartering, or just hanging out. Children were admonished from front windows by their observing parents, grandparents, aunts and uncles, other extended family (not necessarily their own) in Spanish, Italian, Yiddish, or variously accented English. Although not always delivered with a full appreciation of who had done what to whom, the comments on youthful misbehavior were made with commanding vigor and directness. It was usually some variant of, "Stop, or else!" (and the "or else" was likely to be embarrassing, to hurt, or both). We didn't have much privacy, but each of us felt a deep and abiding sense of belonging.

We were privileged to see a diversity of ages and kinds of people: very old and very young; tradespeople, mothers with children, winos, and numbers runners; brown, black, and white (and occasional Asians). The city blocks of the easily identified geography of our youth had natural cadences of time and activity. It made sense to us, and there was a power to it that we somehow shared.

The idea for this book has been part of each of us since the 1950s. Growing up in New York City's Spanish Harlem and Upper West Side, we did not know what special communities we shared. Indeed, it was the resurgence of community organization in the 1960s and 1970s and our own involvement in it—as organizers, teachers, and consultants—that led us to take a more careful look at our roots. We realized that these roots, despite the problems of poverty, racial conflict, gang violence, alcoholism, and drugs, had been a major source of nurturance, strength, and validation for us both.

In each of our neighborhoods, an important part of what made them places of identity and empowerment were elements of ethnic solidarity. Aspects of language and religion, similarities of economic status and life situation, contributed to this solidarity. The contempt of more affluent surrounding communities also contributed to defensive but also supportive mutual aid efforts.

The vicious attack on affirmative action of the late 1990s has thrown the sense of continuity and meaning that we experienced in these neighborhoods into high relief. The systematic disparaging of the validity of ethnic communities, despite very loud political rhetoric to the contrary, is part of the heritage of the 1980s and early 1990s. The recent past has seen an unparalleled emphasis in the media on gangs, drugs, teen pregnancy, disease, and drive-by shootings (especially of people for being in the wrong place at the wrong time) that neglects a vital part of this drama. That part has very much to do with communities of color waging an uphill struggle to protect their integrity and build their power. It is also about two kids growing up with an undeniable belief that people can come together to enrich their lives and increase their influence with the forces that control their destinies. Of the many promises of the twenty-first century, this is not one to be ignored.

This third edition of our book gives us a special pleasure. The revisions keep us up to date in a time of great turmoil, with additional emphasis on case studies, intervention strategies, needed skills, and the most current problems facing each community.

We particularly want to thank the reviewers of the first edition—Robert F. Vernon, University of Indianapolis; Wynne DuBray, California State University, Sacramento; Terry Mizrahi, Hunter College; and Chester H. Jones, the State University of New Jersey–Rutgers—as well as those of the second edition—Glenn E. Rohrer, East Carolina University, and Michael Reisch, University of Pennsylvania—who made a number of valuable suggestions. Also, we are grateful to Adelle Sanders and Andy Bein of California State University, Sacramento, who offered especially useful critiques. Judy Fifer of Allyn and Bacon was supportive and patient throughout the development of this edition.

The exceptional support our text has received indicates its value in these very difficult times. It heartens and reminds us how many of you out there are committed to the struggle for lasting change in communities of color across the nation.

1

A Time of Fear;
A Time of Hope

FELIX G. RIVERA AND JOHN L. ERLICH

What is to be done, and what remedy is to be applied? I will tell you, my friends. Hear what the Great Spirit has ordered me to tell you! You are to make sacrifices, in the manner that I shall direct; to put off entirely from yourselves the customs which you have adopted since the white people came among us; you are to return to that former happy state, in which we live in peace and plenty, before these strangers came to disturb us, and above all, you must abstain from drinking their deadline besonm (liquor) which they have forced upon us for the sake of increasing their gains and diminishing our numbers.... Wherefore do you suffer the whites to dwell upon your lands? Drive them away; wage war against them.[1]

Little did the Delaware leader know that his warning of the destruction of his people would reflect many of the concerns of people of color approaching the turn of the twenty-first century. Indeed, the media attention devoted to violence, gangs, and drug traffic has heightened the popular view of ethnic minority communities (especially poor ethnic communities) as devastated disaster areas that might best be dealt with by eradication. The people who reside in the communities often feel surrounded and under siege.

In this time of declining real wages (for the working poor) and rising rents, more than five million households are paying more than 50 percent of their pretax income for shelter.[2] (The federal standard for "affordable" is no more than 30 percent of a family's income.) Worse, less than one-third of the fifteen million qualified for housing assistance can get it. Indeed, in many cities, waiting lists have long been closed. The necessary funding just is not there. The U.S. Conference of Mayors has noted that, in 1996, 24 percent of requests for shelter from families with children were denied because of capacity limits. These inadequacies fall most heavily on communities of color and further contribute to their sense of isolation and oppression.

Despite these multiple (and increasing) constraints facing communities of color, however, an important undercurrent of organizing activities continues in many of them. Unheralded and largely unappreciated, these efforts are going forward in urban, rural, and changing suburban areas.

Moreover, very little written material is available to guide such efforts among people of color. Until the first edition of this text was published in 1992, a book on community organizing with people of color did not exist. The reasons for this deficiency are multiple, complex, and interwoven. Racism—economic, political, and social—is at the core. Most recent changes in social provisions have brought with them further damage to the reputation of poor communities of color. Never popular, the problems of the poor have suffered from a further reduction in declining societal interest. A brief review of recent diminished attention to the homeless, to cite but one example, makes this trend painfully clear.

Despite the great bulk of research evidence that indicates the sources of oppression and poverty as outside communities of color, the disenfranchised are again being told to shoulder the responsibility for their inability to leap into the middle class. The declining resource base has had its most powerful impact on poor communities of color in relation to such issues as substance abuse, crime, AIDS, substandard housing, teen pregnancy, failing schools, developmental disability, unemployment, and underemployment. As things now stand, it is as if society has chosen poor communities of color to be the scapegoat for much of what is wrong in the United States today.

The proportion of the population represented by people of color needs to be taken into consideration much more openly and honestly. U.S. Bureau of the Census projections for 1996 (middle series) suggest a total population of 265,253,000, of whom 33,611,000 are African American; 2,273,000 are American Indian, Eskimo, and Aleut; 9,728,000 are Asian and Pacific Islander; and 27,804,000 are Hispanic. Thus African Americans represent 12.7 percent of the population, an increase of 10.9 percent since 1990; American Indians, Eskimos, and Aleuts 0.9 percent, an increase of 11 percent; Asian and Pacific Islanders 3.7 percent, an increase of 29.2; and Hispanics 10.5 percent, an increase of 24.7 percent. These numbers and the problems and potentials they represent can only be ignored at the nation's peril. Note that the Census Oversight Committee (and others) have suggested a continuing problem with undercounting the poor and disenfranchised, especially people of color.

The U.S. government's so-called peacekeeping and stabilization efforts in Central America, the Persian Gulf, Africa, and Bosnia have contributed, perhaps unintentionally, to a lowered commitment to racial equality at home. In part, we can attribute this to a sense that people of color (and others "not like us") have absorbed too many of our societal resources and thus our domestic "others" must settle for less. Anecdotes about the undeserved promotion (and hiring) of people of color are legion.

U.S. priorities in foreign affairs, along with the most recent realignment of domestic preferences, have sharply reduced already depleted resources needed to train people to work in community organization and development. Often the rhetoric of diversity has been a smoke screen to dodge funding desperately needed programs in ethnic enclaves. All too many joint police and community antidrug efforts, for example, make a good photo opportunity for those in power, but do little to address fundamental issues of poverty and racism.

Of all social work methods, community organization has been the most resistant to consistent definition, which has further exacerbated the situation. As we have noted elsewhere, community organization has evolved from being the general rubric under which all social work practice beyond the level of individual, family, and small group was subsumed—including grassroots organizing, community development, planning, administration, and policy making—to being the smallest subsegment of macro-level practice (where it exists at all). Perhaps this definitional difficulty is well illustrated by what we believe is one of the better contemporary definitions of community organization:

> *Community Development refers to efforts to mobilize people who are directly affected by a community condition (that is, the "victims," the unaffiliated, the unorganized, and the nonparticipating) into groups and organizations to enable them to take action on the social problems and issues that concern them. A typical feature of these efforts is the concern with building new organizations among people who have not been previously organized to take social action on a problem.[3]*

However, by any definition, it was not until the 1960s that large numbers of schools of social work were willing to regard community organization as a legitimate concentration. Majors in community organization in graduate schools increased from 85 in 1960 to 1,124 in 1969, or from 1.5 percent to over 9 percent of full-time enrollments.[4]

By 1990 the number of students nationwide training to work as organizers had declined significantly. The Council on Social Work Education's most recent statistics show 154 master's degree students (1.8 percent) in community organization (CO) and planning, 417 (4.9 percent) in administration and management, and 101 (1.2 percent) in a combination of CO and planning with administration or management. Despite growing acceptance as a legitimate area of study in social work, urban planning, and labor studies, community organization and planning has been held hostage by the political and social vagaries of a society that has never accepted its strategies and tactics, especially if methods such as public demonstrations and boycotts caused disruption or embarrassment to those in positions of political authority and power.

With the sharp decline in financial support of community-based work (at the community rather than at the individual or small-group level), and the concomitant reduction in academia's willingness to support communities of color in conflicts with established centers of political power, the educational commitment to organizing has been severely undermined. There are currently few field placement opportunities, few courses, and a sparse recent literature. This is particularly surprising in light of documented successes of community organization and development during the 1960s and early 1970s.[5]

Community organizing and community development by people of color have been virtually ignored. Isolated electives and rare articles in the professional journals have done little to fill this void. Work of a multicultural nature has received only slightly more attention. No book is available that addresses a broad range of the organizing efforts currently proceeding in diverse minority communities. This book is an effort to remedy that situation.

What is the current status of community organization practice? The civil rights gains of the 1960s in voting entitlements, public accommodations, and job opportunities, for example, were tempered by the belief that the African American community had gone too far, that its gains were based on unacceptable levels of violence. Quickly forgotten by the white community was the continuing history of violence experienced by African Americans and other communities of color. "What more do they want?" was more than mere inflammatory rhetoric. These gains seemed to threaten white job security, community housing patterns, and long cherished social interaction networks. The bitter residue of racism remains, and the resentment experienced throughout much of the United States has been part of the conservative backlash we are witnessing (as everything from skinheads and antiminority high school violence to English-only public school curricula poignantly illustrates).

Similarly, efforts toward enfranchisement of new voters, changes in immigration laws, and women's and gay rights have also suffered from the limits imposed by methods deemed acceptable and resulting in supposedly reasonable benefits. As long as someone else did the social protesting—and as long as it was far enough away from their homes and places of work—most white people did not complain actively or resist publicly slow, nondisruptive changes. A concomitant shift has marked the reluctant acceptance of the "worthy" among each ethic minority (largely dependent on whose economic interests are being threatened) while at the same time rejecting those without education or job skills or at high risk for drug problems and sexually transmitted diseases.

Not surprisingly, with the emergence of reverse discrimination as a legitimate response to the enfranchisement of people of color, a new consciousness has permeated schools of social work whose espoused philosophy is commitment to aiding poor and oppressed populations. It is no longer fashionable to invite an ex-Black Panther as a speaker for a seminar on social action, or a Young Lord from New York's Puerto Rican community to discuss how they initiated the movement against lead poisoning in New York's slum tenements, or to have Angela Davis address the systematic exclusion of women of color by the women's movement in key policy and strategy sessions. "Bloods" and "Crips" have disappeared from the main menu of educational guest speakers, and even Jesse Jackson no longer is much in demand. Instead, the invited ethnic so-called leaders focus on issues such as creatively funded drug education programs, multicultural day-care and preschool efforts, and the demographics of rapidly expanding minority youth populations around the country.

As funding has evaporated, and the financial success of relatively few people of color—athletes, entertainers, entrepreneurs, selected professionals—is touted in the media, most people of color again find themselves in the not-so-symbolic back of the bus. Ferocious attacks on affirmative action have become not only trendy but expected. Anticipatory retreats from affirmative action, even before political and legal challenges have run their course, are at hand everywhere. Ethnic studies courses, as well as programs, continue to be eliminated and drastically cut back, and inner-city services are also on the chopping block. It would appear that state courts and the U.S. Supreme Court will continue to be called on to roll back many of the civil rights gains of the last forty years.

People of Color and Organizing: A Troubled Alliance

Why has community organization not been more successful in working with people of color? What happened to some of the cross-cultural efforts that appeared to be so productive in the 1960s and early 1970s? Traditionally, much of the writing on community organization attempts to be color blind. It has been our experience and that of many of the contributing authors here that organizers work with specific strategies and tactics applied to different situations, but the methods that combine them rarely—if ever—change.[6]

Alinsky's mobilization model is a good case in point.[7] Too often the level of analysis of a community's problems has been determined by an organizing strategy that identifies a particular strata of people or social problem for intervention, and, by doing so, ignores the racial and cultural uniqueness of the community. We are not writing about conservative or even liberal community organizers but well-intentioned, progressive-thinking organizers who have been victimized by what may be termed "organizers' myopia" because of their single-minded organizing ideology or preordained methodology.[8]

Readily apparent in the readings here is the absence of an easily identified "radical" or "progressive" ideology along class lines. That does not mean the authors are apolitical, far from it. What it does indicate, however, is that issues surrounding race and culture are often more urgent concerns than social class, which historically has often been conceptualized by white theoreticians apart from the dynamics deemed more critical to the self-determination of communities of color by communities of color. Middle-class Asians, Latinos, Native Americans, or African Americans are still viewed as minorities because of a most easily identifiable characteristic: appearance.

Good clothes and an elegant briefcase are not much help when you need a cab in the middle of the night in Chicago or Washington, D.C.

People of color traditionally have been caught between the polarized struggles of conservative and liberal theoretical forces. On the one hand, too many liberal community organizers have emphasized class issues at the expense of racism and cultural chauvinism, relegating them to supposedly logical extensions of the political and economic structure. Much of the neo-Marxist literature has treated race from a reductive, negative posture: "superexploitation" and the "divide and conquer" strategies of individual capitalist employers. On the other hand, many conservative thinkers have emphasized a kind of uniqueness of each community, which divides it from other communities of color, as well as separating those who can "make it" from those who cannot.[9]

These perspectives largely disregarded many questions, including the fact that racism existed long before monopoly capitalism was institutionalized. Racial harmony does not necessarily follow the passing of capitalism, as the persistence of racial antagonism in postcapitalist societies (such as Sweden) demonstrates. The structural analysis that leads to a unified ideological interpretation of racism is thus deficient.

What too many organizers fail to consider is that little or no history or contemporary evidence substantiates that relations established and legitimated on the basis of race were or are identical to those established and legitimated on the basis of class. For example, we cannot explain the increasing violence against students of color on college campuses primarily as a class phenomenon, especially when we recognize that many of these students of color are similar economically to the white students attacking them. By continuing to look at racism mostly as a broad structural issue, organizers underestimate the roles played by schools, churches, social welfare agencies, and other institutions in negatively influencing and changing race relations.

How might we best define the equality and liberation struggles being waged by African American communities? Native American communities? Chinese American and Vietnamese American communities? The communities of women of color? The immediate reaction of most oppressors is based on skin color and other physical characteristics, language, and culture, then class. The oversimplification of the struggles of people of color has led to unwarranted generalizations about their economic, social, political, and cultural behaviors and attitudes as groups.

Writers criticize the tendency of mainstream and radical theorists to divide society into separate cultural and structural domains. They argue that this arbitrary distinction promotes essentialism (single-cause explanations) in thinking about race. Race and culture cannot be separated. They have to be linked to other social processes and dynamics operating in a society that continues oppressing communities because of skin tone. We hold that at least three dynamics—race, class, and gender—are significant in understanding oppression and the roles played by social welfare institutions in that process. None are reducible to the others, and class is not necessarily paramount.[10]

The phenomenological day-to-day realities of race, language, class, gender, sexual orientation, and age help shape ideological perspectives and enforce the hostilities with which one lives (as well as the strengths that make survival possible). The resulting process is difficult to analyze because it manifests itself differently from one community to another across the country, thereby making the task of organizing against these attacks that much more difficult a challenge. These realities do not lend themselves easily to simple categorizations by agents of social change or schools teaching community organization practice. The need for a more integrated and receptive social change paradigm in working with communities of color must be a main goal of organizers.

The conservative tradition in community organizing—especially within social work education—has also had an impact on the way organizers of color and their communities view the political implications of the social change efforts in which they have been involved. The conventional perspective that education should be ideologically value free and politically nonpartisan has been especially evident in community organizing. Typical traditional textbooks on organizing have avoided clear political and moral positions on issues.[11] These books were guided by a professional and largely mechanistic value base.

As Fisher notes,

> *The social work tradition views the community essentially as a social organism; it focuses on social issues such as building a sense of community, gathering together social service organizations, or lobbying for and delivering social resources. It assumes that basically the community's problem is social disorganization. The organizer functions either as an "enabler" to help the community gather itself together or as an advocate to secure additional services for the community. The strategy is gradualist and consensual, which means that organizers assume a unity of interest between the power structure and the neighborhood and assume a willingness of at least some in power to meet community needs.*[12]

In contrast, Friere proposes that "one cannot be a social worker and be like the educator who's a coldly neutral technician. To keep our options secret, to conceal them in the cobwebs of technique, or to disguise them by claiming neutrality does not constitute neutrality; quite the contrary, it helps maintain the status quo."[13]

Many professors of macro practice still resist including discussions of analyzing power and confrontational empowerment, the development of critical consciousness, and racism as fundamental components of community organization. The lack of attention to critical consciousness—that is, how personal and political factors interact with each other and one's work, as well as how values, ideas, and practice skills are influenced by social forces and, in turn, influence them—is both particularly noteworthy and undermining. This neoconservative stance has had the net effect of leaving students of color (as well as white students) confused about their potential roles in their communities and how far they might go in fighting racism and social injustices.

Although the rhetoric of self-determination implies that students are intended to be agents of social change, the reality clearly calls for modest improvements that do not seriously upset the status quo. The tools that might help lead to more fundamental change through a thorough questioning of what is happening and what it means to a community and a person working there are largely absent from the curriculum. Indeed, a number of authors have suggested a general decline in the significance of ethnic communities (or communities in general).

Kreuger argues, "Neighborhoods and communities which have historically buffered the individual and provided human services support from a distance will soon be made economically superfluous. The era of postindustrial corporate dominance will assure that little remains of neighborhood or community identity."[14]

A Paradigm for Organizing with People of Color

The different racial and cultural characteristics present in oppressed and disadvantaged communities represent an unprecedented challenge to organizers as we move into the twenty-first century. We define culture as a collection of behaviors and beliefs that constitute standards for deciding what is, standards for deciding what can be, standards for deciding how one feels about it, standards for deciding what to do about it, and standards for deciding how to go about doing it. A recent history of benign or belligerent neglect has required people of color to mobilize their skills and limited resources in creative ways that challenge prevailing community programs. Although they get little attention or help from mainstream society—indeed, in some areas, overt opposition is more typical—many of those communities are trying to tackle their problems with strategies unique to their situations.

For example, the African American community of West Oakland, California, has attacked the drug problem head on, with many community leaders making themselves visible enemies of major dealers. Nearby, an African American first grade teacher has promised to pay for the college education of her entire first grade class if they maintain a C average and go on to college. The teacher saves $10,000 annually from her modest salary for this fund. In the rural mountains of eastern Puerto Rico there is an exciting revitalization of the community through an energetic community development program. Southeast Asian communities in Boston, New York, Houston, and San Francisco have organized legal immigration and refugee task forces to help fight the arbitrary deportation of undocumented workers. Derelict neighborhoods in New York, Chicago, and Philadelphia are being revitalized through cooperatives and community development activities. Native American tribes are attacking problems of alcoholism through indigenous healing rituals involving the sweat lodge ceremony. Success rates are often dramatic. In the village of Akhiok, Alaska, 90 percent of its adults were chronically drunk. After native treatments, at least 80 percent were able to sustain sobriety. The Latino community in Boston has a grassroots health program called Mujeres Latina en Action, which has successfully integrated third-world health models that include the concept of the extended family in health-care delivery systems. A culture- and gender-sensitive model of community organization is used to reach women in the barrios.

Communities of color traditionally have not been involved in issues related to ecology and the protection of the environment. For many neighborhoods, these are among the last priorities listed of the many problems people face. However, one example deserves special attention, for it may well be a model for similar actions across the country. In California's East Los Angeles, which is predominantly Mexican American/Chicano, a group of Latina mothers was organized by a parish priest in the mid-1980s into militant urban ecologists. They call themselves Mothers of East Los Angeles. They have successfully mobilized against threats to their community, such as (1) the construction of a state prison in a residential area near neighborhood schools, (2) an above ground oil pipeline that would have cut through their middle- to low-income barrio while avoiding much more affluent coastal towns, (3) the local use of dangerous and potentially polluting pesticides, and (4) local construction of a large incinerator. They believe in peaceful tactics and wear white kerchiefs as a symbol of their nonviolent philosophy. They are often seen pushing strollers during demonstrations, and they lobby at the state capitol, engage in letter writing campaigns, and serve as pacesetters for a growing environmental movement in the Los Angeles area among people of color.

From an ethnically sensitive practice perspective, organizing strategies in the Vietnamese or Laotian communities (and with different ethnic groups within these communities) cannot be the same as in Puerto Rican, African American, Native American, or Japanese American enclaves. The experience of one of the editors illustrates this point. In the early 1970s he was organizing in a Mexican American barrio. One of the outcomes of the struggle was the establishment of a storefront information and referral center. In furnishing and decorating the center, several political and cultural posters were displayed, much to the anger of some of the *viejitos* (elders) in the neighborhood. One particular poster featured Emiliano Zapata. Several fathers of the *viejitos* had fought against Zapata during the Mexican Revolution. Although the editor is a Latino, he is not of Mexican descent. However, he does know the conflicting loyalties of Mexico's revolutionary history and should have checked with the community to be sure none of the posters would be offensive. This apparently innocuous mistake set the organizing effort back many months and required the staff to work doubly hard to regain the community's confidence.

Unfortunately, the history of organizing is replete with such examples. Certainly organizers of color must accept a share of the blame. However, the overwhelming majority of organizing writers and practitioners are white males, many of whom come from liberal or radical traditions and most of whom got their theoretical and practice feet wet in the social upheavals of the 1960s. Their apparent successes seemed destined to be color blind. From a community perspective, white radical groups were often more enamored of their political ideologies than they were committed to the needs of specific minority neighborhoods. We experienced many situations in which communities of color were waging important struggles. The Detroit-based battles of African Americans within the United Auto Workers are a prime example. Frequently hovering on the fringes were white radical groups looking to make the struggle their own. They were very critical of the efforts of people of color, accusing them of being culturally nationalistic and methodically not progressive enough. Too often we forget that experiencing racism, economic deprivation, and social injustice are the key relevant politicizing forces in most urban areas. Indeed, it was this kind of elitist attitude that caused many minority organizers to shy away from predetermined ideological postures that seemed to define peoples for them. Even many liberal white groups seemed to disdain poor whites in favor of more visible organizing efforts in communities of color.

Thus it is not sufficient to identify the three classic (and presumably "color-blind") models of community practice—locality development, social planning, and social action—as the foundation within which community organizing with people of color takes place. Factors that must be addressed are (1) the racial, ethnic, and cultural uniqueness of people of color; (2) the implications of these unique qualities in relation to such variables as the roles played by kinship patterns, social systems, power, leadership networks, religion, the role of language (especially among subgroups), and the economic and political configuration within each community; and (3) the process of empowerment and the development of critical consciousness. (This contrasts with what Freire has called "naive consciousness," or a tendency to romanticize intense, satisfying past events and force the same experiences into the future without fully taking into account such multidimensional elements as those just noted.) In addition, the physical setting within which the community finds itself is an essential component for consideration because it plays a significant part in the way people view their situation. The need for a new, revised paradigm is clear and urgent.[15]

One of the most critical factors affecting organizing outcomes hinges on determining how strategies and tactics are played out. These are based on the nature and intensity of contact and influence that help determine the constraints placed on the organizers' (whether indigenous or not) knowledge and identification with the community and when and how technical skills may be brought into play. This "meta approach" helps organizers arrange their strategies and tactics within boundaries that are goal, task, skill, and process specific. We suggest that the degree and nature of contacts is a three-tier process that—for the sake of simplicity—may be conceptualized as contact intensity and influence at the primary, secondary, and tertiary community levels (see Figure 1.1).

The primary level of involvement, which requires racial, cultural, and linguistic identity, is the most immediate and personal in the community. It is the most intimate level of community involvement in which the only way of gaining entry is to have full ethnic solidarity with the community. For example, this level would not be pos-

Community Levels

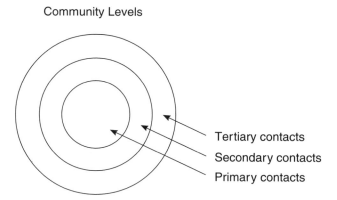

FIGURE 1.1   Organizer's Contact Intensity and Influence

sible for a Chinese American in a Vietnamese or African American area or a Turkish Muslim in an Arab American area.

The secondary level is one step removed from personal identification with the community and its problems. Language—although a benefit and help—is not absolutely mandatory. Many of the functions are those of liaison with the outside community and institutions and service as a resource with technical expertise based on the culturally unique situations experienced by the community. Examples of persons able to work at this level include a Puerto Rican in a Mexican American neighborhood or a person who identifies herself or himself as Haitian in an African American area.

The tertiary level is that of the outsider working for the common interest and concern of the community. Cultural or racial similarity is not a requirement. These organizers are involved primarily with outside infrastructures as advocates and brokers for communities of color. However, their tasks are less that of liaisons than of helpful technicians approaching or confronting outside systems and structures. Clearly, whites and dissimilar people of color may be particularly effective at this level.

Devore, in Chapter 4, has applied our contact model in conceptualizing the strategies and tactics necessary in organizing with Communities United to Rebuild Neighborhoods (CURN). The three levels of contact intensity are applied to a contemporary settlement house community development effort.

Whether organizers should be members of the racial and cultural groups with whom they work has been a subject of major controversy since the mid-1960s, both within and outside communities of color. Sol Alinsky and his Industrial Areas Foundation organizers, for example, often found themselves in the middle of this conflict.[7] However, a careful review of the evolution of their efforts suggests that, in most cases, indigenous organizers (paid or not) played key roles in the success of the organizations they helped build. If communities of color are to empower themselves by giving more than symbolic recognition to the ideal of self-determination and community control, they must search hard for the successful roles played by people within their own communities and the lessons they can teach outside organizers. Furthermore, many emerging communities are underrepresented in local and regional power systems both because they have been stigmatized as overusers of resources and because their languages and customs (the Hmong, for example) demand specialized knowledge and skills. In the broad range of emerging Southeast Asian communities, for example, there are nationalities, ethnic, and subethnic groups whose cultures are quite different from one another and who use an assortment of languages, dialects, and idioms. An outside organizer simply does not stand a chance of gaining rapid access to such unique and insular community groups. The Native American nations speak more than two hundred different languages. Clearly, special care must be taken in recruiting people to work in widely varied Indian communities—on reservations and rancherias, in both rural and urban areas.

The knowledge necessary to understand and appreciate customs and traditions in all communities presents an incredible challenge.[16] Organizing and social change strategies are complex and stressful enough without further exacerbating the community's problems by using organizers who have very limited (or no) awareness of their customs, traditions, and languages. These people have served and should continue to serve effectively in secondary and tertiary roles. But the most successful organizers are those who know their culture intimately—its subtleties of language, mores, and folkways. A white outsider, however sensitive and knowledgeable, simply cannot appreciate all that needs to be considered about a fundamentally different nonwhite culture or subculture. Wannabes, like many political hangers-on, are particularly dangerous because a single serious error can undermine an organizational effort. Some newly emerging communities are so well defended, there would be little chance for an outsider to gain meaningful admission to them, not to mention become a successful organizer. However, cultural and racial similarity by themselves are no guarantor of organizer effectiveness or community acceptance. Indeed, an arrogant, know-it-all insider may be viewed with more suspicion than a similarly styled outsider.[17]

Despite these difficulties, common practice elements may be identified as prerequisites to successful organizing. These principles are not exhaustive, but if organizers take command of these elements, they can increase the likelihood of being effective change agents in their communities. Knowing when and how to mix and phase in these strategies and skill areas is critical to a successful outcome. Organizing has to be conceptualized as a process that is educational for both the community and the organizers.

Organizer's Profile

What follows is a summary of those qualities—knowledge, skill, attributes, and values—that we believe are most important for the success of organizers. The list is an idealized one; those few who have already fully attained the lofty heights described can probably also walk on water. Realistically, it is more a set of goals to be used by organizers and communities together to help achieve desired changes. Note that many of these qualities are addressed later by each contributor in describing a particular community. You will find illustrations and examples of parts of this model in progress throughout the chapters that follow.

1. *Similar cultural and racial identification.* The most successful organizers are those activists who can identify culturally, racially, and linguistically with their communities. There is no stronger identification with a community than truly being a part of it.

2. *Familiarity with customs and traditions, social networks, and values.* A thorough grounding in the customs and traditions of the community being organized is especially critical for those people who have cultural, racial, and linguistic identification, but who, for a variety of reasons, have been away from that community and are returning as organizers.

For example, how have the dynamics between organized religion and the community changed over the last decade? Ignored, its effect may imperil a whole organizing effort. Both defining the problems and setting goals to address them are involved. A number of Latino mental health and advocacy programs regularly consult with priests, ministers, and folk healers about the roles they all play (or might play) in advocating mental health needs. These mental health activists are very clear about the importance of these other systems—formal and informal—in the community's spiritual life. The superstitions and religious archetypes are addressed by a variety of representatives, thereby making the advocacy work that much more relevant and effective. The Native American nations defer to their medicine man and take no actions until he has given approval. Similarly, the Vietnamese, Cambodian, and Laotian communities have strong religious leaders who help define community commitments and directions. At the same time, in these communities, as well as in most other communities of color, historical traditions must be acknowledged and respected.

All too often there exists a cultural gap, as typified by younger, formally educated organizers working with community elders. The elders may be too conservative for the young organizers, or they may disagree about tactics. Knowledge of and appreciation for the culture and traditions will help close the gap among key actors or at least reduce the likelihood of unnecessary antagonisms.

3. *An intimate knowledge of language and subgroup slang.* We separate this dimension from the one just mentioned to emphasize its importance. Knowledge of a group's language style is indispensable when working with communities that are bi- or monolingual. Many embarrassing situations have arisen because of the organizer's ignorance of a community's language style. Approved idiomatic expressions in one area of the community may be totally unacceptable in another. Some expressions have sexual overtones in one community but are inoffensive in others. Certain expressions may denote a class bias that may be offensive to one group of people or another. The pejorative way homosexuals and bisexuals are referred to in some Latino communities represents another important example.

4. *Leadership styles and development.* Organizers must be leaders, but they must also work with existing community leaders and help train emerging leaders. There are significant differences in leadership styles from one community of color to another. Indispensable to the makeup of successful leaders are their individual personalities, how they shape their roles within the organizing task, and how their personal values help shape a worldview. However achieved, leaders should have a sense of power they use respectfully within the community.

5. *A conceptual framework for political and economic analysis.* An understanding of the dynamics of oppression through class analysis is paramount as well as sophisticated knowledge of political systems with their access and leverage points. Organizers must be able to appraise who has authority within the ethnic community as well as who in it has power (often less formally acknowledged). The sources of mediating influence between the ethnic community and wider communities must also be understood. This knowledge fulfills two needs: (1) It helps give organizers the necessary analytical perspective to judge where the community fits in the hierarchy of economic status; and (2) it serves as a tool for educating the community, thereby increasing its consciousness of the roles and functions of the organizer within broader economic and social systems.[18]

6. *Knowledge of past organizing strategies, their strengths and limitations.* Organizers must learn how to structure their organizing activities within a historical framework. Because so little knowledge building is evident in the field, organizers must share their experiences—both positive and negative—to illuminate those techniques that appear to have or have not worked in the recent past.

7. *Skills in conscientization and empowerment.* A major task of organizers in disenfranchised communities is to empower people through the process of developing critical consciousness. How the personal and political influence each other, and the local environment in which they are played out, is a key to this process. It is not enough to succeed in ameliorating or even solving community problems if there is little or no empowerment of the community.

At the same time, the organizer must understand power as both a tool and as part of a process. As Rubin and Rubin write, "Community organizations need not focus exclusively on campaigns to achieve specific goals; they can make building their own power a long-term effort."[19] Power may be destructive or productive in the sense of germinating ideas and concerns and being integrative, or community building. Of course, power is typically experienced in poor communities as both a negative and a positive. The kind of power based on threats is often the most common in disenfranchised areas. When Organizer A makes Target B act in ways it does not wish to act solely because of the sanctions A can levy against B, typically this becomes an imposed "win–lose" situation.[20] A limited special hiring program usually takes this form.

Power may also be a form of exchange: Organizer A and Target B involve themselves in a reciprocal relationship or exchange because both parties have something to win from the process. Exchange is an integrative component of power because it involves some degree of trust in which the final outcome may be "win–win." Coalition building often takes this form. Power may also be defined as love—love of community, lifestyle, or family—that should motivate an organizer and the community. The corruption that often flows from excessive concentrations of power must also be taken into account.

Organizer and community need to view each other as subject rather than object, as learners and as equals. No organizer should enter a community with a sense that she or he has *the* answers. The development of critical consciousness through the process of conscientization may be visualized as a double spiraling helix: Both the organizer and community learn from each other, the problems at hand, and the strategies and tactics they employ (Figure 1.2).[21] The phenomenology of the experience is based on praxis, the melding of theory and experience, for both parties, which in turn makes them stronger actors because their learning is mutual, supportive, and liberating of any preconceived notions one has about the other.

8. *Skills in assessing community psychology.* Organizers need to learn about the psychological makeup of their communities free of stereotypes. Scant attention has been paid to this knowledge area by most community organizers. Creating a methodology without understanding the motivations of the community is risky.

Organizers also need to understand what keeps a community allied and synergized. What is the life cycle of the community? Is it growing, mature, or declining? Are there new arrivals? Have families been in the community for generations? Does

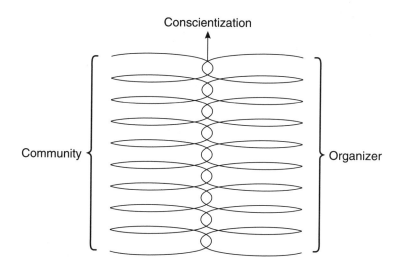

FIGURE 1.2   Development of Critical Consciousness

their language work as a cohesive force or, because of the multigenerational patterns, serve as a problem in getting people together? If the community has experienced a failure recently (such as the loss of a valued school, a religious institution, or health center), what has this done to the shared psychological identification with the community? Does the community feel frustrated and powerless? Or has the loss served to focus anger? If the latter is the case, what strategies may be employed to mobilize the community to action?

9. *Knowledge of organizational behavior and decision making.* Knowledge about organizational behavior and decision making are critical to an organizer's success. The work of Bachrach and Baratz regarding decisionless decisions and nondecisions as decisions has demonstrated its worth in the field. Decisionless decisions are those decision-making strategies that "just happen" and "take on a life of their own." Nondecisions as decisions are defined as "a means by which demands for change in the existing allocation of benefits and privileges in the community can be suffocated before they are even voiced or kept covert; or killed before they gain access to the relevant decision-making arena; or, failing all these things, maimed or destroyed in decision-implementing stage of the policy process."[22]

An awareness of these dynamics is necessary both to be able to ascertain strategies being employed by the institutions targeted for change and as a tactic that may also be employed by the community in its organizing. A thoughtful understanding of organizational behavior may also help community organizations avoid creating the kind of dysfunctional arrangements (such as people who try to control initiatives by hoarding valuable information) that cause members to abandon an organization.

10. *Skills in evaluative and participatory research.* One of the reasons that communities of color have lost some of their political, economic, and legal battles is the increasing vacuum created by the lack of supportive information. Many communities are victimized by data and demographics that have redefined their situations as unmanageable, therefore making them susceptible to mean-spirited external intervention. An expanded role for organizers is needed to include developing skills in demographic and population projections and in social problem analysis. More organizers should develop concepts and theories about the declining social, economic, and political base of communities of color and how people are still managing to survive in times of open hostility and encroachment on their civil rights and liberties. Crime, including that related to drugs, is a major arena for these pressures.

Research continues to be an indispensable and powerful tool for social change. Organizers should pay special attention to the use of participatory approaches in which both researchers and community members are involved as equal participants in securing knowledge to empower the community.[23]

Skill in evaluation research is another indispensable tool for organizers. We are suggesting that evaluative research not necessarily be used to assess program outcomes but to analyze the success and value of different organizing strategies and their relevance in disparate situations. Emerging technologies—such as the Internet and urban databases—must not be ignored.

11. *Skills in program planning and development and administration management.* One of the bitter lessons learned from the War on Poverty had to do with the set-up-for-failure nature of the administrative jobs offered to many people of color. Most had little or no administrative or managerial experience. One of the editors, then little experienced, was offered a position that required him to administer a four-county migrant education and employment training program. With crash courses on organizational behavior, information processing, and budgeting, he met the challenge, but many mistakes were made along the way. Needless to say, the mistakes were widely reported by the program's detractors and administrator's enemies.

Many administrators of color have fallen by the wayside because they were not given the opportunity to sharpen their managerial skills, and thus, a self-fulfilling prophecy of incompetence was validated in the eyes of people who wanted to see these programs fail. Organizers must be aggressive in seeking out this knowledge base and not be deterred by institutional barriers—financial, political, or otherwise—to attaining it. Performing mentoring functions may become increasingly urgent over the next few years as, in President Clinton's phrase, a "bridge to the twenty-first century."

12. *An awareness of self and of personal strengths and limitations.* Reading through our list may raise the question, "Does such a superorganizer possessing all the enumerated skills and knowledge exist?" The answer is both yes and no.

There are people throughout the country with these skills, and many who have most of them. Organizers should know when to seek help, when to share responsibilities, and when to step aside to let others take over. Conversely, skilled and knowledgeable organizers must be open to sharing their expertise with communities and community leaders.

A successful organizer is one who gains respect within the context of the actions being taken, not the individual who is (or appears to be) more knowledgeable than someone else. Honest intentions and abilities are worth more than college degrees. Organizers also need to understand how to react to stress. We all have our ways of coping with conflict. We need to know when our coping is no longer working for us, thereby jeopardizing the community. The danger of burnout is too well documented to be ignored, especially when the risks of taking out our frustrations on the community escalate.

Finally, we would like to caution against the very seductive, but equally dangerous concept of "doing it *for* the community." Not only is this likely to undermine core empowerment building, it also vastly increases the risk of the organizer feeling exploited, or "being eaten alive" by the most important people with whom she or he is working. All too often the result is an organizer who, as an act of self-preservation, abandons a community and provides naysayers with one more "proof" that even the well intentioned do not have the courage of their expressed convictions.

The Readings

The next eleven chapters represent a wide panorama of history, oppression, social problems, organizing, and community development experienced by their respective communities. For this third edition we have added more case studies and identified additional specific skill areas that must be present for organizers to work successfully with their respective communities. Although some might argue this book would have been more coherent if each contributor had rigorously followed a standardized outline, we have taken a different view. Each contributor (or contributing team) was invited to direct attention to the following areas: (1) the historical context of social problems in the community about which they were writing—including their nature, magnitude, and severity; (2) the current state of affairs in their communities—from a personal rather than objective point of view; (3) which skill areas are necessary to work successfully with their communities; and (4) whatever final conclusions they might wish to offer.

Rather than creating a book weakened by a lack of parallel composition across chapters, we believe the mosaic that follows is strengthened by the rich and unique approaches taken by the contributors. Unlike Oscar Lewis, who believed that poor people are largely the same through his misguided notion of the "culture of poverty," the contributors offer a diverse canvas of problems, hopes, dreams, and actions experienced by individual communities.

The contributors have placed each community's social problems within a historical context that is political, social, and economic. They analyze the structural, leadership, power, fiscal, and human issues that have been responsible for making their communities what they are today. They address what they see as the strategies for change in the future: the most effective ways of dealing with their communities' problems and the implications these have for community organization practice and, where relevant, social work education.

Chapter 2, "Community Development with American Indians and Alaska Natives" by E. Daniel Edwards and Margie Egbert-Edwards, presents a culturally sensitive framework for working with American Indians and Alaska Natives. They have edited the case studies and added up-to-date demographic information. Community examples from both reservations and urban areas, expanded information on areas of current concern related to family and child welfare, as well as funding issues are also included. The authors identify the many values shared by Alaska Natives and U.S. Native Americans, which helps define their extensive communities and the compatibility of community development with tribal work, and they identify the process goals for such work. Special attention is given to enhancing community ownership and positive regard through cultural identification. Finally, the authors identify important skills for successful community organization with native people.

Edwards and Egbert-Edwards develop a cultural enhancement/community development model for community organizing with special emphasis on identification with the journey and visions of Native Americans and Alaska Natives. They discuss the dynamics of understanding and implementing the community development process with examples of successful programs in a variety of urban and rural settings and tribes.

"Chicanos, Communities, and Change," Chapter 3, was written by Miguel Montiel and Felipe Ortega y Gasca. The authors analyze the nature of change within the context of Chicano experiences and communities. They put the Chicano experience within a historical perspective, discussing the roles played by community-based organizations in sustaining the Chicano ethos. They assess the movement away from community-based organizations to "profession-centered organizations" and the roles these emerging organizations will play in the Chicano communities as we approach the twenty-first century. Newer references are introduced as the authors analyze such issues as affirmative action and the conflicts between Chicano men and women.

The authors assess and reevaluate the continuity of change in Chicano communities. They also assess the difficulties of sustaining meaningful organizations and change and the importance of dialogue in creating organizations, jobs, and the development of a courageous vision of action.

Wynetta Devore is author of Chapter 4, "The House on Midland: From Inside Out." Devore sets the tone for the survival of the African American family and communities by describing the survival of the African American community within the context of the now popularized notion of "the village." She looks at the history of the settlement house movement using The House on Midland Avenue, which serves as a center for community organizing and development, and, by extension, the village within which it functions. Devore analyzes the community development work being done by Communities United to Rebuild Neighborhoods.

Chapter 5, "Cultural and Political Realities for Community Social Work Practice with Puerto Ricans in the United States," by Julio Morales and Migdalia Reyes, introduces the Puerto Rican community's unique political situation and its ongoing relationships with the U.S. government. Morales and Reyes discuss the roles played by ideology, values, and social change within the Puerto Rican community, along with the dynamics represented by culture and practice issues.

The authors assess the significance of such attributes as respect, honor, dignity, and hospitality in the Puerto Rican community. Similarly, they analyze the nature of the extended family, *personalismo, confianza,* and *espiritismo* and evaluate their importance to organizers. The dynamics of self-oppression are explored with a discussion of their negative outcomes and their implications for change. *Machismo, marianismo,* and other "isms" are considered, as well as the strengths inherent in the Puerto Rican community. Finally, Morales and Reyes introduce the reader to the problems, programs, strategies, and tactics that a successful agent for social change should employ, strongly supported by case studies that look at such issues as HIV and AIDS.

A critical look at the feminist movement and the reasons women of color have been systematically excluded from significant policy-making arenas is taken up in Chapter 6, "A Feminist Perspective on Organizing with Women of Color" by Lorraine M. Gutiérrez and Edith A. Lewis. They define what they mean by women of color, looking at ethnic, racial, social, political, and economic factors that have helped shape that definition. A distinction is made between the interests of women of color and men of color. Additionally, they introduce a feminist perspective, emphasizing power and powerlessness as an integral part of their perspective and as a way for women of color to begin assessing their situation in the United States.

The authors define feminist organizing, introducing a model delineating its dynamics. Issues for feminists organizing with women of color are discussed, as is community organizing by women of color, richly illustrated by updated case examples such as Project Oasis, a project geared to end violence against women of color. Finally, the authors discuss future directions for feminist organizing with women of color, listing practice principles that should be addressed.

Chapter 7, "Organizing in the Chinese American Community: Issues, Strategies, and Alternatives" by Peter Ching-Yung Lee, portrays the complex, multigenerational world of the Chinese in the United States. Lee, in this updated chapter, profiles Chinese American sociodemographic characteristics, their changing values and behaviors, and the implication of these dynamics in the changing nature of their social, economic, and political problems.

The author develops a theoretical framework that looks at classic organizing theories and assesses their relevance or lack thereof for Chinese Americans. Emphasizing the unique cultural experiences of the community, Lee discusses and assesses community organizing strategies through case studies. In conclusion, Lee looks at the efficacy of the social development perspective, assessing its value while emphasizing an integrated sociocultural approach. In the "Analysis and Assessment" section, Lee looks at Chinese community organizations' characteristics and patterns and how they have fared within the community.

Kenji Murase introduces the reader to the sociodemographics of the Japanese in Chapter 8, "The Japanese American Community and Community Organizations." Murase has updated the demographic information since the last edition and has included some projections of demographic trends. He describes the impact of the internment experience on Japanese American community organizations. Major emerging developments discussed are interethnic coalitions, participation in the political arena, campaigning for corporate responsibility, and coalition building at the national level. The chapter ends with a projection of future problems and prospects.

Royal F. Morales is the author of Chapter 9, "The Pilipino American Community: Organizing for Change." He profiles the Pilipino American community's social, cultural, and sociopolitical history. The community is identified as one of the largest-growing Asian communities. The author identifies unique cultural dynamics and the barriers some of these pose to organizing. An organizer profile is introduced that encompasses cultural sensitivities. The author has added case examples for this third edition. Finally, Morales looks at future challenges for schools of social work, social workers, and community activists.

Chapter 10, "Living in the U.S.A.: Central American Immigrant Communities in the United States," by Carlos B. Córdova, looks at the complex history of the Salvadoran, Guatemalan, Nicaraguan, and Honduran communities in the United States. Córdova analyzes those economic and political issues that have forced so many of these people to flee their homelands and the role played by U.S. politics and the Immigration and Naturalization Service. He looks at the structure of Central American communities in the United States and how they function and survive. He analyzes the political power and influence in these communities and the reactions to threats by homeland opponents.

Córdova develops a model of empowerment using Paulo Friere's concept of critical consciousness. The author looks at what needs to be done in the future in the areas of research, immigration reform, counseling services, education, and medical and mental health needs, especially addressing the problems associated with post-traumatic stress disorder. Finally, Córdova addresses the limits of the literature on community organization with Central American refugees and the need to develop new models of practice in these areas as well as to change and adapt existing models of community and economic development. Many fresh examples highlight this new version of the chapter.

Vu-Duc Vuong presents a demographic profile of the Southeast Asian communities and the complexities that exist in working with them—both culturally and linguistically—in Chapter 11, "Southeast Asians in the United States: Accelerated and Balanced Integration." Migration patterns are traced and analyzed beginning with the wealthy elites that left Vietnam in the mid-1970s to the boat people of more recent times.

The author addresses critical issues for these communities, analyzing similarities and differences among Southeast Asian refugees. Critical issues for organizing are discussed, with special emphasis given to problems of English as a barrier to change, lack of political representation, and the distrust that exists because of the legacies of the Vietnam War.

The role played by Southeast Asian women is also addressed by Vuong. Finally, the author introduces strategies for accelerated and balanced integration that include aggressive economic development. A new case study for this edition helps demonstrate his theoretical framework.

Chapter 12, "Community Development and Restoration: A Perspective and Case Study," by Antonia Pantoja and Wilhelmina Perry, is a special chapter on economic and community development within a poor Puerto Rican community. The chapter demonstrates broad community development and restoration approaches that also have wide applicability and relevance to all poor and disenfranchised communities of color. The authors present an innovative model of activist community development. They begin by looking at the many issues and challenges of this kind of capacity building and the need to obtain specialized knowledge. They take the social work profession to task by pointing out its failure in not embracing economic and community development strategies to bring about significant social change.

The authors identify the prerequisites for successful community development workers and define their approach to community development/restoration. The major processes of community development are identified, supported by case studies. Inherent throughout these processes, the authors make clear, is the development of political awareness at the same time they are working in the organizing process. One cannot exist without the other. Finally, the authors discuss future challenges for community developers. Pantoja was awarded the president's Medal of Freedom in 1996 for her many years of community work.

In Chapter 13, "Epilogue: The Twenty-First Century—Promise or Illusion?" we offer our perspectives on the patterns, trends, and possibilities that have been illuminated by all the contributors. The diverse and unique histories, racial and ethnic differences, languages, and cultural patterns are synthesized into a model that addresses the similarities and differences experienced by the communities addressed by the contributors and their implications for successful organizing outcomes. We look at the need for coalition building, with its attendant challenges and rewards, the roles European Americans can play within our communities, politics and legislative reform, and the potentials of the Internet. Finally, we explore the international implications of the struggles by communities of color in the United States.

The appendix introduces updated material from an excellent training manual used by the Center for Third World Organizing, Oakland, California, to illustrate what a community-based social action organization's training material looks like. The material offers an excellent introduction to the range and variety of issues addressed.

Summary

> *No one goes anywhere alone, least of all into exile—not even those who arrive physically alone, unaccompanied by family, spouse, children, parents, or siblings. No one leaves his or her world without having been transfixed by its roots, or with a vacuum for a soul. We carry with us the memory of many fabrics, a self soaked in our history, our culture; a memory, sometimes scattered, sometimes sharp and clear, of the streets of our childhood.*[24]

The struggle to bring about significant social change at the community level continues to be a Herculean task. Despite political rhetoric to the contrary at all levels of government, the gates to social justice are sliding further shut, not open. In the wake of "the end of welfare as we know it," increasing numbers of people of color are being thrown into disadvantage and poverty—homeless, drug addicted, alcoholic, imprisoned, AIDS infected, unemployed, without regular health care, and pushed out of deteriorating schools with few (if any) marketable skills.

As Rice has noted, "The elimination of affirmative action is just the precursor to elimination of all civil rights laws. As announced recently on C-SPAN II, 209 proponents are planning a national strategy and are now considering dismantling Title VII, Title IX, and other federal civil rights laws."[25] Community organization and development with people of color offers a modest vehicle for combating this trend.

We agree with the contributing authors that organizers can make a difference. Although it is never lucrative and rarely romantic, the work can be critical in helping people meet their needs. It can also be a way of enabling people to connect their own histories, the structural changes that confront them, and the future. Perhaps above all it is about empowerment, an empowerment that can be shared by community and organizer.

Notes

1. Delaware leader Neolin advising Indians in the 1760s to be prepared to fight back to protect their culture. Gary Nash, *Red, White and Black: People of Early America* (Englewood Cliffs, NJ: Prentice-Hall, 1974), pp. 302–303.
2. Editorial, "Naked Cities," *The Nation,* 264 (1) (Jan. 7, 1997), p. 3.
3. John L. Erlich and Felix G. Rivera, in N. Gilbert and H. Sprecht (eds.), "Community Organization and Community Development," *Handbook of Social Services* (Englewood Cliffs, NJ: Prentice-Hall, 1981); R. Kramer and H. Specht, *Readings in Community Organization Practice,* 3rd ed. (Englewood Cliffs, NJ: Prentice-Hall, 1983).
4. R. Fisher, "Community Organization in Historical Perspective: A Typology," *The Houston Review* (Summer 1984), pp. 75–87.
5. R. Fisher, *Let the People Decide: Neighborhood Organizing in America* (Boston: Twayne, 1984).
6. H. Boyte, *The Backyard Revolution: Understanding the New Citizen Movement* (Philadelphia: Temple University Press, 1980); G. Frederickson (ed.), *Neighborhood Control in the 1970s* (New York: Chandler, 1970).
7. Sanford Horwitt, *Let Them Call Me Rebel: Saul Alinsky—His Life and Legacy* (New York: Knopf, 1989).
8. Ibid.
9. R. Blauner, *Racial Oppression in America* (New York: Harper & Row, 1972); J. Roemer, "Divide and Conquer: Microfoundations of Marxian Theory of Wage Discrimination." *Bell Journal of Economics* 10 (Autumn 1979), pp. 695–705.
10. E. P. Thompson, *The Making of the English Working Class* (New York: Vintage, 1966); *Harvard Educational Review* (August 1988), special issue on "Race and Racism in American Education."
11. A. Dunham, *The New Community Organization* (New York: Crowell, 1970).
12. Fisher, "Community Organization."
13. Paulo Freire, *Education for Critical Consciousness* (New York: Seabury, 1973).
14. Larry Kreuger, "The End of Social Work," *Journal of Social Work Education* 33 (1) (Winter 1997), p. 24.
15. Editor's Introduction, *Journal of Poverty* 1 (1) (1997) (Binghamton, NY: Haworth).
16. S. Burghardt, "The Other Side of Organizing (Cambridge, MA: Schenkman, 1982); Erlich and Rivera, "Community Organizing and Community Development"; Fisher, *Let the People Decide;* Horwitt, *Let Them Call Me Rebel.*
17. J. Gibbs, L. Huang, and associates, *Children of Color* (San Francisco: Jossey-Bass, 1989).
18. H. J. Rubin and I. Rubin, *Community Organizing and Development* (Columbus, OH: Merrill, 1986).

19. Ibid., p. 235.

20. Ibid.

21. Kenneth Boulding, *Three Faces of Power* (Beverly Hills: Sage, 1989).

22. P. Bachrach and M. S. Baratz, *Power and Poverty: Theory and Practice* (New York: Oxford University Press, 1970).

23. For example, an entire issue of *Community Development Journal* was devoted to participatory research and evaluation, thus stressing its international importance in working with disenfranchised and oppressed communities (Vol. 23, no. 1, Jan. 1988).

24. Friere, *The Pedagogy of Hope* (New York: Continuum, 1994).

25. Connie Rice, "Toward Affirmative Reaction," *The Nation* 254 (2) (Jan. 13–20, 1997), p. 24.

2

Community Development with American Indians and Alaska Natives*

E. DANIEL EDWARDS AND MARGIE EGBERT-EDWARDS

Community organization practice continues to promote Native American self-determination and self-governance in reservation, rural, and urban areas. The number of Native Americans continues to grow as does their diversity. According to the 1990 U.S. Census, the Native American population now numbers approximately 2 million people—less than 1 percent of the total U.S. population. These figures represent a 38 percent increase from the 1.4 million population reported in 1980. Of these 2 million people, approximately two-thirds (1,220,126) reside in off-reservation areas throughout the United States. Only 739,108 Native Americans (38 percent) reside in tribally governed areas including 314 reservations, trust lands, tribal-jurisdiction and tribal-designated statistical areas, and Alaska Native villages. Data from the 1990 U.S. Census included tribal population figures for 542 unique tribes and Alaskan villages. Whether residences are maintained in rural, reservation, or urban areas, Native Americans are influenced by strong cultural ties to their native identity. Professional people will find considerable challenge and stimulation in working with Native Americans and validating their cultural heritage and community development.

---

*The terms "Native American" and "American Indian/Alaska Native" are used interchangeably to refer to the first "native" peoples of this country and their descendants.

Community Approaches: Compatibility with Native American Values

A sense of *community* is important to the culture of American Indian tribal groups. Historically, many American Indian tribes and bands were relatively small in number and culturally bound together by strong community support networks. Daily living and decision making were facilitated by considering the opinions of all tribal members according to well-developed tribal practices and customs.

A review of the community organization literature suggests that "communities provide meaning, a sense of belonging, and well-being" (Martinez-Brawley, 1990, p. 50). Fully functioning communities are those in which there is an appreciation for the capacity of the whole. These communities have a sense of the breadth and depth of members' capacities, their strengths as well as their weaknesses. This capacity promotes "shared responsibility"—shaped by the unique contributions of each member— and strives for equity through collective efforts (McKnight, 1987). Within these communities, members share a sense of solidarity, significance, and security. Solidarity is exemplified in feelings of cohesiveness. Significance is reflected in the contributions of individuals for the collective good. Security is reinforced through the mutuality of relationships and the sense of belonging (Martinez-Brawley, 1990, pp. 14–15).

A sense of community was an important part of traditional American Indian culture. Historically, decision making was facilitated by considering the opinions of all tribal members through well-developed cultural values of individual and tribal acceptance. Positive interpersonal relationships, individual security, and collective solidarity were promoted through the many values shared by Native American people, including the following:

1. *Balance, Harmony, Spirituality.* Native American beliefs in a Supreme Being and continuity of life beyond this "mother earth" experience promoted individual and community responsibility for living in harmony with nature and Native American religious beliefs.
2. *Autonomy.* Native Americans respected the autonomy, worth, and self-determination of each individual person. Each tribal member's contribution was important to the success and well-being of the community.
3. *Solidarity.* Native Americans were expected to respect, understand, and contribute to the well-being of their native families, clans, bands, and tribes. Group consensus in decision making contributed to community well-being.
4. *Knowledge/Wisdom.* Native Americans believed the wise application of knowledge contributed to the well-being of all living things and perpetuation of their communities and cultures.

Respect for and adherence to these values promoted community solidarity and security. Continuing validation of the strength of these relationships has been acknowledged by Martinez-Brawley (1990) in her observation, "Probably the best example of caring in the broad context of community is the collective responsibility assumed by Native American communities for their members" (p. 91).

Native American Community Organization: Compatibility with Locality Development and Community Development Models

The involvement of tribal members in the active work of Native American communities closely resembles the "locality development" model as described by Rothman and Tropman (1987) and the community development model as explicated by Chavis, Florin, and Felix (1993).

An assumption underlying locality development theory is that "community change may be pursued optimally through broad participation of a wide spectrum of people at the local community level in goal determination and action" (Rothman and Tropman, 1987, p. 5). This assumption is compatible with Native American values that advocate respect for the autonomy and worth of every individual, and the importance of each person's contribution to the well-being of the whole in the community decision-making process.

Community development, according to Khinduka (1987), enhances the locality development process by bringing people together, encouraging participatory democracy, and promoting local reasoning and decision-making processes (p. 360). Community development is strengthened through program development. "Community projects . . . strengthen the spirit of unity in a community through enhancement of community feelings, self-reliance, and local leadership" (Khinduka, 1987, p. 36).

Chavis, Florin, and Felix (1993) identify three stages of community development capacity building: (1) expanding the base of citizen involvement; (2) enhancing the leadership pool and augmenting leadership skills; and (3) expanding the information and resource base. All of these strategies are important to the community development and cultural enhancement model advocated for work with Native American communities.

Native American Approaches to Community Problem Solving

In 1985 a national survey of minority people identified many problems affecting the health status of minority people. Subsequently, the U.S. Public Health Service and the National Academy of Health Science formed the "Healthy People 2000 Consortium." Their final report, published in 1990, includes three goals: (1) increase the span of healthy life for Americans; (2) reduce health disparities among Americans; and (3) achieve access to prevention services for all Americans. The American Indian Health Care Association drafted the publication "Promoting Healthy Traditions Workbook" (1990) to serve as a guide to Indian communities seeking to address the goals of the Healthy People 2000 Campaign. This publication proposes to address Indian community health problems through a "Circle of Community Wellness" approach (p. 12). The steps to community intervention are outlined as follows:

1. Conduct assessments to answer questions related to the health status of communities;
2. Mobilize efforts to bring the community together;
3. Create a vision for the future;
4. Create a vision for change;
5. Nurture the vision through program development; and
6. Celebrate the vision and goal accomplishment.

The "Promoting Healthy Traditions Workbook" is a valuable resource for American Indian groups that are addressing the community problems of their people. Whatever approach or combination of approaches is utilized, consideration should be given to both process goals and outcome goals (see Table 2.1).

Examples of Community Development and Cultural Enhancement Approaches

Several Native American urban, rural, and reservation communities have begun to implement community development and cultural enhancement programs. These communities have assumed ownership of their problems, resources, and growth potential. Each tribal member is viewed as both a participant and a contributor to the common good. Communities are reinforcing the importance of individual worth and cultural identity in the development of these programs. We describe some examples of programs in which community development and cultural enhancement success are being achieved next.

Many Native American communities are implementing collaborative efforts to develop "Heritage Centers" for the benefit of tribal members, other Indian groups, and non-Indians. These Heritage Centers house (1) pictorial living histories of their tribal heritage; (2) auditoriums for ceremonial and social dances and powwows; (3) facilities for hosting traditional games and social gatherings; and (4) ceremonial dwellings such as "longhouses" in which healing and traditional ceremonies are held for the benefit of all tribal members. Some centers also house museums, historical tribal arts, modern arts, gift shops to promote sales of tribal arts, and theaters for local plays, ceremonials, and community events.

The Oneida Indian Nation in Oneida, Wisconsin, is directing a community effort on behalf of their 3,000 reservation residents (Boyte, 1984). Tribal members have developed economic resources to employ and support their people and community. Bingo games are generating funds to purchase Indian lands that were lost from the reservation some time ago. Cultural reinforcement efforts are promoting Oneida

TABLE 2.1   Process and Outcome Goals

Recommended for Consideration in Native American Community
Development/Cultural Enhancement Approaches

Process Goals	Outcome Goals

1. Enhance community ownership	A. Identify community problems and resources
	   1. Invite community participation
	   2. Review existing research data
	   3. Conduct needs assessments
	   4. Determine goals and objectives
	   5. Select evaluation approaches
	   6. Report outcomes to the community
	   7. Revise goals and objectives
	   8. Repeat evaluation approaches
	   9. Repeat community reporting measures

2. Enhance positive regard, individually and collectively	B. Include everyone "in"
	   1. Hire competent and committed staff
	   2. Assign responsibilities
	   3. Form task committees
	   4. Recruit and recognize volunteers
	   5. Implement programs
	   6. Modify programs in accordance with evaluation data and revised goals and objectives
	   7. Invite participation from all community members, as appropriate
	   8. Schedule community activities (formal and informal)

3. Enhance positive cultural identification	C. Emphasize cultural values, beliefs, and traditions
	   1. Form cultural committees
	   2. Form "elders" advisory committees
	   3. Include cultural values and traditions in every component of the program
	   4. Program general cultural activities
	   5. Program tribal-specific cultural activities
	   6. Emphasize knowledge/wisdom (current and traditional)
	   7. Enhance leadership skill development

language instruction; construction of a traditional longhouse; traditional Indian ceremonies and dances; a tribal Indian school; tribal cultural classes; home birthing practices; farming; active involvement of elders in community programs; and self-governance after the tradition of the Iroquois Confederacy. This Native American community emphasizes giving, sharing, and cooperating. Cultural classes provide instruction in traditional tribal medicine; giveaways; activities for community elders; and appreciation for nature and all living creatures. Community ownership, individuality, collectivity, and enhanced cultural identification are all important to this community and its vision.

A pressing concern of American Indian urban agencies is expanding financial resources sufficient to meet the increasing demands for social services by expanding urban American Indian populations. The board of directors of the Salt Lake City American Indian Walk-In Center sponsored its first annual American Indian Art Show and Auction in 1996. Participation by American Indian artists more than exceeded expectations. Attendance and support from the American Indian and non-Indian communities were overwhelming. Proceeds from this evening's activities provided funding to meet the increasing social service and counseling needs of American Indian people in the Salt Lake City community.

The Mescalero Apache tribe has "diversified economically in creative ways—partly in response to bad years for cattle and timber in the late fifties" (Trimble, 1993, pp. 272–73). Under the dynamic leadership of tribal president Wendell Chino, the tribal cattle herd continues to grow. A new sawmill has been developed. A reservoir provides recreational and fishing activities as does a resort hotel, golf course, and dude ranch. This success is achieved through efforts addressing the importance of the community.

The Tohono O'odham Tribe approved their tribal education plan in 1987 through a community effort that included "the viewpoints of elders, young people, professionals—*everybody*" (Trimble, 1993, p. 371). The concept of community is historically and currently important to this Arizona tribal group.

One urban community has developed a community approach to enhance the strengths of American Indian people through a variety of Indian and non-Indian activities developed around a cultural enhancement model that emphasizes "four great powers." The goal of this community is to enhance the meaning of life through traditional values of (1) spirituality—living in harmony with the spiritual teachings of tribal groups; (2) intellectual development—positive use of one's mental capacities through the development of knowledge; (3) emotional well-being—development of self-discipline through respect for nature, family, and clan; and (4) physical well-being—achieving holistic wellness by adhering to principles of good health. Among the activities in which community members can participate are the following: martial arts; cultural arts—including beading, weaving, basketry, and leather work; native language skill enhancement; instruction in traditional herbal medicines; drumming circles; sweat lodge ceremonies; and spiritual and vision quests. Treatment options that can be made available to community members include both modern-day medicine/treatment services and spiritual or traditional healers. Respect for "elders" and cultural beliefs are honored through participation in giveaways and a variety of tribal ceremonies.

Window Rock, Arizona High School (Dine Nation—Navajo) has envisioned their student body as a community. Four different types of peer support groups are offered to Window Rock High School students. These include (1) "Staying Straight" groups for those young people in recovery who want to live lives that are chemical free; (2) "Insight groups" for those young people who are experiencing school, family, or relationship problems as a result of drug and/or alcohol abuse; (3) "Support groups" for youth who are negatively affected by drug/alcohol use of significant others; and (4) "Growth groups" for self-development of young people who are not negatively affected by the drug/alcohol use of significant others. All young people at the high school are welcome to participate in the group of their choosing. There is a place for everyone. All the groups offer a nonusing peer support group philosophy. The groups are organized within the school community and have the benefit of leadership and support from adults and peers within that community system (*Positive Self-Esteem Can Protect Native American Youth,* no date given).

Examples of two different Indian communities that have made community commitments to drug-free lifestyles are reflected in the Cheyenne River Sioux Reservation and the Akhiok Alaskan Village on Kodiak Island. The Cheyenne River Sioux Reservation has set a goal to achieve 100 percent alcohol- and drug-free lifestyles among their 5,000 reservation community members by the year 2000. This is a community effort in which a variety of programs are made available to youth and adults to sustain drug-free lifestyles and lend support toward accomplishment of this goal. The Akhiok Alaskan Village on Kodiak Island has achieved a 70 percent adult sobriety rate in the past several years. This achievement represents a substantial increase in sobriety from the baseline of 10 percent sobriety before the village promoted this community effort to achieve sobriety (*Pass the Word,* no date given.)

A Case Study Emphasizing a Long-Term Commitment

The following case study illustrates the implementation of the Community Development/Cultural Enhancement Model. This case study details the community development process over the long term.

The American Indian Community in Salt Lake County, Utah, has stabilized considerably in the past decade. Many Salt Lake County American Indian residents are members of one of the eight predominant tribes in the state of Utah. These tribes include the Northern Ute, White Mesa Ute, Dine Nation (Navajo), Paiute, Northwestern Band of Shoshoni, Goshute, Skull Valley Goshute, and San Juan Southern Paiute. The Indian population of Salt Lake County also includes representation from more than eighty additional tribal groups. Many American Indian people have established permanent residence in Salt Lake County. Some organizations presently serve primarily

American Indian clientele including the Indian Walk-In Center, the Indian Training and Education Center, the American Indian Counseling and Recovery Center, the Indian Health Clinic, and some religious and tribal-based organizations. In the recent past, American Indian community members have come together to address a number of community concerns and to participate in a variety of social, cultural, recreational, and spiritual activities.

In 1988 the Office for Substance Abuse Prevention (OSAP and now CSAP—Center for Substance Abuse Prevention) announced funding for community partnership grants. The Salt Lake County American Indian community had achieved considerable stability and was ready to participate in a collaborative effort of this magnitude. Contacts with the American Indian community were positive and resulted in cooperative efforts with Salt Lake County Division of Alcohol and Drugs and subsequent funding of a five-year OSAP (CSAP) Community Partnership Grant, administered by the Salt Lake County Division of Alcohol and Drugs. A Native American task force was responsible for directing the programs available to American Indians through this funding.

This positive experience led to further community efforts to address community, family, child welfare, and funding issues. A community effort was initiated to respond to a request for proposal (RFP) for funding to support a community alcohol and drug prevention program. An initial community meeting was held at the University of Utah's Graduate School of Social Work. Sufficient interest was demonstrated to plan future meetings.

Process Goals and Outcome Goals

All of the actions taken to this point followed the Community Development and Cultural Enhancement Model advocated by Edwards and Edwards (1988, 1992, 1994, 1995). The actions are also in keeping with the "Circle of Community Wellness" model (1990) advocated by the American Indian Health Care Association.

Enhance Community Ownership

Initial interventions were directed toward enhancing community ownership through broad-based community participation. In the initial planning process two major concerns significantly affected community ownership. One was the location of the community meetings. Although there was considerable comfort in attending meetings at the University of Utah, parking and traffic were often problematic. These factors would likely limit participation of elders and community representatives who lived some distance from the university. The second decision related to which of our community agencies would be the sponsoring agency. After considerable input from those in attendance, the Indian Training and Education Center (ITEC) was selected as the sponsoring agency and designated as the site of future community planning meetings. This agency was located in a more convenient location in south Salt Lake and had ample parking.

Several factors contributed to these decisions. Community meeting locations either encourage or detract from community participation. As indicated in the "Circle of Community Wellness" publication, "a gathering of community members to make important decisions is a long-standing tradition among Indian people" (1990, p. 22), yet community meetings in urban areas "may involve taking risks; like asking people to come together who have never worked together before or who have fought against each other in the past" (1990, p. 22). We knew this to be true of the Salt Lake County community. Broad community participation was, therefore, essential. We hoped the project's goals and objectives would bring people together—if not immediately, then sometime during the process.

It was important throughout the community development process to "enhance positive regard" for participants—individually and collectively—and to "include everyone in." Community development principles were found to be compatible with "process" and "outcome goals" and the cultural procedures recommended in the *Promoting Healthy Traditions Workbook* (1990).

"Traditions of consensus, democracy, and community input" were emphasized throughout this process, but as authors of the *Workbook* have pointed out, "for many reasons, many people are not able to work in this tradition" (1990, p. 23). More community members, however, developed these collaborative skills as they were positively impacted by the vision of this project. Others chose not to participate. It was important to accept the individual decision making of each prospective participant without criticism or backbiting.

Community meetings were attended by Indians and non-Indians. Most participants were familiar with American Indian cultural traditions. There was a willingness to risk involvement and participation by most residents. Meetings were held regularly and cofacilitated by the authors of this chapter and the director of the Indian Training and Education Center. Collaboration resulted in agenda setting, mailing notices and reminders to nonattenders, and general preparation for the meetings. The authors conducted the meetings with considerable support from the ITEC director and other group members. This coleadership relationship was renegotiated several times throughout this process. All community leaders agreed with the position advocated by the *Promoting Healthy Traditions Workbook* (1990) that the chair of the meetings should be "an experienced facilitator...someone who has a neutral role in the community...a respected elder." Our community meetings were facilitated by refreshments; an agenda that welcomed input from community members; updates on work accomplished; appropriate handouts; considerable networking and socialization; extensive good-humored teasing; requests for volunteers for subcommittee assignments; and plans for coming meetings.

Needs Assessment/Research Data Review

The planning committee reviewed existing data from several resources including the Census Bureau, independent community research studies, social service and community agencies, committee representatives, and two recent Native American community needs assessments. All of these data supported information already known to most of the participants; that is, Indian people in Salt Lake County have health, employment, social service, education, social, and cultural needs. Indian people are often overrepresented in statistics indicating problems with alcohol and drug use, incarceration, juvenile justice and adult correction systems, educational attendance and achievement, and dependence on social service systems.

An interesting finding from both recent needs assessments was respondent willingness to participate in programs to identify solutions and develop resources to better meet the needs of Indian people in Salt Lake County. These respondents wanted to be involved in the community development activities.

After reviewing all these data, the steering committee recommended that a survey be formulated related specifically to the purposes of the RFP. The research instrument was developed, pretested, and administered in consultation with the planning committee. Data were tabulated and summarized for presentation at the community meetings. Subcommittees were formed, as appropriate to the recommendations.

Evaluation

All reports were submitted, in detail, at committee meetings. The ITEC staff were responsible for drafting the grant proposal with the planning committee's participation. The ITEC staff were also charged with the responsibility of selecting evaluation approaches.

Reporting Outcomes to the Community

Throughout this process, the community was kept informed through regularly scheduled committee and community meetings. Enhanced community participation was encouraged through written invitations, personal contacts, and shared information.

Enhancing Positive Regard, Individually and Collectively

In keeping with American Indian traditions, considerable effort was directed toward inviting participation of all community members. Goals and objectives were identified. Subcommittees were formed. Tribal chairman, key professional people, and members of the lay community were invited to participate in assignments of their own choosing.

Luncheons and "feasts" were held in restaurants and private homes to celebrate the process and work accomplished. Feasts are traditionally important to both the work and socialization values of American Indian culture. Feasts promote a continued balance in the daily lives of Native American people. They emphasize cooperation, sharing, industriousness, social interaction, and celebration.

Enhancing Positive Cultural Identification

Throughout this community development process, considerable effort was extended to influence positively the cultural identification of community participants and the people served by their agencies. All assignments emphasized incorporation of cultural values, beliefs, and traditions. A cultural content committee was charged with preparing materials that formed the initial cultural thrust of the program. The cultural content emphasized, but was not limited to, important cultural information from the eight major Utah tribes.

In addition to this committee, an elders' advisory committee was formed. This committee reviewed cultural materials prepared for program use and was designated to sanction the work or make recommendations for its modification.

All members of the community were to be kept informed of community activities through the efforts of a media subcommittee. Proposed media methods included (1) publication of a project community newsletter; (2) use of the larger community's media resources; (3) announcements made over the local radio station providing information and programming on a regular basis to the Native American community; (4) utilization of services of a local American Indian–owned artistic design studio; and (5) other resources as appropriate.

The cultural content of project programs related to general American Indian values, beliefs, and traditions but also presented tribal-specific cultural content. For example, the customs observed by Navajo people at the time of death and mourning are quite different from those of the Yurok. Navajos avoid contact with the body of the deceased and traditionally use burial locations some distance from their residences. Yurok people traditionally buried their dead in the center of their villages. Now that Yurok tribal members live on farms and ranches of their own, they often have family burial plots on their own land. Cultural content was proposed to reflect both traditional and modern-day values and practices.

A further goal of the planning committee was to emphasize the attainment and use of knowledge and wisdom—both traditional and current. Traditionally leadership was shared by all tribal members, according to individual and collective strengths and needs. This project sought to further this tradition for all participants, individually and collectively.

What was accomplished throughout the "enhancing community ownership" process included "enhancing positive regard for self" and "cultural identification." There was considerable interaction among community participants. As issues and problems were discussed, committee members offered suggestions based on their own tribal values and understanding and acceptance of the values of other tribal groups with which they were familiar. Differences of opinion were expressed openly and respectfully.

Throughout this project, a vision for the future development of the Salt Lake Native American community was clarified and integrated into the minds and hearts of the community participants. The vision was nurtured in community and committee meetings. The community development and cultural enhancement program brought people together. Personal and professional relationships were developed and enhanced. Participatory democracy was experienced through community decision making.

Whether or not the grant was funded, the Salt Lake Native American community created a vision of what could be accomplished through a community development and cultural enhancement model. Community members committed themselves to continue their support of the Native American community through future interpersonal and professional collaborative "journeys."

A Case Study in Process

As we indicated earlier, the 1990 U.S. Census reports that almost two-thirds of the American Indian population is now residing in urban areas. With the increasing migration to urban areas, there is an increased need for community organization efforts to address the family and child welfare needs of this population. Most major American cities offer services to Indian people through American Indian Centers such as the Walk-In Center in Salt Lake City, Utah. The Indian Walk-In Center offers a variety of services including individual and family counseling, emergency resources and referrals, and social and cultural activities.

As the population of American Indians has grown, so has the awareness of and use of social services. Each community's needs are unique and demand a thorough review of these needs, existing resources and community interest, and support for the development of resources to address these issues. One such need was identified in the Salt Lake community, that is, the need for education, training, and dissemination of information regarding the American Indian Child Welfare Act. This act was passed by Congress in 1978 and sought to address problems associated with the removal of Indian children from their homes and their subsequent adoption in homes of non-Indian people ("The Destruction of Indian Families," 1974). A review of the implementation of the 1978 Indian Child Welfare Act was accomplished in 1988, and although the review showed that some progress had been made, achievement of the goals of the act was uneven across the United States (Plantz, 1989).

In 1996 a community meeting was held in Salt Lake City to address Indian child welfare issues important to this community. This meeting was accomplished with the assistance of a legal intern from one of the Salt Lake City legal aid society offices and the support of the American Indian Walk-In Center staff and American Indian and non-Indian social workers, judges, attorneys, and paraprofessionals. Issues were identified and a committee was formed. Meetings were held with the Utah State Social Services staff and Indian tribal and social service representatives. Plans are under way (1) to provide ongoing training to state and other social service agencies; (2) to recruit American Indian families for substitute care responsibilities; and (3) to recruit American Indian social workers to fill direct-line and supervisory positions in social service agencies.

All of these goals are crucial to the effective implementation of the American Indian Child Welfare Act in Salt Lake City. Social workers must be familiar with required child welfare procedures. Communities must be educated regarding child and parental rights. Compliance with this act must be monitored. Advocacy is crucial to the continuance of the American Indian Child Welfare Act.

As often happens with social legislation, congressional mandates may be legislated without provision of sufficient funds to achieve the full intent of the legislation. It has taken considerable time, education, and advocacy for the Indian Child Welfare Act to achieve more appropriately the intent of the legislation.

During the 1996 congressional session, legislation was introduced that would have had detrimental consequences for the intent of the American Indian Child Welfare Act. American Indian and non-Indian social work advocates have been successful in defending the intent of the American Indian Child Welfare Act, and some negotiation has been forthcoming that will ideally protect and continue the implementation of this act's provisions ("U.S. Senate Holds Hearings on ICWA Amendments," 1996).

Social work advocates and community organizations must continue to actively support legislation that protects American Indian family and tribal heritage. In spite of the continued and ongoing high turnover of social work staff in the public social service sector, continued education and advocacy on behalf of this act must be maintained. Continued community development activities such as those undertaken by the Salt Lake American Indian community are crucial to promote the best interests of American Indian children, families, and their cultural heritage.

Community Organization Practice Skills Important to the Community Development/ Cultural Enhancement Model

Implementation of this model includes judicious and continuous use of professional community organization skills. None of these skills should be neglected. Some, however, must take into consideration the cultural values and traditions of American Indian people.

1. *Leadership* positions are not actively sought by many competent, qualified American Indian people. Leaders are often recruited from participants on an ongoing basis. Leadership must be shared. Major roles must be fulfilled by those having both informal and formal sanction of the community. Leadership assignments must be given to those who will follow through and provide a framework that welcomes and involves participation from all community members. Recognition should be given to all participants—one person should not be singled out for recognition more than another even though that person contributes more significantly to the project. Extensive individual recognition may embarrass traditional Indian people and result in withdrawal from project participation. When people offer suggestions for implementation, they should

be invited to provide leadership in developing these suggestions. This is often a way in which American Indian people offer to "volunteer."

2. *Planning* before meetings and subcommittees is imperative. Community meetings must provide opportunities for networking, socialization, feedback from elders, and attention to work. In order to accomplish all these goals, preplanning is essential.

3. *Sharing* the planning, work, and credit is important to maintain participation. Many American Indian people will not volunteer for assignments, especially in front of their peers. Leaders must recognize community members' talents and invite members to assume chairmanship and committee assignments. When committee members do not accept their share of the work assignments, it is not unusual for this to be pointed out indirectly in a committee meeting, with some pressure placed on the "reluctant" contributors. Young adults should be welcomed as potential leaders. It is the responsibility of the Native American adults to train and support youth in the development of youth leadership abilities.

4. *Communication* is essential. Welcome and respond to both nonverbal and verbal communication. Elders may take considerable time offering their opinions. Listen. Summarize community meetings. Emphasize assignments, the next meeting, and other matters important to the group's business. Express appreciation for the attendance and participation of everyone.

5. *Problem solving* will require attention to *negotiating* and *conflict management.* There is much "history" involved in conflicts among specific tribal groups. Some reservations include more than one tribal group. Some of these tribal "combinations" were prereservation "enemies." They have histories of conflict with one another. There are often problems between "enrolled" and "terminated" members of the same tribe. There are family histories that involve cultural conflicts and ill will. Many of these are known to only a few people. But these are barriers to community development. There are differences of opinion regarding the community project itself. Who will lead? Where will the project originate? Who will comprise the "board of directors"? What is an agency's history—individually and collectively—with these people? Two major issues will affect the process of problem solving, negotiation, and conflict management. One is the worth and value of the community project. The second is whether the shared leadership includes people with whom there is already a trusting/working relationship.

6. *Goal accomplishment* is greatly facilitated when as many community members as possible are consulted and their input is included in the project. An effective leader must honestly seek consultation from every constituency as well as involvement from professionals who can be supportive of the project. *Consultation* must also be ongoing with the elders of an American Indian community with both formal and informal role assignments and recognition given to this valued segment of American Indian people.

7. *Decision making,* like leadership, must be shared. If not, the program may be limited to one agency and one staff—with little involvement or support from the community. If a program operates independently, from a single agency base, it often contributes to the detriment of community building and cultural enhancement.

Personality Traits Important to the Implementation of the Community Development and Cultural Enhancement Model

The implementation of the community development and cultural enhancement model relies heavily on the maturity and personality traits of all community participants—not just the leader(s). American Indian people are community oriented. Individually and collectively, their personality strengths must support the community development and cultural enhancement model.

1. Community members must be *visionary*. Spiritually, American Indian people have strong, positive ties to the visionary attributes of their personalities. All community members must see the program or components of the program from a committed visionary stance. This means they truly see, feel, and experience the goals, work, and potential accomplishments.
2. The community project must be conceptualized as a *journey*. American Indian people enjoy the journey (process) as much as they appreciate the outcome. Individual growth is valued and subtly recognized throughout the process. Collectivity is nurtured and celebrated. Community members are reluctant to terminate satisfying community journeys.
3. American Indian community members must continue to build their *inclusionary* traits. Ideally, leaders genuinely welcome participation and involvement from others. There is a selflessness in evidence when people recognize the importance of the community project or goals and submit themselves to the will of the group in working toward accomplishment of these community goals. One can imagine the conflicts that occur when there are negative histories or unresolved relationship issues among Native American people who are committed to the same community goals. Resolution of these conflicts may take considerable time to accomplish.
4. Over time, *honest investment* in goal accomplishment and all aspects of the program's development may result appropriately in subjugation of personal issues to the success of the program.
5. All of the above may successfully contribute to *understanding, diffusing, and resolving criticism and divisiveness,* which, unfortunately, are altogether too common in programs undertaken within American Indian communities. There is often legitimate basis for criticism (or unfinished history) that could be addressed. Acknowledging the criticism will do much to diffuse it. Offering to accommodate or include positive recommendations can propel positive energy toward the program's goals and objectives.
6. *Motivation* and commitment to the American Indian community and project are often framed by the *high-energy* investment of community members. All participants should be encouraged to "enjoy" the hard work, the association and togetherness, and the successes and challenges. *Good humor* and positive interactions will motivate continued involvement and personal growth of community members

at all levels of participation. Feasts and other socialization activities are appropriate to celebrate accomplishments and redirect community efforts.

Secondary Community Development

There are often many benefits that communities enjoy in accomplishing goals and objectives through implementation of "community development and cultural enhancement" models. Primary benefits are the realization of the goals of the specific projects. Secondary benefits are often seen in community togetherness and the enhanced networking of individuals, groups, and agencies. Many secondary benefits have been noted in Salt Lake County since efforts were established to implement this community model. Among these are the following:

1. One agency has established an "Elder's Advisory Committee" that identified elders in Salt Lake County, assessed needs, and developed a program to address these needs. An Elder's Committee is now established, with program responsibility being invested by the elders themselves.
2. Groups for Indian youth have been developed at elementary schools through volunteer efforts of professional social workers and graduate social work students. Parents are also involved in these group efforts, with one elementary school sponsoring its first annual "American Indian Community Powwow and Dinner" activity.
3. The first annual American Indian Motivational Youth Conference was implemented as a result of suggestions from American Indian teens participating in a Youth Leadership program. Representatives from three western states attended this conference.
4. The first Annual American Indian Art Show and Auction was successful in fundraising for family and individual counseling at the Indian Walk-In Center.
5. An American Indian Child Welfare Task Force has been organized to address American Indian family and child welfare issues.
6. There has been active outreach to all of the major tribal groups represented in the state of Utah.
7. Information has been readily shared throughout the community regarding these projects. Youth, adult, and elder participation has been invited and expanded throughout the community.

Summary

It is important to emphasize both the community development and cultural enhancement aspects of this model. Native American people have experienced the benefits of community in their traditional heritage. They have considerable history, knowledge, and wisdom, much of which can be applied to the community challenges of today. Native American people are committed to self-determination and self-governance, values that complement community organization principles. They find much satisfaction in identification of "visions" important to the success of their people. They have rekindled the hope of the "journey" (process) that has been so effective in past community accomplishments. Many challenges remain in the broader society and within Native American communities. This community development approach, with its emphasis on cultural enhancement, has the potential for reinforcing the identification and achievement of the visions of Native American people—individually and collectively.

References

Boyte, H. C. *Community Is Possible: Repairing America's Roots.* New York: Harper & Row, 1984.

Census Bureau Completes Distribution of 1990 Redistricting Tabulations to States, CB91-100. *U.S. Department of Commerce News,* Washington, D.C., March 11, 1991.

Chavis, D. M., Florin, P., & Felix, M. R. J. "Nurturing Grassroots Initiatives for Community Development: The Role of Enabling Systems," in *Community Organization and Social Administration: Advances, Trends and Emerging Principles,* T. Mizrahi & J. Morrison (Eds.). New York: Haworth Press, 1993.

"The Destruction of Indian Families." *Indian Family Defense: A Volume of the Association on American Indian Affairs,* 1974.

Edwards, E. D., et al. "Community Organizing in Support of Self-Determination within Native American Communities," *Journal of Multicultural Social Work, 3*(4), 1994.

Edwards, E. D., et al. "A Community Approach for Native American Drug and Alcohol Prevention Programs: A Logic Model Framework," *Alcoholism Treatment Quarterly, 13*(2), 1995.

Edwards, E. D., & Edwards, M. E. "Alcoholism Prevention Treatment and Native American Youth: A Community Approach," *Journal of Drug Issues, 18*(1), 1988: 103–114.

Edwards, E. D., & Edwards, M. E. "Native American Community Development," in *Community Organizing in a Diverse Society,* F. G. Rivera and J. L. Erlich (Eds.). Boston: Allyn & Bacon, 1992.

Khinduka, S. K. "Community Development: Potentials and Limitations," in *Strategies of Community Organization: Macro Practice,* F. M. Cox et al. (Eds.). Itasca, Ill.: F. E. Peacock, 1987.

Martinez-Brawley, E. E. "Power, Influence, and Leadership in the Small Community," in *Perspectives on the Small Community.* U.S.A.: NASW Press, 1990.

McKnight, J. "Are Social Service Agencies the Enemy of Community?" *Social Policy,* Winter 1987.

Pass the Word. A resource booklet published by the Native American Development Corporation, Washington, D.C., no date given.

Plantz, M. C. "Indian Child Welfare: A Status Report," *Children Today,* 18, (January/February 1989).

Positive Self-Esteem Can Protect Native American Youth. A resource booklet published by the Native American Development Corporation, Washington, D.C., no date given.

Rothman, J., & Tropman, J. E. "Models of Community Organization and Macro Practice Perspectives: Their Mixing and Phasing," in *Strategies of Community Organization: Macro Practice,* F. M. Cox et al. (Eds.). Itasca, Ill.: F. E. Peacock, 1987.

Scott, S. *Promoting Healthy Traditions Workbook: A Guide to the Healthy People 2000 Campaign.* St. Paul, Minn.: American Indian Health Care Association, 1990.

Trimble, S. *The People: Indians of the American Southwest.* Santa Fe: School of American Research Press, 1993.

"U.S. Senate Holds Hearings on ICWA Amendments," *NICWA News,* Summer 1996.

"We, the First Americans." U.S. Department of Commerce, Bureau of the Census, September 1993.

3

Chicanos, Community,
and Change

MIGUEL MONTIEL AND FELIPE ORTEGO Y GASCA

As Alice discovered, nothing is more "curiouser" than change. Often change is viewed as synonymous with "progress": movement toward reason and justice stressing equality as the core of justice (Ginsberg, 1953, p. 68). Men and women have power to the extent they change the circumstances of the time.

Why do some people resist change while others rush to greet it? William Blake identified resistance to change as "mind-forged manacles." It is true that each of us guards a gate of change most of us are reluctant to open. Nevertheless, each of us makes concessions to change, consciously or unconsciously, with or without consent.

Purposive change—the power of "intervention oriented toward improving or changing community institutions and solving community problems" (Cox et al., 1979, p. 3)—is the theme of this chapter. We explore the part played by Chicano organizations, particularly since the 1960s, in influencing change.*

To understand how change occurs in Chicano communities, let's consider what is meant by "community." It is simply a group of people sharing similar interests and goals. Warren (1972) refers to community as action organized to "afford people daily local access to those broad areas of activity which are necessary in day-to-day living" (p. 1). Often towns and cities are referred to as communities even though the

*The information on organizations comes from Gonzales's and Meier's dictionaries (see References) and from the experiences of the authors, who have witnessed many of the organizational developments over the years. Hispanic dictionaries include only a fraction of Hispanic organizations, because many organizations spring into being between the time a directory is submitted for publication and the time it appears in print.

residents may not share common interests and goals. The notions of community—culture, religion, work, education, war, and power (Cox et al., 1977, pp. 1–11; Mercer, 1956, p. 27)—have served "to gratify man's desire for community and for the cherished legitimacy that community alone can give to authority, function, membership, and loyalty" (Nisbet, 1973, p. 446).

What have been the process, progress, and direction of change in the Chicano community? What part have Chicano organizations played in change? What are the prospects and projections for Chicano communities and organizations? And what challenges can be expected as Chicanos approach the next millennium? What needs to be done to make things better? These are the questions we explore here. We begin with a brief profile of the Mexican American community, and the place of the barrio within it, and follow with a discussion of the evolution of organizations and the issues they attempted to address.

The Mexican American (Chicano) Community

The Mexican origin population of the United States is growing rapidly. Hispanics (Mexicans, Puerto Ricans, Cubans, and other Spanish-speaking peoples) now constitute about 9 percent of the total U.S. population, or more than 22 million people—an increase of 53 percent from the 1980 count. About 60 percent (13.5 million) are Mexican Americans, and about half of these are recent immigrants arriving over the last two decades. Compared with the general population, Hispanics are more concentrated, with 87 percent living in ten states as compared with 54 percent in the total population. The highest percentage of Hispanics among the population has remained within the Southwest (Texas, New Mexico, Colorado, Arizona, and California) with the majority (12 million) living in the states of California and Texas (U.S. Bureau of the Census, 1991).

Compared with the total U.S. population, Mexican Americans are younger (23.8 years vs. 32.9 years), more fertile (3.6 children for women aged 35–44 vs. 2.5 for white women), and seemingly beset with more problems (18.8 percent female-headed households vs. 14.3 for the Anglo cohort). Similarly, there are higher rates of delinquency, school dropouts, violent deaths, and alcohol-related diseases even though the life expectancy of Mexican Americans is similar to that of Anglos. Although Mexican American males had the highest labor force participation of any group, they had relatively higher rates of unemployment (9.2 percent vs. 6.1 percent for the total population). Median income was almost $9,000 less than the median of the total population, and women received the lowest wages of any group except Puerto Ricans (Bean et al., 1985, p. 57–75; Skerry, 1993; U.S. Bureau of the Census, 1991).

In many areas of the Southwest, Mexican culture has lingered despite the overwhelming dominance of Anglo society. It is in the barrios where the culture has been kept alive and vibrant. Mexican barrios have provided temporary continuity to their land of origin similar to that of the Jewish ghetto described by Louis Wirth (1928).

A barrio, however, is not necessarily a community, which doesn't mean it isn't. The word *barrio* is an imprecise term for a cluster of Chicanos principally because it is fraught with negative perceptions of poverty and impotence. The breakup, or more appropriately the segmentation of barrios, as with ethnic villages, has been created partly because of the movement of the middle class to the suburbs. According to Sennett and Cobb (1972), the integration of white ethnics "meant integration into a world with different symbols of human respect and courtesy, a world in which human capabilities are measured in terms profoundly alien to those that prevailed in...their childhood" (pp. 17–18). The same applies to Mexican Americans. Nevertheless, barrios do serve an important function particularly for newly arrived immigrants. The barrios are the communities with the greatest need for organization and leadership.

The Evolution of Chicano Organizations in the United States

To understand change and the role that Mexican American organizations have played in the Chicano community since the 1960s we need to examine the historical record. The period from 1848 to 1960 can be seen as three stages, each contributing cumulatively to the evolution of Mexican American organizations and Chicano consciousness.

Early Mexican American Period: 1848–1912

This was a period of transition for Mexican Americans. Although no accurate record of the number of Mexican citizens in the territory demarcated by the Treaty of Guadalupe-Hidalgo in 1848 exists, estimates range from 75,000 (McWilliams, 1968) to 350,000 (Ortego y Gasca, 1981). Additional Mexicans became residents of the United States as a result of the Gadsden Purchase in 1853. These were the first Mexicans to cope with becoming Americans in their own land.

These events marked the end of a historically Mexican community and the beginning of a consciousness as Mexican Americans. During this period, Chicanos resisted the one-way process of acculturation and assimilation. Conquest, segregation, a distinct language and culture, and, to some extent, skin color kept Mexican Americans from full participation in the American experience.

There were, of course, many organized groups within the Mexican community before the conquest in 1848. For example, the Penitentes (Brothers of Our Father Jesus of Nazareth), carryovers from the original Spanish settlers, began organizing in the late 1700s in what is now New Mexico and Colorado. After the conquest, however, Mexican Americans saw the need for organizational strength to ward off Anglo American onslaughts. The massive land transfers, legal and illegal, from Mexican to Anglo hands, the conversion of Mexican people into a pool of cheap labor, and laws like the California "Greaser Act" of 1855 were some of the tangible effects of discrimination, and resistance organizations were formed in response. In addition to the many mutual aid societies were radical organizations headed by figures like Juaquin Murrieta and Padre Martinez. One such organization, El Guante Negro Mutualista, was a secret society dedicated to robbing the rich and helping the poor. In 1894, twelve years before the formation of the NAACP, the first successful organization for Mexican American rights was formed in Tucson, Arizona, under the banner of Alianza Hispano Americana. Its mission was to defend Mexicans against the bad will extant in American society. These are the events that set the agenda of the times. The year 1912, when New Mexico and Arizona were admitted into the union, marks the end of this period.

Later Mexican American Period: 1912–1940

Between 1912 and 1930, fleeing the turmoil created by the Mexican Revolution of 1910 and attracted by the lure of mining jobs and manufacturing, more than 1.5 million Mexicans crossed into the United States. Ernesto Galarza, a scholar and an early organizer in the farm workers' cause, called this one of the greatest migrations in the history of the world. Although as many as one-third of this number (including bona fide American citizens) were "repatriated" to Mexico during the 1930s, it is from this rapid expansion of the Mexican American community that the current Chicano population draws its numeric strength.

This period is also marked by Mexican American efforts to become Americans, shedding, if need be, their "Mexicaness" including their language to become part of the American mainstream. Leading the effort to promote English and help its members become good American citizens was the League of United Latin American Citizens (LULAC) organized in 1927 in Texas. LULAC, one of the more significant organizational efforts with a membership of approximately 100,000 members, has a long list of civil rights, labor, and educational accomplishments.

Modern Mexican American Period: 1940–1960

This was the period when Mexican Americans searched for America and discovered two Americas—White America and the Other America, as Michael Harrington (1978) described it. Some 500,000 Mexican Americans served in the armed forces during World War II and earned a significant number of medals of honor. Yet after the war, Mexican Americans learned painfully that "color" was still the way white America defined good Americans. In the apartheid system of the United States, Mexican Americans could not cross the color line.

In South Texas in 1947, a Mexican American soldier who died in battle during World War II but whose body had only then been recovered was denied burial in a municipal cemetery. This (and other related events against returning soldiers) precipitated the formation of the American G.I. Forum, a powerful militant organization of Mexican American veterans.

Two important court cases enjoined by LULAC laid the legal foundation for the involvement of Mexican Americans in the civil rights movement of the 1960s. In

1945 Gonzalo Mendez of Orange County, California, brought suit against the public schools of Westminster to end segregation of Mexican American students. Judge McCormick ruled for Mendez, and the ruling was affirmed on April 14, 1947, by the Ninth Circuit Court. In 1948 a similar case was affirmed against the Bastrop School District in Texas. Both cases were important precedents in the 1954 Supreme Court ruling on *Brown* v. *Board of Education.*

In 1955 the Alianza Hispano Americana—then more that sixty years in existence—established a civil rights department headed by Rafael Guzman, an early scholar of the Chicano movement. The Alianza joined with the American Civil Liberties Union (ACLU) and the NAACP to further the civil rights of all minorities (Gonzales, 1985, pp. 8–17). In 1957, for example, the *Alianza* magazine informed Mexican Americans that Charlotte C. Rush, patriotic education chairman of the Denver chapter of the Daughters of the American Revolution, didn't "want a Mexican to carry old Glory" in a parade at the State Industrial School for Boys. She believed that only "American boys" should carry the flag despite the fact that the boy originally chosen was an American of Mexican descent.

Only until the civil rights movement of the 1950s and 1960s did Americans began to realize that nineteenth-century theories of acculturation did not tell the full story of minorities in America. An America founded on a homogeneity of values rooted in the English tradition is giving way to an America founded on cultural pluralism (Lubdomyr, 1975). That was the situation of the Mexican American at the threshold of the 1960s.

The 1960s and Beyond

A taxonomy for "Chicanos, Community, and Change" since 1960 does not evolve neatly by decades. The patterns seem to fall from mid-decade to mid-decade. The momentum of the 1950s carries well into the 1960s and the consciousness of the Chicano movement, faint though stirring, begins well before the 1960s. Although the beginning of the Chicano movement is not the beginning of the civil rights struggle for Mexican Americans, it begins a time of self-determination and a disruption of the traditional Americanization process. It is out of this resolve that the plethora of Chicano organizations emerged, dedicated to "going it alone" (at least for a while) rather than trying to "satisfy the man." Three organizational epochs since the 1960s are identified: (1) the Chicano Renaissance, (2) economic development, and (3) Hispanicity. The 1990s, characterized by an alarming trend in the breakdown of families, polarization between men and women, and antiminority shifts in public policy may frame yet a new organizational epoch.

The Chicano Renaissance

This period during the 1960s and early 1970s is the beginning of Chicano resistance activities in the arts, academia, and politics. During this period, Chicanos became involved in numerous projects, abortive and successful, in collaboration and in opposition with the "establishment." It was a time of turmoil, confusion, and opportunity. It was a time when Chicanos tried to enter the American system on their terms.

One of the most effective organizing efforts in the Mexican American community was led by the Industrial Areas Foundation (IAF), a training network established by Saul Alinsky in 1940. IAF-trained organizers built the Community Services Organization and the Farm Workers Union in the late 1950s and early 1960s. Chavez, Roybal, Corona, and many other Mexican American organizers were influenced by Alinsky's confrontational tactics.

In the late 1950s and early 1960s organizers in California and Texas began aggressive activities in state and national politics. For example, under the leadership of Bert Corona (and with assistance from the Jewish community), the Mexican American Political Association (MAPA) achieved the incorporation of East Los Angeles and the election of Edward Roybal, an instrumental figure in the formation of several national organizations, to the U.S. House of Representatives. During this time, similar activities were initiated by Henry B. Gonzales, the eccentric and courageous U.S. representative (who became the chairman of the Banking Committee) from San Antonio, Texas.

In spite of strong opposition from growers and the Teamsters Union and a history of failed attempts to organize farm workers, Cesar Chavez established what is today known as the United Farm Workers Union, an affiliate of the AFL-CIO. Chavez's organizing genius included utilizing powerful religious Mexican symbols like the Virgin de Guadalupe to network diverse groups of farm workers, appealing to the liberal community, and using Gandhian nonviolence and fasting to keep the peace and make it difficult for the growers to retaliate. Until recently, Chavez maintained a loyal following. Shortly before his death in 1993, however, competing unions, lack of enforcement of the Labor Relations Board in California, and litigation setbacks began to affect the power and membership of the Farm Workers Union.

In the mid-1960s, radical organizations led by charismatic leaders sprang up throughout the Southwest. Most important were Reyes Lopez Tijerina's Alianza Federal de Pueblos Libres in New Mexico, Rodolfo "Corky" Gonzales's Crusade for Justice in Colorado, and Jose Angel Gutierrez's Raza Unida Party in Texas.

Chavez's nonviolent posture stands in stark contrast to the militant tactics of the flamboyant Protestant minister Tijerina, the leader of the Alianza, who fought to have Spanish land grants restored to the original Mexican settlers in New Mexico, Colorado, and Texas. The Alianza lost its base when violence erupted in a courthouse raid in Rio Arriba County in northern New Mexico. The story of what happened varies depending on to whom one talks; however, the raid did destroy the movement and Tijerina was imprisoned.

Exhibiting a similarly strong nationalistic orientation, Rodolfo "Corky" Gonzales, a former boxer and powerful charismatic leader, inspired the passions of Chicano youth through his Crusade for Justice. The yearly Youth Liberation Conference sponsored by the Crusade of the 1970s had a powerful, long-lasting impact on the more radical elements of the Chicano movement. It is from these conferences that El Plan

Espiritual de Aztlan emerged, which outlined a "declaration of self-determination" for Chicanos in the Southwest. "Nationalism," Gonzales claimed "is a tool for organization, not a weapon for hatred" (Marin, 1975).

Under the leadership of the firey Jose Angel Gutierrez, the Raza Unida Party gained electoral victories in several communities in Texas where Mexican Americans held majorities, thus challenging, at least for a short period, the dominance of the Democratic Party in the Chicano community (Meier & Rivera, 1972). Several prominent Chicano leaders have accused the Raza Unida Party of reverse racism. Important during this period also were the organizing activities of the Chicano students under the MECHA banner, which led to the formation of numerous Chicano studies programs in universities across the country.

The emerging Chicano intelligensia, some based at fledging Chicano studies departments, began to search for a more accurate depiction of the Chicano community. Up to this time, the social sciences had depicted Chicanos as deficient, and policy was aimed at transforming Mexicans into a narrow middle-class success model (Montiel, 1978). Padilla (1987) claims that because of its diversity and insignificant community participation, however, Chicano studies advocates created an idealized vision of the Chicano community. Focus on community, Padilla argues, reflected a desire on the part of Chicano intellectuals to participate in the struggle for equality at a grassroots level (pp. 9–10).

During the 1960s and early 1970s, Chicanos proposed bold visions of a bilingual/bicultural society to be maintained by Hispanic institutions; only a handful have survived. The most ambitious was the Hispanic University of America in Denver in 1972. Although headed by New Mexican U.S. Senator Joseph Montoya, the drive to secure funding comparable to that of congressional funding for black colleges did not materialize. The Chicano movement did not create bilingualism or biculturalism in American society; both were there from the beginning of Anglo American society on the Atlantic frontier. The Chicano movement (with the significant influence of exiled Cubans) did raise discussion of these issues to the level of national policy, however, culminating in the Bilingual Education Act of 1968.

In the late 1960s, Chicanos began to organize caucuses within various professional organizations. In social work, for example, the Trabajadores de la Raza led by Paul Sanchez helped organize chapters in cities in the Southwest and Midwest. Chicano-oriented schools of social work were established at San Jose State University (where Sanchez became the first dean) and New Mexico Highlands University. The Trabajadores also had a part in curriculum changes and redirecting social service delivery systems. Many Chicano agencies began as advocacy agencies but ended as social services agencies because of their dependence on external funding. Many professional groups organized during this period became institutionalized in the 1980s. Nevertheless, although blatant negative stereotypes of Chicanos have gone by the wayside and institutions give token service to Chicano concerns by establishing what have been generally ineffective bilingual programs, there is no bilingual/bicultural society.

The Economic Development Period

The economic development era took hold in the mid-1970s and continues to the present. During this time, the focus of reform efforts shifted from global and idealistic aspirations for social justice of the 1960s to gaining economic and political advantage for Chicanos at the national level. Enhanced activity in Washington, D.C., created, at least temporarily, a paucity of leadership at the local level. In the 1970s, a more systematic approach toward solving problems appeared to be taking place. The tactics of the radicals were rejected. Government and philanthropic organizations such as the Ford Foundation encouraged the establishment of Chicano agencies that would work within the system. There is little question that the rejection of many charismatic leaders led to greater opportunities for the moderate leaders that followed.

Activists (as opposed to agency heads) continued to confront established institutions on many of the same issues raised during the 1960s. Invariably these confrontations lead to concessions, usually not for confronters but for others who waited in the wings. The relationship between confrontation and change is never direct. Institutions never admit that the change results from pressure. As a university administrator stated about a prominent leader, the prize goes to those who are "acceptable to the establishment." The 1970s are filled with examples of this phenomenon: The Raza Unida Party enhanced opportunities for Mexican Americans in the Democratic Party; MECHA opened the universities for newly graduated Ph.D.'s; demonstrations and disturbances in the inner cities created opportunities for economic development corporations; the Tierra Amarillo raids in New Mexico enhanced opportunities for Hispanic New Mexican politicians.

The most prominent organizational phenomenon of the 1970s was the formation of community development corporations (CDCs) in poor minority neighborhoods in the late 1960s and early 1970s. Their goal was to develop "sources of strength and confidence in those neighborhoods" and alleviate "the economic and social distress caused by the malfunctioning of the private sector and the shortcomings of the public sector" (Search, 1975). These corporations were designed to quiet the disturbances in the inner cities. Today, the more than one hundred CDCs (some controlled by Chicanos but most by blacks) are supported largely by federal programs and private foundations (especially Ford), although the ultimate goal is to be self-supporting through profit-making ventures.

The Mexican American Legal Defense and Education Fund, (MALDEF), spearheaded by the LULAC network with moneys from the Ford and Marshall Field Foundations, came into its own during this period. MALDEF's civil rights activities have touched every area of Mexican American life from education to women's rights. The Ford Foundation has figured prominently in the organization and funding of other organizations including the Hispanic Policy Development Institute and the Inter-Agency Consortium for Hispanic Research, two national Hispanic organizations. Interestingly enough, these groups are headed by non-Hispanics.

The Industrial Areas Foundation's (IAF) influence on the Mexican American community was again felt in the mid-1970s, first in Texas, later in California, and more recently in Albuquerque, New Mexico, and Phoenix, Arizona. There is a strong link between the IAF, at the time led by Fred Ross, and the formation of various Mexican American organizations (e.g., CSO, MAPA, the Farm Workers Union, and subsequent organizations like the Hispanic Caucus and NALEO [The National Association of Latino Elected and Appointed Officials]). The IAF has also served as a catalyst for the formation of various Mexican American organizations. This pattern is manifested in the formation of other Hispanic organizations. The union organizing efforts of leaders like Barraza and Lacayo spawned ideas for the development of the National Council of La Raza and a string of Community Development Corporations such as Chicanos Por La Causa in Phoenix and TELACU in Los Angeles, as well as several offshoots of the Council. Similar threads can be traced to the development of organizations like LULAC, the American G.I. Forum, La Alianza Hispanoamericana, and most recently El Concilio de America.

The resources provided by the War on Poverty and the unions helped develop networks that remain to this day. For example, the National Council of La Raza hosted over 125 affiliates and 8,000 participants at their annual meeting in Detroit in 1993. It is not surprising that organizational life in the Mexican American community is dominated by relatively few individuals connected through a national network (a network, however, that touches only a small segment of Chicano and Mexican communities in the United States).

The Age of Hispanicity

In the 1980s many of the concerns of the 1960s were institutionalized. It was the epoch of Hispanicity, a period when many important Chicano leaders of the 1960s became outcasts, when it became possible to form a Hispanic congressional caucus, and when national Hispanic organizations gained prominence. It was also a period when corporations and political leaders at the highest levels saw the convenience of aggregating Spanish-speaking groups, and from one day to another Mexican Americans and other Spanish-speaking groups were referring to themselves as Hispanic.

During the 1980s, "leadership" became important in Hispanic communities. MALDEF, LULAC, and the United Way of America initiated leadership programs to help Hispanics develop the skills needed to serve on agency boards. In 1988 representatives from various Hispanic leadership programs established the National Network of Hispanic Leadership Programs aimed at the formation of a national leadership training agenda.

Although still important, community-based organizations are giving way to profession-centered organizations. Local and national organizations have sprung up in business, health, education, welfare, and the arts. In the professions there are Hispanic organizations for accountants, executives, personnel managers, psychologists, and nurses.

The National Hispanic Quincentennial Commission was organized to plan a national program commemorating the 500th anniversary of the Hispanic presence in the Americas. IMAGE (The National Association of Hispanics in Government) established a commission to assess the status of Hispanics in the Department of Defense. Hispanic corporate executives organized the National Hispanic Corporate Council, a Fortune 500 group, to create opportunities for Hispanics within corporations. A similar group of executives, headed by former New Mexico governor Jerry Apodaca, established the Hispanic Association for Corporate Responsibility. The development of professional groups tied to their mainstream professional organization points to a shift in strategies for change in the 1990s and beyond. Everywhere Hispanic groups with ties to their mainstream organizations are being formed to tackle specific pieces of the Hispanic agenda.

Although general membership organizations like LULAC still "cover the waterfront" in voicing their concerns for Chicanos, more and more of the particular issues of the Hispanic agenda are taken up by organizations with specific rather than general membership. The organizations of the 1980s operated more like pressure groups held together by narrow goals and objectives than the broad-based advocacy groups of the past.

Organizations oriented toward promoting individual or professional interests are a recent phenomenon in the Chicano community. They are indicative of the growing diversity (and fragmentation) of the Chicano community and of the emergence of a professional and merchant class. The contrast between the pragmatism of the 1980s and the idealism of the 1960s was a source of great tension among the poor, the working class, and the middle class; between immigrants and Chicanos; and among the various Hispanic groups.

There has been some dissatisfaction with national efforts of organizations like the National Council of La Raza because some critics claim they are removed from the pulse of the local communities, they are influenced far too much by non-Hispanics and particularly corporate interests, and their advocacy is geared more toward individual interests than to that of their affiliates. In many instances national agencies are more and more involved in running programs rather than advocating for local efforts. These concerns have spurred organizing efforts such as those of Miguel Barragan, a pioneer in the development of the Chicano CDCs, who has organized El Concilio de America, an organization in Northern California with over 185 affiliates, some of which belong to both the National Council of La Raza and El Concilio. El Concilio's aim is to establish a Hispanic development fund for Hispanic self-determination, thus avoiding the control that agencies like United Way have exerted on Hispanic organizations. It is not surprising that these maverick efforts have angered those Hispanic groups and individuals who have finally managed to maneuver themselves into the mainstream.

Most Hispanic organizing efforts are staff dominated and little attention is paid toward developing leadership within the communities where the organizing takes place. Organizers and agency heads in many Hispanic communities do not live in the communities in which they work and rarely do they experience the indignities endured by residents of those communities. The dilemma facing the professional organizer is one of credibility, to have people believe him or her when the organizer speaks about dropouts, segregation, and housing. This is not to derogate the role of community agency organizers but to highlight the inevitable conclusion that although the individual circumstances of many Mexican Americans have changed, the social circumstances of barrios and communities—the targets of community organizers— have not changed dramatically.

Dissatisfied also are many Hispanic women, particularly with their level of participation in organizations of the Mexican American community. Numerous parallel groups for women like the Chicana Forum, MUJER, The Hispanic Women's Conference of Arizona, and the Mexican American Women's National Association, to name just four, have emerged in the last few years. Gonzales was one of the first women to raise this issue. Interstate Research Associates (IRA), an important nonprofit research and consulting firm founded on the idea of self-determination, she claimed, was out of touch with the women's movement: "Most notable was the lack of female representation in its leadership hierarchy. Mexican American women...questioned the lack of women in IRA's decision-making process. More and more they felt that IRA's problem solving excluded the problem of women" (pp. 106–107).

The 1990s and Beyond

During the 1990s, Chicanos have continued their organizing activities, many of them centered on politics and the professions. Various trends, however, both internal and external to Chicanos, have begun to influence their organizing efforts. We touch briefly on some of the more important policy issues including immigration, "official English," and affirmative action as well as newly emerging trends that threaten the Mexican American community.

Immigration and Naturalization Service (INS) apprehensions increased from 139,000 in 1966 to more than 1.3 million in 1985, and 95 percent were Mexican nationals. That same year the illegal immigrant population was estimated at 5 million (Bean et al., 1985). This phenomenon has led to a great deal of anti-immigrant sentiment as reflected in initiatives like California's Proposition 187, which proports to protect U.S. citizens from economic and other hardships attributed to the presence of illegal immigrants. The proposition makes it illegal for government agencies to provide health, education, and welfare services to illegal immigrants and punishes individuals who deal in the manufacturing and distribution of false documentation. In similar fashion the federal government has stepped up efforts to curtail illegal entry through enhanced law enforcement efforts including the addition of federal agents along the U.S.-Mexican border.

Official English initiatives motivated by concerns over costs and fears that policies that promote bilingual education and voting not only fragment American culture, but also retard economic and political equality of immigrants. Thus far thirteen states have enacted legislation declaring English as the official language, but only Arizona's Proposition 106 goes beyond the symbolic by calling for English to become the official language of the ballot, the schools, and most government functions. The proposition ("An initiative measure proposing an amendment to the constitution of Arizona relating to the English language providing that English is the official language of the state of Arizona and amending the constitution of Arizona by Adding Article XXVIII") was declared unconstitutional in the lower courts, but is scheduled to be heard before the U.S. Supreme Court.

Affirmative action policies initially viewed as legitimate mechanisms to reverse discrimination are now seen by many as mechanisms of reverse discrimination (Gamwell, 1996). There are numerous court cases (e.g., *Adarand Constructors Inc.* v. *Pena*), legislation, and referendums that have begun to curtail if not eliminate affirmative action policies. California Proposition 209, for example, approved by the California voters in 1996, is the most decisive statement against affirmative action to date (*Phoenix Gazette,* 1996). This proposition, which is currently being argued in the courts, bans preferences for women and minorities in contracting, government hiring, and college enrollments. The University of California Regents actually anticipated the proposition by eliminating preference enrollments in the U.C. system. These actions have jeopardized enrollments, scholarships, and other advantages afforded to minorities.

Despite the many political assaults against affirmative action, the chairman of the U.S. Equal Employment Opportunity Commission, Edward Casillas, reports that Hispanic men earn 64 cents for every dollar earned by white men, and Hispanic women with college degrees earn less than white men with high school diplomas. Most telling, however, is the statistic which indicates that of the 100,000 active cases at the EEOC, fewer than 2 percent are cases of reverse discrimination against whites. Furthermore, between 1990 and 1994 only about 3 percent of the court decisions on employment discrimination were reverse discrimination cases.

Perhaps the most serious issue facing the Mexican American community is the fragmentation of the family. *The Monthly Vital Statistics Report* of the National Center for Health Statistics of June 1996 indicated that 43 percent of Hispanic births were nonmarital. The expected increases in the number of teenagers in the Mexican American population will surely increase the number and proportion of births to nonmarried Mexican American women. Moynihan reports that one-parent families are the norm. "The vast majority of them will live with just their mothers, and over half of them will be poor" (70 percent of Hispanics as compared to 46 percent of whites). He speculates that "family structure may now prove to be the principal conduit of social class status" as well as the "primary setting in which social capital (education, access, mobility) . . . is amassed or dissipated" (p. 221).

Another source of internal pressure centers on the ever escalating rifts between Chicano men and women. Gloria Molina, exploiting the dissatisfaction of women and what Skerry (1993) referred to as "elite-network" politics—developed from outside money and with weak community ties practiced by Los Angeles politicians like Alatorre and Torres—got herself elected to the Los Angeles County Board of Supervisors. Similar rifts are evident in organizations such as the National Association for Chicana and Chicano Studies where the splits between men and women, "straights" and gays have made the organization ineffective and probably short lived. These same rifts are evident in virtually every campus with Chicano men and women professors, who seem more intent on attacking one another than confronting the institutions that have excluded them in the past. These academic conflicts are narrowly focused conflicts, far removed from the day-to-day life of most Mexican Americans whose struggles are concrete and immediate.

What can be said of the 1980s is that it was a time of institutionalization for Hispanics. In this period we witnessed the demise of the charismatic leaders of the 1960s; the proliferation of Hispanic professionally oriented organizations; increased visibility of Mexican Americans within the broader community; the seriousness with which they are taken as consumers; dissatisfaction with the status quo among Hispanic women; and the amnesty bill, which at once legalizes illegal immigrants and makes it more difficult for illegal "aliens" to live in the United States. The 1990s are characterized by the attempts to separate ethnicity and public policy as reflected in affirmative action, anti-immigrant sentiments (including U.S. Hispanics), and the "English only" movement. The fragmentation of the family and the divisions between men and women are the new realities that organizing efforts will have to take into consideration.

Assessments and Revaluation

In the new science of chaos, consideration of data focuses on the sensitivity to initial conditions. That is, from the initial conditions we cannot predict the outcome. This is an appropriate consideration in assessing and revaluating Chicanos, community, and change during the last thirty-five years (1960–1995).

The initial conditions that engendered the tumult of the 1960s—poverty, unemployment, housing, failed foreign and domestic policy—are still with us, exacerbated by demographic imperatives that augur the realizations of all past apocalyptic visions, especially those of Malthus.

Have things changed for the better since the 1960s? The individual circumstances of many Mexican Americans have changed dramatically. Many make more money, live in better homes than their parents, are better educated, and generally enjoy a higher standard of living than they did as children. Dramatic changes have occurred at the national level also. National organizations like MALDEF, the National Council, and NALEO have fulfilled one of the most important goals of the 1960s: to get into the national agenda. In the 1990s we have seen national organizations like GI Forum and SER move their headquarters from the Southwest to Washington, D.C., providing further testimony to the prominence of Chicanos in the national scene. There also have been significant gains in national representation in the U.S. Congress and a proliferation of Spanish-speaking radio and television stations primarily controlled, however, by Cuban and Mexican interests.

Despite these efforts, the situation has not changed appreciably for most Chicanos. The level of Chicano participation in electoral politics continues to be low (de la Garza et al., 1985), and broad-based Hispanic political organizations have not learned how to hold their politicians accountable. And it may be as Skerry (1993) claims that some Mexican American politicians, because they are beholden to interests outside their communities (as the Los Angeles clique just mentioned), want it that way. The Chicano population is young, poor, and growing rapidly, and a significant sector is beset with seemingly insurmountable problems including crime, drugs, teenage pregnancy, and dropouts. Chicano communities have become more segregated, income distribution is lopsided, and indicators of family life are increasingly pathological. We seem to be living in a society ill equipped to grapple with these problems.

Is the relative lack of progress the fault of leadership or of organizations? Perhaps it is both. Still the fault may lie, as Marc Antony intoned, not in the stars but in ourselves. We expected the miraculous from our ordained leaders and perhaps the impossible from our organizations. We expected a larger response from mainstream America. In *Forgotten People* Sanchez (1938/1967) wrote about the pledge to his people made by the U.S. government in the Treaty of Guadalupe-Hidalgo—a pledge to help his people lift themselves up by their bootstraps. Instead, Sanchez wrote, "It [has taken] away our boots." The Chicano movement, unlike previous Mexican American movements, made a clarion call for change to come from Mexican Americans themselves, not externally or benevolently from government. This does not mean that government has no role to play. On the contrary, government has a large role to play because it was, after all, government that in 1848 made Mexicans an internal colony.

Chicano organizations did not spring into being sui generis. Although most often formed in opposition to historical oppression, Chicano organizations nevertheless modeled their structures on organizations consistent with their experience in the United States. As Franz Fanon (1967) observed in *Black Faces/White Masks,* having experience with few other models, invariably the liberated turn to models with which they are familiar.

Still, the objectives of Chicano leaders and organizations were sufficiently radical to alarm mainstream America and even some Mexican Americans. That's why the term *Chicano* describes a generation whose sociopolitical directions veered sharply from the historical trajectory of the Mexican American experience. And it is quite possible that the term *Chicano* will die with the generations of the 1960s.

Organizations are oftentimes ephemeral, chimeras of a hopeful vision. The durable artifacts of change are most often the ideas that give birth to change, ideas written down on clay tablets, or parchment, or codices, or books for future generations to ponder and by which to judge the efficacy of the past.

The most fertile and perhaps the most dynamic period of the Chicano movement was the Chicano Renaissance. Its most enduring contributions are found in education and the cultural arts. Loosely, the decade of the Chicano Renaissance can be likened to an Iliad of Chicano assaults on mainstream America. By extension, the decade from 1976 to 1985 can be regarded as the Odyssey of Chicanos navigating through the rocks and shoals of mainstream America on the "final lap home," as Ricardo Sanchez, the Chicano poet laureate of Aztlan, phrased it.

Unfortunately, that meaning is being lost as the Chicano community grapples with the notion of Hispanicity introduced in 1986. Are they Chicanos (or Mexican Americans) or Hispanics? More than three-fifths of the Hispanics in the United States are Chicanos. Yet many are concerned that by subsuming themselves under the Hispanic rubric, they will lose their edge in numbers to Cuban Americans, who make up less than 5 percent of the U.S. Hispanic population but, like Jewish Americans, are influential beyond their numbers in the population. (Unless educated and mobilized, however, numbers alone are not a good indicator of power.)

Since 1986 Chicanos have been receding into the backdrop of American culture as an ethnic group; they are being culturally if not economically assimilated into the mainstream. High school textbooks still do not reflect the ethnic mosaic that is the American experience. Chicano high school students do not question this; neither do their parents. The Chicanos of this generation are busy professionalizing their lives, fashioning them on the templates of the dominant culture, and they have apparently lost interest in Chicano politics, particularly the politics of protest.

The Mexican American heteroclites who fashioned and shaped the various canons of the Chicano movement seem forgotten now. Here and there, *chispas* of those thoughts flow and fan the movement's flame for a flickering moment. The Chicano movement is a distant mirror to a time now denigrated by mainstream thought. Chicano intellectuals fashioned a heuristic tradition for the proper study of Chicano life and culture. Has it all been for naught?

No, we do not think so. The Chicano movement integrates a vision of past and present. The renewed sense of pride in their bicultural heritage has helped Mexican Americans better understand the sociopolitical context of their lives in the United States. More and more, national and local Chicano organizations (in concert with other Hispanic organizations) are influencing the national agenda. This was evident in the Bush appointments of the Texan Lauro Cavazos and the New Mexican Manuel Lujan as the first Mexican Americans to cabinet rank, and the Clinton appointments of Henry Cisneros, a prominent Chicano politician from Texas, to HUD and Federico Pena, the former mayor of Denver, to the Department of Transportation. Skerry (1993) raises a critical political consideration for Mexican Americans: do they follow the immigrant ethnic politics pursued by other ethnic groups or do they follow the racial minority politics of African Americans?

It may be, however, that the demographic imperative will be the demise of the Hispanic agenda. At the moment, there appears to be little planning for that eventuality. When that moment comes, Hispanics will not need an ethnic-specific agenda, because the public agenda will become their agenda. If this does not happen, internecine conflict will surely follow.

Conclusion

The problems that confront Chicanos are the problems of most Americans—environment, war, education, employment, poverty, the population explosion, and most recently unbridled government and corporate corruption. These problems, according to Morgenthau (1970), result from deliberate policies pursued by powerful interests (pp. 39–40).

Chicano organizations have been influenced by the same forces, perhaps to a greater extent, that influence mainstream culture, and Chicano leaders are vulnerable to the power brokers—interests that set the broad direction of economic and government policy. It is not only the powerful interests that prevent Chicanos from forging a better life, however; it is also the lack of strong families, strong friendships, ethical priests, viable communities, and strong vocations. It is the deterioration of these forces that allows "leaders" to lead while separated from the communities they represent. Accountability is absent.

The fragmentation in the Chicano community mirrors that of the larger society. The distorted concept of democracy that sets up a competitive system for the limited societal resources with little concern for the "common interest" makes it most difficult to organize. Chicano organizations often work at cross purposes with one another, and they often miscommunicate one another's motives. Given these circumstances, it is difficult to lay out a strategy for organizing. Noam Chomsky (1977) blames a "system of ideological control which aims to make the issues seem remote from the general population and to persuade them of their incapacity to organize their own affairs or to understand the social world in which they live without the tutelage of intermediaries" (pp. 4–5).

However it is possible to articulate a philosophical and ethical stance on the world that can guide action. It should rightly be an action that confronts the realities of the Chicano experience. And although we have attempted to highlight some of these realities, there are fundamental issues that would need to be explored in great depth if the Chicano reality was to be understood in its full significance. The works of Paulo Friere (1970), the Brazilian philosopher; Tomas Atencio, a New Mexican sociologist and activist; and the organizing of the IAF symbolized by the work of Ernesto Cortez are instructive in this regard. At the core of Freire's teaching is the idea that the ontological vocation of a human being is to be subject. Humans' reason for being rests on establishing horizontal relationships brought about through a confrontation with the reality of their situation—nature, institutions, and other humans. They can achieve their vocation through a critical consciousness—a depth of understanding in the interpretation of problems that lead toward changing themselves, the world, their relationship with others, and their culture. A critical consciousness within the Chicano community is possible, Freire would argue, only through a reflection of humans in the context of their cultural environment, that is, the place of Chicanos in American society; the eras both of Mexico and America and the interaction created by the confrontation of two cultures; the extent they are involved in the creation of their own history and culture; and the obstacles that need to be overcome. Education and organizing would need to focus on the development of a critical consciousness, and action would be based on Chicanos viewing themselves as social and political beings capable of accessing and acting on the world.

Tomas Atencio's (1978) reflections expand on an understanding of Chicano consciousness. He believes that the core of the problem facing Chicanos is the disharmony between Anglo and Chicano values: one set instrumental (e.g., goal oriented), legitimate, and systematic; the other moral, nonlegitimized, and unsystematic, but linked to myth. He refers to myth as the primal forces of society that serve to give meaning to cosmic and social phenomena. It is the separation of modern culture from its myth that has led to distorted ideologies that support negative irrational political motives. Cultural action must be based on the Chicano experience uncovered through personal history, oral history, folklore, and art—*el oro del barrio.*

It is through dialogue that people become aware of their myths and to the external forces that lessen or aid "fulfillment and freedom." Atencio (1988) uses the idea of the *resolana*—sunlight reflecting light off the walls where men gather to talk—as the metaphor for enlightenment. The spiral of thought and action that evolves from individuals to groups leads to consensual validation objectifying a body of knowledge from everyday experiences. It is "this body of knowledge that is used as education and ultimately objectified as a basis for action," an action where people respond (and not react) to their world. Atencio has been implementing these ideas in one of the barrios of Albuquerque in the Resolana Learning Center.

The tedious organizing process of the Industrial Areas Foundation (IAF) as described by Skerry (1993) consists of transferring "informal, primary groups between friends and neighbors into the instrumental ties binding members of a formal organization" (p. 210). The process requires an understanding of the disjuctures between democratic and Judeo-Christian values and the reality facing not only Mexican Americans or Hispanics but all segments of American society, black or white, rich or poor. Thus Cortez (1987) argues that people's concerns transcend ethnicity and, as a matter of fact, has criticized Mexican American civil rights activists of the late 1960s and early 1970s because of their "ethnic exclusivity."

In San Antonio, Houston, and El Paso, people were concerned with flooding and deterioration, education, and utility bills. Cortez's method of organizing is based on organizing people and not communities. Power relies on broad-based organizing that requires money and many organized people, not single individuals. What is needed is a strategy and vision that Cortez claims "comes out of our institutions and . . . Judeo Christian tradition and democratic values." IAF's goal is to establish self-governing institutions and a political culture that can hold institutions accountable. It is not surprising that IAF organizing depends on linkages with religious organizations, particularly the Catholic church.

Realistically, given the existing power arrangements and the available means to counter them, it is difficult to envision anything from American institutions other than token changes. There are no quick fixes and there are no Chicano messiahs. In the final analysis, it is Chicanos who must set the example of just and democratic behavior. Only then can the example be set for the next generation.

References

Atencio, T. (1978). *Phenomenology and social research: A theoretical discussion of a proposed method.* Unpublished manuscript. University of New Mexico.

Atencio, T. (1988). *Resolana: A Chicano pathway to knowledge.* Ernesto Galarza Commemorative Lecture. Stanford Center for Chicano Research. Stanford University.

Bean, F. D., Stephen, E. H., & Optiz, W. (1985). The Mexican origin population in the United States: A demographic overview. In de la Garza, R. O., Bean, F. D., Bonjean, C. M., Romo, R., & Alvarez R. (Eds.), *The Mexican American experience: An interdisciplinary anthology.* Austin: University of Texas, pp. 57–75.

Brischetto, R., & de la Garza, R. O. (1983). The Mexican American electorate: Political participation and ideology. Occasional Paper No. 3 in *The Mexican American Electorate Series.* San Antonio: Southwest Voter Registration and Education Project.

Casellas, G. (1995–96). America's continuing need for affirmative action. *The Journal of Intergroups Relations,* 4, 3–11.

Chomsky, N. (1977). *Language and responsibility.* New York: Pantheon Books.

Cortez, E., Jr. (1987, February). Changing the locus of political decision making. *Christianity and Crisis,* 47 (1), 18–22.

Cox, F. M., Erlich J. L., Rothman J., & Tropman J. E. (Eds.). (1977). *Tactics of community practice.* Itasca, Ill.: F. E. Peacock.

Cox, F. M., Erlich J. L., Rothman J., & Tropman J. E. (Eds.). (1979). *Strategies of community organizing: A book of readings.* Itasca, Ill.: F. E. Peacock.

de la Garza, R. O., Bean, F. D., Bonjean, C. M., Romo, R., & Alvarez R. (Eds.). (1985). *The Mexican American experience: An interdisciplinary anthology.* Austin: University of Texas.

Erlich, J. L., & Rivera, F. G. (1979). The challenges of minorities and students. In Cox, F. M., Erlich J. L., Rothman J., & Tropman J. E. (Eds.), *Strategies of community organizing: A book of readings.* Itasca, Ill.: F. E. Peacock.

Fanon, Frantz. (1967). *Black skins, white masks.* Trans. Charles Lam Markmann. New York: Grove Press.

Freire, P. (1970). *Pedagogy of the oppressed.* New York: Herder and Herder.

Gamwell, F. (1996). Affirmative action: Is it democratic? *The Christian Century,* 113, 77–81.

Ginsberg, M. (1953). *The idea of progress: A revaluation.* London: Methvens.

Gonzales, S. A. (1985). *Hispanic American voluntary organizations.* Westport, Conn.: Greenwood Press.

Harrington, M. (1978, January 29). *New York Times,* p. E–17.

Limon, J. (1974). El primer congreso Mexicanista de 1911: A precursor to contemporary Chicanismo. *Aztlan* 5 (1 & 2).

Lubomyr, R. W. (1975). *Encyclopedic directory of ethnic organizations in the United States.* Littletoy, Colo.: Libraries Unlimited.

MALDF. (1994). *Information on proposition 187* [Pamphlet].

Marin, C. (1975). Rodolfo "Corky" Gonzales: The Mexican-American movement spokesman, 1966–1972. *Journal of the West,* 14 (4), pp. 107–120.

McWilliams, C. (1968). *The Mexicans in America: A student's guide to localized history.* New York: Teacher College Press.

Meier, M. S. (1987). *Mexican American biographies: A historical dictionary, 1836–1987.* New York: Greenwood Press.

Meier, M. S., & Rivera, F. (1972). *The Chicanos: A history of Mexican Americans.* New York: Hill and Wang.

Mercer, B. E. (1956). *The American community.* New York: Random House.

Montiel, M. (1978). *Hispanic families: Critical issues for policy and programs in human services.* Washington, D.C.: National Coalition of Hispanic Mental Health and Human Service Organizations.

Morgenthau, H. (1970, September 24). The end of the republic? *New York Review of Books,* pp. 39–40.

Moynihan, D. P. (1996). *Miles to go: A personal history of social policy.* Cambridge, Mass.: Harvard University Press.

Nisbet, R. (1973). The social philosophers, community and conflict in western thought. New York: Thomas Y. Crowell.

Ortego y Gasca, F. D. (1981). *Backgrounds of Mexican American literature.* Austin, Tex.: Caravel Press.

Padilla, R. V. (1987). *Chicano studies revisited.* Occasional Paper No. 6. El Paso: University of Texas, Chicano Studies Program

Phoenix Gazette. (November 6, 1996). "California voters end affirmative action," p. E–1.

Sanchez, G. I. (1967). *Forgotten people: A story of New Mexicans.* Albuquerque, N. M: C. Horn. Originally published 1938.

Search. (1975, Winter). *A Report from the Urban Institute,* 5, 5–6.

Sennett, R., & Cobb, J. (1972). *The hidden injuries of class.* New York: Vintage Books.

Skerry, P. (1993). *Mexican Americans: The ambivalent minority.* New York: Free Press.

U.S. Bureau of the Census. (1991, June). Race and Hispanic origin: 1990 census profile. Washington, D.C.: Author.

Warren, R. L. (1972). *The community in American* (2nd ed.). Chicago: Rand McNally.

Wirth, L. (1928). *The ghetto.* Chicago: University of Chicago Press.

4

The House on Midland:
From Inside Out

WYNETTA DEVORE

The Village

The African proverb "It takes a village to raise a child" has become familiar to the American public with the publication of First Lady Hillary Rodham Clinton's (1996) book entitled *It Takes a Village and Other Lessons Children Teach Us*. In the introductory chapter Clinton explains that she chose the African proverb for the title "because it offers a timeless reminder that children will thrive only if their families thrive and if the whole society cares enough to provide for them" (p. 12).

Published in the midst of the presidential campaign, responses to the book were often shortsighted with little understanding of the concept of village as a personal place in which children may thrive. Clinton describes it as a place of caring adults who are dedicated to children's growth, nurturing, and well-being. The American public is called forth to join together in behalf of the children.

Historians (Bennett 1964; Franklin 1967) who have examined the black experience in Africa before slavery, during slavery, and after freedom came describe the early African family as the basis of social organization. The enlarged family, the clan, developed in the same village or community. These communities were bound together by kinship, religion, and art, which was a life expression much like religion. In this environment, the elderly, the sick, and the infirm received care. Children could play safely in these caring villages, which were surrounded by gardens and fields.

There have been lively discussions in the historical and social science literature questioning the survival of African cultural patterns in family life, religion, and music

62

in the United States. Franklin (1967) comments that "perhaps the survival of African-isms in the New World was as great as it was because of the refusal of the members of the dominant group in America to extend, without reservations, their own culture to the Negroes whom they brought over" (p. 41). This dominant group, through the peculiar institution that was slavery, denied Negroes the joy of family life. Marriage among slaves was unrecognized and stable relationships were discouraged because they tended to interfere with the potential for sale and the availability of women for procreation (Lincoln, 1967).

Although he was not looking for evidence of African retentions or responding intentionally to the proverb, Billingsley (1968) presents the African American family as a social system set in a network of mutually interdependent relationships. These include the immediate community along with the wider society. His "village" includes schools, churches, taverns, newspapers, neighborhood associations, lodges, fraterni-ties, social clubs, age and sex peer groups, recreation associations, and small busi-nesses, such as barber shops, beauty parlors, restaurants, pool halls, funeral societies, and various organized systems of hustling. In the present these hustlers may be viewed as the ever present drug dealer.

Billingsley (1968) augments the community list with a delineation of the major institutions that help set the conditions for family life in the community. Among these are a subsystem of values, as well as political, economic, education, health, welfare, and communications institutions. The family with its children are joined to-gether into a system, community, village. In many African American communities this commitment to a village response to the care of children is evident in community centers that provide activities related to the needs of children and their families.

This chapter calls attention to a particular grassroots organization that has iden-tified a particular community of need and the children who reside there. The work of this group is examined using perspectives from Kretzmann and McKnight (1993), Rivera and Erlich's (1992, 1995) paradigm for organizing with people of color, the layers of understanding for ethnic-sensitive practice, and an ethnic-sensitive gener-alist practice (Devore and Schlesinger, 1996).

The Settlement House Movement

The early history of community social work presents evidence of a unique method for improving the health of residents in the poor communities of London, England. Young people from the prosperous suburbs of Oxford and Cambridge "settled" in in-ner-city London, where activities were centered in the neighborhoods around Toyn-bee Hall, a center for community service. The settlement movement's most noted program in the United States was in Chicago where Hull House responded to the needs of new immigrant populations. In New York City the Church Settlement House served a population that was Irish, German, French, Italian, and Jewish. The San Francisco Settlement Association served working-class families who had Irish and

German ancestry. These settlements and others provided a range of activities for young and old members of the community. These activities were related to physical health, economic welfare, educational instruction, social skills, political awareness, and religion (Husock 1993).

During this same era of the 1880s and 1890s, African American communities were developing mechanisms that would be identified as self-help. Pollard (1979) identifies the church and the school as focal points of help. Churches could be depended on to make contributions to the needs of the aged and children who had been orphaned. Informal systems of help developed during slavery were focused on ministry and human feeling. These experiences were viewed as the duty of the community rather than a right of the recipient. Each of these responses to need may be observed in the present as the development of self-help. This oppressed population was able to realize there was a need for collective responsibility.

Leaders emerged from these movements that were pressing for political and social consciousness within the community. These individuals articulated the need for security, dignity, and self-fulfillment for themselves and others. Often without background in business or training in economics they attempted to organize the community into communal enterprises. Some were successful; others failed. Various societies sponsored by churches came to the fore. Other community groups were supported by membership dues; still others were mutual benefit societies. This caring goal was evident in secret societies for men, such as fraternities and lodges. Service to the community and the payment of dues were required for membership. In return, members could be assured of support during times of illness or at death. The training received as members of these organizations cultivated talent needed for individual and community development. The community organization presented in this chapter holds unique elements of the settlement house movement, as well as perspectives of self-help.

A New Settlement House Perspective: The House on Midland Avenue

Howard Husock (1993) provides a more detailed historical perspective that explores the work of settlement houses and their advocates during the Progressive and New Deal eras of U.S. history. These houses provided structure and activities for large numbers of people, young and old, in poor neighborhoods. The leaders were clear in their motives: to expose the poor to more middle-class values such as saving and character development.

Husock (1993) calls attention to a settlement house organized in 1902 and still active today. Grace Hill Neighborhood Services, loosely affiliated with the Episcopal Church, remains a member of a movement once a major part of our approach to improving prospects for the poor and their neighborhoods. A Grace Hill program, Member Organized Resource Exchange (MORE), presents a model of community cooperation and self-help. To receive assistance, members of the exchange must contribute services such as care for children or ailing adults, car repair, or assistance with moving. The network does not use cash; service is the medium of exchange. Neighbors have joined together to help themselves with the support of the community settlement house.

In the present, the settlement house is more often thought of in historical terms if considered at all. Toynbee Hall and Hull House (Addams, 1910) are chapters in the early history of social work and social welfare. Still there is evidence of a continuing life for the settlement house movement in New York City (Kraus and Chaudry, 1995) and in Syracuse, New York. This chapter presents the case study of a house in Syracuse, New York, that serves as a center for community organizing and development.

The house is on Midland Avenue and may be identified by the red door that opens to children in the neighborhood three afternoons a week. Inside the children find "The Library," two rooms devoted to their academic and recreational needs. There are stacks of books, fat, thin, large, and small. A computer provides a resource for games for fun and enrichment. In the kitchen older children meet regularly with a Cooperative Extension agent who provides training that helps them become nutrition counselors for their peers. Geneva Hayden is the householder. This is the home she shares with her husband now that their children are adults with homes of their own.

The Hayden family has lived in the Midland Avenue neighborhood for the last twenty-eight years. During that time the neighborhood has changed as have so many others in Syracuse and other cities of similar size. Hayden thinks of the early years and comments, "When we moved here years ago, it was beautiful. Everybody in the neighborhood knew each other. Now it's much worse. People are scared to come to our community. Used to be the kids were always playing. The kids had a curfew then. They would see the sun going down, they—not just one of them but all of them— knew what they had to do. They knew they should be making it home" (Kim, 1995).

The U.S. census (Bureau of the Census, 1990) describes this community as one in which the majority of residents' households are African American earning up to $18,000. Very few earn more than $30,000 and only six households earn more than $75,000. Data reveals that within this population 1,878 persons lived above the poverty line in 1989; 1,365 persons in all age categories lived below. Those who are employed find work as laborers in specialty operations or health and educational services. The Syracuse community is home to a community college and two four-year institutions of higher education. In addition there are three public hospitals and one facility for veterans. Each offers positions that require a minimum of skills but steady employment.

In this small village most residents rent houses built in the 1930s or earlier; certainly this is an older housing stock. Landlord neglect gives greater evidence of age; houses need paint, roof shingles are missing, windows need repair, sidewalks are in disrepair. Residents of these mostly three-bedroom homes paid a median rent of $433 in 1989.

The Hayden home is in good repair. Mrs. Hayden sits on her pleasant porch and looks out on the neighborhood-village. Leaving the porch, she has become a good neighbor as she reaches out to the children and the elderly in the vicinity. Young men, without visible employment, have responded to the call for a block cleanup day. They have found her to be a resource as well as a confidante. Before retirement Hayden was a kindergarten teacher's assistant in a neighborhood school. The experience gave her particular insights into the lives of young African American children. Children in these classrooms were in need of the skills that provide the foundation for success in continued education, but in addition there was the pressing need for the development of social skills. Angry, hostile young children were in need of nurture and direction that was lacking in many of their homes. They needed love and attention; they needed a safe place. "The Library" became the safe place. It was only the beginning of this unique settlement movement.

The Midland Avenue house is a family home, yet it fulfills uniquely the initial concept of the settlement house. Toynbee Hall "settlers" were members of the middle class who moved into impoverished communities so they might join with the residents in efforts that would improve living conditions (Lundbald, 1995). Geneva Hayden is a different "settler." This is her home community. She is not an outsider, come to improve living conditions. This is her home, her neighborhood, her village.

Organizing the Village: Communities United to Rebuild Neighborhoods (CURN)

Communities United to Rebuild Neighborhoods (CURN) is a community association that is the organizational home for "The Library" and other neighborhood-village activities. A $1,247 grant from the Central New York Community Foundation was used to purchase supplies for the first neighborhood cleanup campaign. The foundation is unique as a funding source for nonprofit community organizations in the central New York community. Contributions are received from the community at large, from donors "of all colors and all ages, from high school students to retirees" who give individually, as part of a family, or as a business (The giving effect, 1996).

In a special effort the foundation provided funding for community groups willing to consider adopting the capacity-focused model of community development developed by John Kretzmann and John L. McKnight (1993). This community organizing model questions the value of familiar, traditional responses to devastated communities that focus on community needs, deficiencies, and problems. It is their belief that these processes have generated a variety of responses from social welfare and human service delivery systems. Although well meaning, for the most part, these responses tend to support a neighborhood environment in which residents begin to believe the client role is the most appropriate for use in their associations with community resources.

Capacity-Focused Development

Kretzmann and McKnight (1993) question the value of such a problem-focused response to community concerns. Rather, they present capacity-focused development as an alternative to more familiar modes of community intervention. Capacity-focused development calls for initial activity that creates a map of community assets which includes the gifts of individuals, citizens' associations, and local institutions.

CURN has recognized the gifts of a landlord who cares about his property, the tenants, and the community, and young men who help with block cleaning, gardening, or street fairs as community assets. Active older residents contribute skills acquired in their youth as they work with children in the community garden. Less active senior citizens sit on their porches and watch out for the children. These individual gifts are placed in the center of the community assets map.

Like many other declining low-income neighborhoods, there are few informal social associations. However, the church remains as a stable asset providing spiritual support for single adults and families. Unfortunately, the churches in the CURN neighborhood have been reluctant to accept the invitation to become a part of the community change effort. However, churches outside the immediate community have shared their gifts of space and service as volunteers.

Continuing to respond to capacity-focused mapping process, more formal community institutions have been identified. A community school building has been used for a summer reading program funded by Laubach Literacy and the Nike Corporation. Children spent the summer in a classroom "Reading for Sneakers." At the end of the summer children who participated received sneakers. The community public library branch provided space for the closing celebration. The school continues to offer space for fall and winter programs.

The Center for Community Alternatives, a prevention organization, with a program targeting children at risk, has joined with CURN in developing a community garden that has been the pride of the neighborhood. The program is located in the neighborhood school along with CURN programs. Students in the Alternative program may live in the immediate community or in other areas of the city. All of the students participate in the gardening program. As suggested earlier, older residents have joined with the children in planning, planting, weeding, and harvesting. Children have come to look forward to work in the garden; more reluctant young gardeners have secretly asked when there would be another trip to the garden.

During the summer of 1996, there was no garden vandalism, flowers were picked and vegetables gathered only by members of the Midland Avenue community. Children and adults safeguarded their work. Plans are under way to acquire the use of more land in the summer of 1997. Owners of vacant lots have offered their land. These offers place them on the map as persons with assets to share with the community. Their gift is land. The Center for Community Alternatives has offered to extend its gift of access to land, plants, seeds, and tools.

Syracuse University found a place on the community map as students in the graduate-level social work education program worked with Geneva Hayden on a grant proposal that would fund a "Summer Fun" program. An award of $2000 supported the program as a supplement to the reading program. In addition, the university has donated space for committee meetings.

Organizations such as the university, the Center for Community Alternatives, the city school district, the public library system, and cooperative extension are among the groups that are a part of the design of the entire community. Enlisting them in the capacity-focused effort calls for them to take greater responsibility for the health of this particular neighborhood-village.

Individuals, associations, and institutions are at the core of capacity-focused community development (Kretzmann and McKnight, 1993), which is indeed unlike the more familiar programs (Perlman and Gurin, 1972). During a visit to Syracuse, sponsored by The Community Foundation, John Kretzmann commented, "The focus has always been on needs and problems of the communities and the solution to those needs being a massive infusion of government aid. There is a new kind of leadership. The focus is local and how to rediscover strengths and resources within the community. There are no cookie cutter answers. You need to adapt within the community" (Kim 1995).

The initial success of Communities United to Rebuild Neighborhoods (CURN) comes from understanding and believing participants have the ability to build their own agenda. They understand they will need to address the neglect of community institutions that has contributed to the community's descent. At the same time they recognize the community must take responsibility for its own contributions to the decline.

Added to the demographics presented earlier related to housing and employment, there is a high rate of crime and violence, drug and alcohol abuse, and little evidence of academic achievement as the dropout rate fails to decline. This community has accepted the capacity-focused model and Hayden claims, "We are going to take his (John's) advice... make a plan and see what we can do to build up this area" (Kim, 1995).

The capacity model calls for community work from the inside out. If the change effort is to be successful then the capacities, gifts of individuals at the center, who are at the margins of the larger society, must be identified and released. An inventory of community capacity identifies individual skills ranging from care for the sick or elderly, child care, office skills, construction and repair skills, food preparation, to hairdressing or sewing.

Residents of the CURN neighborhood, children, youth, and adults, have demonstrated community skills as they organize and conduct rummage sales, held a May Day celebration that crowned a young king and queen, worked together in the garden, and planned for a Halloween party for small children. These residents have capacities that are identified and released.

Persons who serve as CURN block captains are developing skills in identifying individual and community needs, which they present in meetings of the organization.

Together, these developing leaders make decisions about appropriate responses to identified challenges. Mapping the assets of individuals, community, and local associations and taking inventory and releasing individual capacity of individual residents are tasks CURN has begun and expects to continue in its push for rebuilding the neighborhood. The capacities of other residents are yet to be identified and released.

A measure of CURN's success in identifying and releasing capacity is a licensed Christian day-care center called "JC's Place." The child-care and administrative skills of Briget Jones have enabled her to provide a service for working parents in the community. Child care is Briget Jones's skill and her gift to the community. Mapping, identifying, and releasing individual gifts is the core activity of the capacity model.

The Rivera-Erlich Paradigm

In earlier editions of this book, editors Felix G. Rivera and John L. Erlich (1992, 1995) have, like Kretzmann and McKnight (1993), wondered about the traditional models of community development (Rothman, Erlich, & Tropman, 1995; Tropman, Erlich, & Rothman, 1995). Their concern was with the assumption that the three most familiar models (locality development, social planning, and social action) were color blind and therefore useful in any community.

They have indicated that when working in communities of color certain factors needed to be addressed. These include (1) the racial, ethnic, and cultural aspects of the community; (2) the implication of this uniqueness in particular communities; and (3) the process of empowerment and the development of a critical consciousness. Given this perspective on community work with ethnic minority communities, Rivera and Erlich add that considerable attention must be given to the strategies and tactics used in accomplishing community change. Three levels of contact are suggested, and like Kretzmann and McKnight they begin at the center of the community, the most personal, most intimate level.

At this primary level, the same racial, cultural, and linguistic identity is required. Hayden, who is the president of CURN, holds these characteristics. Her level of involvement is intense as she uses her primary-level identity to open neighborhood doors that have been closed to others. She is a "settler," a respected member of the community.

Persons working with the community at the secondary level do not need to be members of the same ethnic group but must be closely aligned to the community and sensitive to its needs. Tasks to be accomplished include serving as liaison with the outside community and institutions and taking the role of facilitator when the community experiences extraordinary instances of discrimination in the larger community.

The third level of contact may held by the "outsider" who shares the concerns of the community. Ethnic group membership is not at issue, but particular skills are. These skills relate to the need to be able to approach and confront entrenched societal institutions and structures. Access to power gives the person making tertiary contacts a valued asset to the community.

The Rivera-Erlich (1992, 1995) levels of intervention may be viewed as activity that parallels the mapping of the capacity-focused model. Both call for the community to be at the center of attention. Kretzmann and McKnight (1993) have entitled their work *Building Community from the Inside Out.* They expect the community will identify and release the capacities of its individual members. Rivera and Erlich look to a particular person, the organizer, to be at the center and provide a profile with the expectation that these leaders will come from the community with qualities that will enhance their potential for successful community change. Among the qualities suggested are a similar cultural and racial identification, a familiarity with community customs and traditions, social networks, leadership skills, and skills in program planning, development, and administrative management.

In the case study presented here, The Community Foundation provides potential community leaders with the opportunity to participate in leadership development seminars. Members of CURN, including Mrs. Hayden, have attended these seminars acquiring the skills suggested by Rivera and Erlich. Each model for community intervention presented thus far has a commitment to rethink tactics and strategies used in the past. Although Kretzmann and McKnight do not claim to identify communities of color for intervention, this community in Syracuse has found it useful.

The Layers of Understanding for Ethnic-Sensitive Practice

Ethnic-sensitive practice was introduced by Devore and Schlesinger in 1981. The perspective called for social workers to pay greater attention to the impact of ethnic group membership on individual behavior and experience in family and community. Since then any number of educators and practitioners have responded to the call to make adaptations in practice.

They have come to recognize the need to consider the impact of the ethnic reality, behaviors found at the intersection of ethnic group membership and social class, that tell individuals how to govern their relationships with parents and other family members, the young, the old, and with the community at large.

Practice responses and adaptations to ethnic minority groups has claimed considerable attention to the neglect of other ethnic groups. We are concerned about this turn of events but appreciate the attention that has been paid to neglected groups that have had and continue to have experiences with discrimination and oppression (Schlesinger & Devore, 1995).

Attention will be paid here to the African American community introduced earlier. It will allow us the opportunity to examine the layers of understanding that are an essential component in ethnic-sensitive practice. These layers are a convergence of the knowledge, values, and skills that are at the foundation of social work practice and provide guidelines for ethnic-sensitive social workers

Social workers who relate to neighborhoods similar to Midland Avenue may be assured of greater success if they pay attention to the layers. Neighborhood groups should expect that those who enter at the secondary or tertiary level (Rivera & Erlich, 1992, 1995) or find themselves placed on the community assets map as representatives of local institutions (Kretzmann & McKnight, 1993) have these layers of understanding as part of their practice repertoire.

The layers of understanding are: (1) social work values; (2) a knowledge of human behavior and the social environment; (3) knowledge and skill in the understanding of the agency or institution they represent; (4) self-awareness with emphasis on "who am I in the ethnic sense?"; (5) the impact of the ethnic reality with particular attention to this community's injuries that have been inflicted by racism and poverty; and (6) the route to the social worker—a conceptualization which recognizes that members of this community are most likely to find themselves in client roles through coercive routes set in motion by schools or the courts (Devore & Schlesinger, 1996). The incorporation of these layers into community practice enriches the relationship between practitioner and community.

Ethnic-Sensitive Generalist Practice

The Council on Social Work Education has developed curriculum policy statements that require a generalist foundation at the undergraduate and graduate levels. The generalist practitioner may be found in any number of social service delivery systems that call members of the Midland Avenue community clients. Each elementary school in the Syracuse city school district has at least a part-time social worker. Social workers join with other professionals and educators as members of the staff of a high school program for adolescent girls who are pregnant or have infant children. Generalist workers relate to the community as members of the staffs of Salvation Army and Catholic Charity programs. Each has the opportunity to relate to this community through work with individuals and families, and in collaboration with other agencies such as public assistance.

The ethnic-sensitive generalist model considered here is drawn from the structural approach to practice originated by Wood and Middleman (1989). Two assumptions are basic to this approach: (1) individual problems are not to be seen as individual pathology; rather they are manifestations of inadequate social arrangements; (2) a response to the need for change is the obligation of all social workers no matter where they may find themselves in the practice community. From this flows a frame of reference that includes work with individuals, small groups, policy makers, interested persons, or community institutions.

The layers of understanding and an assortment of appropriate roles are added to the structural frame of reference to form a generalist perspective for ethnic-sensitive practice. The CURN case study continues to provide examples. An article in a local newspaper told the story of Geneva Hayden and The Library (Kim, 1995). Two children visiting the library were mentioned in the article, Jabreem and Fatima. During this time in The Library the children were working with the letter of the day: "M." Meal and milk were identified.

These children may be placed in the first quadrant of the generalist model. They are children who are in need of assistance beyond the services that can be provided in this settlement house setting. An agency social worker or CURN members may move on to second quadrant work by involving these children and others in similar family situations in more library activities, other neighborhood activities, or encouraging their parents to involve them in programs in nearby community centers.

CURN has taken on third quadrant tasks as they have written grants for funds that would support leadership training for adults and after-school and summer programs for children. Other funds are raised through rummage and yard sales. They are very aware of developing social policy and participated in the Children's March on Washington in the spring of 1996.

Local institutions provide the resources needed for fourth quadrant work. In addition to the community agencies already mentioned may be added PEACE, INC which has senior citizen programs that have included community children, and two family centers that provide counseling and join with CURN in seasonal celebrations. These are assets, gifts of the local community.

Miley, O'Melia, and DuBois's (1995) generalist approach to practice includes roles that may be used by practitioners as they carry out the several functions of practice. The roles suggested for community work include planner, activist, and outreach. At the same time roles for work with individuals and families include enabler, broker, advocate, and teacher.

The ethnic-sensitive generalist practitioners' work included work with individuals and families, small groups, policy development, fund-raising, and grant writing. This work may be accomplished with the assistance of community and local resources committed to this ethnic minority community. To accomplish these tasks the generalist has a variety of roles available. These activities are embedded in the layers of understanding discussed earlier. The generalist may find a place in the capacity-focused model as a representative of local institutions or accomplish primary contact tasks if one holds membership in the ethnic community. Secondary and tertiary contact tasks of the Rivera-Erlich paradigm (1995) may be accomplished as well.

Summary

A unique settlement house was the first home of CURN. The "settler" was the householder, Geneva Hayden. This house in the center of the community has served as a library for neighborhood children, a learning center for nutrition education, and a meeting place for CURN.

The community work of this grassroots organization has been examined in relation to several models for community work. Capacity-focused work calls for the development of a community assets map which locates individual, community, and local assets. In addition, an inventory of capacities identifies skills held by individuals that may be released for individual and community growth. The Rivera-Erlich paradigm (1995) calls attention to the need to review the usefulness of familiar models for community organization with the understanding that these are not color blind as once presumed. They posit three levels of contact for community practice. Secondary and tertiary tasks may be done well by social workers or others who do not reside in the community but are committed to its future.

Finally, the ethnic-sensitive perspective has been presented, including an examination of the layers of understanding and an ethnic-sensitive generalist practice. This is the model for practice that needs to be incorporated by social workers who work in communities of color such as Census Tract 54 in Syracuse, New York. These workers need to be flexible as communities begin to work from the inside out, setting their own agendas.

References

Addams, J. (1910). *Twenty years at Hull House.* New York: New American Library.

Bennett, L., Jr. (1964). *Before the Mayflower: A history of the Negro in America.* Chicago: Johnson.

Billingsley, A. (1968). *Black families in white America.* Englewood Cliffs, NJ: Prentice-Hall.

Bureau of the Census. (1990). *1990 Census of Population and housing characteristics for census tract and block numbering areas. Syracuse NY MSA.* Washington, DC: U.S. Department of Commerce.

Clinton, H. R. (1996). *It takes a village and other lessons children teach us.* New York: Simon & Schuster.

Devore, W., & Schlesinger, E. G. (1996). *Ethnic-sensitive social work practice.* (4th ed.). Boston: Allyn & Bacon.

Franklin, J. H. (1967). *From slavery to freedom: A history of Negro Americans* (3rd ed.). New York: Knopf.

The giving effect. (1996). Central New York Community Foundation annual report.

Husock, H. (1993, Fall). Bringing back the settlement house. *Public Welfare, 51,* 16–25.

Kim, N. (1995, November 14). Making a neighborhood a better place to live. *The Herald Journal,* pp. C1, C2.

Kraus, A., & Chaudry, A. (1995, Fall). The settlement house initiative: Merging Head Start and daycare in New York. *Public Welfare, 53,* 34–43.

Kretzmann, J. P., & McKnight, J. L. (1993). *Building community from the inside out: A path toward finding and mobilizing a community's assets.* Northwestern University: Center for Urban Policy Research.

Lincoln, C. E. (1967). *The Negro pilgrimage in America.* New York: Bantam Books.

Lundbald, K. S. (1995). Jane Addams and social reform: A role model for the 1990s. *Social Work, 40* (5), 661–669.

Miley, K. K., O'Melia, M., & DuBois, B. L. (1995). *Generalist social work practice: An empowering approach.* Boston: Allyn & Bacon.

Perlman, R., & Gurin, A. (1972). *Community organization and social planning.* New York: Wiley.

Pollard, W. L. (1979). *A study of black self-help.* San Francisco: R & E Research Associates.

Rivera, F. G., & Erlich, J. L. (1995). *Community organizing in a diverse society* (2nd ed.). Boston: Allyn & Bacon.

Rothman, J., Erlich, J. L., & Tropman, J. E. (1995). *Strategies of community intervention* (5th ed.). Itasca, Ill: F. E. Peacock.

Schlesinger, E. G., & Devore, W. (1995). Ethnic-sensitive social work practice: The state of the art. *Journal of Sociology & Social Welfare, 22* (1), 29–58.

Tropman, J. E., Erlich, J. L., & Rothman, J. (1995). *Tactics and techniques of community intervention* (3rd ed.). Itasca, IL: F. E. Peacock.

Wood, G. G., & Middleman, R. R. (1989). *The structural approach to direct practice.* New York: Columbia University Press.

5

Cultural and Political
Realities for Community
Social Work Practice
with Puerto Ricans
in the United States

JULIO MORALES AND MIGDALIA REYES*

Ideology, Values, and Social Change

In the late 1950s and early 1960s, the Puerto Rican Association for Community Affairs
(PRACA) sponsored youth conferences for Puerto Rican high school and college students. The theme of the conferences was "Aspire and Attain," and the organizers, many
of them social workers, contributed their time to reach young Puerto Ricans and involve them in community work. PRACA's efforts served as a backdrop to the creation
(in 1962) of ASPIRA, the first Puerto Rican–controlled private social service agency
in the United States. Both groups stressed the importance of a college education, a

*Drs. Morales and Reyes both have MSW degrees with concentrations in community social work. Dr.
Morales's community organization skills have facilitated his founding Puerto Rican Studies projects and
numerous social service agencies and programs in New York, Massachusetts, and Connecticut. Dr. Reyes
has extensive experience in community social work with women of color.

positive sense of identity, knowledge of Puerto Rican history and culture, and a commitment to contributing to the Puerto Rican community.

By the late 1960s and early 1970s, as Puerto Rican Studies programs took root in New York and New Jersey colleges, a more progressive ideology developed.[1] This ideology urged a rejection of traditional learning and teaching. It suggested new theoretical constructs that encouraged more collective methods of working, defined new sources of knowledge, discarded ideologies that condoned colonialism and forced assimilation, and designed theoretical constructs that looked at the power of macro forces on poor and powerless people. More recently, Puerto Rican Studies programs have generated new ideas to integrate racism, ethnocentrism, classism, sexism, and heterosexism within the Puerto Rican experience.

Community social workers can play a major role in addressing and integrating shifting paradigms as they deliver services to Puerto Rican client systems. To do so they must confront their own and others' tendencies to blame *vicsurs*[2] and look for new ways to empower Puerto Ricans and other oppressed peoples. As part of their community organization processes, social workers must validate the contributions and struggles of their client systems. Using *grupos de conocimiento* or *grupos de intercambio* (planned group discussions) may be an effective strategy. These *grupos* examine the forces of institutionalized oppression and the strengths that individuals and communities bring to the everyday reality of people's lives.

For example, a group of elderly Puerto Ricans could be encouraged to share stories about living in Puerto Rico and why they migrated to the United States. Many may say they had to try elsewhere because of the inadequate employment opportunities in Puerto Rico. The community social worker could facilitate further discussion by asking provocative questions to stimulate people to open up about their experiences: "Did you find the employment opportunities you sought? What challenges did you encounter once you left Puerto Rico?" Such discussions with older Puerto Ricans yield interesting anecdotes that underscore their hard work and high aspirations for themselves and their families. This type of exchange is emotionally charged and can act as a springboard for elderly Puerto Ricans to confront and challenge stereotypes and become more assertive about their rights. It would be helpful to encourage the elderly to share their experiences with their children, grandchildren, and other younger members of the family and community.

There is great diversity among Puerto Ricans. Some may not view themselves as oppressed, marginalized, or discriminated against. Others may blame themselves for the social, economic, and political problems they face. Community social workers need to address these beliefs, connect private and personal troubles to public problems, and foster positive identities within the larger Puerto Rican community.

An ideology that empowers clients must also question the societal priorities and forces that have led to large discrepancies in income and wealth distribution among North Americans. In the 1980s, poor people in America experienced a 9.8 percent decrease in income while the affluent enjoyed a 15.6 percent increase, according to a congressional study.[3] Similar studies document that 40 percent of America's wealth is owned by 1 percent of the population; 44 percent of Americans share just 2 percent of the wealth.[4] Poverty is especially concentrated among Latinos and even more so among Puerto Ricans.[5]

According to demographic projections, the face of America will look more and more Latino in the near future. Indeed, soon Latinos will be the largest minority group in the United States. On January 30, 1997, the *New York Times* stated what many Latinos have been suspecting for years: In the United States, Latinos are poorer than Asians, than blacks, and than whites:

> *Census data show that for the first time the poverty rate among Hispanic residents of the United States has surpassed that of blacks. Hispanic residents now constitute nearly 24 percent of the country's poor, up eight percentage points since 1985. Of all Hispanic residents, 30 percent were considered poor in 1995, meaning they earned less than $15,569 for a family of four. That is almost three times the percentage of non-Hispanic whites living in poverty. Of the poorest of the poor, 24 percent were Hispanic.* (p. 1)

The article goes on to say, "These are not just statistical blips. Overall, income for Hispanic households has dropped 14 percent since 1989, under $22,900 from about $26,000, while rising for black households."

The U.S. Census Bureau statistics for 1995 record the median income for Puerto Ricans living in the United States as $20,929 compared to $23,609 for Mexican Americans, $26,558 for Central and South Americans, and $30,584 for Cuban Americans. The Census Bureau also records that 36 percent of people of Puerto Rican heritage living in the United States live below the poverty level versus 32.3 percent of Mexican Americans, 25.8 percent of Central and South Americans, and 17.8 percent of Cuban Americans. A major problem confronting Puerto Ricans and other Latinos is their invisibility and powerlessness. They are conspicuously absent in the media, in the political arena, in governmental appointments, in the professions, and in academia.

Community social workers need to project genuine caring for people and strive continuously to enhance, integrate, and interpret knowledge, skills, and values when working with Puerto Ricans and other oppressed groups, To some extent, this parts from the social work ethos of impartiality, neutrality, and objectivity. It means placing the problems of an individual or community within the context of larger social, economic, and political problems and generously sharing such knowledge with the client and action systems.

History of the Americas and Puerto Rico

Many historical accounts of Puerto Rico, Latin American nations, and the United States start with Columbus's so-called discovery of a new world in 1492. These accounts reinforce a decidedly European perspective on history and exemplify institutionalized ethnocentrism and racism by dismissing the fact that indigenous people preceded Columbus and European populations by thousands of years.

The Europeans who settled in North America brought millions of black African natives to sell as slaves in the Americas and the Caribbean. In the United States and other countries, white people justified the killing of the people they called Indians and the enslavement of Africans by viewing these populations as subhuman heathens. Later, European Americans would view the Indians and Africans as racially and culturally inferior, a misconception that exists to this day.

Puerto Ricans are a racially mixed people of Europeans, indigenous natives called Tainos, and Africans. The United States began to occupy Puerto Rico in 1898 after winning the Spanish-American War. The U.S. government and military establishment had long viewed the island as an essential territory to obtain because of its strategic position and economic value.[6]

The Foraker Act of 1900 established an American-controlled government in Puerto Rico. The U.S. president appointed the governor of the island and the upper chamber of the legislature. Economic control followed. A diversified agricultural society was turned into an economy based on a sole crop—sugarcane—dominated by U.S. absentee businesses. Very-low-paying jobs, the seasonal nature of work in the sugarcane fields, shipping monopolies, a tax system that favored U.S. businesses, and an economy based on exporting goods led to poverty so severe that by 1940, Puerto Rico became known as the "Poor House of the Caribbean."[7]

An effort to industrialize Puerto Rico's economy, called Operation Bootstrap, was seen as a remedy. American capital quickly moved in to enhance a factory system that guaranteed owners seven years of tax exemptions, a cheap labor force and political stability not associated with other Third World countries.... Operation Bootstrap did not provide enough of the labor-intensive work it had promised. Instead, it has favored pharmaceutical, computer and other capital-intensive industries. Factory owners often leave Puerto Rico when their tax exemptions expire and find cheaper labor in other Third World countries.[8]

Public Law 600, passed in 1950, gave the Puerto Rican people the power to structure a government that would allow them some local economy. The U.S. Senate committee that wrote the legislation emphasized the subordination of Puerto Rico to the federal government. In 1952, 47 percent of Puerto Rico's registered voters approved a constitution that created the current Commonwealth of Puerto Rico. It is important to underscore that "Congress may repeal Public Law 600, annul the Constitution of Puerto Rico, and veto any insular legislation which it deems unwise or improper. From the perspective of constitutional law the compact between Puerto Rico and Congress may be unilaterally altered by the Congress."[9]

According to Pedro Caban, Public Law 600 maintained the economic regulations of the Foraker Act and "created a set of social institutions and arrangements that enhanced the prospects for long-term, corporate investments and profitability."[10] Also, it accelerated Puerto Rico's integration into the United States, providing U.S. corporations with an economy based on minimum-wage jobs.

"In 1976, Congress amended the tax exemption policy for United States firms with branches in Puerto Rico. The revised tax code, known as Section 936 of the U.S. Internal Revenue code, permits U.S. subsidiaries in Puerto Rico to repatriate profits to the United States and receive a federal tax credit."[11] Section 936 maintain the island as a profitable investment site. "In 1988, U.S. firms in Puerto Rico realized profits of $8.9 billion."[12]

Even though Puerto Rican economy relies heavily on Section 936, the Puerto Rican population continues to suffer economically:

> *Puerto Rico's per capita income is less than one-third that of the United States ($5,157 in 1988, or about 47 percent of the per capita income of Mississippi, the poorest state); unemployment unofficially strikes about 25 percent of the labor force; and labor participation rates are extremely low, about 41 percent. . . . In 1979, nearly two-thirds of Puerto Rico's population earned incomes below the poverty level.[13]*

It is often because of these reasons that outmigration continues. This is not the only reason World War II's economy created a great demand for labor in the United States, however. Because of the anti-immigration laws passed by Congress in the 1920s, immigrants could not enter the United States to fill the need. Puerto Ricans, U.S. citizens since 1917, were recruited to fill the labor shortage, especially in the cities and farms of the Northeast.

Mass migration is indeed an integral component of the Puerto Rican experience in the United States. Prior to the 1940s, the Puerto Rican population in the United States totaled approximately 70,000. The 1995 census projections estimate that 2.73 million Puerto Ricans reside in the United States. Sixty-eight percent live in the Northeast; 9.4 percent in the Midwest; 14.9 percent in the South; and 7 percent in the West. Puerto Ricans are 12.1 percent of all Latinos in the United States and among the fastest growing population.

In Puerto Rico, unskilled workers often compete with one another and with undocumented workers from neighboring Caribbean nations. In the United States, they compete for scarce jobs because manufacturing, farm work, and jobs in light industry have dried up or relocated. Ironically, even though Puerto Rican migrants now tend to have more formal education than past immigrants, many continue to experience economic hardship. The jobs available today require more specialized education, training, and skills than those in the past. In 1910, 90 percent of Americans did not finish high school, but they could find jobs and prosper. This is no longer true. Even skilled positions such as clerical workers, bank tellers, telephone operators, machinists, and other blue-collar workers, which provided upward mobility in the past, are almost obsolete. Electronically advanced and information-processing industries require jobs with different levels of education and training. The global economy continues to have an impact on Puerto Ricans both in Puerto Rico and in the United States.

Culture and Practice Issues

The Taino, European, and African mixture, the geography and topography of the island, and a history of oppression and colonization by both Spain and the United States have combined to create a culture that is different from American, Spanish, and other Latino cultures.

For four hundred years, Spain imposed its language, religious beliefs, values, and culture on the people of Puerto Rico. Influences of the indigenous and African cultures altered these systems, however. Thus, dominated by Spain, and later by the United States, Puerto Ricans have long lived in a colonized and oppressed society. Many have been conditioned by ideologies that systematically perpetuate structures of inequality. Nevertheless, the history of Puerto Rico demonstrates that the people have developed powerful survival mechanisms, reflected in their culture. These include a spirit of resiliency, a strong sense of peoplehood, and a readiness for action when organizers tap their leadership and resourcefulness. To avoid stereotypical thinking, it is important to stress that Puerto Rican communities and individuals vary. Certain socioeconomic factors, such as industrialization, urbanization, and modernization, and differences in social class membership, such as levels of formal education, skin color, place of birth, sexual and emotional orientation, and length and place(s) of residence, affect the varying relation of Puerto Ricans to their traditional cultural patterns.

Confianza *and* Personalismo

Confianza means trust and culturally established acceptable boundaries for interpersonal behavior. *Confianza* evolves and allows for *relajo* (joking around) and for bonding. *Confianza* must be earned. Assuming prematurely that one has it is often culturally unacceptable. Establishing trust, an essential component of social work practice with Puerto Ricans and others, requires approaches that may be new to social workers who have never worked with this population.

Personalismo is a culturally supported expectation of "personalizing" individual contact in important relationships. No matter how much a social service system claims it is concerned about people, Puerto Ricans need to feel the caring personally. Community workers must understand this pattern because getting Puerto Ricans to become involved in local organizing efforts may depend on their feeling connected, in a personal way, to the organizer. Face-to-face contact is important in all community organization work, but it can be crucial in organizing Puerto Ricans.

Community social workers are more likely to win over the constituency by demonstrating they care. An effective way to demonstrate this is by socializing in the Puerto Rican and Latino communities and spending time with the action group involved in the organizing efforts. This may mean drinking coffee together, sharing pictures of each other's families, attending parties and church services, shopping at local stores, and eating lunch in neighborhood restaurants.

Respect, Honor, Dignity, and Familismo

Traditionally, Puerto Rican feelings of pride and self-esteem are rooted in family and community and culturally related to the concepts of respect, honor, and dignity. Respect is shown by being polite, attentive, discreet, and sensitive to the needs and feelings of others. People's essence or personality may be regarded as more important than a person's social group. Respect is shown to neighbors and acquaintances, regardless of social class or community standing, by addressing them as Doña or Don (Madam or Sir) followed by their first name (e.g., Doña Juana, Don José); by using the formal "you" (*Usted*); by calling adult strangers Mr., Miss, or Mrs.); by not joking or jiving without people first developing *confianza;* by avoiding eye contact when culturally appropriate; and by showing that one cares about other people's opinions, contributions, and feelings.

Familismo is a distinctive cultural tradition of Puerto Rican populations that places the family at the center.[14] According to Delgado et al. (1982), loyalty, emotional closeness, and interdependence are common overriding descriptors of the Puerto Rican family. Even in Puerto Rican communities in the United States, *hijos de crianza, compadres, comadres, padrinos, madrinas,* and close friends, especially those migrating from the same town in the island, are also recognized as members of the family.[15]

A cultural expectation of *familismo* is a person's relationship with the community. For example, hospitality is captured in the phrase *mi casa es su casa* ("my house is your house"). Puerto Ricans also demonstrate a strong sense of *familismo* through the cultural expectation that family members take care of each other. Ritual and rules on how children relate to adults, on dating, and on interrelationships between partners and spouses are also of importance. For example, many Puerto Ricans demonstrate honor for parents, grandparents, aunts and uncles, and godparents by asking for their blessing (*bendición*) when entering or leaving their presence.

The traditional extended family, or the new combination of extended and nuclear family, and some community systems tend to be based on a patriarchal kinship network replete with the traditional male/female role expectations that are tied to concepts of respect and honor. This kinship network often poses challenges for women, especially those who do not follow traditional values, and for gay males, lesbian women, and transgendered people who often encounter family and community conflict because of sexism, heterosexism, and homophobia.

Religion and Spirituality

The mixed heritage of Puerto Ricans has led to a blending of indigenous and African religious customs with Catholicism. American Protestantism has also strongly influenced spirituality and religion in Puerto Rican communities. Most Puerto Ricans identify themselves as Catholic, but many, especially the poor, practice Pentecostalism, an evangelical form of Protestantism.

African and indigenous religious and spiritual influences are evident in many Puerto Rican communities, where some people frequent *botanicas,* shops that sell candles, statues, incense, body oils, herbs, and other paraphernalia used for healing purposes and to obtain protection from spirits, saints, and ancestors. These practices are part of *espiritismo,* which is influenced by fifteenth-century Catholicism, European Kardecism, and Santeria, an African Yoruba religion.[16] Catholic and Protestant clergy obviously have clout in the Puerto Rican communities and are important in community social work. *Espiritistas* and *Santeros/as* also need to be recognized in social work practice because of their influence in the lives of many Puerto Ricans.

Machismo *and* Marianismo

Puerto Rican society, like most societies, maintains ideologies, values, behaviors, and institutions that condone and perpetuate oppression toward certain social group members. Historically, cultural and religious values and the manifestations of *machismo* and *marianismo* have prevented equality between males and females by maintaining rigid delineations of how males and females are socialized. Although some manifestations of *machismo* are perceived as positive, males are socialized to be dominant, independent, and controlling. They are perceived as superior to women and generally expect and obtain greater privileges. Traditionally, a major assumption of *machismo* is the financial responsibility of men for their families and the protection of women, especially wives, mothers, and sisters. Often men, particularly poorer men, perceive and/or experience a loss of both power and maleness and shame and dishonor if they cannot provide adequately for their families even if due to unemployment, underemployment, or discrimination.

Although abuse is against the law in Puerto Rico, as in the United States, manifestations of *machismo* can lead to such behavior. Most Puerto Rican men are not abusive, however. Social workers are unfamiliar with delivering services to Puerto Rican men. They need to challenge their knowledge and stereotypes about *machismo.* For example, a Puerto Rican man from a rural region may not exhibit any negative manifestations of *machismo,* but a middle-class urban Puerto Rican man might. Furthermore, negative behaviors must be understood before they can be changed. When is desertion, abuse, or neglect a function of societal maladies? How can social workers use the cultural characteristics of honor, dignity, and respect to enhance the power of women? How can *grupos de conocimiento (grupos de intercambio)* be effective in challenging *machismo?* Organizing Puerto Rican men is a challenge that few community social workers have undertaken.

Marianismo is a cultural ideology and practice that, like the whore-madonna dichotomy in many other cultures, divides women into two exclusive categories: the saintly devoted mother, wife, and sister(s), and the sinful, coldhearted, and promiscuous "others." *Marianismo* ultimately models "female behavior" to harmonize with and represent the virtues of the Virgin Mary.[17] This value system can place women in positions of power because it assumes that women are spiritually superior to men.[18]

Marianismo is critically linked to the cultural expectations of women marrying, having children in a heterosexual relationship, and taking care of others in spite of their personal needs and requirements.[19] *Marianismo* may also be conceptually applied to the parents' protective position in regard to their daughters' virginity in order to maintain the honor of, and respect for, the family. Traditional female gender roles often lead to overt heterosexualism and homophobia in Puerto Rico and Puerto Rican communities in the United States. Although sexual taboos have relaxed in recent years, and an increasing number of young unmarried women are becoming sexually active, strict gender roles and close supervision of female children may still lead to marriages at young ages or early common law and consensual living arrangements. Rigid traditional female gender roles and expectations can lead some Puerto Rican women, as well as gay males, lesbians, and transgendered people, to migrate from Puerto Rico to the United States where tolerance and equality are expected.

An important component of *marianismo* is the relationship among women friends. Although emotional and physical closeness among women is encouraged and perceived as a socially approved mechanism to diminish contact with men, behavior presumed to be lesbian is generally not tolerated. Nevertheless, a lesbian woman or gay male, especially those who migrate from Puerto Rico, may need to develop deep attachments to their ethnic communities to cope with and survive ethnocentrism, racism, and internalized colonization. Greene (1994) suggests that this is "particularly problematic if the family, community, and/or traditional cultural values are perceived or selectively interpreted as rejecting a lesbian or gay sexual orientation."[20]

The other face of marianismo is *hembrismo*. In Puerto Rico, *hembrismo* (from the word *hembra* used to denote female gender) has been reclaimed by many feminists as a healthy challenge to *marianismo* because traditionally *hembrismo* has been perceived as congruent with feminist ideology. Nevertheless, this concept has also been used with a negative connotation to describe women who take on some manifestations of *machismo* and demonstrate that they too can be independent and controlling.

Self-Oppression

Environmental and institutional challenges and implications of beliefs and behavior may be best understood within the context of religious, linguistic, social, political, and economic colonization and oppression. As a result of centuries of oppression and colonization under Spain and the United States, many Puerto Ricans have internalized negative stereotypes of themselves and/or other Puerto Ricans. Paulo Freire and Frantz Fanon describe and explain these behaviors in their classic work on the effects of oppression and colonization.[21]

Strengths

As a society, Puerto Ricans value hospitality, cooperation, and sharing, as well as a collective humanism that appeals to a sense of justice and fairness. Because of the racial mix that constitutes this population, racism may be less of an issue than in other client groups.[22] These culturally sanctioned patterns and principles enhance community organizing.

The tradition of close-knit extended families serves as a source of community strength and stability. This cultural strong point can be used effectively by involving family members in community organization activities, such as adolescents in tutoring programs and adults in tenant organizing. Organizing projects involving housing, jobs, education, and other macro issues that benefit entire families, especially their children, have a better chance of attracting Puerto Rican participation.

Problems and Programs—Strategies and Tactics

Although some middle-class Puerto Ricans hold jobs that pay enough to cover basic needs and provide fringe benefits such as health insurance, paid vacations, and medical leave, many Puerto Ricans in the United States confront problems rooted in poverty and discrimination. Poverty is associated with political powerlessness that, in turn, minimizes the ability to compete for resources. The traditional American values of competition and individualism, along with America's history of ethnic and racial rivalries and discrimination, clash with Puerto Ricans' values of cooperation and collectivism.

> *Most importantly, competition in the United States is less than perfect ... politicians and bureaucrats often side with those having greater access to power, not those having greater needs.... A society needing less unskilled work, stressing profit and middle-class comfort, and generally accepting cuts in social programs and services will have little empathy for Puerto Ricans and other oppressed populations. The high price of housing and necessities; national trends of unskilled jobs moving out of large cities where Puerto Ricans are concentrated; gentrification and continued automation add to Puerto Rican poverty.[23]*

Homelessness, a lack of decent and affordable housing, a high school dropout rate, HIV/AIDS, chronic unemployment or underemployment, substance abuse, discrimination, teen pregnancy, attacks on bilingual and affirmative action programs, the English First/Only movement, limited access to society's resources and institutions, and a deficit of culturally and linguistically sensitive health and social services—an endless list of problems confronts Puerto Ricans in the United States.

Although these problems seem overwhelming, all lend themselves to community organization intervention. Mobilizing needs to capitalize on the efforts of past struggles. Coalition building, not competition with other oppressed groups, is necessary for success. The political process must be targeted for change because that is where decisions affecting Puerto Ricans and other poor people are made. Organizers need to address and challenge prejudices such as sexism and heterosexism that characterize certain marginalized communities. These attitudes, however, must be confronted with sensitivity to cultural norms and values and only after a relationship of trust and *confianza* have been established.

Specific Strategies

Ideally, social workers in the Puerto Rican community are bilingual, bicultural, and progressive advocates with strong community roots. They make community empowerment a community goal, offer a repertoire of community organization skills, and possess a theoretical understanding of macro forces and dynamics. They also familiarize themselves with cultural and value differences and factor them into their organizing strategies. Furthermore, they understand that problems and possible solutions must address the values and ethics of the social work profession and those of the community, action group, sponsoring agency, target group, and client group.

The way a problem is defined determines its possible solution. The assessment process is inevitably grounded in a framework of the values of those defining the problem. For example, teen pregnancy can be viewed from many perspectives. Some regard it as a crisis in morality, a health-care issue, or a reflection of the powerlessness of underprivileged young people. Based on problem definition, possible solutions include pastoral counseling, family planning education, expansion of prenatal health services, and advocacy for progressive abortion policies. When discussing teen pregnancy, some people concentrate on the economic hardships to young parents and their families. Others highlight the societal burdens created. Many connect it to the feminization of poverty. Some connect it to the need for better utilization of the funding the U.S. Congress allocates to the Pentagon and to corporate welfare. Conflicts that arise from the ideological and emotional value-laden definitions of a particular problem are difficult to address and may lead organizers to either work on less controversial issues or to tackle tough ones and accept the consequences. Sometimes, depending on the issues, effective community social work intervention requires the use of a community needs assessment approach that could lead to policy development; allocation of funding toward the creation of social service programs; and/or the establishment of research projects or coalitions where Puerto Ricans are one of several entities developing appropriate strategies for addressing community problems.

It is equally important for organizers to assess and try to increase resources available to Puerto Ricans while realizing the resistance they are likely to face from constituencies at the neighborhood, local, regional, or national levels. At times, community social workers will face opposition from Puerto Ricans who may feel threatened both by a potential loss of their own leadership and their limited resources as new leadership emerges.

Community social workers with the characteristics and skills just described are not plentiful. A challenge for social work education and practice, therefore, is to actively recruit, retain, and graduate committed Puerto Ricans and teach transcultural community social work knowledge and practice skills that will enable Puerto Rican and non–Puerto Rican social workers to work effectively with this population group. Obviously this requires a diversified classroom and field education faculty with adequate representation of Puerto Ricans.

Organizing Strategies

The poverty, powerlessness, racism, ethnocentrism, and numerous social ills such as homelessness, substance abuse, and criminal activity that grow out from these forces have led to the full-plate syndrome facing many Puerto Ricans and other marginalized communities. Efforts to counteract this syndrome, such as community-based social service programs for Puerto Rican families and populations and culturally competent social work education and training, are either inadequate or nonexistent. To effect meaningful change for Puerto Rican communities, community social workers need to focus on certain pressing issues such as intercommunity rivalries and power imbalances stemming from greater levels of need, lack of political representation, tokenism, or invisibility of Puerto Ricans in positions of power, such as on agency boards and their administrative units. For example, addressing educational issues for Puerto Rican children in public schools may be more difficult when Puerto Ricans are not proportionately represented on school boards or as school principals.

The saliency of issues in a specific community obviously influences this work. Assessing and intervening in a crisis, for instance, may lead to decisions around short-term organizing efforts that can, in turn, serve as springboards for future intervention. Clearly, an agency employing community social workers can respond to a local tragedy by encouraging residents to express their feelings collectively about the event and harness the emotional energy to call attention to injustices and challenge policy. For example, when a hit-and-run driver who held an influential job killed a young Puerto Rican girl in Hartford, Connecticut, the Puerto Rican community was outraged at the lenient treatment of the driver. The anger led to forums on racism and classism and to organized marches and vigils. As a result of that process, new leaders emerged, and they assailed the criminal justice system with criticism. Although immediate changes did not result, the experience of responding in a unified and organized way—one voice for the entire community—was empowering and led to other opportunities for organizing.

Seizing the moment is appropriate, important, and can lead to building on the momentum created by events such as tragedy or success. For example, the tragedy of Hurricane Hugo led many community social workers to raise money for grass-roots agencies wishing to help hurricane victims in Puerto Rico. The shock and pain of gang-related deaths in Puerto Rican communities have prompted organizing activities around empowering people to access resources leading to safety and increased community involvement in combating violence in their neighborhoods. Such efforts make agencies and community social workers appear more humane, supportive, and help them be perceived as allies in the eyes of the community.

Community social workers must gather much information about the community with which they are involved. Demographic information on population, age, gender, employment indicators, poverty, housing, and other matters is necessary and important. Knowledge of the community history, neighborhood associations, human services, cultural groups, religious institutions, perceived leadership, and how the community is viewed by Puerto Ricans and non–Puerto Ricans should also be gathered, interpreted, and utilized as a part of the assessment and intervention process.

We cannot overstate the importance of selecting appropriate locations and meeting times, assuring transportation and child care, and utilizing effective communication and language skills in the organizing process. At times, speaking in Spanish only is effective. Other times, English may be more appropriate when addressing second-generation Puerto Ricans. Even then, however, using a bicultural method of intervention may help create a more efficient and productive outcome. Often, both languages may need to be spoken. Translations must be accurate. Communicating effectively means being clear and not assuming that people understand what is being expressed. It goes beyond the language(s) being spoken. The language must be appropriate to the group one is working with. This may mean addressing people as Don or Doña, avoiding or explaining professional language and technical terms, and utilizing idiomatic expressions.

Community social workers must be willing to knock on many doors and go to where the client system lives, socializes, or gathers and where the action systems are. This may mean visiting many neighborhoods and human service groups and asking to speak at PTAs, church services, clubs, or organizations. Working with and through community leaders and identifying and helping promote emerging leadership is crucial. Involving people in agenda setting, translating, designing leaflets that are culturally relevant, making phone calls, and writing letters empowers them. Giving people credit for their efforts and appropriately praising their work encourages participation.

Much organizing demands working long hours and planning or attending evening meetings. Planning enjoyable activities and celebrating small victories is part of the community social work process. Sometimes providing snacks during a meeting is appropriate; at other times it takes away time and energy from the meeting. Ethnic food and music may attract more participants, however, especially if the entire family is invited.

The following cases illustrate organizing efforts that highlight these and other skills and strategies that proved appropriate in direct community social work with Puerto Ricans in the United States or in community social work from that Puerto Ricans and others have benefited.[24]

Organizing Church Constituents—A Pentecostal Example

"I knew that I needed to get people to trust and like me. Singing at the services helped a lot," said Ada Suarez, an energetic and highly committed community organization student who graduated from the University of Connecticut School of Social Work (UCSSW). While completing her second year of practice, Ada wanted to harness the potential strength of the members of a large Puerto Rican Pentecostal Church in Hartford. Ada had been raised as a Pentecostal in Puerto Rico and believed organizers could cultivate the spiritual mandate of Pentecostals, to do God's work, and use it as the basis for organizing strategies around church and community improvements.

Churches are not typical social service agencies. They usually have no social workers on staff. As a member of the Puerto Rican Studies faculty at UCSSW, Dr. Julio Morales agreed to supervise Ada.[25] Culturally, college professors are respected as experts, and Ada's pastor welcomed access to this valuable resource along with Ada's help.

In her role as a community social worker, Ada visited homes of people she identified as potential community leaders, met with church elders, and served as a mentor to some of the church's youth. As part of a needs assessment, she distributed a questionnaire to the membership at various meetings and church gatherings that asked for information about members' needs and concerns. Ada shared the survey responses with the congregation during a church service and developed a set of recommendations. "Some brothers and sisters want to write better in Spanish, some want to learn English, and others want help in finding work or better jobs.... Some committees want help in functioning better at meetings, and others want to know more about how to help people.... The youth want to discuss school issues, and some church elders wish to learn how to be better leaders in and out of the church."

Ada brought teachers from the public school system into the church to teach literacy and English as a second language. With assistance from the Puerto Rican Studies faculty, Latino and Latina students at UCSSW, and community leaders, Ada organized workshops in leadership skills development, vocational training, résumé writing, job interviewing skills, and public assistance eligibility. Ada made sure church members were involved in planning and, wherever possible, in conducting the workshops.

Ada also introduced controversial projects such as HIV/AIDS workshops. She encouraged young people to talk about their feelings of isolation in school and the community as a result of the Pentecostal church's strict moral codes, which forbid such typical adolescent behaviors as listening to popular music and going to the movies. In addition, she encouraged the women of the congregation to become more assertive and independent and to seek equal representation with men on the board of elders. Some church members were not comfortable with the graphic language used by HIV/AIDS workshop speakers and the possible changes Ada proposed for the adolescents and women. In response, she explained, respectfully and diplomatically, that because members work with drug addicts and prisoners, some had expressed interest in knowing more about the AIDS epidemic. Ada then led a discussion of why certain language might be appropriate for certain subjects and asked members to suggest less offensive terms. Obviously Ada earned the congregation's *confianza*. Not everyone agreed with her, but she was respected and trusted.

As a result of Ada's work, women did join the board of elders, and the youth group continues to meet. Ada consciously used culturally relevant strategies. She maximized the participation of groups of people that had not been previously involved and respectfully tackled controversial issues. She imparted community organization skills to church members by helping them articulate their needs, involving them in agenda setting and sharing leadership. She also moderated struggles emanating from changes, helped church members design and disseminate flyers, and led discussions on forming committees and selecting organizing strategies. To spark discussion and increase member involvement in these sessions, Ada employed colorful visual aids, such as videotapes and slides. Sometimes images can leave a lasting impression and emphasize points more effectively than words.

English First/Only

Few issues have mobilized Puerto Ricans as much as fighting against the English First/Only bills introduced in Connecticut numerous times. Massive community organizing efforts and strategies continue to defeat this proposed legislation. Opponents of the bills acknowledge that English Only initially sounds appealing because learning English is essential for acclimating to American society. Still, English is already the nation's dominant language, and such bills take on ethnocentric and racial overtones. They can curtail civil rights and eliminate or tightly restrict necessary bilingual services such as emergency health and police responses. Organizers against the bills have mobilized Spanish-speaking media, written letters and editorial responses to local and state media, organized debates, and created coalitions with Latino and Latina leaders who have access to the community and to resources. The emphasis has been on a multiplicity of community organization strategies that have included calling attention to the adverse effects of what initially appears to be sound legislation. Motivating people to attend and testify at hearings and bombarding neutral legislators with calls, letters, and telegrams have proved effective. Organized rallies before and during hearings call further attention to the Puerto Rican community's logic in opposing this movement. English Only and antibilingual education bills were last introduced, and defeated in committee, in 1996.

Research, Consultation, and Evaluation as Community Social Work Tools for Action

In 1992, Dr. Morales was hired by the Bridgeport school system as a consultation/researcher to study why Puerto Rican youngsters drop out of school. As a community social worker, he knew that if the research were to lead to changes, a strong and diverse community team to which he would be accountable had to be organized. Fortunately, the Ford Foundation, which sponsored the study, supported broad community participation.

A collaborative team, with broad Puerto Rican representation, was formed. Dr. Morales reported directly to them. They were encouraged to help develop all research instruments and were trained to interview Puerto Rican youths who had dropped out, young Puerto Ricans who were at risk of dropping out, and those who were achieving. Parents, teachers, administrators, social workers, and other staff members were also interviewed in order to obtain the broadest level of participation and support, as well as raise awareness. All questionnaires addressed community and school factors that contribute to dropout. Too often dropping out of school is blamed only on students and their families. Numerous community forums were organized to disseminate findings and gain more input on problems and solutions. The collaborative "owned" the study and continued meeting and advocating for programs flowing from the study's recommendations long after the research project ended. Programs addressing school policies, teacher training, and a Puerto Rican Studies curriculum have been initiated as a direct result of the study.

School Integration

On April 26, 1988, legal action was taken by the Puerto Rican Legal Defense League, the Connecticut Civil Liberties Union, and other legal entities on behalf of Hartford's schoolchildren against the state of Connecticut. The U.S. Census Bureau identified approximately 48 percent of Hartford public school children as poor. Ninety-one percent of these children were black or Latino. The Hartford school system was overwhelmed by the demand to educate a student population drawn almost exclusively from the poorest families in Hartford. Students from neighboring towns and suburbs are primarily white and upper or middle class. The court case is known as *Sheff* v. *O'Neill*. (Sheff is an African American student and O'Neill was governor of Connecticut in 1988.) Latino students, overwhelmingly Puerto Rican, comprised more than 50 percent of Hartford's public school enrollment, and yet no information was available about what Puerto Rican parents knew about this important case, which could change public education in Hartford and elsewhere.

A research class taught in the spring of 1993 became involved in interviewing Puerto Rican parents in an effort to determine Puerto Rican awareness of the case, attitudes toward integration, and knowledge about potential integration strategies. Students and Dr. Morales interviewed 187 people in Hartford's El Mercado, a Puerto Rican shopping center, and during parent-teacher organization meetings in two of Hartford's schools. Generally, Puerto Ricans with children in the public schools knew almost nothing about *Sheff* v. *O'Neill* and could not define concepts such as mandatory versus voluntary busing, magnet schools, regionalization, or school vouchers. After each interview, interviewees were given definitions of the concepts used during the interview. The findings were publicized, and schools were encouraged to hold meetings (in Spanish and in English) on the topic. Because integration is often viewed in black and white terms, interviewers asked Puerto Ricans how they identified in terms of color. They were given the choices of white, black, or *trigueño* (tan). Seventy percent identified themselves as *trigueño*.

Research can be a powerful strategy for alerting communities about important issues, for learning about the Puerto Rican community, and for advocacy. Carefully translated instruments must be used. Interviewees must be interviewed in the language they prefer. Conversing with people after the interviews is an excellent tool for raising consciousness related to issues addressed by the research.

Addressing HIV/AIDS

Puerto Ricans in Connecticut and elsewhere are almost four times more likely than European Americans to be AIDS patients.[26] The need to organize around AIDS prevention, education, and services in Puerto Rican communities cannot be overstated. Sometimes this can best be done by concentrating solely in Puerto Rican neighborhoods. Other times, depending on the goals or issues, working jointly with other communities can be more effective and lead to future collaborations.

Traditional and nontraditional methods of bringing attention to this pandemic should be utilized. Between 1986 and 1990, Puerto Rican students used research as a tool for raising consciousness around AIDS. They interviewed Puerto Rican store owners or employees of Puerto Rican grocery stores, beauty salons, or other businesses in Puerto Rican neighborhoods to assess their knowledge of AIDS. They were given information on AIDS and asked to share it with their customers. Hundreds of Puerto Rican churchgoers were interviewed after Sunday services. The information obtained as a result of this research effort was brought to the attention of policymakers, AIDS activists, and AIDS organizations. The findings have also been disseminated at conferences and published in *Multicultural Services for AIDS Treatment and Prevention,* a book edited by the Puerto Rican Studies faculty involved in this research.[27]

Working with a community organization class in 1990, Dr. Morales helped organize the Greater Hartford Coalition for Needle Exchange. This was a very controversial undertaking that attracted organized and fierce opposition. AIDS often forces people to confront their values and moralistic judgments. Coalition members reviewed and summarized the sparse literature on needle exchange, wrote position papers, lobbied Hartford city council members, testified at community meetings, and met with elected state representatives. This coalition is often credited for expediting legal needle exchange programs in Hartford and elsewhere in Connecticut.

Latinos/as Contra SIDA (Latinos/as Against AIDS), a Hartford community-based organization, has pioneered innovative methods to mobilize AIDS awareness in communities. Among these is a yearly AIDS radiothon utilizing local radio stations and national and statewide Puerto Rican entertainers, who perform during an entire day in late spring. Park Street, in the heart of the Puerto Rican community, is closed off. Stages are erected and local leaders mobilized to spread the message of AIDS prevention. Merchants contribute money, food, prizes, and other resources. Stores are encouraged to distribute AIDS information, and volunteers are organized to canvass buildings, streets, and other places where people gather. Puerto Ricans are asked to contribute their pocket change to support Latinos/as Contra SIDA (LCS). Radio stations invite people to Park Street to enjoy the music and dance and become involved in the fight against AIDS.

A broader collaborative strategy utilized over the past eight years has been organizing AIDS vigils. High school choirs and church youth choruses have been asked to perform during the vigil to ensure the participation of youth. Collaboration in AIDS work has been facilitated by having the vigils sponsored by four key community-based organizations offering AIDS services in Hartford: LCS, AIDS Project Hartford, AIDS Ministries Program, and the Urban League of Greater Hartford. Those organizations invite other private and public groups to cosponsor the vigil. Cosponsors are expected to duplicate and distribute flyers, commit themselves to sending more than five people to the vigil, and not hold other AIDS activities on the eve of the vigil.

The vigil is a helpful tool for minimizing conflict and rivalry among the primary sponsors. Other strategies for enhancing cooperation and collaboration include having joint socials for staff and board members and expecting board membership in the organizations to share representatives. In this manner, secrecy is minimized and successful strategies are shared, duplicated, coordinated, or jointly sponsored.

Summary of Strategies and Conclusion

The community social work interventions discussed here stress coalition building, consciousness raising, educating people on how to draw from their strengths, and creating political awareness and empowerment. The importance of cultural sensitivity, knowledge of specific communities, strong research skills, and alternative paradigms for understanding history and political power have been highlighted. Advocacy tools include educating potential funders and board members and agency personnel of human service agencies that deliver services to Puerto Ricans; having experts and grassroots organizers testify at public hearings; holding public demonstrations; and training and developing community leaders. All have been included in the case studies we have discussed. Personal involvement and the inclusion of friends, relatives, neighbors, and clients in the political arena must also be part of community social work intervention.

Organization is political. At times, personnel in Puerto Rican and non–Puerto Rican agencies may choose not to initiate or participate in organizing efforts if the activities are perceived as potentially risky to their programs, their own agencies, or agency funding. Ada Suarez was successful in much of her work, but churches can be a tool for either supporting victim-blaming ideology, dependency, sexism, and heterosexism or for helping liberate Puerto Ricans. Many institutions may find obstacles to the use of tactics that directly confront employers, politicians, landlords, school officials, or other powerful systems that discriminate or disempower Puerto Ricans. It may be easier for some agencies or churches to support maintaining affirmative action, increasing access to employment, education, business opportunity, bilingual and multicultural education, protecting social welfare benefits, and strict health and sanitary housing codes. Given the needs of most Puerto Rican communities, community social workers need to accept such support. Most important, they need to question continuously a system that seems to create conditions that promote or perpetuate poverty and to seek to address short- and long-range goals and strategies for liberation for all marginalized populations.

Future community social work with Puerto Ricans must also include organizing to challenge federal and state policies that may lead poor people further into poverty even as government promotes social welfare reforms. Supporting national health insurance, guaranteed child care, employment at "living" wages, especially for single mothers, decent and affordable housing, transportation, quality education, and the civil rights of lesbian women, gay males, and bisexual and transgendered people are all appropriate and essential responsibilities for community social workers.

More than 50 percent of Puerto Ricans are women and 10 percent are gay or lesbian. Validating diversity within the Puerto Rican community strengthens us as a people. Organizing the unemployed, the "disappearing" Puerto Rican male referred to earlier, the homeless, and the uninsured are challenges community social workers must pursue.

Schools of social work have a special responsibility to hire Puerto Rican faculty and administrators and to actively recruit Puerto Rican and Latino students. Puerto Rican course content in social work school curricula must be visible, both as special courses and infused throughout the curriculum. Moreover, social work students must engage in community social work as a prominent social work intervention method. It has been an important part of social work history. Unfortunately, it was not given adequate attention in the late 1970s, 1980s, or 1990s. As we approach the millennium, we face much political backlash against social work policies and programs. Let us seize the moment to organize against that backlash and help usher in a progressive era as part of the first decade of the twenty-first century.

During the next century the meaning of diversity and minority status will change dramatically. Community social workers must demonstrate confidence and competency in delivering services to diverse population groups. Furthermore, just as caseworkers must address macro forces as they respond to individual client needs, community social workers must consciously address the importance of organizing style and the culture, social class, and values of the clients they work with. This implies learning how to address *vicsurs* blaming ideology at all levels and tapping into the strengths of people.

Notes

1. See Julio Morales, "Puerto Rican Studies and Social Careers," and Josephine Nieves et al., "Puerto Rican Studies: Roots and Challenges," in *Toward a Renaissance of Puerto Rican Studies,* eds. Maria Sanchez and Antonio M. Stevens-Arroyo (Highland Lakes, NJ: Columbia University Press, 1987); also see Julio Morales, "Puerto Rican Studies: An Example of Social Movements as a Force Towards Social and Economic Justice," in *Towards Social and Economic Justice,* eds. David Gil and Eva Gil (Cambridge, MA: Schenkman, 1985).

2. The literature has used the word *victims* to describe groups or members of groups who have suffered injustices, been subjected to oppression, destruction, injuries, or mistreatment usually by members of other groups with greater power. Because the word *victims* does not capture the resiliency, strengths, and struggles of victims who have survived, despite the oppression, the literature is also using the word *survivors.* We dislike the word *victims* but clearly understand that members of oppressed groups have not always survived. For example, according to David E. Stannard in "Genocide in the Americas" (*The Nation,* October 19, 1992), between 60 and 80 million people from the Indies to the Amazon perished before the seventeenth century as a result of the European colonization of the Americas. Furthermore, millions of African slaves died during their forced crossing from Africa and their enslavement in the Americas. Although most women survive the violence they are subjected to, often by their partners, thousands are killed every year. Here we are using *vicsurs* to capture the spirit of both the victims' and survivors' perspectives and call attention to this issue.

3. See Martin Tochlin, "Study Shows Growing Gap Between Rich and Poor," *New York Times,* March 2, 1989, p. A-24; also see Robert Pear, "Study Shows Health Gap Widens Between the Affluent and the Poor," *New York Times,* July 8, 1992, p. A-1; and "Evidence Indicates the Rich Got Richer During the '80s," *San Juan Star,* March 5, 1992, p. 1.

4. See Bob Kaplan, "Who's Worth More—America's Richest 400 Families or Its 40 Million Poorest," *New England Prout Journal,* December 1986.

5. United States Government, *U.S. Census 1990* (Washington, DC: General Accounting Office, 1990).

6. Manuel Maldonado-Denis, *Puerto Rico: A Socio-Historic Interpretation* (New York: Random House, 1972).

7. John Gunther, *Inside Latin America* (New York: Harper & Brothers, 1941).

8. From Julio Morales's "The Elusive American Dream," written for the *Hartford Courant*, pp. C-1–C-4, Commentary, August 10, 1986. Also see Julio Morales, *Puerto Rican Poverty and Migration* (New York: Praeger, 1986).

9. See Pedro Caban, "Redefining Puerto Rico's Political Status," in *Colonial Dilemma: Critical Perspectives on Contemporary Puerto Rico,* p. 21, eds. Edwin Melendez and Edgard Melendez (Boston: South End Press, 1992).

10. Ibid., p. 22.

11. Ibid., p. 28.

12. Ibid., p. 29.

13. Ibid., p. 30.

14. M. Delgado and D. Humm-Delgado, "Natural Support Systems: A Source of Strength in Hispanic Communities," *Social Work,* 27, 1982, pp. 83–89. Also see *Women of Color: Integrating Ethnic and Gender Identity in Psychotherapy,* pp. 114–138, eds. L. Comas-Diaz and B. Greene (New York: Guilford Press, 1994).

15. *Compadres* and *comadres* are close friends among the adults, established as a result of the baptism of a child. *Padrino* means godfather, and *madrina,* godmother (of the baptized child). *Padrino* and *madrina de boda* are best man and maid of honor at a wedding. *Hijos de crianza* means "children by raising" and is usually translated as stepchildren.

16. See Raul Canizares, *Walking with the Night* (Rochester, VT: Destiny Books, 1993).

17. See M. Reyes, "Women's Studies Programs in Latin America: A Source of Empowerment." Unpublished doctoral dissertation, University of Massachusetts, Amherst (1992).

18. See J. Carrier, *De los otros: Intimacy and Homosexuality Among Mexican Men* (New York: Columbia University Press, 1995).

19. In Reyes, "Women's Studies Programs in Latin America: A Source of Empowerment."

20. See *Women of Color: Integrating Ethnic and Gender Identity in Psychotherapy,* pp. 389–427.

21. See Paulo Freire, *Pedagogy of the Oppressed* (New York: Continuum, 1981). Also see Frantz Fanon, *Black Skin, White Mask* (New York: Grove Press, 1967), and *The Wretched of the Earth* (New York: Grove Press, 1968).

22. Puerto Ricans on the island and the United States are not totally free of racism. For example, in his autobiography, *Down These Mean Streets,* Piri Thomas describes the pain he experienced because he was the darkest child in the family. John Longres's article, "Racism and Its Effects on Puerto Rican Continentals," *Social Casework* 55, No. 2 (1974), discusses a preference among many Puerto Ricans for lighter skin. Nevertheless, it is next to impossible to be racist in the North American sense when there is so much variation in skin color (and hair texture) within Puerto Rican families. Puerto Ricans often call someone *negro* or *negra* (black) as a sign of affection and love. Referring to someone as *negro(a)* has nothing to do with color, and to be *jincho* (too white) is sometimes perceived as unattractive.

23. Competition for resources—jobs, housing, scholarships—can lead to conflict between oppressed groups. Organizers must avoid such possibilities. See "Black Puerto Rican Conflict: The Inevitable Systemic Outcome," in Morales, *Puerto Rican Poverty and Migration.*

24. For further organizing and advocacy strategies, see Julio Morales, "The Clinician as Advocate: A Puerto Rican Perspective," in Mizio and Delaney.

25. The Puerto Rican Studies Project at the University of Connecticut School of Social Work was founded by Dr. Julio Morales. Dr. Reyes directed this project for nine years. The project was created to address the need for culturally sensitive social work practitioners in the Puerto Rican community, to recruit, retain, and graduate Puerto Rican and other Latino graduate social work students and to train social work providers throughout Connecticut and southwestern Massachusetts. Before the project was initiated in 1980, the University of Connecticut School of Social Work had graduated 25 Latino students (1946–79). From 1980 to 1990, it graduated 140.

26. Julio Morales and Marcia Bok, eds., *Multicultural Human Services for AIDS Treatment and Prevention* (New York: Haworth Press, 1992).

27. Ibid.

6

A Feminist Perspective
on Organizing with
Women of Color

LORRAINE M. GUTIÉRREZ AND EDITH A. LEWIS

Although the presence of women of color in the United States is growing (Armott & Matthaei, 1991), our distinctive perspectives, problems, and potentials have rarely been addressed within the field of community organizing. As educators, activists, and practitioners of community practice and multicultural social work, we believe this limited perspective can have negative effects on both women of color and those who wish to work within their communities. In this chapter we present a feminist approach to organizing with women of color in order to suggest how race and gender issues can be worked on simultaneously. The issues and practice principles we present here are relevant for both women of color and European American women organizing in communities of color.

Women of Color: Who Are We?

The term *women of color* has been adopted by many African American, Latina, Asian, and Native American women in the United States as a way of unifying what we have seen as commonalties between us, especially in contrast to the experiences of European American women in our society (Comas-Diaz & Greene, 1994). However, the acceptance of this umbrella term does not indicate that we do not recognize the differences between and within racial and ethnic groups. Understanding the specific historical experiences and cultural expressions of different groups of women of color is as important as understanding ways in which we are similar. All women of color have been affected by the domination of the larger society, but this has taken different forms with different groups: the experience of reservation life creates a different social context from slavery or forced deportation. Women of color have tended to draw strength from their ethnic minority communities, but this can be expressed quite differently within each group. Therefore, although this chapter is about women of color in general, it is important to keep in mind that differences exist between these groups that must be recognized and used when working within specific communities.[1] Understanding differences and similarities is particularly important in the development of multiethnic coalitions or when the organizer is from a different background than the majority of the women involved.

Although the specific ethnic and racial groups encompassed by this umbrella term differ in many respects, together we share similarities in terms of our strengths, low status, and power. Women of color experience the double jeopardy of racism and sexism in our society. We are hampered by average earnings lower than that of white women, by overrepresentation in low status occupations, and by a low average level of education (Armott & Matthaei, 1991). Correspondingly, women of color are underrepresented in positions of power within our government, corporations, and nonprofit institutions (Comas-Diaz & Greene, 1994; Gordon-Bradshaw, 1987; Zambrana, 1987).

These statistics suggest ways in which our powerlessness as a group has very direct and concrete effects on our daily experiences. Lack of access to many social resources is both a cause and effect of powerlessness. The poverty rate of women of color is two to three times that of white women: 36.5% of all black women and 31.2% of all Latinas live below the poverty line, in contrast to 12.7% of all white women (U.S. Census, 1992). Therefore, women of color are more likely than white women to suffer from conditions of poor or no housing, insufficient food and clothing, and inadequate access to health and mental health services and to be located within low-income and physically deteriorating communities (Gordon-Bradshaw, 1987).

Women of color also share similarities in terms of strengths and coping strategies. Within our own communities we have developed values and behaviors that have allowed us to survive in the face of oppression. Economic necessity has led women of color to participate in the labor market at higher rates than European American women. Although this role has not always been voluntary, it has helped us to develop ties and a sense of self outside of the family and has reduced our economic dependency on men. Women of color are also likely to have strong family ties and ties with other women in our community to whom we can go for concrete and emotional support. These informal ties can be a form of strength. Another common-

---

[1]It is beyond the scope of this chapter to detail the specific historical and cultural conditions particular to the experience of women within each ethnic minority group. The bibliography includes resources that organizers can use in order to learn about specific populations and communities of women of color.

ality is a strong connection to spirituality, through formal or informal religion, which has helped us to survive (Comas-Diaz, 1994; Gilkes, 1986; White, 1981). This history of coping and surviving within a hostile world has led many women of color to perceive themselves as strong and capable of dealing with adversity.

Existing models of community practice need to recognize these ways in which women of color differ from white women and from men of color. Organizers have most often recognized the impact of powerlessness on women of color from the perspective of institutional racism while overlooking the role of gender inequity in influencing the life chances of women of color. Similarly, the strengths of women of color are also often ignored in community work. When women of color are viewed solely as members of their racial or ethnic group and gender is not taken in account, community organizers may alienate women of color and reinforce ways in which sexism, both in the larger society and within ethnic minority communities, is a form of oppression (Aragon de Valdez, 1980; Armott & Matthaei, 1991; Weil, 1986; Zavella, 1986).

A feminist perspective, which assumes that issues of power and powerlessness are integral to the experience of women of color, can address this oversight. It proposes concrete and specific ways in which community organizers can work with women of color by increasing their power on a number of different levels and by drawing on their strengths. The goal of this approach is to eliminate the social conditions that are oppressive to women of color by increasing their influence in our society. However, the historical tension between European American feminists and communities of color has led some to reject this method without looking closely at ways in which differences can be dealt with and used constructively to the benefit of women of color. In this chapter we attempt to bridge this gap by outlining the assumptions of the feminist perspective and the practice principles it involves, describing ways in which feminist organizing has excluded women of color, and presenting a reformulation of feminist organizing for use with women of color. Although we anticipate that our ideas may be controversial, it is our belief that feminist methods are a framework for ensuring that attention is given to both sexism and racism when organizing with women of color.

Defining Feminist Organizing

Community work has always played an important role within the feminist movement in this country. Nineteenth-century feminists were leaders in the abolitionist movement, the suffrage movement, social settlements, and the progressive movement. Community organizing has been equally important in more recent feminist movements, especially those coming from a radical rather than liberal perspective (Nes & Iadicola, 1989; Weil, 1986). This organizing has focused primarily in work for improving women's health, for ending violence against women, and for increasing economic opportunities for all women (Morell, 1987; Schechter, 1982; Withorn, 1984).

The overarching goal of feminist organizing is the elimination of permanent power hierarchies between all people that can prevent them from realizing their human potential. The goal of feminist organizing is the elimination of sexism, racism, and other forms of oppression through the process of empowerment which "seeks individual liberation through collective activity, embracing both personal and social change" (Morell, 1987).

Recent research on feminist organizing has begun to identify ways in which it differs from other models of community practice. Most often this research has used participant observation methods to identify the values and practice principles on which feminist organizing is based (Hyde, 1986). These are the most common characteristics of feminist organizing:

1. A *gender lens* is used to analyze the causes of and solution to community problems. Sexism is assumed to be an important force in the experiences of all women and at the root of many problems. All women are thought to be a part of a "community" of women, as well as members of their own specific community (Bricker-Jenkins & Hooyman, 1986; Gould, 1987; Hyde, 1986; Kopasci & Faulkner, 1988; Morell, 1987; Zavella, 1986).

2. Attention is paid to the *process of practice,* in an effort to create organizations based on feminist principles (Hyde, 1990). As described by the Women Organizers Project (Joseph et al., 1989), "Feminist organizing is based on values and actions carried out in a democratic, humanistic framework . . . [it] must affect the conditions of women while empowering them." Efforts are made to make feminist movement organizations "safe spaces" where women can escape the larger and more oppressive external social environment. This has most often involved developing feminist organizations based on the principles of collectivity and gender equality in which women can support and develop the confidence and skills necessary to increase their political power (Bricker-Jenkins & Hooyman, 1986; Hyde, 1990).

3. *Empowerment through consciousness raising* is characteristic of feminist organizing efforts. Empowerment is a process of increasing personal, interpersonal, or political power so individuals can take action to improve their lives (Bricker-Jenkins & Hooyman, 1986; Collins, 1990; Gould, 1987b; Gutiérrez, 1990; Kieffer, 1984; Longres & Mcleod, 1980; Morell, 1987; Pernell, 1985; Pinderhughes, 1983; Schechter, Szymanski, & Cahill, 1985; Simmons & Parsons, 1983). Empowerment theory assumes that society consists of separate groups possessing different levels of power and control over resources (Gould, 1987b). Recognizing the way in which power relationships affect daily reality and understanding how individuals can contribute to social change is the process through which empowerment takes place (Friere, 1970; Gutiérrez, 1990; Longres & McLeod, 1980).

Consciousness raising contributes to empowerment by helping individuals make this connection between personal problems and political issues. By examining the nature of their lives, women can begin to understand the commonalty of their experience and its connection to community and social issues. Consciousness raising can be carried out in one of two formats: group discussion or praxis, the integration of action and reflection. An important outcome of consciousness raising is an understanding of ways in which women, individually and in groups, can begin to change the social order (Bricker-Jenkins & Hooyman, 1986; Friere, 1970; Gutiérrez, 1990; Rosenthal, 1984).

4. A major assumption is that the personal is political, therefore organizing often takes a *"grassroots," bottom-up approach.* Organizing efforts must often grow out of issues that are impinging on women's daily lives. The development of alternative services for women is integral to this method. As described by Withorn (1984), "for the past 15 years, to be a feminist has meant to engage in service work as much as it has meant to do the things which are normally defined as political." Alternative services such as support networks, health clinics, shelters, and hotlines are critical elements of feminist organizing (Hyde, 1990; Withorn, 1984).

Fannie Lou Hamer's work in the Mississippi Democratic Freedom Party during the 1960s is but one example of using a grassroots approach to affect change. This movement, originally built on consciousness-raising efforts regarding racial segregation in the South, expanded to include other social and political issues facing poor, rural, and urban families. Eventually the party gained national recognition, although it remained true to its interest in expanding the rights of those who have been ignored by political circles across the country. The legacy of the Mississippi Democratic Freedom Party can still be seen in the interests of presidential candidates making campaign speeches in smaller, more rural, areas of the United States.

5. Efforts are made to bridge differences between women based on such factors as race, class, physical ability, and sexual orientation with the principle that *diversity is strength.* According to this model, "feminist practitioners will not only strive to eliminate racism, classism, heterosexism, anti-semitism, ableism, and other systems of oppression and exploitation, but will affirm the need for diversity by actively reaching out to achieve it" (Bricker-Jenkins & Hooyman, 1986). As described in the following section, this principle has often been difficult to put into practice.

6. *Organizing is holistic.* It involves both the rational and nonrational elements of human experiences. Emotions, spirituality, and artistic expression are used as tactics for unifying women and expressing issues. Involvement in social change is considered organic, not an adjunct, to women's lives. The use of puppets and street theater in the women's disarmament movement is one example of this tactic (Linten & Witham, 1981).

This brief discussion of feminist organizing indicates some of the ways it can be used when working with women of color. Feminist theory provides a means for understanding ways in which racism, sexism, and classism have an interactive impact on the lives of women of color (Armott & Matthaei, 1991; Collins, 1990). It also suggests a method for directly addressing how we are affected by conditions of powerlessness. By placing a value on multiethnic and racial coalitions, it assumes that women of color should play an important role in the movement. However, as discussed in the following section, this coalition has historically been the exception, rather than the rule.

Issues for Feminist Organizing with Women of Color

Problems and Issues

The feminist movement of the United States has excluded women of color in three ways: by an inability to acknowledge its racist tenets and foundations; by ignoring the issues that primarily affect women of color; and through difficulties with integrating other "voices" into the formulation of feminist theory and practice. Lack of attention to these three conditions has led the feminist movement in the United States to provide a platform for European American women while ignoring the contributions of women of color to feminist concerns.

The inability to address racism in the feminist movement has been documented by numerous scholars (Dill, 1987; Giddings, 1984; Hooks, 1981; Solomon, 1982; Spelman, 1989). Although the movement has advocated paying critical attention to the domination of women in their historical and political contexts, only recently has it done so when examining its own formation. Hooks (1981) notes two instances of this historical racism. Elizabeth Cady Stanton, a leader of the suffragist movement of the turn of the century, identified the rights of white women to vote as being distinct from those of other men or women of color in this way:

> *If Saxon men have legislated thus for their own mothers, wives and daughters, what can we hope for at the hands of Chinese, Indians and Africans? . . .*
> *I protest against the enfranchisement of another man of any race or clime until the daughters of Jefferson and Hancock are crowned with their rights.*

In the early 1900s, during a meeting of the General Federation of Women's Clubs, the president, Mrs. Lowe, stated her own reluctance for the integration of African American women into the clubs on the following basis:

> *Mrs. Ruffin belongs among her own people. Among them she would be a leader and could do much good, but among us, she can create nothing but trouble.*

Yet during this era, African American male scholars and activists such as Frederick Douglass and Henry Garnett were welcome in white women's social circles as speakers.

Recent feminist scholarship demonstrates how racism in the contemporary women's movement has interfered with the involvement of women of color. Although many white leaders of the women's liberation movement gained an awareness of gender inequity through their involvement in the civil rights movement, they were unsuccessful in working collaboratively with women of color (Evans, 1980). Because feminist movements have often presented gender as the sole form of oppression, women of color have perceived their experiences with racism or ethnocentrism as being ignored (Gould, 1987b; Reid, 1984). Only recently have efforts been made to incorporate issues of racism and other forms of oppression into the women's movement (Gould, 1987b; Weil, 1986).

A second impediment to the involvement of women of color has been the nature of the issues selected for mobilization. Because the majority of the leaders of the movement emerged from the European American middle class, their life experiences have influenced the direction of the movement (Kopasci & Faulkner, 1988). Women of color, who have traditionally had high rates of labor force participation, often could not identify with the emphasis placed by feminists on the right of women to enter the workplace. Many of these women attributed their low wages to racism, rather than sexism; therefore the issue of comparable worth based on gender had little meaning.

One example of the exclusion of women of color and their problems from the women's movement of the United States is given by Williams (1988). In describing incidents of sterilization of women of color, she noted:

> *I was reminded of a case I worked on when I was working for the Western Center on Law and Poverty about eight years ago. Ten black [and] Hispanic women had been sterilized by the University of Southern California-Los Angeles County General Medical Center, allegedly without proper consent, and in most instances without even their knowledge. Most of them found out what had been done to them upon inquiry, after a much-publicized news story in which an intern charged that the chief of obstetrics at the hospital pursued a policy of recommending Cesarean delivery and simultaneous sterilization for any pregnant woman with three or more children and who was on welfare. In the course of researching the appeal in that case, I remember learning that one-quarter of all Navajo women of childbearing age—literally all those of childbearing age ever admitted to a hospital—have been sterilized.*

Feminist organizing regarding reproductive rights has more often focused on issues of access to abortion than on the sterilization of women of color. A more inclusive formulation of the issues involved in reproductive rights would involve both access to contraception and abortion *and* the ability to exercise one's reproductive capacity.

The third impediment to the participation of women of color is the willingness to acknowledge other "lenses" or "voices" through which the experiences of women can be analyzed. The emergence of a number of theories about the status of women in the United States has resulted in criticism for their lack of application to those other than white women (Giddings, 1984; Hooks, 1981; Solomon, 1980; Spelman, 1989). Contemporary theories of the women's movement are only now acknowledging the existence of an ethnic labor market structure, as in the case of Chinatown women (Armott & Matthaei, 1991; Loo & Ong, 1987). They further fail to acknowledge fully the oppression of men of color, or differences in family or gender roles in some ethnic communities (McAdoo, 1981; Segura, 1987; Solomon, 1980).

Community Organizing by Women of Color

Lack of participation in feminist movements does not mean that women of color have not been active in their own communities: organizing by women of color in the United States has a rich and diverse history. An example of this involvement is the organization of Black Women's Clubs in the United States a century ago. Through women's clubs, African American women such as Ida B. Wells Barnett took leadership roles in the organization of their communities. At the end of the nineteenth century, these clubs organized nursing homes, day-care centers, and orphanages because the need for assistance with the care of children and the aging was of critical concern to African American women in families during this period. Women's clubs were also involved in social action against lynching and sexual assault. The National Urban League, in which women had an important founding role, was another example of a community of color organizing nationally to address the problems and concerns of people of color in the United States.

These organizations, supported and developed by women of color, had goals of benefiting all society, not just their own target ethnic group. Macht and Quam (1986) note:

> [T]he contributions of these groups did not stop with the Black community. They also played a vital role in World War I. The Committee on Women's Defense Work of the Council for National Defense consisted mainly of Black women. It helped care for families of absent soldiers, gave comfort kits to the soldiers, helped conserve and enlarge the food supply, and formed canning clubs. The Committee also brought attention to the high infant mortality rate in this country. It discovered a need for better community health services. To correct these problems, the Council set up programs to weigh and measure infants and provide them with milk. In addition, the Committee sought to improve recreational facilities available to youth and pushed for nurse's training for Black women. Medical personnel for Black people had always been woefully inadequate; the committee compiled and circulated a list of hospitals where Black women could be trained." (p. 96)

Women of color in these and other organizations did not view their work as affecting only their constituencies. Their work allowed for the incorporation of additional perspectives that would assist all families.

Organizing by women of color has been based on existing networks of family, friends, or informal and formal *ethnic community* institutions. Gilkes (1981, 1983) notes in her research on African American women community organizers that these women were deeply embedded in black communities and became active because of their commitment to their communities. Barrera (1987) describes the extra activities willingly taken on by Latina professionals and paraprofessionals. These individuals, he notes, have developed organizations and political interest groups and have served as interpreters of the wider society to those Latinos with limited access to it.

Other examples of community organization in long-standing ethnic communities are the mutual aid societies. The Hui among the Chinese, the Ko among the Japanese, and the Tribal Councils among the Native Americans have all served as vehicles for assisting individual ethnic group members, families, and entire communities through the establishment of business loans, funerals, and community programs. Organizing with women of color from a feminist perspective must acknowledge, work within, and build upon these rich traditions.

Examples from the Field

Feminist organizing methods place a high value on experience-based knowledge. Effective feminist organizing with women of color builds on this base by drawing on two sources: techniques based in feminist efforts and those from the tradition of women of color organizing within their own communities. The following examples indicate ways in which these traditions have been integrated.

The Network Utilization Project (NUP)

The NUP project was developed by one of the authors in her work with women in a small midwestern city. The purpose of the project was to use the strengths of African American families as an intervention for empowerment. We did this in a variety of ways. First, the project was designed to be community based. All participants lived in the same geographic proximity and had frequent interaction. Second, the project focused on the small group as a primary form of interaction. In this way, women had an opportunity to meet with each other on a weekly basis in a small group that did not require that they either physically or psychologically remove themselves from their community of origin.

A third principle underlying the NUP project was that women of color in communities of color were a part of both those communities as well as extended family networks. It was necessary for these networks to be acknowledged in any change effort undertaken by the women, either individually or in groups. Each decision for change was met with an analysis of its possible consequences for the participants, their families, and the host community.

Lastly, it was assumed that experiences with individual problem resolution could be expanded to community problem resolution. It was in this effort that the program was most effective (Lewis, in press). NUP participants, through group meetings, organized a Tenant's Council in one of the city's low-income communities, were instrumental in closing down a city-funded agency that had not provided service to the community although it was being paid to do so, and participated in the organization of a citywide organization for low-income women's rights. The Network Utilization Project activities moved participants from developing a sense of personal empowerment to bring about change in their communities as well.

Project Oasis

Safe home networks were created early in the battered women's movement to provide short-term emergency shelter to victims of spousal abuse and their children. The core of such a program is volunteers who agree to shelter battered women and their families within their homes for a limited period of time (Schechter, 1982). Safe home programs have most often been used in white middle-class areas and rural areas and have rarely been developed within low-income minority or urban settings.

Project Oasis was an attempt to bring this form of feminist organizing into multiracial and multiethnic urban communities. The goal of Project Oasis was to end violence against women in these communities through the provision of advocacy, counseling, and shelter services, and through community education, legal advocacy, and the development of self-help networks. The program was initiated by one of the authors while working with a larger organization that offered counseling and community organization programs for all victims of crime in a large northeastern city.

Developing a safe home network for women of color involved modifying the structure it had taken in other localities. The organizer was able to draw on the natural support networks of women of color within each community. She found that it was not unusual for women of color to shelter sisters in need, but that this sheltering was often done with expectations of reciprocity. Few low-income families could afford to provide financial support for a woman and her children. Therefore, this program gained funding which allowed them to reimburse volunteers for room and board so women who had the desire to help others were given the financial means to do so.

The program was ethnically and racially integrated in terms of staff on all levels, and efforts were made to administer it collaboratively. The director and 50 percent of the staff were women of color. Personal attributes and a commitment to using a feminist perspective in working with women of color were considered more important qualities for staff and volunteers than actual academic training. Staff and volunteers were involved in all aspects of administration, particularly in the area of program planning and outreach. The goal was to develop a structure in which the women on the staff could grow and learn from each other.

Working within this multiethnic environment was a challenge for all of those involved in the program: many of the white staff and volunteers had never worked in an environment in which women of color had the leadership roles and many of the women of color had never been in a position in which they were allowed to take a major role in the development of programs. In an effort to deal with these issues, and others that emerged in this kind of program, much attention was paid to staff development and training. On the basis of principles of feminist management (Hyde, 1990), each month all-day staff retreats were scheduled in which team building and organizational activities were carried out. Responsibility for these meetings was rotated among the different staff and units. These efforts were successful to the degree to which they opened up lines of communication and provided a structure for shared responsibility and collaboration among staff and volunteers. However, they did not prevent or eliminate the emergence of conflicts or issues present in any multiethnic organizing effort.

The multiethnic and urban nature of this program also affected the location and development of safe home. Many safe home networks established within white middle-class settings have focused their efforts on volunteer recruitment within the feminist community. Project Oasis was most successful when focusing outreach to organizations within minority communities: churches, Asian merchant associations, schools, health clinics, Head Start centers, and multiservice community centers. These organizations saw Project Oasis as an asset to the community and provided us with support and assistance. As a method for feminist organizing, Project Oasis was most successful in educating the community regarding violence against women and providing shelter. It also was effective in empowering individual women to became involved in helping others, volunteering, and testifying at public hearings. In these ways, women of color became more directly involved in ending violence against women.

Community Development in West Africa

The roots of feminist organizing among women of color are drawn from the African, Latin American, Asian, and Native American diaspora. Often when one travels to other countries and experiences different forms of organizing among women, one can recognize elements that have been retained by women of color in the United States. These experiences suggest ties between the organizing of women of color in the United States and internationally. We can learn a lot from these examples of organizing, especially ways to unite women across differences in language, class, or religion.

One of the authors was recently involved in community development work with women in Ghana, West Africa. When participating in a consortium of over forty-five different women's organizations in the Greater Accra area, the author was struck by several "familiar" experiences. First, the women who represented several ethnic groups, religions, and languages were careful to make certain that all participants were welcomed and included in discussion and represented on consortium subcommittees. This inclusion was also directed to the men who participated. Second, the women could discuss their differences openly and set aside topics, ideologies, and actions that could irrevocably derail meeting the common goals of the consortium. For example, when discussing their stance concerning the International Year of the Women Platform—which was potentially divisive in relation to religious differences—a decision was made for each individual organization to address the platform separately and on its own time, rather than addressing it as a consortium issue. The consequences of this action allowed those organizations that supported the platform elements to operationalize them in the individual organization's work without imposing them on the overall coalition. The goal was to meet the collective will of the organization.

Future Directions for Feminist Organizing with Women of Color

Practice Principles

The purpose of this chapter is to explore ways in which knowledge concerning feminist organizing methods and an understanding of the issues relevant to women of color can be integrated toward developing a new and more inclusive organizing strategy. What do these examples and the preceding discussion tell us about feminist organizing with women of color? We believe the following practice principles can provide directions for future work:

1. *Organizers must have intricate knowledge of and willingness to participate in the woman's ethnic community.* This first involves knowledge of its institutions and how they work for or against women. Churches, community centers, schools, and social clubs can be avenues for accessing women of color and effecting change within the community. Organizing requires an analysis of societal institutions, including the one represented by the organizer, and how they might ultimately benefit or hurt the women being organized. Gaining this knowledge could involve learning more about specific communities of color through reading and participation in community events (Kopasci & Faulkner, 1988). Working with women of color requires an understanding of the cultural context.

In an effort to become involved in the community, one of the group facilitators of the NUP project participated in activities sponsored by the local community center. She worked weekly with the children of the community in enrichment programming for several months before proceeding to organize the women. During this time, she became aware of community members' patterns of interaction, their relationships with agencies in the city, and other potential issues in the community. Community members and group participants had the opportunity to meet and talk with the community worker and to watch her interact with their children. Many of the initial participants later mentioned that their decision to participate in the project was directly related to their approval of the facilitator's work with their children and presence in the community.

2. *Effective feminist organizing with women of color requires that women of color be in leadership roles.* Too often attempts to use these techniques with women of color have taken the unidirectional "outreach approach": communities of color are targets of feminist efforts, rather than active participants. When this approach is used, women of color often resist these efforts or can undermine them (Kopasci & Faulkner, 1988; Schechter, 1982). In both of the case examples described here, women of color acted as the organizer of the activity within the community and used "community expertise" to guide their work. Although we were outsiders, our experience as women of color assisted our entree into community. As women of color we were capable of assessing strategies of feminist organizing and making them more compatible with the minority community in which the women worked. This is similar to Rivera and Erlich's description of secondary level contact within the community in this book.

Feminist organizations that would like to carry out more organizing with women of color will need to incorporate women of color as active participants and leaders *before* taking on this kind of work. This kind of collaboration may require redefining the kind of work they do and their attitudes toward institutions such as the church and family. The history of attempts at collaboration suggest that effective work involving European American feminists and women of color requires identifying how racism and goal setting may exclude women of color from feminist efforts. Therefore successful collaboration will require that European American women change their interactions with women of color. This kind of organizational work embraces the tenet of feminist organizing that "diversity is strength."[2]

3. *The organizer must be willing to serve as a facilitator and to allow the problem to be studied through the "lens" or "vision" of women of color.* This requires allowing this vision to alter the way the organizer herself views her work and sharing that new information with others hoping to organize and work within communities of color. An organizer who is from a different racial, ethnic, or class background than the women must recognize how her life experience has colored her perceptions. Her definitions and perceptions should not dominate the organizing effort. It is important that her work involve secondary or tertiary contact with the community: taking the role of facilitator or consultant while developing and working with local leadership.

In the Network Utilization Project described earlier, the initial design of the project was to separate individual from community concerns. We initially believed that the group members would work on individual problem resolution for a period of eight weeks and then, having established a pattern of interaction within the group, be able to work cooperatively on analysis and resolution of a community concern. It became clear within the first two meetings that the project could not separate individual from community concerns. As one participant put it: "My individual problems *are* the community's problems." The flexibility to alter the design based on the

---

[2]White feminists interested in working more effectively with women of color might find the books and articles in the bibliography particularly useful.

realities of the community allowed the group to continue to work toward resolution of its identified goals, not those of the facilitator/researcher.

4. *Utilize the process of praxis to understand the historical, political, and social context of the organizing effort.* This means that the organizing process will inform not only the organized community but the "community" of the organizer as well. Praxis involves an analysis of the process and outcome of organizing efforts. When this technique is used the outcome of a tactic is often less important than what the community and organizer learn about the nature of the problem being addressed. In this way community issues are often redefined.

Community organizers must engage in an ongoing process of praxis in their work in order to recognize their own biases and assumptions in working with communities. How, for example, do their own social, historical, and political experiences influence their understanding of the communities they are working in and their assumptions about what strategies are effective in these communities? How do the organizers change their own behavior and communicate that transformation to members of the wider society as a result of community work? How are effective strategies developed within the community of color transmitted for use to the wider society?

The involvement of women of color in the battered women's movement provides another example of this principle. When many feminist shelters observed that they were unsuccessful in reaching women of color, many defined the problem as that of inadequate outreach. When outreach was unsuccessful, women of color in some localities provided feedback to many shelter programs that their approach was alienating and foreign to communities of color. Those problems that have been most successful with women of color have been those that addressed their own racism, classism, and ethnocentrism in the development of alternative programs (Schechter, 1982).

5. *An effective strategy for organizing women of color is the small group.* The literature on empowerment and feminist organizing suggests that small group interaction can play a critical role (Gutiérrez, 1990; Pernell, 1985). The small group provides the ideal environment for exploring the social and political aspects of "personal" problems and for developing strategies for work toward social change (Schechter et al., 1985). Therefore, feminist organizing often begins with interactions between women in small groups (Hyde, 1986).

On a national level, women of color have been using this strategy to improve conditions in ghettos and barrios based on a "house meeting" strategy (*Sunday Chicago Tribune Magazine,* 1988). For example, Clementine Barfield's work with SOSAD (Save Our Sons and Daughters) in Detroit began with a small group of individual mothers who had experienced the loss of a child through a violent death in the inner city. The formation of many similar small groups has built coalitions that have become an influential force in lobbying for gun control and related issues.

6. *Women of color who are involved in feminist organizing must anticipate the possible backlash from within their own community of origin, the wider society, and the* *feminist movement.* These sources of conflict will affect the outcomes of the organizing effort. The extent to which the worker/organizer anticipates conflict related to group interaction, the possibility of internalized oppression, wider society strategies to destroy the community change effort, and similar issues will often determine whether the efforts are successful.

Women of color have often worked effectively as organizers, but often at great expense to their physical and emotional health (Gilkes, 1983). Organizing around issues shared with European American women may place the organizer in additional jeopardy within the ethnic community, due to the notion that organizing groups of women can be divisive (Aragon de Valdez, 1980). Strategies such as mapping out the benefits and drawbacks of sharing a community change effort are necessary when these linkages are desired. Efforts often will require dealing directly with incidents of homophobia or sexism within communities of color.

When the consequences outweigh the benefits, alternatives to the proposed organizing effort must be identified. In some cases, this may mean that organizers who are not community members must continue their work outside the ethnic community and share strategies with organizers who are inside the ethnic community (Kopasci & Faulkner, 1988). Women of color inside the community can look to other women of color across the country involved in organizing efforts for support as well. Pat Collair's efforts at organizing rural southern poor women rely not only on work with these women, but also with other women involved in similar grassroots change efforts. This continued communication is one way of dealing with the problem of the emotional drain related to issues of racism and sexism in community organization.

7. Feminist organizers must recognize ways in which women of color have worked effectively within their own communities. Women of color have traditionally been involved in activities to benefit their community. Feminist organizers should work with these indigenous leaders and learn from them the most effective ways of working in particular communities. Working with existing leaders may involve feminist organizers in different types of activities from those in which they may usually engage. For example, existing community leaders may be active in church-related activities or in working with municipal agencies (Bookman & Morgan, 1986) to provide necessary survival services. Organizers can learn from these women ways in which they have found to survive and leverage political power.

It is more important than ever to recognize and facilitate effective organizing efforts among women in communities of color. Poverty levels in the United States, which have always disproportionately affected families of color, are at pre-1965 levels for women and children. Homelessness, originally theorized to be a problem of unemployed men, is now a serious problem for poor women and their families as well. Current initiatives to block the rights of immigrants and their children, and efforts to eliminate affirmative action policies, directly affect women of color. Women of color account for increasing numbers of new AIDS/HIV cases. Many of the reasons for organizing efforts of the 1800s for people of color have been resolved (inability to vote, legalized housing and job segregation, restricted access to banks and insurance companies, etc.). The mutual aid societies and African American women's clubs, however, may be still be used as entry-level points to women of color. Just as the early African American Women's Clubs of the 1880s began with a concentration on anti-lynching strategies and later expanded to problems facing the general society, so can the mutual aid societies form a basis for organizing on both the micro and macro levels for women of color.

Conclusion

A feminist perspective on organizing with women of color is one way to address how sexism and racism have a profound effect on our lives. Knowledge based on feminist organizing suggests very specific ways in which organizers can move individual women from feelings of powerlessness and apathy to active change. However, this model of feminist organizing must be modified when working in communities of color. Feminist organizers must recognize how their life experience might differ from that of community members and therefore be willing to accept the problem definitions and strategies developed by women of color. Another technique requires recognizing how historical conflicts between feminist and antiracist movements may affect interactions between white women and women of color and point to ways of opening up a dialogue that will work toward creative resolution of these conflicts.

Traditional feminist organizing has usually moved in one direction only: from the organizers representing the white middle-class community to the community of color. For example, little of the literature on feminist organizing or community organizing describes the activist roles of women of color within our communities. As students, we learned of our contributions to social change only through reading the popular African American press (e.g., *Ebony, Essence, Black Digest*) and local ethnic press or through oral tradition within our communities.

As suggested by Rivera and Erlich in this volume, the most appropriate role for European American organizers with woman of color would be that of consultant rather than direct grassroots organizer. In this chapter we reinforce this perspective by suggesting that in order for this work to be effective, the flow of information about the best ways to engage in organizing activities with women of color is to adopt a multidirectional approach: from the individual women of color, through their families, informal institutions, and back to the feminists representing the wider society. In this way, feminist community organization techniques can contribute to the empowerment of individual women and to their involvement in solving the problems of all women of color.

References

Aragon de Valdez, T. (1980). Organizing as a political tool for the Chicana. *Frontiers, 5,* 7–13.

Armott, T., & Matthaei, J. (1991). *Race, Gender, & Work: A Multicultural History of Women in the United States.* Boston: South End Press.

Barrera, M. (1987). Chicano class structure. In R. Takaki (Ed.), *From Different Shores: Perspectives on Race and Ethnicity In America* (pp. 130–138). New York: Oxford University Press.

Bookman, A., & Morgan, S. (1986). *Women and the Politics of Empowerment.* Philadelphia: Temple University Press.

Bricker-Jenkins, & Hooyman, N. (1986). *Not for Women Only: Social Work Practice for a Feminist Future.* Silver Spring: NASW.

Burton, L., & Bengston, V. (1982). Research in minority communities: Problems and potentials. In R. Manuel (Ed.), *Minority Aging: Sociological and Social Psychological Issues.* New York: Greenwood Press.

Collins, P. (1990). *Black Feminist Thought.* Boston: Unwyn Hyman.

Comas-Diaz, L. (1994). An integrative approach. In L. Comas-Diaz & B. Greene (Eds.), *Women of Color.* (pp. 287–317). New York: Guilford.

Comas-Diaz, L., & Greene, B. (1994). *Women of Color.* New York: Guilford.

Dill, B. T. (1987). Race, class and gender: Prospects for an all-inclusive sisterhood. In R. Takaki (Ed.), *From Different Shores: Perspectives on Race and Ethnicity in America* (pp. 204–214). New York: Oxford University Press.

Evans, S. (1980). *Personal Politics.* New York: Vintage Books.

Friere, P. (1970). Cultural action for freedom. *Harvard Educational Review, 40,* 205–225, 452–477.

Friere, P. (1973). *Education for Critical Consciousness.* New York: Seabury Press.

Giddings, P. (1984). *Where and When I Enter: The Impact of Black Women on Race and Sex in America.* New York: William Morrow.

Gilkes, C. (1981). Holding back the ocean with a broom: Black women and community work. In Rodgers-Rose, L. F. (Ed.), *The Black Woman* (pp. 217–233). Beverly Hills: Sage.

Gilkes, C. (1983). Going up for the oppressed: The career mobility of Black women community workers. *Journal of Social Issues, 39* (3), 115–139.

Gilkes, C. (1986). Building in many places: Multiple commitments and ideologies in Black women's community work. In A. Bookman & S. Morgan (Eds.), *Woman and the Politics of Empowerment.* Philadelphia: Temple University Press.

Gordon-Bradshaw, R. (1987). A social essay on special issues facing poor women of color. *Women and Health, 12,* 243–259.

Gould, K. (1987a). Life model vs. role conflict model: A feminist perspective. *Social Work, 32,* 346–351.

Gould, K. (1987b). Feminist principles and minority concerns: Contributions, problems, and solutions. *Affilia: Journal of Women and Social Work, 3,* 6–19.

Gutiérrez, L. (1990). Working with women of color: An empowerment perspective. *Social Work, 35,* 149–154.

Hooks, B. (1981). *Ain't I a Woman: Black Women and Feminism.* Boston: South End Press.

Hyde, C. (1986). Experiences of women activists: Implications for community organizing theory and practice. *Journal of Sociology and Social Welfare, 13,* 545–562.

Hyde, C. (1990). A feminist model for macro practice: Promises and problems. *Administration in Social Work, 13,* 145–181.

Joseph, B., Mizrahi, T., Peterson, J., & Sugarman, F. (March, 1989). *Women's Perspectives on Community Organizing: A Feminist Synthesis of Theory and Practice.* Paper presented at the Annual Program Meeting of the Council on Social Work Education, Chicago.

Kieffer, C. (1984). Citizen empowerment: A developmental perspective. In J. Rappaport, C. Swift, & R. Hess (Eds.), *Studies in Empowerment: Toward Understanding and Action* (pp. 9–36). New York: Hawthorn Press.

Kopasci, R. & Faulkner, A. (1988). The powers that might be: The unity of white and black feminists. *Affilia, 3,* 33–50.

Lewis, E. (in press). Ethnicity, race and gender: Training and supervision issues in the treatment of women. In B. De Chant, J. Cunningham, J. Lazerson, & R. Perls (eds.), *Women, Gender and Group Psychotherapy.* New York: American Group Psychotherapy Association Monograph.

Lin Fu, J. (1987). Special health concerns of ethnic minority women. *Public Health Reports, 102,* 12–14.

Linten, R., & Witham, M. (1981). With mourning, rage, empowerment and defiance: The 1981 Women's Pentagon Action. *Socialist Review, 63,* 11–36.

Longres, J., & McLeod, E. (1980). Consciousness raising and social work practice. *Social Casework, 61,* 267–627.

Loo, C., & Ong, P. (1987). Slaying demons with a sewing needle: Feminist issues for Chinatown's women. In R. Takaki (Ed.), *From Different Shores: Perspectives on Race and Ethnicity in America* (pp. 186–191). New York: Oxford.

Macht, M., & Quam, J. (1986). *Social work: An Introduction.* Columbus, Ohio: Merrill.

McAdoo, J. (1981), Black father and child interactions. In L. Gary (Ed.), *Black Men* (pp. 115–130). Beverly Hills: Sage.

Morell, C. (1987). Cause is function: Toward a feminist model of integration for social work. *Social Science Review, 61,* 144–155.

Nes, J., & Iadicola, P. (1989). Toward a definition of feminist social work: A comparison of liberal, radical, and socialist models. *Social Work, 34,* 12–22.

Pernell, R. (1985). Empowerment and social group work. In M. Parenes (Ed.), *Innovations in Social Group Work: Feedback from Practice to Theory* (pp. 107–117). New York: Hawthorn Press.

Pinderhughes, E. (1983). Empowerment for our clients and for ourselves. *Social Casework, 64,* 331–338.

Reid, P. (1984). Feminism vs. minority group identity: Not for black women only. *Sex Roles, 10,* 247–255.

Rosenthal, N. (1984). Consciousness raising: From revolution to re-evalution. *Psychology of Women Quarterly, 8,* 309–326.

Sarri, R., & du Rivage, V. (1985). *Strategies for Self-Help and Empowerment of Working Low-Income Women Who Are Heads of Families.* Unpublished manuscript, University of Michigan, School of Social Work, Ann Arbor.

Schechter, S. (1982). *Women and Male Violence: The Visions and Struggles of the Battered Women's Movement.* Boston: South End Press.

Schechter, S., Szymanski, S., & Cahill, M. (1985). *Violence against Women: A Curriculum for Empowerment.* (Facilitator's Manual). New York: Women's Education Institute.

Segura, D. (1987). Labor market stratification: The Chicana experience. In R. Takaki (Ed.), *From Different Shores: Perspectives on Race and Ethnicity in America* (pp. 175–185). New York: Oxford.

Simmons, C., & Parsons, R. (1983). Empowerment for role alternatives in adolescence. *Adolescence, 18*(69), 193–200.

Solomon, B. (1976). *Black Empowerment.* New York: Columbia University Press.

Solomon, B. (1980). Alternative social services and the black woman. In N. Gottlieb (Ed.), *Alternative Services for Women* (pp. 333–345). New York: Columbia University Press.

Solomon, B. (1982). Empowering women: A matter of values. In A. Weick & S. Vandiver (Eds.), *Women, Power and Change* (pp. 206–214). Silver Springs: NASW.

Spelman, E. (1989). *Inessential Woman: Problems of Exclusion in Feminist Thought.* Boston: Beacon Press.

Stack, C. B. (1974). *All Our Kin.* New York: Harper & Row.

Sunday Chicago Tribune Magazine. (1988, Oct. 16). Fighting back: Frances Sandoval and her mother's crusade take aim at gangs, pp. 10–24.

U.S. Census of the Population. (1992). *Volume 1: Characteristics of the Population.* Washington, D.C.: U.S. Department of Commerce.

Van DenBergh, N., & Cooper, L. (Eds.). (1986). *Feminist Visions for Social Work.* Silver Spring: NASW.

Weil, M. (1986). Women, community and organizing. In N. Van DenBergh & L. Cooper (Eds.), *Feminist Visions for Social Work* (pp. 187–210). Silver Springs: NASW.

White, B. (1981). Black women: The resilient victims. In A. Weick & S. Vandiver (Eds.), *Women, Power and Change* (pp. 69–77). Washington, D.C.: NASW.

Williams, P. J. (1988). On being the object of property. *Signs: Journal of Women and Culture, 14* (1).

Wilson, J. (1987). Women and poverty: A demographic overview. *Women and Health, 12,* 21–40.

Withorn, A. (1984). *Serving the People: Social Services and Social Change.* New York: Columbia.

Zambrana, R. (1987). A research agenda on issues affecting poor and minority women: A model for understanding their health needs. *Women and Health, 12,* 137–160.

Zavella, P. (1986). The politics of race and gender: Organizing Chicana cannery workers in Northern California. In A. Bookman & S. Morgan (Eds.), *Women and the Politics of Empowerment.* Philadelphia: Temple University Press.

Resources for Learning More about Women of Color and Feminist Organizing

Bookman, A., & Morgan, S. (1986). *Women and the Politics of Empowerment.* Philadelphia: Temple University Press.

Cross, T., Klein, F., Smith, B., & Smith, B. (1982). Face-to-face, day-to-day—Racism. In G. Hill, P. Scott, & B. Smith (Eds.), *But Some of Us Are Brave,* pp. 52–56. Old Westbury, N.Y.: Feminist Press.

Joseph, G., & Lewis, J. (1981). *Common Differences.* Boston: South End Press.

Kopasci R., & Faulkner, A. (1988). The powers that might be: The unity of white and black feminists. *Affilia, 3,* 33–50.

Moraga, C., & Anzaldua, G. (1981). *This bridge Called my Back: Writings of Radical Women of Color.* New York: Kitchen Table Press.

Wolverton, T. (1983). Unlearning complicity, remembering resistance: White women's anti-racism education. In C. Bunch & S. Pollack (Eds.), *Learning Our Way: Essays in Feminist Education.* Trumansburg, N.Y.: The Crossing Press.

7

*Organizing in the
Chinese American
Community: Issues,
Strategies, and
Alternatives*

PETER CHING-YUNG LEE

As our communities become more diverse, it is important to observe and understand the history we share as well as the unique experiences of the different groups. Asian and Pacific Islander Americans are a diverse and rapidly growing minority population in the United States. They or their ancestors have originated from more than thirty different countries spread across the majority of our planet ranging from Hawaii through the Indian subcontinent. The rapid population growth for Asian and Pacific Islanders in the United States is primarily due to the large influx of immigrants from China since the late 1960s; from Korea, the Philippines, and India since the early 1970s; and more recently from Hong Kong, China, Taiwan, and Southeast Asia. In many ways, the major Asian or Pacific Islander groups are different from one another as well as from other races. As a people of color who represent a multitude of distinctive languages and cultures, Asian and Pacific Islander Americans also face political and economic oppression, which results in an array of problems and issues associated with discrimination. The new conservatism of the 1980s and

117

the reform of welfare laws in the 1990s also promise to make Asian and Pacific Islander Americans' struggles for justice more difficult than ever. Community organization practice is one professional field in which efforts can be made toward resolving these problems. Although the human services literature related to the people of color has received much recent attention, the scarcity of literature on the community organization practices of minorities, and on organizing strategies and tactics of Chinese Americans in particular, created the need for this chapter.

The framework and contents of this chapter are based on three areas of knowledge: (1) sociocultural and political-economic dynamics of minority populations; (2) theoretical frameworks; and (3) knowledge and strategies relevant for professional action. Accordingly, the chapter is divided into three major sections. The first part examines the status of Chinese Americans in terms of historical background, sociodemographic changes, cultural values, problems and issues, and human service needs. The second part provides an introduction to community organizing of Chinese Americans by identifying key elements of a basic framework. By applying a case study approach, our purpose is to analyze further the state of community organizing among Chinese Americans in Santa Clara County in Northern California to illustrate the wide range of areas that can be subsumed under the community organization practice. This chapter also diverges from current community organization literature in one important respect—its emphasis on transcultural practice. Therefore, the final part of the chapter concludes with a discussion of community intervention strategies from social development and cross-cultural perspectives and the prospects for the future.

Chinese Americans: A Profile

Ethnicity in itself is a complex variable that involves knowledge, expectations, attitudes, social norms, and experiences. It is not a stable variable because its significance changes as persons become acculturated and socially adapted to the dominant culture. For persons or groups in varying stages of adaptation, ethnicity could have subsequent varying effects on their changing problems and needs. One particularly relevant target population in this context is Chinese Americans whose cultures, traditions, assimilation patterns, and coping mechanisms may have profound implications for the professional practice of community organization. With nearly two centuries of immigration history, Chinese Americans have come to the United States from different parts of the world in search of better lives. Although there is a frequent and strong stereotyped notion among policy makers, researchers, professionals, and the public that the Chinese are all alike, the reality is that the Chinese are a heterogeneous population with very diverse cultural, political, economic, and social circumstances. Discussing community organizing in the context of cross-cultural practice requires an outline first of general trends and characteristics of Chinese Americans as an ethnic group in the United States.

Current Sociodemographic Characteristics

Reliable statistical data on Chinese Americans in the United States are either rare or nonexistent. Yet this group is one of the fastest growing ethnic minorities in the country today. Since the 1980 census, the population of the Chinese Americans, up 85 percent since 1970, has emerged as the largest group among Asian and Pacific Islander populations in the country.[1] According to the 1990 U.S. Census, the largest number of immigrants to the United States is Chinese, who have an average annual growth rate of around 7 percent, numbering 1,648,000 (22.6 percent of all Asian and Pacific Islander Americans) and accounting for 0.7 percent of the total U.S. population.[2] If the current trend continues, the Chinese American population will number over 3 million by the year 2000, which may account for over 1 percent of the total projected U.S. population.

The 1990 census also provided basic sociodemographic information on Chinese Americans. The Chinese Americans are primarily an urban-oriented population concentrated in metropolitan areas. A majority of Chinese Americans live in three states: California (about 40 percent), Hawaii (10 percent), and New York (20 percent), with the other 30 percent or so scattered over the remaining forty-seven states. The concentration of Chinese Americans in the West is not surprising because large Asian and Pacific Islander populations already reside there.[3]

Given prior and ongoing accelerated Chinese immigration to the United States, it is not surprising to note that more than two-thirds (70 percent) of the current Chinese American population is foreign born. As for those who were born outside of the United States—the so-called first generation of Chinese Americans—nearly two-thirds of them came from Taiwan or mainland China (65 percent), 12 percent came from Hong Kong, 16 percent from Southeast Asia, and the remaining 7 percent from other parts of the world.[4]

Average age for the Chinese Americans is nearly the same as the national average (median age of 29.6 years for Chinese compared with 30 years for the nation).[5] The Chinese family composition of 3.7 persons, on the average, is slightly higher than the national average of 3.3 persons, partly because a higher percentage of Chinese elderly and children live with family members.[6] Chinese women have a lower fertility rate than do U.S. females in general, as well as a lower divorce rate.[7] In addition, out-of-wedlock childbearing, as measured by the ratio of births to unmarried women per 1,000 total live births, occurs least often among Chinese women.[8]

Chinese are among the highest ranked Asian American groups in terms of socioeconomic status. For example, the 1980 census documents that most Chinese Americans were solid middle class, with an average family income of $22,600, higher than the national median income of $19,900. A similar trend was also observed in the 1990 census. However, this difference is somewhat misleading because it is partly a function of their having more working family members. And a disproportionate number of Chinese Americans reside in areas with a high cost of living (California and Hawaii, for instance), which may force many individuals to work at more than one job. In addition, the poverty rate among Chinese was only slightly lower than the national average (14.5 percent) in 1993 because of persistent nationwide unemployment, low wages, and a slow recovery from the last recession.

The Chinese American emphasis on education is well known and clearly reflected in the census data. In educational attainment, Chinese Americans are one of the best educated groups in the United States. For example, nearly three-quarters of Chinese Americans who are age 25 and older have graduated from high school. Respectively, more than two-fifths (44 percent) and nearly one-third (30 percent) of Chinese men and women in the United States have completed college education, thus far exceeding the national rates of 20 percent and 13 percent for men and women respectively.[9]

Changing Values and Behaviors: What Are We?

What does it mean to be Chinese in America? This question would no doubt invite a wide variety of responses. When a profile of a given ethnic group is presented, it may stray across the invisible boundary that separates profiles from stereotypes. With this caution in mind, the following general description explores some cultural values and behavioral norms that may be helpful in understanding Chinese Americans and their community.

1. When trying to understand Chinese American values and behaviors, one must begin with the concept of self in Chinese American terms. Whereas Western concepts of self place the individual at the center, with all other relationships arranged around the self, the Chinese people perceive the self as part of a set of interpersonal relationships of which the family system is the core. Contemporary Chinese families in America are predominantly nuclear ones consisting of a married couple and their children; their role composition is simpler when compared to the traditionally extended ones. For the great majority of Chinese Americans, the provision of a sense of security, intimacy, unity, acceptance, and mutual support by the family is still found to be indispensable to modern life.[10]

2. With their social organization centered around family and kinship, the Chinese have traditionally held on to the concept of *jen,* or benevolence, which encompasses filial piety and fraternal love. In etymology as well as in interpretation, *jen* is always concerned with human relationships. Basically, *jen* is translated variously as *goodness, benevolence, humanity,* and *human-heartedness. Jen,* therefore, is rooted in human sentiment as well as in a fundamental orientation of life. It is associated with loyalty (*chung*)—loyalty to one's own heart and conscience—and reciprocity (*shu*)—respect and consideration for others.

3. Within the traditional Chinese community system, the well-known Five Relationships include that of ruler-subject, father-son, husband-wife, elder-younger brothers, and friend-friend.[11] Three of these are family relationships; the other two are usually conceived in terms of the family models. For this reason, the Chinese society regards itself as a large family. Thus familial relations provide a model for Chinese social behavior. The responsibilities ensuing from these relationships are mutual and reciprocal. They have been the reason for the strong sense of solidarity not only in the Chinese family, but also in social and community organizations. Thus the group, rather than the individual, is the major unit of society. In addition, the parent-child relationship (that is, the father-son relationship in the traditional sense) often takes priority over the husband-wife spousal relationship. The parent-child relationship tends to be characterized by mutual obligation within a vertical power hierarchy. Benevolent parents are those who do what is best and appropriate for their children, even at the expense of personal needs. Although the extent of Chinese parental sacrifice and fulfillment of duties varies, it is reasonable to generalize that Chinese culture continues to perpetuate a powerful pressure on parents, as well as children, to think of the family first.[12] For example, divorce is generally considered a social embarrassment and only as a last alternative, an attitude that may be changing among the younger generation of Chinese Americans.

4. The concept of obligation in Chinese culture is also crucial in the context of community. In American society, the tendency toward reciprocity, for example, is weighed heavily toward contractual obligation. Within Chinese culture, obligation is important and is generally incurred through ascribed roles or status, even though kindness or helpfulness is received from other people. Therefore, obligation often becomes the basis for reciprocal relationships between peers and within families, as well as community social networks. Although social relationships are based primarily on the preservation of harmony and suppression of conflict, obligation to different individuals, families, or groups may conflict and can become a source of great anxiety. In Chinese culture, in which interdependence is much emphasized, the perceived or actual withdrawal of support may shake the individual's basic trust and confidence and raise one's anxiety over being alone. Thus the fear of losing face or support can be a very strong motivating force for one's conformity, and family or group-oriented behavior is strongly approved.

5. Of further importance is the great emphasis on mutual dependence rather than individual independence and antagonism. That is, role fulfillment is a cardinal virtue in Chinese culture. Everyone should learn to play his or her proper role in various interpersonal relations in society. By establishing correct interpersonal relationships in all aspects of life, it is then possible to achieve an orderly and peaceful society.

6. Many first-generation Chinese Americans feel they may be the last generation in America to feel a strong connection with traditional values and customs.[13] They are in many ways a link between the past and future and feel a sense of responsibility to pass on the traditional way of thinking, although they often find this a difficult task. Their own children, as products of a very different environment, tend to be much more individualistic in their decision making. Still, most first-generation Chinese Americans consider it their obligation to be good role models for the younger generations.[14]

7. Although most new immigrant Chinese accept responsibility for the welfare of their aging parents, they do not expect their children to take care of them. In fact, today's Chinese immigrants are perhaps the first generation to assume they will be on their own after retirement, and many are beginning to make financial preparations for their old age. By the same token, many also expect their children to fend for themselves when they grow up, a marked change in attitude from their parents' generation. Although many first-generation Chinese Americans do not want to exert as much influence over their children's lives as their own parents did, they still have high expectations for them. And, whatever they may expect of their children, Chinese Americans still consider their families a valuable source of moral support.

8. Children's education is another paramount consideration for Chinese American parents. Central to the Confucian thinking is the Chinese belief in the perfectibility and educability of human beings. This is why the emphasis on education became one of the most prominent features of Chinese culture, particularly for many first-generation Chinese immigrant parents who worry that their children do not excel academically and often invest generously in education-related programs and activities.

The Chinese Community: Then and Now

We now turn to an overview of the historical dynamics of Chinese immigration to the United States. Even though the United States has traditionally identified itself mostly with Europe, an important component of the political or social change perspective has been an increased awareness and understanding of cultural diversity. Therefore, within the cross-cultural framework proposed here, it is crucial to understand functioning or particular behaviors of Chinese Americans in the context of contemporary American society. Many Chinese Americans are still victims of discrimination and social prejudice. By tracing some historical facts, we examine examples of some of the most important racist legislation that significantly hindered the political, social, and economic development of the Chinese American community.

In Search of Origin: Some Historical Background

The Pioneer Chinese

Since the Chinese began to arrive in the United States as early as the mid-seventeenth century, the nature and size of the Chinese population have varied widely.[15] Before the 1800s, the number of Chinese immigrants remained relatively small, and many of them served as "importing Chinese workers" in Hawaii. However, the unstable political and miserable social conditions in China, along with the discovery of gold in California during the late 1840s, motivated Chinese immigrations in increasing numbers. By 1860, the census reported 34,933 resident Chinese, a figure that rose to 63,199 in 1870, 105,465 in 1880, and peaked at 107,488 in 1890.[16] More significantly, these early Chinese immigrants were mostly male (94.9 percent according to the 1860 census) and were frequently praised for their cleanliness, thrift, industry, and orderly behavior.

Most of these newest minority were poorly educated, strong, young, single males from rural areas in China, who were attracted by labor contractors, steamship companies, and plantation owners. But from the time of their arrival, these immigrants suffered from economic exploitation, political oppression, social and legal injustice, and subhuman treatment. For example, the California Foreign Miner's Tax Law of 1853 allowed for the collection of taxes almost exclusively from Chinese miners between 1853 and 1870. During the first four years of its enforcement Chinese miners paid 50 percent of the total revenues obtained from working in gold mines. During the next thirteen years, the rate was increased to 98 percent.[17] The Exclusion of Chinese Witness Act of 1854 (reaffirmed in 1871) prohibited Chinese persons from serving as witnesses in actions or proceedings wherein a white person was a party. In addition, no Chinese were permitted to testify or present evidence in favor of or against any white person. Clearly, this legislation put Chinese in a judicially unprotected situation.[18]

Continued Oppression

Before the turn of the century, there were about twenty-seven men for every woman among the Chinese in America. This was primarily the direct result of the so-called Restriction of Chinese Female Immigrants Act of 1870, which prevented the entry of Chinese females into the United States. What this meant for white perceptions of Chinese newcomers is probably familiar enough. Forced into Chinatown ghettos, these men joined together in clan associations and secret societies to obtain some sense of familiarity, security, and solidarity. Meanwhile, the alarming imbalance in the sex ratio also meant that the Chinese communities in America at the time were almost incapable of producing a second generation of American-born Chinese. It was not until 1950 that the American born made up more than half the total Chinese population in the United States, and even this growth came about only through the much larger number of immigrants who entered since the 1940s, thanks to gradual but important relaxations of the immigration laws.

In the economic depression of the mid-1870s, the Chinese became the scapegoat for white laborers who lost their jobs. Legal and legislative action was taken in an attempt to diminish Chinese competition in the labor force. In fact, the Naturalization Act of 1870 excluded Chinese from obtaining U.S. citizenship and forbade the entry of laborer's wives. Subsequently, the Chinese Exclusion Act of 1882 was passed to stop the immigration of Chinese laborers and to continue the denial of citizenship to the Chinese. A series of laws followed the Act of 1882, culminating in the 1924 Asian Exclusion Act, designed to shut out all Asian immigrants in a clearcut case of institutional racism.

The Geary Act of 1892 (upheld by the Supreme Court in 1893) extended all existing laws restricting Chinese immigration and was later extended further to restrict all Asian immigrants. In 1913 California became the first state to pass the Alien Land Law, also called the Webb-Henry Act of 1913. This act prohibited land ownership and limited to three years the leasing rights of aliens ineligible for citizenship.

It was not until 1943 that the so-called Magnuson Act finally repealed the Chinese Exclusion Act of 1882. Finally, the McCarren-Walter Immigration Act of 1952 changed exclusion to restriction for all Asian immigrants and gave them the citizenship they had long been denied. For more than a century and through repressive legislation, the result of injustice was a steady decline in the Chinese population and a concomitant repression of their basic human rights and fair participation in the dominant white society.

A Turning Point

Time has brought more social equality and opportunities. Consequently, the old stereotypes have waned, and the image and Chinese Americans as a group have improved considerably in recent decades. This change gained increased momentum in the mid-1960s as the result of the most radical immigration law, passed in 1965 (Public Law 89-236), finally giving fair and equal immigration opportunity to Chinese. The abolition of the quota system through this 1965 legislation established an annual ceiling of 20,000 immigrants for each Asian country. As a result, an influx of immigrants arrived from all walks of life and different parts of Asia.

The law's emphasis on family reunification attracts thousands of new Chinese immigrants who are either parents or children of U.S. citizens. Unlike Chinatown residents, the majority of these more recent immigrants from Taiwan, mainland China, or Hong Kong came to the United States as students pursuing advanced degrees. And the policies of admission based on occupational preference also absorbs a large proportion of professional immigrants. Many of these students who became qualified professionals actually formed a second wave of Chinese immigration to the United States, beginning in the 1950s. This 1965 law was based on a shift in the American public's image of Asian Americans from yellow peril to model minority.

Starting from Zero

Since the end of Vietnam War in 1975, another distinct ethnic Chinese group from Southeast Asia began to arrive in the United States in large numbers as refugees under the so-called Indochina Migration Refugee Assistance Act of 1975. The majority of these ethnic Chinese are refugee populations resembling other refugee groups (e.g., Vietnamese and Cubans) who were forced to leave their homelands and settled in the United States. Further, their resettlement experiences are similar in many ways to those of other Asian immigrant groups. This population has faced adjustment problems such as cultural change, acculturation stress, and intergenerational conflict, including negative public attitudes in the United States.[19]

Changing Problems and Needs: From Chinatown to the Suburbs

The marked increase in the Asian and Pacific Islander American population, especially since 1965, has created a fluid, rapidly changing mixture of peoples. The Asian and Pacific Islander American populations are now becoming more heterogeneous as new immigrants alter their composition and cultural unity. By the same token, the Chinese communities in America are perhaps much less homogeneous than they appear to the casual observer. As the largest Asian group, the overall picture for the Chinese American community, then, is that the Chinese American population has continued to increase substantially since 1965 because of immigration, and this influx of Chinese immigrants has concentrated itself in a relatively small number of urban areas.

The earliest immigrants came as coolie labor to work on farms, in mines, and on the railroads. They came with no expectations of staying, but they ended up settling down in North America. Originally, the Chinese community was expressed in the term *Chinatown,* which continues to have both a geographic and social reality. Early immigrants stayed and raised their families in Chinatowns, where the old ways held sway. Chinatown first grew out of a desire to maintain closeness, preserve cultural values and traditions, and help its residents become self-sufficient. However, misunderstood and mistrusted by the mainstream, the Chinese who lived there did so as a society within a society. Ironically, the anti-Chinese movement forced the entrenchment of Chinatown, which in turn strengthened the controls of traditional associations, resulting in the establishment, rather than the destruction, of the Chinese community.

Although many Chinese immigrants have succeeded in making their dreams realities, they, like earlier immigrants, live in two worlds. Their workplace is often predominantly white, but they live in a "Chinese community," where Chinese goods, Chinese newspapers, and Chinese television programs are readily available, including a special Chinese edition of the yellow pages. This is what could be called a divided existence: they work in one culture, but live in another. As a result, many new immigrants are not forced to venture outside of the Chinese community. Consequently, the conflict between personal identity and social identity may affect first-generation Chinese Americans and their children. It can be a trying emotional struggle.

Furthermore, successes of Chinese immigrants have also led to an interesting new phenomenon: the rise of a new stereotype of the Chinese Americans as overachievers in science or business. Now greater numbers of young Chinese Americans are entering nontraditional fields outside of science and business. They are gaining recognition in music (cellist Yo-Yo Ma and violinist Cho-liang Lin), literature (novelist Amy Tan rose to fame with *The Joy Luck Club*), broadcasting and journalism (TV anchor Connie Chung), and in public life (former California state secretary March Fong Eu; Julia Chang Bloch, the first Chinese American to serve as a U.S. ambassador; and Elaine Chao, the former head of the United Way of America), to name a few. Like earlier immigrants to America, Chinese Americans are now striking a balance between maintaining their cultural heritage and assimilation, and everyone is the richer for it.

The American-born generation faces unique problems of its own as well. They naturally assimilate much more readily into the mainstream of American life than their parents. The Chinese language is almost extinct among children of Chinese immigrants. Having been brought up in America's predominantly English-speaking environment, they have little motivation to learn the language of their parents. Loss of linguistic heritage is not the only problem faced by the Chinese in America. In the eyes of their parents, younger Chinese Americans are losing touch with their cultural roots and traditional values. It is generally agreed that the strong family ties and filial piety so cherished in traditional Chinese culture have lost their authority with younger Chinese Americans.[20]

The model minority myth, coupled with the rising economic prowess of Pacific Rim Asian countries and the corresponding downturn of the American economy, has given rise to an increase in anti-Asian sentiment and violence. The case of Vincent Chin sadly demonstrated the impact of such campaigns. Chin, a 27-year-old Chinese American engineer, was bludgeoned to death by two white unemployed auto workers in Detroit. The two men, who were merely fined and put on probation by the judge, mistook him for Japanese, whom they blamed for their unemployment. In recent years, violence against Asian refugees and immigrants who compete for scarce resources in low-income communities has also dramatically increased.

Among other new issues facing the Chinese American community is the emerging phenomena of so-called little overseas students from Taiwan and Hong Kong.[21] Many of these families brought their children here for the sake of better education and the security of property and investment in America. The burden of care for these youngsters, ranging in age from 6 to 15 in most cases, often rests on the shoulders of the mothers, friends, and relatives while fathers return to their jobs in Taiwan or Hong Kong most of the time. Most of these families left their homelands with high hopes, only to face the grim reality of adjustment in American society. As young and inexperienced immigrants, many of these students face legal problems when their visas expire, in additional to language difficulty and learning barriers. Some juvenile delinquency and gang activities have started to appear among the new Chinese youth in junior and senior high schools around the urban communities.

Therefore, the human service needs of the current Chinese Americans stem from an aggregate of new and old problems. On the one hand are the problems of incomplete structural assimilation common to a visible minority group like Chinese Americans who has coexisted uneasily for several generations with a white majority that has never totally accepted it. On the other hand, the fact that current Chinese Americans are overwhelmingly foreign born may lead to problems arising from a lack of cultural assimilation. For example, the new immigrant Chinese may not know how to utilize social services; the second-generation Chinese American may still be asked when he or she immigrated to the United States.

Because of the large proportion of recent immigrants among most Asian American groups, we must have a clear notion of the community experiences of these people. For example, what is the nature of the ethnic community and its social support system? Does such a community support system exist and, if it does, has it managed to remain viable in view of the great influx of immigration since 1965? Can the organizing experience of Asian American communities (such as the Chinese), which do have well-established community organizations, be generalized to the more recently arrived groups? How important are the family and the ethnic community in providing help? Do Chinese Americans fail to utilize social services provided by the majority community? Has community organization been successful in working with Chinese Americans? What effect has the new immigration had on the older Asian American communities? It is also important to know what specific community-organizing strategies and tactics have been applied to the Chinese American community. This may affect the overall service needs of these communities. From this overview of what we need to know about Chinese American community, it should be clear that determining how strategies and tactics are practiced is one of the most critical factors in community organizing.

Chinese American Community Organizing Experience

Theoretical Framework

An analysis of literature in the field of community organization indicates that some of the most common theories include system theory, conflict theory, theories of political economy, theories of group politics and influences, theories of social change, theories of personality and attitude formation, and theories of management and administration. The importance of a sociocultural perspective in community-organizing strategies has now begun to be explored. It cannot be assumed the strategies and tactics that are effective with the majority community will be applicable to the same degree with the ethnic community. Synthesizing some of this recent body of knowledge indicates several working principles relevant to the Chinese community. From an application perspective, the current changing patterns of the Chinese American community may be understood in terms of these theoretical perspectives.

Empowerment as a Relevant Paradigm
The first fundamental assumption on which the theoretical framework is based is this: There are a limited number of basic human problems for which all peoples at all times and in all places must find some solution.[22] Within the practice of community organization, a pluralistic American society requires a special awareness of the cultural beliefs, values, and behaviors of the ethnic community and the adaptation to its cultural milieu. The major thesis is that individuals, families, and groups in Chinese American communities have been subjected to negative valuations from the mainstream society to such an extent that powerlessness in the community is pervasive. Thus, when working with the Chinese American community, organizers must consider the structure and process of service delivery systems that have the greatest potential for facilitating empowerment of minority groups.

Individual and Community Worldview
A community is said to exist when interaction between individuals has the purpose of meeting individual needs and obtaining group goals. In all societies, physical, psychological, and social needs are met through the creation of social systems. Particular

structures within systems are called institutions, and these become basic features of a community. In a pluralistic society, both ethnic individuals and their community's worldview need to be understood.

Worldview refers to the values and beliefs one holds about the world. These values and beliefs are manifested in actions and behaviors. For minority people and their communities, worldview may include degree of acculturation, impact of social oppression on the group as well as the individual, and the extent of opportunities to interact with people from one's own culture as well as from the dominant culture.[23] Further, there are specific ways in which a client's worldview may influence social services, such as help-seeking behaviors, formulations of problem assessment, and strategies for problem resolution.

Cultural Deprivation and Discrimination

Many empirical reports have generally portrayed ethnic minorities in a negative manner, regularly finding them disadvantaged or deficient in some way. This is the "cultural deficit model," which rests on the assumption that norms and cultural patterns of minority groups that varied from those of the majority culture are for the most part deviant and destructive and lead to a self-perpetuating "cycle of poverty and deprivation."[24] Ethnic minorities are kept in a subordinate and disadvantageous position because it serves the interests of the dominant group to maintain such a stratified system. People of color come to believe misinformation about their particular ethnic group and thus believe their mistreatment is justified. Racism, then, is the systematic, institutionalized mistreatment of one group of people by another based on racial heritage. Therefore, inequality is a result of a struggle or competition for resources, privileges, and rewards that are in short supply. The "deficit hypothesis" has increasingly been challenged, and serious questions have been raised concerning the methodological adequacy of ethnic research in the United States.[25]

The Cultural Difference Model

Minority individuals, including Chinese Americans, must learn to function in two environments: their own culture and that of the mainstream society. The cultural difference model posited that each minority culture is unique and should be viewed as an independent and internally consistent system. Therefore, each minority culture can be understood in its own context rather than judged according to its similarity to or difference from the majority culture.[26] This perspective can become somewhat complicated in view of the fact that ethnic cultures, and indeed their communities, are contained in the majority culture. Further, the cultural difference model drew criticism based on its inability to explain how minority community members who were socialized within this totally distinct cultural context were able to function within the bounds of the majority society and its institutions.[27] The question is: According to which cultural standard ought ethnic communities be assessed? From the standpoint of community intervention, the answer is clear—the culture from which the community is an integral part must be seen in its own terms. What is important is the attempt to evaluate and understand ethnic community behavior in the social and cultural context in which it occurs.

The Model Minority Myth

The once predominant media caricatures of Chinese and Chinese Americans as the inscrutable coolie, the powerful kung fu masters, the effeminate Charlie Chan, the evil Dr. Fu Manchu, or the exotic Suzy Wong are gradually giving way to more subtle but equally damaging image and stereotypes. The emerging picture of Chinese Americans, like other Asian groups, as hard-working, highly educated, family-oriented, and financially successful—in short, a "model minority"—appears benign at first, even beneficial. The pervasive perception that Asian Americans are making it, even surpassing whites despite their minority status, is resulting in a growing discriminatory backlash against their model minority status.

A closer examination of the facts, however, gives us a better picture of reality. For example, the higher figure of the average family income for Asian Americans (and for Chinese Americans as well) in the 1990 census dramatically changes if adjusted for the number of workers per family. As we indicated earlier, because Asians generally have more workers per family, the total income of a family reflects less per individual. Further, nearly three-quarters of Asian Americans live in the urban areas of San Francisco, San Jose, Los Angeles, New York, and Honolulu, where the incomes and cost of living are correspondingly much higher.

Even though immigrants from Hong Kong, Japan, Korea, and Taiwan tend to come from wealthier and more educated backgrounds, the more recent immigrants from Southeast Asia do not mirror the image of instant success that the media and general public perpetuate. These hundreds of thousands of Southeast Asian refugees, many of them ethnic Chinese, suffer not only from language barriers and limited employment opportunities, but also from emotional and psychological trauma and disorders.

There is no denying that Asians often rise to the top of their college classes and then earn recognition on the job as diligent and dependable workers and professionals. But many Asian Americans hoping to climb the corporate ladder face an arduous ascent. Statistics reflect the difficulty that Asian Americans face in moving into the ranks of management.[28] They are frequently victims of lingering stereotypes that depict them as passive and self-effacing with poor social and communications skills—traits that would rule them out for management.

The Cross-Cultural Perspective

Growing evidence indicates that human service interventions, when conceived in a cross-cultural framework, can be effective within a minority clientele system.[29] A cross-cultural approach can contribute a great deal to community organizing with minorities by providing another, potentially fruitful way of thinking about the practice of community organization. Basically, this model acknowledges cultural differences in social norms, behaviors, values, and traditions and promotes a more effective assessment and understanding of human services utilization and naturally occurring sociocultural forces (such as social support networks) within ethnic communities. Another realm in which a cross-cultural perspective is essential is in helping the community practitioner be aware of both minority and majority cultures, points of contact between them, and the process by which cultural standards influence the community.

Santa Clara County: A Case Study

Asian and Pacific Islander Americans comprise a significant portion of the population in Santa Clara County of the San Francisco Bay Area. Chinese Americans, who represent the largest Asian and Pacific Islander groups in the county, and their community-organizing strategies and tactics are the main focus of our examination. Primarily by using secondary analysis, we first provide a brief sociodemographic description of the county, followed by the assessment of issues and problems relative to the Chinese community organizations.

Located south of San Francisco, Santa Clara County, also known as Silicon Valley, is a world-renowned center of the computer-electronics industry. Between 1980 and 1985, nearly half of all new jobs in the nine-county region of Northern California were created in Santa Clara County.[30] But economic success has its price, and the county budget is feeling the strain of growth and social change. It assumes one of the largest social welfare budgets of all California counties, partly because of the growing number of Asian immigrants and other poor people.[31] With the nation and especially the state of California becoming more culturally pluralist, it is important to examine and understand some of the significant factors that account for the Chinese community's organizing effort in interacting with mainstream society.

Santa Clara County is one of the fastest growing counties in California. Since 1965, this high-tech–oriented county has experienced a large influx of Chinese professionals, immigrants, students, and businesspeople. The Chinese population in Santa Clara County includes a broad range of socioeconomic levels and degrees of acculturation. Immigrants, refugees, and the American born are all present in the Chinese population of the county. In addition, some portion of the Indochinese refugees, although coming from Vietnam, Cambodia, and Laos, in fact are ethnic Chinese.

In Santa Clara County today, the Chinese population is largely integrated into the county, and there is no equivalent of the Chinatown of San Francisco. In 1980, almost three-quarters (71 percent) of the total county population was white, with Hispanics as the second largest group, accounting for 17.5 percent of the total population. By 1990, the census data indicated that whites accounted for far less than three-quarters (69.1 percent) of the total; the Asian population increased dramatically from 8 percent in 1980 to 17.5 percent of all Santa Clara County residents (total county population = 1,497,577) over this time period.[32] Chinese Americans numbered 65, 924 (4.4 percent) in 1990, which represented the largest Asian population in Santa Clara County.

Similar to national patterns, the Asian American population is one of the most educated and economically advantaged groups in the county by virtually all objective indices of socioeconomic status. This condition is especially evident in terms of educational attainment: Almost all of the Asian population (97.2 percent) 25 years old and over were at least high school graduates in 1990, significantly above the national rate.[33] Because of Silicon Valley's reputation as the world's center for high technology, it is not surprising that the Asian population as a group has the highest percentage of college graduates (50.2 percent). Asian Americans are among the highest ranked county populations in terms of income. In 1989, for example, per capita income for Asian persons 15 years of age and above was $21,218, compared with $28,333 for whites, $19,996 for blacks, and $15,247 for Hispanics, which is again distinctive among Asian Americans and the country as a whole.[34]

A notable aspect of the Chinese experience in Santa Clara County is the fact that some Chinese are descendants of one of the oldest immigrant groups in this area and other Chinese are among the newest immigrants to the area. The early Chinese worked in various industries in the valley as construction workers, miners, and agricultural laborers. Many were employed as domestics by wealthy families. During the labor struggles of the 1870s, state laws and local ordinances were passed prohibiting the employment of Chinese in various industries and forbidding them to buy land or to intermarry with whites. After the racial quotas were eliminated in the 1960s, a new wave of Chinese immigrants arrived, and for the first time intact Chinese families immigrated in large numbers. Because of the concentration of computer and allied high-technology industries in Santa Clara County, more highly trained Chinese professionals have been drawn to this area since the 1970s.

With its diverse population and high-tech economic clout, Santa Clara County has become an area of great political importance. Generally, it has been faithfully Democratic, a reflection of its working-class history. But as home prices soar and more affluent people steadily move in, Santa Clara's changing sociopolitical environment will definitely shape the character of problems and issues in the Chinese American community. Continuing our focus on Santa Clara County, we examine next the scope and nature of organizing strategies relevant for the Chinese American community.

Organizing Strategies: Assessment and Discussion

Community Organizations and Community Organizing

A total of twenty-five community organizations in Santa Clara County, ranging from service oriented to social and recreational, were identified. In order to further understand organizing strategies and tactics of the Chinese community fully, it is necessary to analyze the several types of community organizations and activities as they are practiced in Santa Clara County. In so doing, note that organizational characteristics serve as the classification basis in this case study approach.

First there are clan associations, or "family associations." Originally, these clan associations derived from the lineage communities so prevalent in China, and ideally united all persons who bear the same surname. In the early days of Chinese immigration, the clan associations became a special kind of immigrant aid society, providing the newcomer with food, shelter, protection, advice, even employment.[35] Furthermore, the clan leaders often assumed the authoritative role, settling disputes, arbitrating disagreements, and in general containing interclan differences within the kinship fold. Until the recent arrival of large number of immigrants, the Chinatown clan associations, still prevalent in the New York, Oakland, and San Francisco areas, had been declining in power and authority because of the aging of their members and the acculturation of the younger American-born Chinese. Even though clan associations were present in the early part of this century, however, Santa Clara County does not have a single clan association at this time.

A type of association functionally similar to the clans but structurally different and based on a common dialect or district is also commonly found in Mainland China or Taiwan. This is the community organization generally called *tung hsiang hui* (same village/township/province association), or *hui kuan* (society or club). The two terms are often used interchangeably, except the latter is usually applied when the organization has its own office or building.

In many ways, these community organizations are similar to those immigrant aid and benevolent societies established by Germans, Irish, Jews, and other Europeans in America. In fact, a coordinating organization of all these district-oriented associations came into being about 1850 with the name *Chung Hua Hui Kuan* (Chinese Society). In 1901 this organization was incorporated under California state law as the Chinese Consolidated Benevolent Association in San Francisco.[36]

Traditionally, the *hui kuan,* like the clan association, exercised community leadership by conducting arbitration, mediating hearings between disputing parties, and managing and collecting debts of its members, including charging various fees for its services. With membership exceeding three thousand recent refugees from Southeast Asia, Chinese Mutual Assistance Association of Santa Clara County is a good example of such an organization. However, all other like-minded community organizations, such as San-Dong Association, San Francisco Tung-Pei Association, Hu-Nan Association, Hakkas Association, and Taiwan Association, are organized primarily for the purpose of social networking only. Their memberships range from a few hundred to a few thousand as well.

The third type is the human service–oriented organization, which is devoted to providing socioculturally sensitive services in meeting the needs of the Asian community. This is primarily an ethnic-sensitive practice approach, which includes community organizations such as the Asian Law Alliance (ALA), American Cancer Society's Asian Task force, the Center for Southeast Asia Refugee Resettlement, the Crosscultural Community Services Center (CCSC), and the Asian Americans for Community Involvement, Inc. (AACI).

As Chinese American community workers deal with problems in their own community, they are increasingly becoming aware of the shared needs and problems with other Asian and Pacific Islander communities. This critical factor is the major moving force that led to the creation of Asian Americans for Community Involvement, Inc., which was officially incorporated on November 27, 1973. Funded on the basis of the importance of solidarity in a common struggle for social justice, AACI has become the largest nonprofit advocacy, education, health, and human service organization dedicated to the welfare of Asian Pacific Americans in Santa Clara County. Providing more than 45,000 client visits annually, AACI has over eighty professionals and paraprofessionals who provide a wide array of human services to nine Asian ethnic communities, including the Chinese community. AACI has actively engaged in organizing the Asian American community to support its human services, health, and mental health programs for American born as well as for new immigrants from China, Hong Kong, Indochina, Southeast Asia, Taiwan, and so on.

Many of the AACI's board members and professional social work staff are known Chinese American community leaders, whose knowledge and skills in organizational development, community outreach, coalition formulation, networking, fund-raising, and interorganizational planning were effectively utilized in organizing local and statewide campaigns. For example, one of AACI's major advocacy efforts was to eliminate stereotyping of Asian Americans in textbooks and to promote a new commitment toward an accurate presentation of Asian American contribution to American society. In cooperation with school boards and state departments of education, AACI operated on both local and state levels to create the Textbook Screening Committee, an organization that actively screens for overt and subtle elements of racism and sexism. When this state committee faced the threat of elimination in 1980, AACI took a leadership role first in forewarning the community and later in rallying a unified voice of eighty-two groups statewide to preserve the committee. This coalition later evolved to become the Asian Pacific American Coalition, USA (APAC), a national organization aimed at producing a united voice to articulate common concerns and to advocate effectively on behalf of Asian Pacific Americans.[37]

The diversity of Asian Pacific elders is also apparent in contrasting the extent to which Asian Pacific populations in the United States consist of the foreign born. When the proportion of foreign-born Asian elders is further assessed, the largest groups are from Chinese backgrounds, with the Japanese and Filipino behind.[38] It is not surprising, therefore, that the fourth type is target population–oriented community organizations such as Self Help for the Elderly, Taiwanese Elderly Association, and Chinese Senior Club of Santa Clara County. With the exception of the Taiwanese Elderly Association, whose primary function is social and recreational, the other two organizations frequently require and enlist the intervention of professional social workers. In such circumstances, community organizers are expected to play a great variety of practice roles, particularly because these elderly self-help–oriented community groups lack organizational skills, political influence, human service technical expertise, and money. Much of the organizer's time may be devoted to rectifying this imbalance through education and advocacy. And the lack of funding is often made up through the concerted use of large numbers of community members, including family and community volunteers.

The Chinese written and spoken language continues to be of importance especially among Chinatown-centered Chinese in urban areas and among first-generation Chinese Americans. Skillful community organizational strategies among the Chinese Americans are specifically reflected in their effort to establish bilingual/bicultural education for their children. Almost entirely carried out by volunteer efforts, parents and teachers devote considerable time and resources to a frantic expansion of Chinese schools and classes. The results are impressive. Established in 1978, a coordinating organization—Association of Northern California Chinese Schools—is by far the largest community organization in the county and currently includes 85 member schools with a total student population well over 15,000.[39] Among them, 35 schools are located within the boundary of Santa Clara County. Generally speaking, the program goals for the Chinese schools include academic achievement, language proficiency, and cultural appreciation.

It is clear that organizing efforts such as the establishment of Chinese schools require considerable commitment and dedication of many groups of professionals and concerned parents. The Chinese schools, well organized through volunteer efforts and like the church before them, have played and will continue to play a significant role in helping bring different groups and individuals within the Chinese community together.

Known for being the world's computer-electronics industry capital, Santa Clara County is home to many Chinese American engineers and scientists who play significant roles in the rapid growth of the wide-range technology development in the professional and business community. Naturally, a few Chinese organizations have taken on new purposes and functions to provide a forum for exchange and networking, and above all, to promote cooperation among sociopolitically concerned Chinese American engineers to enhance their image in and contribute to the American society.[40] Examples of such community-oriented nonprofit organizations include the Chinese Institute of Engineers, USA, the Monte Jade Science and Technology Association, and the Chinese American Economic and Technology Development Association. In addition to sponsoring annual conferences, these socially sensitive organizations also work closely with other Asian American organizations for social welfare and political fundraisers, as well as providing scholarship for Chinese American high school and college students.

Since the mid-1980s, new development for political action has been taking place in the Chinese American community in the county. Chinese Americans began to mobilize resources in supporting Chinese and other Asian American candidates for local political offices and succeeded in electing a number of members of local county boards of supervisors, city councils, and school boards.

In addition to promoting and exercising electoral rights, direct representation of Asian Americans in government agencies ensures political participation. Along with other Asian community leaders, many members of the Chinese community have been appointed to city and county commissions on human relations, the status of women, juvenile justice, library, drug abuse coordination, and many more. Others have served on the state-level board of education, Council on Mental Health, and Equal Educational Opportunities Commission. The list of involvement is extensive and continues to grow as more members in the community are encouraged to pursue these important posts. Asian Americans for Community Involvement (AACI) and Chinese American Voters Education and Promotion Council are two prime community organizations that provide the basis for advocacy and coalitions in the political arena.

Analysis and Assessment

The Chinese in America are learning how to pool their considerable resources together for a common goal, something many see as quite atypical of Chinese in general. It is a commonly shared opinion among the Chinese that they are not a cooperative people among themselves. A closer look at their community organizations appears to support this view. For example, in the Los Angeles area alone, there are more than three hundred different Chinese organizations. They are organized primarily based on differences in political views, places of origin, family clan, professions, and so on.[41]

Traditionally, Chinese immigrant elites have managed to establish a kind of added legitimacy to their leadership and control by winning unofficial but practically useful recognition from white civic elites. However, the old order must contend not only with the mounting opposition of the community's respectable professionals and American-born younger and middle-aged Chinese Americans, but also with the new breed of more socially concerned community leadership.

Organizational Characteristics and Functions

Our purpose is to examine Chinese community organization's characteristics and patterns of behavior in contrast to their American counterparts and to show how those patterns have fared in the Chinese American community. The community organizations illustrated here are all private and nonprofit. Nearly all were found to be delivering services to Chinese Americans and have extensive involvement with the Chinese community (i.e., serving Chinese American elderly, having Chinese American staff and board members). In fact, among the twenty-five community organizations, Chinese board members were the majority, comprising more than 90 percent of the boards' membership. It should be noted that the idea of kinshiplike solidarity is still important among the Chinese Americans, for alleged local origin, kinship, and quasi kinship are obviously prevalent bases for many of their community organizations.

The aims and activities of these community organizations in Santa Clara County mostly differ from those of the past, although some of their functions remain similar. For example, some of the current Chinese organizations' services include outreach programs and aggressive publicity regarding available services to the Chinese as well as to the other Asian groups, as in the case of the Crosscultural Community Services Center. With the exception of Chinese schools, most of these community agencies were not located near the ethnic neighborhoods of the Chinese community, reflecting the fact that accessibility is not the major issue because of the marked increase of mobility among the Chinese Americans in the county. The newer organizations developed by the Chinese in Santa Clara County are therefore neither extensions of traditional ones (except in the case of the Chinese Mutual Assistance Association of Santa Clara County, which is entirely composed of ethnic Chinese from Southeast Asia) nor reactions to those of the white majority.

Thus in Santa Clara County, for instance, the newer community organizations such as the Taiwanese Association and the Chinese American Economic and Technology Development Association are not managed in the traditional Chinatown-connected style. The same is true of the Taiwanese Chamber of Commerce and Chinese American Culture Center, which contributes much to social welfare and to interorganizational planning and networking.

Strategies and Tactics Underlying Practice

Organizers in Santa Clara County choose to work with the Chinese American community on the basis of several criteria: common cultural patterns (such as speaking the same Chinese dialect or coming from the same place of origin); specific issues or concerns (for instance, new immigrants, youth employment, and voter registration); targeted population (elderly people); business associations and mutual support; or the objectives of a social movement (e.g., Asian Americans for Community Involvement). Social movement are increasingly of interest to the Chinese community because their concerns transcend the boundaries of the ethnic community and because the nature of their advocacy and the solidarity they engender bring them increasingly to public attention. They often face the dilemma common to most organizing strategies—the need to produce tangible results while promising some deferred social betterment. As in the case of Asian Americans for Community Involvement, Inc., social movements combine cause orientation with service orientation. For these reasons, agencies like AACI must constantly guard against goal displacement.

The Chinese community organizations just discussed are concerned with improving sociopolitical conditions, the delivery of needed services, enhancement of the coping mechanisms of target populations, and strengthening community participation and integration. These objectives, however, frequently conflict with one another. The establishment of a multiservice center, for example, may be achieved much more effectively without resorting to broad community involvement. There is also an underlying tension between the advocacy of the service-oriented approach and a political or action orientation. For this reason, action-oriented organizations— Asian Americans for Community Involvement, Inc., for example—have added a multitude of services as supports to their action platforms.

Organizer's Roles

One of the critical skills of an organizer is the capacity to build effective relationships with the Chinese community, whether involved with the task of developing community cohesiveness or developing new services. Without attempting to be exhaustive, and at a risk of omission or distortion, we list the roles that are readily identifiable in the above mentioned case illustrations:

Activist
Advocate
Communicator
Community leader
Cultural broker
Developer
Educator
Enabler
Expert
Interpreter

The most impressive feature of our observation is that a social developer role of the organizer has already begun to exist in the Chinese community organizations. The role assumes, first, not only that the problems of people are imbedded in social structural arrangements but also that a rational problem-solving framework is necessary to community intervention. Second, the role is founded on knowledge of social change and commitment to cultural values, which generate expectations that community involvements need to be created. Third, in the case of these community organizations such as AACI, associations for the elderly, and Chinese schools, the role performed by the worker was generally carried out in some integrated way. The techniques and strategies of various traditional macro roles, for example, administration, community organizer, planner, even the policy developer, were viewed as similar to, or at least complementary to or integrated with one another. Essentially, the orientation of the social developer is working toward adaptation and culture building rather than contest or conflict.

Acculturation Issues

Another issue relevant to the organizing strategies is the level of acculturation. In community organization, the enormous variance associated with differences in environmental context, geographic region, or acculturation is often underestimated. As time goes on, the Chinese in America will undoubtedly develop more community organizations based on ties other than kinship and local origin. But three observations are in order. First, the Chinese kinship and locality organizations will persist for a long time to come. Second, in spite of finding little attraction in such organizations, the newer generations of American-born Chinese will be positive in initiating or joining cause-oriented activities, especially if the causes are politically correct. Finally, more Chinese Americans are ready to associate with non-Chinese groups on the basis of social, political, or professional interest.

Bilingual/Bicultural Services

Over the last decade and a half, we have seen an emerging need for bilingual/bicultural services and socioculturally sensitive care for the elderly. It is particularly critical and stressful for the Chinese elderly immigrants whose productive lives were lived in their native land and who have maintained familial and social networks in a traditional Chinese cultural environment. Although the recent upsurge of interest in the health and social problems experienced by the Asian elderly population has been evident, services available to Chinese elders and their needs in Santa Clara County are sparse. An examination of the elderly's perceptions of the social environment and the processes through which Chinese elderly attain social services may lead us to a better understanding of the consequences of coping mechanisms on health, quality of life, and general well-being.

As can be seen, many of the Chinese community organizations in the county are so-called indigenous organizations and have become diversified and broad based. Some groups are easily distinguished by their alliance with different political parties in Taiwan and mainland China; others are oriented toward local, state, and national politics. Some organizations are geared to the interests of first-generation immigrants, and others to the service needs and problems of the American-born Chinese. However, one thing stands out clearly: the human service needs of Chinese Americans are largely unmet. As mentioned earlier, Chinese Americans do not utilize services as much as might be expected based on the size of the Chinese community. Further, our survey of Chinese community organizations in the county indicates that underutilization is due partly to the lack of responsiveness of the human service delivery system to provide culturally sensitive and bilingual services.

Conclusion and Implications

When the first Chinese arrived in America to labor as railroad workers and miners, little did they know they would stay. They had come to make better lives and then hoped to return home to China. For many years, the Chinese were a silent and invisible minority in the United States. For the rest of America, they were a mysterious people living on the fringes of society, living secret lives behind the walls of Chinatown. Today, more than a century later, their descendants, as well as more recent waves of Chinese immigrants, constitute a dynamic and creative force in a pluralistic American society. Their contributions in scientific research and business are well known, and now their influence is growing in other fields as well. Chinese Americans have overcome many barriers, but the final stumbling block on the road to complete citizenship is politics. Long hesitant to assert their voice in government, the Chinese have been reluctant to get involved in politics. As their voice begins to be heard, they will have more freedom to forge a new and different image for themselves, without the burden of confining stereotypes, new and old.

Beyond the issues and problems of the Chinatown itself—some of which are typical of all poor ethnic enclaves in American cities, others of which are peculiarly Chinese—loom the attitude and action of the larger society. The Chinese community's myth of social propriety, communal self-help, familial solidarity, and a low crime rate was a carefully nurtured mystique, prepared to counteract the vicious stereotype of coolie laborers, immoral practices, and inscrutable cunning that characterized America's racism. But discrimination and prejudice are still kindled in the United States. Thus Chinese Americans are constantly reminded that all their efforts at convincing mainstream America that they are a peaceable, law-abiding, family-minded, and docile people who have contributed much and asked little in return might be for naught. In time of crisis they too might suffer the same fate that overtook the highly acculturated Japanese Americans during World War II: incarceration. History, however, does not simply repeat itself. As illustrated in our analysis, a new "Chinatown" community is emerging, as well as new sorts of Chinese Americans who try new solutions to old problems. Attention has shifted from factors within the individual to those of the social system.

We see as fruitful two major themes relevant to strategies of community organizing in the Chinese American community. A "social development orientation" takes as its basic tenet that an ethnic minority's social and economic status, personal and group dignity, political power, and general well-being depends on the capacity building of the people involved. In working with the Chinese American community, we would also propose using a cross-cultural perspective, which begins from the assumption that there are indeed differences among all groups in U.S. society; each has its own unique tradition, culture, ways of living, and, in some cases, language. The cross-cultural perspective can foster a greater sensitivity to the role that culture and values play in community organization of ethnic peoples.

The Social Development Perspective

From a social development perspective, the community organizer's primary role is to seek qualitative growth and to that extent the remedial task is secondary. The primary base, then, is on conditions conducive to qualitative growth with greater emphasis on how societal structures are related to better human functioning. Therefore, in the context of community organization practice with Chinese Americans, political, social, economic, and technological structures of society are studied with a view to channeling their contribution to human betterment and quality of life.

1. From the social development point of view, the element within the community organization that appears to have the greatest potential as an organizing strategy is the concept of community control. In the social development model, citizen involvement is essential to achieve a solution to problems in the Chinese American community. This perspective further stresses that human service delivery systems should function as social action programs, as in the case of AACI in Santa Clara County. Therefore, efforts at social change or institution building should reflect the priorities and sense of urgency of the ethnic community served, and the system should take an active, aggressive role in that changing process. In order to achieve this, control should be taken out of the hands of the professional community worker and invested in a community representative. A perhaps more potent force is the recognition that a sense of empowerment, of group effort and belonging, and of being able to take greater control over one's destiny is an important source for further community solidarity and development, as well reflected in the organizing effort of the Chinese schools.

2. A related issue is the problem of short-term strategies. Although the ultimate goal for ethnic minorities in America is large-scale social development, experience suggests that this will require unremitting effort over an extended period of time, perhaps even generations. To begin with, we need more research in almost all areas involving the Chinese community: essential demographic data, needs assessments, intergenerational relations, culture and ethnic identity, mental health, community functioning, discrimination, the costs of racism on Chinese Americans and all other Americans, family structure, human service delivery system, and ethnic resources, to name a few. Further, a group of concepts might be selected relevant to important practice issues, such as effective community-based networks, organizational development techniques, the use of grassroots staff, client and community participation, leadership skills, public speaking skills, lobbying efforts, as well as conflict management.

3. For the Chinese American community at the current stage of development, the integration of leadership between first and second generations, between grassroots volunteers and professionals, and between social and political groups must be made to form a solid foundation for positive ethnic identity and all necessary social action programs. Although the ultimate goal of leadership development is to effect the positive social changes in the Chinese community, both older and younger generations of Chinese Americans must learn to respect each other, taking account of their differences in language abilities, political orientation, sociocultural values, and mentality.

In leadership development, a new awareness of our own diversity as a people must be the acknowledged reality of the Chinese community in the 1990s and beyond. In particular, the newly arrived immigrants must recognize that Chinese Americans, along with all other ethnic minority groups, have experienced a very painful history of oppression. For this reason, Chinese American community leadership must be given the opportunity to explore and understand the complexity of American multicultural society and its historic, social, and economic makeup. They too need to have a better understanding of their own Chinese diversity before they can begin to understand and interact effectively with other cultures.

4. In the Chinese community, there will continue to be problems associated with the gradual decline of the informal, indigenous natural resources and support network that have traditionally taken care of many community problems. Realistically, the Chinese American community will have to develop professional systems of services as the alternative forms of community-based service organizations. During this transitional phase, professional social workers with extensive experience in the Chinese American community can assume a special role of responsibility and leadership. For example, community organizers can serve as social developers to find ways to provide alternative services that are socioculturally sensitive and appropriate. Because many Chinese-specific community organizations are often linked in unstructured and ad hoc ways, a great deal of attention must also be directed to the management of relationships between and among organizations.

5. Philosophy and method, objective and technique have to be joined. The social development framework in community organizing requires not only a social change perspective and integrated strategies, but also interrelationships between these factors. The social developer must employ a variety of techniques or skills and generally be concerned with accountability, including cost efficiency and coordination. The role of the social developer is essentially concerned with the impact of social policies, programs, interorganizational relations, and administrative procedures on meeting the social needs of the ethnic community.

The Cross-Cultural Perspective

Within the cross-cultural framework proposed here, the crucial issue is to understand the functioning or particular behaviors of the Chinese community in the context of American society, although with a readiness to evaluate and propose change in terms of more universal standards.

1. A cross-cultural perspective views the behavior and problems of minority persons as expressions of their history and life conditions and can best be understood in terms of the customs and values of each of their cultures in a contemporary American pluralistic society. From a community practice standpoint, this conceptual model has important heuristic promise. Given the complexities of defining culture, the idea that ethnic minority groups in American society have separate and distinct cultures is, given the historical, anthropological, and sociological data, a tenable hypothesis. Although the case for the Chinese American group is perhaps more readily apparent, culture-bound community variables or categories must be modified until they are truly descriptive of the behaviors of the Chinese community. In community organization, there may be some categories that are in fact universal, or at least equivalently descriptive across cultures. But some basic categories, such as notions of roles and relationships, deviance, and power and empowerment, may require substantial rethinking and modification.

2. The cultural adaptiveness of the Chinese American community must be investigated. A beginning step in this direction will require a deep and sensitive awareness of the Chinese community's cultural beliefs, values, and behaviors. Further, community organizers will need to understand Chinese Americans' adaptation to their own cultural milieu, regardless of whether they are American or foreign born. In short, community organizers must first assume a traditional social work value of nonjudgmentalism when working with the Chinese community, one that allows an empathic grasp of how Chinese culture and social position influence their phenomenology in the community. In addition, bilinguality is clearly preferred, although supportive roles for English-speaking monolinguals may well emerge.

3. Human service programs aimed at the Chinese community have to take into account the crucial role of stigma and shame associated with problems such as cancer and mental illness, as indicated by community investigations.[42] Such shame may lead to denying the seriousness and prevalence of problems in the community. To address this issue effectively, community and other human service professionals must begin by working in institutional and community settings, developing programs with, for example, Chinese schools and other community centers, and establishing regular meetings (preferably in the hub of the Chinese community like the Chinese American Culture Center in Santa Clara County) where an exchange of information and a sharing of perspectives can take place.

Conclusion

The new conservative politics of the 1990s, reflected through the so-called contract with America, the attack on affirmative action, and recent welfare reforms, is ironically providing an incentive for Asian and Pacific Islander Americans to increase their commitment for social justice. Although it can be argued that Asian and Pacific Islander Americans are such a minority that organizing them is futile, Asian groups must play a proactive and leadership role in organizing their communities. Asian groups will continue to face many obstacles as they attempt to organize and to influence their communities: developing consensus on issues, generating interest among their diverse community organizations and members, influencing the thinking of political leaders whose attitudes have already been formed.[43] Those who are committed to the field of community organization, especially in working with ethnic minority groups, must continue to contend with these perspectives and dilemmas. This chapter has described integrated sociocultural approaches to community organization practice in social work. Nevertheless, this work must remain highly attuned to the political and social change context in which it is carried out.

Notes

1. U.S. Bureau of the Census (1996). *Statistical Abstract of the United States.* Washington, D.C.: U.S. Government Printing Office.

2. Ibid.

3. U.S. Bureau of the Census (1993). *U.S. Census of Population: 1990, General Population Characteristics.* Washington, D.C.: U.S. Government Printing Office.

4. Wen Lang Li (1993). "The Changing Patterns of Overseas Chinese in the United States" *The World Journal,* March 21.

5. Karen Huang (1991). "Chinese Americans." In N. Mokuau (ed.), *Handbook of Social Services for Asian and Pacific Islanders.* New York: Greenwood Press, pp. 79–96.

6. Ibid.

7. L. Mangiafico (1988). *Contemporary American Immigrants: Patterns of Filipino, Korean, and Chinese Settlement in the United States.* New York: Praeger.

8. Selma Taffel (1984). "Characteristics of Asian Births: United States." *Monthly Vital Statistics Report* 32(10), 1–16. Also see U.S. Bureau of the Census (1993). *Statistical Abstract of the United States.* Washington, D.C.: U.S. Government Printing Office.

9. Ibid.

10. Francis L. K. Hsu (1981). *Americans & Chinese: Passage to Differences.* Honolulu: University Press of Hawaii. Peter C. Lee et al. (1984). "Group Work Practice with Asian Clients: A Sociocultural Approach." In Larry E. Davis (ed.), *Ethnicity in Social Group Work Practice.* New York: Haworth Press, pp. 37–48. Karen Huang (1991). "Chinese Americans." In Noreen Mokuau (ed.), *Handbook of Social Services for Asian and Pacific Islanders.* New York: Greenwood Press, pp. 78–96.

11. Hans Kung and Julia Ching (1989). *Christianity and Chinese Religions.* New York: Doubleday.

12. Karen Huang (1991). "Chinese Americans."

13. Winnie Chang (1991). "No Longer Silent." *Free China Review* 41(12), 5–18.

14. Ibid.

15. W. S. Tseng and D. Y. H. Wu (eds.) (1985). *Chinese Culture and Mental Health.* San Diego: Academic Press. Betty Lee Sung (1967). *The Story of the Chinese in America.* New York: Collier Books.

16. Bay Area Social Planning Council. (1971). *Chinese Newcomer in San Francisco: A Report and Recommendation.* San Francisco: Author.

17. Bok-Lim C. Kim (1973). "Asian Americans: No Model Minority." *Social Work* 18, 157–169.

18. S. M. Lyman (1974). *Chinese Americans.* New York: Random House.

19. Noreen Mokuau (ed.). (1991). *Handbook of Social Services for Asian and Pacific Islanders.* New York: Greenwood Press.

20. S. S. H. Tsai (1986). *The Chinese Experience in America.* Bloomington: Indiana University Press.

21. Peter C. Y. Lee (1991). *Little Overseas Student: Needs Assessment in Santa Clara County.* A research report submitted to the Coordinating Council for North American Affairs, San Francisco; Helena T. Hwang and Terri H. Watanabe (1990). *Little Overseas Students from Taiwan: A Look at the Psychosocial Adjustment Issues.* Unpublished master's thesis, University of California, Los Angeles; Teresa Watanabe (1989). "Child Dumping: Taiwan Teens Left to Struggle in U.S." *San Jose Mercury News,* March 26, 1989.

22. Florence R. Kluckhohn (1967). "Dominant and Variant Value Orientations." In Clyde Kluckhohn and Henry A. Murray (eds.), *Personality in Nature, Society, and Culture.* New York: Knopf, pp. 342–357.

23. Noreen Mokuau (1988). "Social Work Practice with Individuals and Families in a Cross-Cultural Perspective." In Daniel S. Sanders and Joel Fischer (eds.), *Visions for the Future: Social Work and Pacific-Asian Perspectives.* Honolulu: University of Hawaii School of Social Work.

24. Daniel P. Moynihan (1965). *The Negro Family: The Case for National Action.* Washington, D.C.: U.S. Department of Labor; Diane de Anda (1984, March-April). "Bicultural Socialization: Factors Affecting the Minority Experience." *Social Work,* 101–107.

25. William T. Liu (ed.) (1982). *Methodological Problems in Minority Research.* Chicago: Pacific/Asian American Mental Health Research Center.

26. Diane de Anda (1984). "Bicultural Socialization: Factors Affecting the Minority Experience."

27. Charles A. Valentine (1971). "Deficit, Difference, and Bicultural Models of Afro-American Behavior." *Harvard Educational Review* 41, 137–157.

28. Winifred Yu (1985, September 11). "Asian Americans Charge Prejudice Slows Climb to Management Ranks." *Wall Street Journal;* James C. Ma and Peter C. Y. Lee (1986, July 7). "Asian Americans Climbing the Executive Ladder Need Feedback." *San Jose Business Journal.*

29. Enrico E. Jones and Sheldon J. Korchin (eds.) (1982). *Minority Mental Health.* New York: Praeger; Larry E. Davis (ed.) (1984). *Ethnicity in Social Group Work Practice;* Doman Lum (1986). *Social Work Practice & People of Color: A Process-Stage Approach.* Monterey, Calif.: Brooks/Cole; Noreen Mokuau (ed.) (1991). *Handbook of Social Services for Asian and Pacific Islanders.*

30. Stephen Green (ed.) (1993). *California Political Almanac.* Sacramento: Information for Public Affairs.

31. Ibid.

32. ABAG Regional Data Center (1992). *Santa Clara: San Francisco Bay Area Census Tracts.* San Francisco: Association of Bay Area Governments.

33. Ibid.

34. *A Community Challenged: A Public Report on Human Needs in Santa Clara County.* United Way of Santa Clara County, 1989.

35. Francis L. K. Hsu (1981). *Americans and Chinese: Passage to Differences.* Honolulu: University Press of Hawaii.

36. Francis L. K. Hsu (1971). *The Challenge of the American Dream: The Chinese in the United States.* Belmont, Calif.: Wadsworth.

37. Asian Americans for Community Involvement, Inc. (1993). *Annual Report.* San Jose, Calif.: Author; APAC-USA (1986). *Achievements & Activities.* Sacramento, Calif.: Asian Pacific American Coalition, USA.

38. Noreen Mokuau (ed.) (1991). *Handbook of Social Services for Asian and Pacific Islanders;* Gwen Yeo (1995). "Ethical Considerations in Asian and Pacific Islanders" *Clinics in Geriatric Medicine* 11(1), 139–152.

39. J. L. Lee (1994, February 19). "Association of Northern California Chinese Schools: An Organizational Analysis." *The World Journal.* p. B5; Association of Northern California Chinese Schools (1996). *Annual Report of the Chinese Schools Association.* San Jose, Calif.: Author; Chinese American Educational Research & Development Association. (1996). *Balancing Academic Achievement & Social Growth.* San Jose, Calif.: Author.

40. Chinese American Economic and Technology Development Association (1993, November 27). "New Development Prospect of the Pacific Rim Nations in the 21st Century." 1993 Annual Conference, Burlingame, California, November 27.; Chinese Institute of Engineers, USA. (1992, January 25). "The Role of Technology for the Common Growth of the U.S. and the Pacific Rim Countries." Second National Convention, San Francisco Airport Hotel.

41. Isaiah C. Lee (1992). "The Chinese Americans—Community Organizing Strategies and Tactics." In Felix G. Rivera and John L. Erlich (eds.), *Community Organizing in a Diverse Society.* Boston: Allyn & Bacon, pp. 133–158.

42. Hector B. Garcia and Peter C. Y. Lee (1988). "Knowledge about Cancer and Use of Health Care Services among Hispanic and Asian American Older Adults." *Journal of Psycho-*

social Oncology 6 (3/4), 157–177; Roger G. Lum (1982). "Mental Health Attitudes and Opinions of Chinese." In Enrico E. Jones and Sheldon J. Korchin (eds.), *Minority Mental Health,* pp. 165–189.

43. See Phillip Fellin, *The Community and the Social Worker.* Itasca, Ill.: F. E. Peacock, 1995.

Additional Sources

W. G. Brueggemann, *The Practice of Macro Social Work.* Chicago: Nelson-Hall, 1996.

Patrick J. Burkhart and Suzanne Reuss, *Successful Strategic Planning: A Guide for Nonprofit Agencies and Organizations.* Thousand Oaks, Calif.: Sage, 1993.

Fred M. Cox, John L. Erlich, John E. Tropman and Jack Rothman, *Strategies of Community Organization.* Itasca, Ill.: F. E. Peacock, 1987.

Virginia Cyrus (ed.), *Experiencing Race, Class, and Gender in the United States.* Mountain View, Calif.: Mayfield, 1993.

Phillip Fellin, *The Community and the Social Worker.* Itasca, Ill: F. E. Peacock, 1995.

Eileen Gambrill and Robert Pruger (ed.), *Controversial Issues in Social Work.* Boston: Allyn & Bacon, 1992.

D. F. Harrison et al., *Cultural Diversity and Social Work Practice.* Springfield, Ill.: Charles C. Thomas, 1996.

Francis L. K. Hsu, *Americans & Chinese: Passage to Differences.* Honolulu: University Press of Hawaii, 1981.

B. Lakey et al., *Grassroots and Nonprofit Leadership: A Guide for Organizations in Changing Times.* Philadelphia: New Society, 1995.

Peter C. Y. Lee, "Social Welfare of Hong Kong, Singapore, and Taiwan: Progress and Challenge," *American Journal of Chinese Studies* 3(2), October 1996, 225–233.

Peter C. Y. Lee, "Understanding Death, Dying, and Religion: A Chinese Perspective."

Peter C. Y. Lee, Gordon Juan, and Art B. Hom, "Group Work Practice with Asian Clients: A Sociocultural Approach." In Larry E. Davis (ed.), *Ethnicity in Social Group Work Practice.* New York: Haworth Press, 1984, pp. 37–48.

Don C. Locke, *Increasing Mutual Understanding: A Comprehensive Model.* Thousand Oaks, Calif.: Sage, 1992.

Noreen Mokuau (ed.), *Handbook of Social Services for Asian and Pacific Islanders.* New York: Greenwood Press, 1991.

Armando T. Morales and Bradford W. Sheafor, *Social Work: A Profession of Many Faces.* Boston: Allyn & Bacon, 1992.

Larry L. Naylor (ed.), *Cultural Diversity in the United States.* Westport, Conn.: Praeger, 1997.

Daniel S. Sanders (ed.), *The Developmental Perspective in Social Work.* Honolulu: University of Hawaii Press, 1982.

Ronald L. Taylor, *Minority Families in the United States: A Multicultural Perspective.* Englewood Cliffs, N.J.: Prentice Hall, 1994.

8

The Japanese American
Community and
Community
Organizations

KENJI MURASE

The current image and status of Japanese Americans represent a remarkable transformation of the public's perception of one ethnic minority population. Little more than fifty years ago, they were an unwanted minority perceived as incapable of being assimilated into U.S. society. This view is epitomized by a declaration made on the floor of the Congress that people of Japanese ancestry born in this country were "not citizens of the United States and never can be.... There is a racial and religious difference they can never overcome. They are pagan in their philosophy, atheistic in their beliefs, alien in their allegiance, and antagonistic to everything for which we stand" (*Congressional Record*, February 23, 1942).

These attitudes had provided the rationale for anti-Japanese legislation in the early 1900s that prevented Japanese immigrants from owning land, prohibited them from intermarriage, denied them the right to become American citizens, and excluded them from entering the United States. This history of virulent anti-Japanese sentiment was to reach its height after the outbreak of World War II when 120,000 Japanese Americans, of whom two-thirds were American citizens, were removed from the West Coast and interned in concentration camps in the interior (Weglen, 1976). The basis for their incarceration was the belief that Japanese Americans could not be trusted to be loyal to the United States and therefore were to be treated as potential spies and saboteurs.

Consider then the status of Japanese Americans today. In just fifty years, they have been transformed from an unwanted minority, incarcerated during World War II as potential subversives, to a group that is often characterized as a model minority. By almost any standard, Japanese Americans are now firmly established as middle-class Americans. Their mean income is higher than that of white Americans; they are among the highest educated of all minorities; they are overrepresented in the professions; the vast majority live in predominantly white neighborhoods; and currently more than half of all new marriages involving Japanese Americans are with Caucasians (Kitano, 1993).

Japanese Americans also present the paradox of a group that has maintained its ethnic identity while becoming structurally assimilated into the life of the larger society. Their experience can be seen as a departure from the European immigrant experience in which a zero-sum relationship prevails between assimilation and retention of ethnicity, that is, in which ethnic identity weakens as structural assimilation strengthens (Fugita & O'Brien, 1991). By contrast, Japanese Americans have been able to maintain high levels of ethnic consciousness and ethnic community involvement while becoming structurally assimilated into the dominant society.

Sociodemographic Characteristics

Unlike other Asian Americans, the population of Japanese Americans has remained relatively stable over the past several decades. In the 10-year period 1980 to 1990, the number of Japanese Americans increased by only 21 percent to a total of 847,562 (U.S. Bureau of the Census, 1991). In the same period, Filipinos increased by 82 percent, Chinese by 104 percent, Koreans by 125 percent, and Vietnamese by 135 percent. These differences in population growth reflect a marked decline in immigration from Japan at a time of rapidly increasing immigration from other Asian countries. The low immigration rate from Japan is also reflected in a higher proportion of U.S. born in the Japanese American population (68 percent) than in the case of Filipino Americans (36 percent), Chinese Americans (31 percent), Korean Americans (27 percent), and Vietnamese Americans (20 percent) (U.S. Bureau of the Census, 1991).

The 1990 Census reports that the following states had the largest concentration of Japanese Americans: California (312,989), Hawaii (247,486), New York (35,281), Washington (34,366), and Illinois (21,831). Other states with substantial populations of Japanese Americans are New Jersey, Texas, Georgia, and Colorado. In Hawaii, Japanese Americans comprise almost one-fourth of the state population.

Of all Asian Americans, Japanese Americans have the highest median age (36.5 years) compared to Asian Indians (29.4 years), Chinese (32.2 years), Filipinos (36.3 years), and Koreans (29.1 years). With an average of 2.7 persons per household, Japanese

Americans have the smallest household among all Asian Americans compared to Asian Indians (2.9 persons), Chinese (3.1 persons), Koreans (3.4 persons), Filipinos (3.6 persons), and Vietnamese (4.4 persons) (U.S. Bureau of the Census, 1993).

More than one-third of Japanese Americans have completed four or more years of college, compared to one-fifth in the general population. The level of educational attainment among Japanese Americans no doubt contributes to their having the highest median family income ($51,550) of any group. Moreover, among all Asian Americans, Japanese Americans had the lowest proportion (3.9 percent) in the age 65 and over group who were reported to be living below the poverty level in 1990 (U.S. Bureau of the Census, 1993).

Cultural Heritage

Any understanding of Japanese Americans requires an appreciation of the continuing influence of their cultural and historical legacy. More than anything else, the survival and achievements of Japanese Americans is a tribute to the enduring power of their cultural legacy. Despite the passage of time, traditional cultural values and practices continue to play a significant role in the lives of contemporary Japanese Americans.

An important component of the Japanese cultural legacy is an ethical system rooted in Confucian traditions transplanted to Japan from China during the seventh century (Reischauer, 1981). At the center was the notion of obligation and loyalty to one's family. The family and not the individual comprised the basic unit of society. Each family member was assigned a definite position in a hierarchical scale that bound him or her to others in a network of moral duties and rules for proper conduct. Thus the survival of the family, rather than the fulfillment of an individual member's needs, took precedence in the family system.

Family stability, as reflected in a low divorce rate, is another indicator of the persistence of traditional cultural values. Compared with other Western traditions, Japanese American conceptions of marital roles place greater emphasis on family-centered duties and responsibilities, with less emphasis on individualistic views of love and romance. Moreover, the strong network of families in Japanese American communities serves both as a social support for family cohesion by providing a buttress against the stresses found in all marriages and as a barrier against divorce.

A significant new phenomenon is an increasing out-marriage rate. Among the immigrant first generation (*Issei*), the out-marriage rate was less than 2 percent. The out-marriage rate for the second generation (*Nisei*) generation was 4 percent, in contrast to the 20 percent out-marriage rate of second-generation European ethnics. But by the late 1970s, out-marriage among the third generation (*Sansei*) had jumped to more than half of all new marriages. Among the fourth generation (*Yonsei*), the out-marriage rate may be expected to be even higher as the acculturation process continues (Iwasaki-Mass, 1992).

History

The initial period of Japanese immigration to the United States was from 1880 to 1924 when some 400,000 were admitted as an alternative to admitting the Chinese, whose entry was sharply restricted by the Chinese Exclusion Act of 1882. The *Issei* (first-generation) immigrants answered the need for a continuing supply of cheap and reliable labor by the agriculture, railroad, lumber, and mining industries that were flourishing in the American West. Despite their significant role in the economic development of the West, the Japanese, as well as other Asian immigrants, were subjected to humiliating acts of racial discrimination and even mob violence. There were segregated schools for Japanese children in San Francisco, laws prohibiting interracial marriage, antialien land laws preventing ownership of property, trade union restrictions on entry into skilled crafts, and diversion into employment that was noncompetitive with white workers (Daniels, 1988). Moreover, as Asians the *Issei* were barred from U.S. citizenship, which meant they were excluded from the American political process and left defenseless against discriminatory legislation. In 1924 the U.S. Immigration Act shut the door on Japanese immigration completely for nearly 30 years, until 1952 when the McCarran-Walter Immigration Act allowed an annual quota of 185 immigrants from Japan.

Community Life

The racism of the larger society led to the emergence and maintenance of a parallel community that was in many respects self-contained (Fugita & O'Brien, 1991). An extensive ethnic community infrastructure evolved that comprised protective mutual aid associations, rotating credit unions, religious institutions, newspapers, language schools, and cultural and recreational associations. This community structure continued the functions of socialization of members in traditional Japanese ways and the maintenance of ethnic community cohesion in the face of external threats. This community as developed by the immigrant *Issei* generation remained largely intact and served to nurture the American-born *Nisei* generation until the outbreak of World War II.

Historically, the Japanese in America have a tradition of organizing formal associations for the purpose of taking collective action to protect or advance their interests. Early immigrants in agriculture formed unions and engaged in work stoppages and boycotts as leverage to gain improved wages and working and living conditions. As early as 1907, Japanese and Chinese coal miners participated in collective action against coal mine operators in Wyoming (Ichioka, 1988). Soon after their arrival, Japanese immigrants formed mutual aid associations such as rotating credit unions and burial societies. Farmers' cooperatives were organized to share the costs of seeds, fertilizers, and tools, as well as to market their crops. Other voluntary organizations, such as language schools and music and dance groups, were formed to transmit the traditional cultural content from the old country to their children.

The early community organizations of the *Issei* generation primarily served economic and sociocultural interests rather than political purposes. Not until the *Nisei* generation reached adulthood did community organizations serve political ends. For example, the Japanese American Citizens League (JACL), founded in 1929, petitioned Congress to amend the Cable Act to permit *Nisei* women, who had married alien Japanese, to regain their citizenship and to permit Asian-born men who had served in the U.S. armed forces in World War I to be granted citizenship. Increasingly, the JACL entered the political arena to make representations on behalf of Japanese Americans before governmental bodies and the legal system. In the period before the outbreak of World War II, the JACL was engaged in strenuous efforts to stem the tide of rising anti-Japanese hostility resulting from rapidly deteriorating U.S.-Japan relations. However, after the Japanese attack on Pearl Harbor, there was little the JACL could do to counter the wave of hysteria and hate that would engulf the country and lead to the eventual exclusion of Japanese Americans from the West Coast and their internment in concentration camps.

The Internment of Japanese Americans

For Japanese Americans the internment in concentration camps during World War II is without question the one historical event that universally defines and symbolizes the Japanese American experience. When Japanese forces attacked Pearl Harbor in December 1941, some 125,000 people of Japanese ancestry lived along the Pacific Coast. Approximately two-thirds of this population were American citizens. Despite assurances from military intelligence sources and the Federal Bureau of Investigation that there was no danger of subversion by Japanese Americans, President Franklin Roosevelt acceded to the demands of the military, powerful agricultural and commercial interests, and racial bigots and issued an executive order authorizing the removal of all Japanese Americans from the West Coast. Although the United States was also at war with Germany and Italy, no similar order was applied to German or Italian Americans.

Internment is perhaps the one word that best evokes an understanding of what it is to be a Japanese American. Whether internment was personally experienced by the *Issei* and *Nisei* generations, or retold and learned by the *Sansei* (third) and *Yonsei* (fourth) generations, all Japanese Americans have been profoundly affected by what happened to America's Japanese during World War II. The shared experience of being uprooted and removed to concentration camps produced a deep sense of collective identity that persists regardless of Japanese Americans' subsequent dispersal to all parts of the country. The kinship of experiencing a common tragedy for an immutable physical trait, that of bearing the face of the enemy, and the humiliation and hardships endured during the internment contributed to their everlasting sense of group identity.

The Concentration Camps

Ten concentration camps were located on deserts and wastelands in Arizona, Arkansas, California, Colorado, Idaho, Utah, and Wyoming. Each camp held from 7,600 to 18,800 residents, housed in tar-paper-covered barracks, which, according to military regulations, were suitable only for combat-trained troops and then only on a temporary basis. For Japanese Americans, these barracks served as long-term housing for a period of close to four years. An average of eight people were assigned to a 20 by 25 foot "apartment." Communal kitchens, dining halls, and bathhouses provided little or no privacy. The camps were surrounded by armed guard towers and barbed wire. At one camp, several internees were shot and killed, though not during attempted escape; they died when guards fired into unarmed public demonstrations (Weglen, 1976).

Psychologically, the internment was a devastating experience (Nagata, 1993). To the *Issei* the forced evacuation and detention symbolized a repudiation of their years of toil and sacrifice for their children. For the *Nisei* the internment meant rejection by a nation to which they had pledged allegiance. Repression of the painful internment experience was a common reaction. It was not until their children, the *Sansei,* gave legitimacy to expressions of outrage about the injustice of the internment that the *Nisei* could confront and come to terms with their own deeply buried emotions. Only then could they join in the movement with the *Sansei* to seek redress and reparations for the physical and psychological damages inflicted by the internment.

Rebuilding the Community

The end of World War II and the closing of the concentration camps in 1945 signaled the beginning of a new era in Japanese American history. Upon their release Japanese Americans returned to re-create their former communities, which had been destroyed by their removal and internment. There followed a difficult process of recovery and rebuilding of their economic base, their social institutions, and their network of relationships to sustain a viable community life.

With an economic base reestablished primarily in small businesses and service occupations, Japanese American community workers then addressed broader community concerns such as poverty, health care, housing, and social services. Over time a network of indigenous community-based services and support systems evolved to meet the economic, social, and psychological needs of the community (Murase, 1985). This indigenous community care and support system comprised institutions such as churches, credit unions, prefectural associations, and social and cultural organizations, as well as individuals such as ministers, priests, doctors, lawyers, teachers, shop-keepers, and others respected in the community. Their role as community caretakers represented an extension of the traditional attitude and practice of collective responsibility embedded in their cultural legacy.

The Resurgence of Community Organizing

The heightened militancy and demand for redefinition by minorities of color that characterized the civil rights movement of the 1960s had a strong impact on the Japanese American community leadership. The struggles of African Americans, Hispanic Americans, Native Americans, and other minorities of color raised among Japanese American community activists a consciousness of the broader legal and social relevancy of their historical internment legacy.

In the late 1960s Japanese American community leaders were alerted to threats posed by the Emergency Detention Act of 1950, which authorized the imprisonment, without trial, of persons regarded as security risks in times of national emergency. To carry out its provisions, the Department of Justice had designated six sites for detention camps. In the political climate of the times, with the Black Power movement, the assassination of Martin Luther King, Jr., riots in the ghettos, and the anti–Vietnam War movement, there were ominous signs that dissenters could be rounded up and interned.

As past and only victims of American concentration camps, the Japanese American community felt a special obligation to take the leadership in the removal of a law that threatened to abridge the civil rights of other Americans. Accordingly, Japanese American community activists initiated the formation in 1968 of a National Ad Hoc Committee for Repeal of the Emergency Detention Act. During its three-year campaign, the committee mobilized the support nationally of civil rights groups, labor unions, religious organizations, governmental bodies, and the media. Two Japanese Americans in the Congress, Senator Daniel Inouye and Representative Spark Matsunaga, introduced bills in their respective chambers, and President Richard Nixon signed a bill into law on September 25, 1971, that would henceforth prohibit the detention or imprisonment of citizens without due process of law (Okamura, 1974).

Redress and Reparations

Unquestionably, the most significant community organizing effort among Japanese Americans during the period of the 1970s and 1980s was their national campaign to secure redress and reparations for their internment during World War II. This campaign involved every segment of the Japanese American community, and the unified support commanded was without historical precedent. From the original formal approval in 1978 by the Japanese American Citizens League for a national campaign to take the Japanese American case to the American public, to the signing of the Civil Liberties Act of 1988, took ten long years of persistent effort.

The first stage of the campaign was to bring the issue before the American public, which was largely uninformed about the World War II experience of Japanese Americans. Key players in this educational process were the veterans of the celebrated 442nd Regimental Combat Team composed of Japanese Americans, which was the most decorated military unit in World War II. Japanese American members of the Congress (Senators Daniel Inouye and Spark Matsunaga and Congressmen Norman Mineta and Robert Matsui) were instrumental in securing legislation to establish the Commission on Wartime Relocation and Internment of Civilians. The commission conducted public hearings to assess whether any wrong was committed by the government in interning Japanese Americans and to recommend remedial action to Congress.

In its final report issued in February 1983, the commission concluded that the internment of Japanese Americans was not justified by military necessity as claimed by the government in 1942 (U.S. Commission on Wartime Relocation and Internment of Civilians, 1982). It recommended to Congress that the government issue an official public apology and award a one-time compensatory payment of $20,000 to each of approximately 60,000 surviving internees. Legislation to implement the commission's recommendations took five additional years of sustained organizing of pressure by the Japanese American community before President Reagan signed the enabling Civil Rights Act of 1988.

Impact of the Redress Movement

The significance of the redress movement is that it served to revive and reinforce the collective ethnic identity of Japanese Americans (Takezawa, 1995). For the few surviving *Issei,* redress represented a vindication of their belief in the rewards of toil and sacrifice for their children. For the *Nisei,* the redress drive served as a catharsis that helped to heal the wounds inflicted by the internment experience. For the *Sansei,* the redress effort revealed the history of their community and their perceived status in American society. Through their cultural reconstruction of the past in the redress campaign, Japanese Americans redefined their past and the present in terms of what it means to be Japanese Americans and what it means to be a minority in American society. Essentially, their reassessment of the internment experience raised the level of political consciousness among Japanese Americans, that is, an awareness that although racism and war hysteria were the driving forces underlying the internment, it was also aided and abetted by their own political naïveté, their political passivity, and their political impotence.

In retrospect, the historical transformation of ethnicity among Japanese Americans can be seen as occurring in four distinct stages (Takezawa, 1995). The first stage, before World War II, was characterized by the primordial attachments of the immigrant *Issei* generation to their cultural roots in Japan. There followed a second stage of ethnic stigma brought about by racial discrimination and social isolation from the larger society. The third stage was dominated by the shared suffering of forced removal from their homes and internment in concentration camps, solely on the basis of their racial ancestry, during World War II. In the final stage, with the vindication of their constitutional rights established by the redress victory, Japanese Americans could repudiate the guilt and shame of internment and affirm and acclaim their ethnicity.

Current Directions in Community Organizing

The lessons learned by Japanese American community organizations in the 1970s and 1980s were to shape the character of their community organizing in the 1990s. There continued to be ethnic-specific, locality-based organizing directed to addressing endemic urban issues such as affordable housing, public safety, quality education, children and youth services, and services to the elderly. However, currently emerging developments suggest that Japanese American community organizations are striking out in new directions. Illustrative are efforts in the areas of interethnic coalitions, participation in the political arena, advocacy for corporate social responsibility, and coalition building at the national level.

Interethnic Coalitions

As a direct outgrowth of the civil rights movement, Japanese Americans who were previously self-defined in terms of their specific ethnicity came to confront their own racial identity and status in a political environment of heightened racial consciousness. Along with Chinese, Filipino, and Korean Americans, Japanese Americans embraced the panethnic concept of "Asian American" in which both assimilation and ethnic particularism were supplanted and transformed (Espiritu, 1992). The designation "Asian American" was a convenient political label that reflected their common historical experience of being subjected to exclusionary immigration laws, restrictive naturalization laws, labor market segregation, and patterns of ghettoization by a society that perceived and treated Asians as all alike.

Japanese American activists saw in the Asian American concept a rallying point for raising political consciousness about the problems besetting all Asian American communities and for asserting demands on public institutions for legislative remedies and resources. Among their commonly sought objectives have been bilingual ballots, bilingual education, redistricting of political boundaries to reflect demographic realities, equal employment opportunities, immigration reform, and economic development (U.S. Commission on Civil Rights, 1992).

Political Participation

The successful campaign to repeal the Emergency Detention Act of the 1970s and the campaign for internment redress and reparations of the 1980s impressed on Japanese American community organizations the importance of representation in legislative bodies. The key players in both campaigns were Senators Daniel Inouye and Spark Matsunaga and Representatives Norman Mineta and Robert Matsui. It was also clear to the Japanese American community leadership that their legislative victories were made possible only with the massive support of other civil rights and ethnic minority organizations.

In the 1990s political participation has moved increasingly toward collaborative efforts between Japanese American and other ethnic minorities in the local political arena. The Japanese American experience in Monterey Park, a suburb of Los Angeles, is an instructive case example of Japanese American participation in the emergence of minority politics and multiethnic alliances to secure representation in the local political process (Horton, 1995).

Monterey Park was the first city in the mainland United States with a majority Asian American population and the first female Chinese American mayor. With the arrival of Chinese immigrants in the 1980s, Japanese Americans had lost their previous position of dominance in the local Asian community. Unlike Mexican Americans, they lacked the numbers to achieve power and representation as Japanese Americans. As part of a rapidly expanding Asian population in a predominantly Latino area, the Japanese American leadership viewed the dramatic increase in the Chinese population as a potential resource for Asian American power and an opportunity to form alliances with Latinos on this basis. As a result of such alliances between Asian Americans and Latinos to unite behind selected Asian candidates, there was a significant expansion of Asian representation in the Monterey Park city government in the 1980s and 1990s.

Monterey Park exemplifies the emergence in the 1990s of a politics of diversity: a movement toward empowerment of immigrants, ethnic groups, and women and their incorporation into a local political system that had once been the exclusive province of white males. The Monterey Park experience also provides a lesson that the politics of diversity must be a politics of incorporation and inclusion, including the encouragement of social and political participation, education, and language skills that are the necessary tools for citizenship and equality in a society of immigrants.

Corporate Responsibility

One of the repercussions of Japan's ascendancy as an economic power has been a growth of anti-Japanese sentiment in the United States. The American public has been particularly sensitive to the impact of Japanese-owned corporations operating in this country. The Japan Pacific Resource Network (JPRN) is a unique community-based advocacy group that has taken the initiative in confronting Japanese-owned companies with the issue of their corporate social responsibility, especially in relation to minority employees and minority consumers. JPRN first attracted media attention in 1986 by calling a press conference to denounce derogatory remarks made by the then prime minister of Japan about racial minorities in the United States (Ishi, 1987).

In 1996 JPRN coordinated a visit to Japan for representatives of the National Organization for Women to participate in a rally before a shareholders' meeting of Mitsubishi Motors Corporation. The rally was organized by JPRN with assistance from Japanese women's groups to protest allegations of sexual harassment at the company's plant in Illinois. The rally not only raised the issue of Japanese corporate behavior in overseas operations but also exposed the linkage to underlying attitudinal and structural problems of gender relations in Japanese corporations as well (MacGregor, 1996).

At the local level, in the San Francisco Bay Area, JPRN initiated in 1990 a dialogue between the leadership of the African American and Japanese American communities to ameliorate tensions between the two communities. Organized as the African/Asian American Roundtable, the organization facilitates dialogue to promote positive relationships between the African and Asian American communities. Through joint efforts in advocacy, public educational forums, and participation in cultural activities, the roundtable has become an effective force for amicable relations between communities that have historically viewed one another with distrust and hostility (Lang, 1990).

Coalition Building at the National Level

Japanese American organizations were among the prime movers in providing the initiative and resources for the formation of several national coalitions of Asian American organizations. Leadership Education for Asian Pacifics (LEAP) was founded in 1982 by a diverse cross section of the Asian American community of Southern California. From its inception LEAP has focused on the development, strengthening, and expansion of the leadership role of Asian Pacific Americans in all sectors of society. LEAP evolved out of a recognition that many Asian Pacific Americans with training and qualifications have lacked opportunities historically to fully realize their potential at the highest levels of leadership in mainstream America. LEAP seeks to achieve its mission of enhancing leadership among Asian Pacific Americans through leadership training, community development and empowerment, and public policy research and education.

LEAP's Community Development Institute (CDI) was established in response to issues and concerns of emerging Asian Pacific American immigrant communities. Focusing on Southeast Asian and Pacific Islander populations, the CDI offers a multifaceted approach in developing indigenous leadership and, at the same time, enabling existing community organizations to respond to the need for social services and economic development in these emerging communities.

LEAP's Public Policy Institute was established in 1992 as an ethnically inclusive community-based public policy center with the goal of increasing the ability of

Asian Pacific Americans to impact the decision-making and policy formulation process from which they have been traditionally excluded. To date, LEAP has published a series of highly acclaimed and influential reports on issues affecting Asian Pacific Americans, including *The State of Asian Pacific America: Economic Diversity, Issues and Policies* (1994); *The State of Asian Pacific America: Policy Issues to the Year 2020* (1993); *Beyond Asian American Poverty: Community Economic Development Policies and Strategies* (1993); *Common Ground: Perspectives on Affirmative Action and Its Impact on Asian Pacific Americans* (1995); and *The State of Asian Pacific America: Reframing the Immigration Debate* (1996).

Another example of collaboration between Japanese American organizations and other Asian American organizations is the National Asian Pacific American Legal Consortium, a nonprofit, nonpartisan organization whose mission is to advance and protect the legal and civil rights of Asian Pacific Americans through litigation, advocacy, public education, and public policy development. Its priorities include anti-Asian violence prevention and education, voting rights, immigration, naturalization, affirmative action, language rights, and the census. In its anti-Asian violence work, the consortium monitors and documents hate-motivated incidents and publishes an annual anti-Asian violence audit (National Asian Pacific American Legal Consortium, 1996). Based in Washington, D.C., the consortium is affiliated with three major civil rights legal organizations in cities with significant Asian Pacific American populations: The Asian American legal Defense and Education Fund (New York City), the Asian Law Caucus (San Francisco Bay Area), and the Asian Pacific American Legal Center of Southern California.

Future Problems and Prospects

The destiny of Japanese American community organizations is likely to be shaped by demographic trends, the continuing legacy of the internment experience, the role of the National Japanese American Citizens League, and the larger context of the status of Asian Americans in society.

Demographic Trends

Demographic trends suggest that the rate of growth of the Japanese American population will continue to decline at the same time there is increasing dispersal away from the ethnic enclaves into the wider mainstream. This process of structural assimilation will be reinforced by an increasingly higher rate of out-marriage, which is now well over one-half of all marriages. These demographic trends will have significant consequences for Japanese American community organizations.

The prospect is that there will come a time when Japanese Americans on the West Coast will no longer reside in an identifiable ethnic community, such as now exists in cities such as Seattle, San Francisco, San Jose, and Los Angeles. This means Japanese Americans will no longer comprise the critical mass necessary to support and sustain local ethnic-specific institutions and organizations, such as churches, social services, social and recreational voluntary associations, and small businesses. Japanese Americans will then have to rely on either other Asian American or mainstream institutions and organizations.

Another likelihood is that as Japanese Americans become more structurally assimilated, they, like contemporary Americans of European origin, will become more sensitive to the importance of recognizing and preserving a sense of symbolic ethnicity. Japanese American community organizations will have an important role in encouraging and supporting a renewal of interest in language study, a revival of traditional cultural arts and practices, and a revisiting of the history of the Japanese in America.

The Internment Legacy

Any consideration of the future role of Japanese American community organizations cannot ignore the singularly distinctive nature of the Japanese American experience as survivors of the internment (Nakanishi, 1993). A collective response to their past victimization is an obligation to be vigilant to any situation that re-creates their tragic past and to rise to the defense of other groups whose loyalties are questioned and who become the targets of racial hostility and violence.

As a case in point, during the 1990–1991 Persian Gulf War, Japanese Americans were among the few groups that publicly protested the conduct of the Federal Bureau of Investigation in detaining Arab American community leaders for questioning, in a manner ominously reminiscent of the period following the outbreak of World War II when Japanese American community leaders were rounded up and detained.

The internment legacy imposes on Japanese Americans an understanding that the internment was not an aberration in American history but an expression of the racism deeply imbedded in American history and culture. The internment must thus be seen as a product of the same culture that lynched African Americans in the South, invented Jim Crow practices, and wrote the Chinese Exclusion Act of 1882. Therefore, the redress payment and certificate of apology from the U.S. government to Japanese Americans for their internment cannot be the end of the struggle but only a symbolic beginning in the process of making the Japanese American community whole. True redress must be interpreted to mean that payment in full will not be complete until the elimination of all practices, institutions, and ideologies that serve to maintain racial subordination in any form.

Role of the Japanese American Citizens League (JACL)

In virtually all major Asian American community organizing efforts, at both the local and national levels, the JACL has performed a key role in contributing its leadership and resources. Founded in 1929 to fight discrimination against people of Japanese ancestry, the JACL continues to be the preeminent Japanese American civil and human rights advocacy organization. Among its current national objectives are to promote equal opportunities through vigorous support for antidiscrimination initiatives, affirmative action programs, and immigrant rights; to disseminate information and materials for public education about the Japanese American internment experience; to promote positive portrayals of Japanese Americans in the media; to empower the Japanese American community to work for social justice and prevent tragedies such as the World War II internment experience; and to promote and preserve the Japanese American cultural heritage and values and sense of community (Yip, 1996).

Today, with over 25,000 members in 100 chapters throughout the country, the JACL is positioned to perform a central role in shaping the future status of Japanese Americans and other Asian Americans. With its proven record of legislative and legal accomplishments, its experiences and resources can now be directed toward influencing the national political and legal process on behalf of all Asian Americans. Both alone and in coalition with other organizations and communities dedicated to eradicating bigotry and discrimination, the JACL is armed with the capacity to exercise influence on the national scene in advancing civil and human rights for all sectors of society.

Role as Asian Americans

The future role and status of Japanese Americans is inextricably linked to developments affecting all Asian Americans. Based on recent trends, the Asian American population is projected to be close to 20 million by the year 2020 (Asian Pacific American Public Policy Institute, 1993). This population has and will continue to enrich the United States culturally, socially, and economically. However, there are also severe problems—growing racial conflicts, poverty, underemployment, and limited accessibility to the political process—that affect Asian Americans and must be addressed (Ming, 1995).

The growth of the Asian American population, along with the growth of other minority groups, is transforming the United States into a pluralistic society. As an integral part of the Asian American collectivity, Japanese Americans will have a special role in providing leadership and resources in efforts to recognize and promote multiculturalism and intercultural sensitivity within existing legislation, programs, and agencies.

In the area of civil rights protections, especially laws that protect minorities against discriminatory practices, there remain issues not adequately addressed by existing laws—laws that have been developed historically in the context of black-white relations. For example, in higher education, protection is needed against restrictive admissions quotas based on race. In employment, a glass ceiling prevents Asian Americans from moving into management positions; unfair personnel practices are based on language and culture; and restrictions limit opportunities and advancement in self-employment or small business enterprises. In the political sphere, Asian

Americans need greater access to the electoral process through redistricting and appropriate bilingual materials.

Given the large proportion of Asian Americans who are immigrants or refugees, support is needed for programs to help Asian newcomers to adjust and become integrated into their communities in order to become full and productive members (Hing & Lee, 1996). Demographically, as Asian Americans became a larger proportion of the current and emerging diversity, they need to become more actively engaged in policymaking that promotes quality of life enhancement for all people.

In their relationship to other people of color, Japanese Americans may face difficult choices regarding issues that can potentially unite and issues that threaten to divide. For example, with other Asian American and Hispanic American communities, a common agenda could focus on issues of bilingual education, immigration reform, and employer discrimination against foreign-born or non–English-speaking employees. The same issues, however, could alienate African Americans, especially during periods of declining public resources and shrinking private sector opportunities. But a firm commitment to civil rights legislation and enforcement, equal opportunity in hiring and promotion, and revitalization of inner cities could unite Japanese Americans and other Asian Americans with African Americans, as well as with other people of color (Asian Pacific American Public Policy Institute, 1993).

Summary

The history of the Japanese American community holds far-reaching implications for the future of other communities of color. The Japanese American experience provides an instructive lesson on the mercurial nature of public attitudes about an ethnic minority population. During World War II, Japanese Americans were outcasts, perceived as a threat to national security and summarily interned in concentration camps without due process of law. Today, they are considered a model minority to be emulated by other minorities.

The experience of the Japanese American community is also instructive as an example of how an ethnic minority group can impose its collective will on the forces of history and shape its own destiny by sheer force of determination and character. Following their release from the concentration camps, Japanese Americans prevailed over immense adversities to rebuild their communities and to become again productive members of society. Ten years of perseverance ensued before their national campaign succeeded in gaining redress and reparation from the U.S. government for the injustices of their internment.

Lastly, the experience of the Japanese American community is a testament to the enduring power of ethnicity in forging community cohesion and sustaining survival. Demographic trends, however, will severely test the bonds of ethnicity as the Japanese American community undergoes continuing dispersal and an increasing rate of out-marriage. Further, with time the legacy of the internment will cease to be as decisive in defining Japanese American ethnic group identity. The viability of the Japanese American community organizations will then be determined in large part by their role in relation to the larger Asian American community.

The Japanese American community, recognizing their common historical experience of racial subordination, is obliged to contribute leadership and resources to collaborative efforts with other Asian American communities to protect and advance the civil and human rights of all minorities. Ultimately, then, the future status of the Japanese American community is bound up with and inseparable from the destiny of all other Asian American communities.

References

Asian Pacific American Public Policy Institute. (1993). *The state of Asian Pacific America: A public policy report.* Los Angeles: Asian Pacific American Public Policy Institute, Asian American Studies Center, University of California at Los Angeles.

Civil Rights Act of 1988. P.L. 100–430, 102 Stat. 1619 to 1636.

Congressional Record. (1942, February 23), pp. A768–A769.

Daniels, R. (1988). *Asian America: Chinese and Japanese in the United States since 1850.* Seattle: University of Washington Press.

Espiritu, Y. L. (1992). *Asian American pan-ethnicity: Bridging institutions and identity.* Philadelphia: Temple University Press.

Fugita, S. S., & O'Brien, D. J. (1991). *Japanese American ethnicity: The persistence of ethnicity.* Seattle: University of Washington Press.

Hing, B. O., & Lee, R. (Eds.). (1996). *Reframing the immigration debate.* Los Angeles: LEAP Asian Pacific American Public Policy Institute, Asian American Studies Center, University of California at Los Angeles.

Horton, J. (1995). *The politics of diversity: Immigration, resistance and change in Monterey Park, California.* Philadelphia: Temple University Press.

Ichioka, Y. (1988). *The Issei: The world of the first generation Japanese immigrants, 1885–1924.* New York: Free Press.

Ishi, T. (1987). *Naksone's racial remarks and international dynamism in race* race *relations.* Oakland, CA: Japan Pacific Resource Network.

Iwasaki-Mass, A. (1992). Interracial Japanese Americans. In M. Root (ed.), *Racially mixed people in America* (pp. 265–279). Newbury Park, CA: Sage.

Kitano, H. H. L. (1993). *Generation and identity: The Japanese Americans.* Needham Heights, MA: Ginn Press.

Lang, P. (1990, October 31). Bay area Blacks, Asians decry Japanese remark. *San Francisco Chronicle,* p. A17.

MacGregor, H. E. (1996, June 28). The weapons of choice in Japan: U.S. women. *Los Angeles Times,* p. B13.

Ming, P. G. (Ed.). (1995). *Asian Americans: Contemporary trends and issues.* Thousand Oaks, CA: Sage.

Murase, K. (1985). Alternative mental health service models in Asian Pacific communities. In T. C. Owan (Ed.), *Southeast Asian mental health: Treatment, prevention, service, training and research* (pp. 229–260). Washington, DC: U.S. Government Printing Office.

Nagata, D. K. (1993). *Legacy of injustice; Exploring the cross-generational impact of the Japanese American internment.* New York: Plenum.

Nakanishi, D. T. (1993). Surviving democracy's "mistake": Japanese Americans and the enduring legacy of Executive Order 9066. *Amerasia Journal 19*(1), 7–35.

National Asian Pacific American Legal Consortium. (1996). *Audit of violence against Asian Pacific Americans: The consequences of intolerance in America.* Washington, DC: National Asian Pacific American Legal Consortium.

Okamura, R. (1974). Background and history of the repeal campaign. *Amerasia, 2,* 73–94.

Ong, P., & Hee, S. J. (1993). The growth of the Asian Pacific American population: Twenty million in 2020. In *The state of Asian Pacific America: Policy issues to the year 2020.* Los Angeles: LEAP Asian Pacific American Public Policy Institute, Asian American Studies Center, University of California at Los Angeles.

Reischauer, E. O. (1981). *The Japanese.* Cambridge: Harvard University Press.

Tokezawa, Y. I. (1995). *Breaking the silence: Redress and Japanese American ethnicity.* Ithaca: Cornell University Press.

U.S. Bureau of the Census. (1991). *Race and Hispanic origin.* In *1990 Census profile,* No. 2. Washington, DC: U.S. Government Printing Office.

U.S. Bureau of the Census. (1993). *1990 census of population, Asians and Pacific Islanders in the United States* (PC-3-5). Washington, DC: U.S. Government Printing Office.

U.S. Commission on Civil Rights. (1992). *Civil rights issues facing Asian Americans in the 1990s.* Washington, DC: U.S. Government Printing Office.

U.S. Commission on Wartime Relocation and Internment of Civilians. (1982). *Persons justice denied.* Washington, DC: U.S. Government Printing Office.

Weglen, M. (1976). *Years of infamy: The untold story of America's concentration camps.* New York: William Morrow.

Yip, A. (1996, August 2). Defining Asian Americans. *Asian Week.*

9

The Pilipino American Community: Organizing for Change

ROYAL F. MORALES

The challenges of the approaching twenty-first century are more critical than ever for the Pilipino communities in the United States.[1] Attacks on immigrants, so-called welfare reform, and increased racism make organizing in our community more important than ever. In reviewing the literature on Pilipino community organizing and development, one finds very few articles, perhaps because the few Pilipino and non-Pilipino organizers do not consider this area interesting despite the many activities of "social work organizations." Maybe it is also because the schools of social work and other institutions are not targeting the Pilipino community, which is often identified as a "model minority" and is not seen as needing organization and mobilization.

This chapter presents some community organizing experiences and observations and discusses and explores some tools, strategies, and principles utilized to respond to the various human service needs of the community. Based on my professional and personal experiences as a social worker and community activist in Los Angeles, I see the areas to be covered as: demographic growth pattern and profile of Pilipino Americans; human service needs and problems; waves of immigration and history; and some community organizing issues, concerns, and recommendations.

Community Profile and Problems

The Pilipino American community, like other groups, is rapidly growing and is confronted with social, health, economic, and welfare problems symptomatic of those faced by the greater society. Often denied, hidden, and pushed aside by the community itself and by the mainstream health and welfare institutions, these difficulties are further complicated by negative stereotypes, the model minority myth, and the glass ceiling.

In Los Angeles, the United Way conducted a study of several Asian and Pacific Islander groups, including Pilipino Americans. Summarizing its findings, the report on the Specific Service Needs of Each Asian Pacific Community listed priority needs and recommendations in terms of the following categories:

- Community resource development and advocacy
- Health and mental health services
- Services for the elderly
- Family services
- Services for youth
- Employment and language education

The specific needs and service recommendations for Pilipino Americans were as follows. Among youth, identified needs include delinquency prevention programs, gang outreach, recreational activities, and stay-in-school efforts. Pilipino elderly need social recreation services, transportation, and health and nutritional counseling. Also important are job retraining, legal aid, single parent counseling, shelter for abused women, low-cost housing, and child care. Military wives and mail-order brides of interacial marriages may also experience social adjustment problems. New immigrants and undocumented aliens are in need of legal assistance.

All four identified priority needs would be most effective if delivered from agencies with a Pilipino focus, from a multiservice center within the community. Youth centers similar to Search to Involve Pilipino Americans (SIPA) in Central Los Angeles are needed in other areas of high Pilipino population. Increased bilingual staffing is also important.[2]

The 1960s marked the beginning of dramatic population growth of Pilipinos in America, thus the reference to the Pilipino American experience "from colonials to immigrants to citizens." The growth is closely tied to several historical events: population explosion and implosion in the Philippines; the push-pull forces of people immigrating to other countries; and the impact and influence of the U.S. Immigration Act of 1965. The act (1) redefined and broadened the various categories of immigrants focusing primarily on professionals ("brain drain") and family reunification; (2) shifted the geographic source of new immigrants to Asia and Latin America; and (3) increased the quota of immigrants from the Philippines to a maximum of 20,000.

For the Philippines, the quota increase, from 100 (1946) to 20,000 led a flood of people to apply for immigration to the United States and other parts of the world, and the push-pull forces of immigration caused the population shift to be quick and dramatic. Consider the following growth pattern of Pilipino Americans for three decades in Los Angeles, California, and the United States:

	LA City	LA County	California	USA
1970	18,625	33,459	138,859	344,060
1980	43,713	100,849	357,492	744,690
1990	88,889	223,276	731,585	1,406,770

Given this trend, the Asian American Health Forum, Inc., of San Francisco projected that by the year 2020, the population of Pilipinos in the United States will be 3,354,990.[3] If this projection is startling, so is the dramatic growth of Pilipinos throughout the United States, as of 1989 and compared with 1980 census data of selected states:[4]

Hawaii	168,682	Washington	43,799
Illinois	64,224	Virginia	35,067
New York	62,259	Texas	34,350
New Jersey	53,146	Maryland	19,376

Bill Tamayo indicated that the visa waiting list in the Philippines as of January 1992 was 472,714, much more than in Mexico,[5] and that over 60,000 immigrated to America in 1992; and the other cause is a 5.0 fertility rate of Pilipino Americans between 1986 and 1990. In addition, it is clear that the population distribution of Pilipino Americans can be characterized as concentrating in the urban inner-city enclaves and dispersed into the suburban areas of the various states. Over 70 percent are foreign born and primarily speak Pilipino (Tagalog), which is the third most spoken language in California and in the top six in the United States.[6]

Some preliminary but significant social, economic, and education data from the 1990 census are as follows:

Poverty: 9 percent, as compared with 7.1 percent in 1980

Unemployment: 8 percent in 1989 as compared with 4.8 percent in 1980

Median household income (2 or more workers): $25,696, compared with $21,926 in 1980, and the Asian Pacific Islander MHI of $36,100, in 1989

Education: High college education, next to the Japanese and Chinese American educational levels

The lack of current data and the delay in reporting by the Census Bureau is unfortunate and detrimental to the needed response for human services and related socioeconomic needs of Pilipino Americans. As in the past, by the time census reports are out, the problems have multiplied and the planning and organizing are delayed and useless because they are obsolete.

Overview of the Waves of Immigration

Fully understanding the Pilipino American experience requires a brief overview of U.S.-Philippine history and relations. Often unknown and misunderstood by the greater society, the Pilipino American experience and community are about struggles, survival, and victory. This is a story that has to be told and told again as a significant and important part of the American history of multiculturalism.

At the conclusion of the Spanish-American War and the defeat of the Spanish Armada at Manila Bay in 1898, the United States cheaply "acquired" the Philippines from Spain as provided for in the Treaty of Paris. In addition, another provision of the treaty was for the victor, the United States, to decide the political fate and future of the new colony. Thus began the U.S.-Philippine "special and unique relationship" that lasted for almost a century.[7] To Pilipino nationalists and historians, the "sealed fate" handed down by Spain was detrimental to the social, economic, and political well-being of the country.

The first wave was the colonial workers, recruited and imported between 1900 and 1934 under the Sacada system, a replica of the eighteenth-century indentured servitude applied to Europeans. During this period strong anti-Japanese feelings and attitudes resulted in laws decreasing the immigration of this Asian people. Their absence left a need for replacements—the Pilipinos filled the requirement for young, single, able-bodied, noneducated workers for the plantations of Hawaii and the vegetable-citrus farms of California and other Western states. Over 100,000 were imported as the "brawn power" in addition to the thousands of students and government-supported *penstonados* who while in America learned the skills of administering political and educational programs and services for their developing country.

Like their immigrant predecessors during the Depression years, the Pilipinos, limited in their use of English, "neither citizens nor aliens," faced racism, exploitation, and oppression. Faced with hard labor and low pay, they were unwanted by the labor organizations, and from one season to the next, they moved as contract laborers throughout the West Coast. Perceived as competitors, they were threats to economic prosperity, as they were "taking away jobs" and were social threats for "marrying white women"; this translated into personal and institutional racism, which ended in bloody anti-Pilipino race riots. Having no civil rights, Pilipinos were not allowed to own property, to marry white women, or to vote and were ghettoized; in the end a law was passed repatriating the Pilipinos to the Philippines. Few Pilipinos took up the offer because it meant their return to the United States would be illegal.

Carlos Bulosan's *America Is in the Heart* and Carey McWilliams's *Brothers Under the Skin* depict this part of the story of the Pilipino in America. This wave, through difficult times and sacrifices, contributed to America and the agribusiness and city entrepreneurs; they paid their taxes and shared their cultural values and traditions; with their hard-earned money, they educated relatives and helped their families build homes and start businesses.

The second wave started after Philippine independence (1964) and into the Cold War of the 1950s, and as a result of U.S.-Philippine military and economic agreements. Each year, according to the agreement, thousands of young, able-bodied males were recruited into the armed forces, especially the navy, to serve on ships and at various military academies and naval installations throughout the world. Known as brawn military power, their job classifications qualified them for menial jobs—in the galleys, in the cabins, and in the kitchen and yard of the White House. Other types of jobs and upward mobility were slow in coming.

Timothy Ingram's October 1970 article in *Washington Monthly,* "The Floating Plantation," presents the hard struggles and condition of life of the Pilipino in the navy. Like the old-timers and pioneers, the Pilipinos in the armed forces contributed to the mission of America, "making the world safer" and enhancing the status of the country as a military power. They also established community enclaves on various military installations and bases, thus keeping their value of family togetherness for support. They also sent money to those left behind for their education and related family needs. The sons and daughters of this wave are now filling up colleges and universities. Moreover, they pay their taxes and enhance the multiculturalism of the country.

A third parallel wave of immigrants started in the late 1950s and escalated dramatically and rapidly in the 1960s. As indicated earlier, the push-pull forces included the socioeconomic and political turmoil in the country during this period: poverty, high unemployment, the Vietnam War, martial law, and the unprecedented impact of the U.S. Immigration Act of 1965. The professional immigrants—medical doctors, Ph.D.s in the social sciences, dentists, engineers, accountants, pharmacists, and lawyers contributed to the brain drain of the country while it was developing.

This wave provided yet another dimension to the multiculturalism of the United States and the Pilipino American community. Rich in education, talent, and youth, Pilipinos are contributing to the development of the country—through taxes, community enclaves, and organizations, business development, and political activities. Their children are in universities and are making their presence known with their money and status.

The fourth wave is known as the "political exiles and asylees," referring to the impact of the ten-year martial law under the presidential administration of the late Ferdinand E. Marcos. This occurred during the 1970s and 1980s as thousands (more than 15,000) left the Philippines or were forced out because of the imposition of martial law. This wave included politicians, military personnel, intellectuals, teachers, students, and community activists against the new order. With their political perspectives, resources, connections, and resolutions, they organized and developed organizations with a primary goal: to topple Marcos and bring democracy back to the Philippines. This segment of the Pilipino American community educated and enlightened America to the economic and political plight of Pilipinos, articulated issues, established businesses, and paid their taxes.

1970s: Decade of Events

In the late 1960s and into the 1970s, after the L.A. Watts riots and the movement for civil rights, ethnic studies, and affirmative action, our involvement began with community organizing in response to community conflicts and problems. Facing up to the challenges of the time as a social worker for a youth agency supported by the United Way, I joined the ranks of the activists whose watchwords and slogans were: eliminate ghettoism, racism, alienation, violence, and economic poverty; and end the Vietnam War. It was an era of trying to win two wars: the war in Vietnam and the war on poverty in America—both great dilemmas, unsatisfactorily resolved.

Targeting South Central Los Angeles, the focus of community organizing was to resolve and respond to age-old community problems: economic and educational disparities, institutional racism, ethnic relationships, and structural and organizational changes toward community empowerment. One-to-one approaches and segmented methods of human service were insufficient, we later found out. The combination of macro and micro approaches—community organizing and empowerment of the community—would have lasting results.

Personally and professionally, I found a gap and a weakness. My social work preparation and training in community organizing was limited and lacking in experience. After so many years in the community, I used the fruitful and practical experiences in community collaboration and interethnic relationships as a basis for work with the Asian and Pacific Islander and the Pilipino American communities.

The search for answers, approaches, and community support in the Asian and Pacific Islander communities was assisted by a conference held at UCLA in the early 1970s, called ACT I, Asians Coming Together. The conference brought together human service workers, students, community representatives, teachers, and other observers from the various Asian American communities. Participants at this gathering, including myself, started with questions, suspicions, and guarded confrontations. Fortunately, with patience and understanding, ACT I ended as a community vehicle for constructive dialogue on common problems, issues, and program development. For me it was the beginning of ethnic awareness and interaction with the greater Asian American community.

It was the turning point of my lasting associational and organizational involvement with the minority movement, leading to social activism among the Pilipino American community. The experience and feelings associated with ACT I were summarized by one of the Pilipino-American leaders: *Any pagsasabing tapat ay pagsasamang maluat* ("a sincere dialogue guarantees a lasting association").

A decade of "happenings," the 1970s were also a time of lasting contributions, of strong bonds between the campus and the community in organizing for responsive leadership and cooperative activities. For me, the promise, dreams, and visions were translated into the thrust and challenges of organizing developing organizations, and serving on boards or in leadership positions of the Council of Oriental Organizations (COO, later to be renamed Council of Asian Pacific Organizations) and its service arm, the Oriental Service Center (currently headed by a Pilipino American); the Asian American Education Commission of the Los Angeles Unified School District (currently headed by a Pilipino American); the Los Angeles Day of the Lotus Festival (still being celebrated); the Asian American Community Mental Health Training Center (now defunct because of Reaganomics); the Search to Involve Pilipino Americans (SIPA, currently headed by a Pilipino American); a now defunct Pacific Asian Coalition, headed by a Pilipino American; and the currently active Asian Pacific Planning Council (APPCON).

Through the years, other involvements and activities led us to assist educational groups in the development of Asian American studies and the writing of syllabi and ethnic/culture-sensitive materials for elementary and college levels. In 1974, *Makibaka: The Pilipino American Struggle,* which I authored, was published as an introductory book on the Pilipino American experience and history. It served as a reference to contemporary community problems, and it encouraged other Pilipino Americans to write their experiences and related stories.

Related organizing/learning activities include the directing of the Asian American Community Mental Health Training Center (AMTRAC), which was established through the collaboration of the Asian American Social Workers, community members of the Asian American communities, students, and faculty members of the local School of Social Work, which was funded by the National Institute of Mental Health (NIMH). The center provided needed scholarships, training, mentoring, field work placement, and supervision of over 180 students of Asian and Pacific Islander heritage for a decade. The center, as a community-based organization (CBO), was a base for networking between the campus and the community; a forum for discussing issues and related social work and community concerns, for activism and advocacy; and leadership development, for both students and community representatives.

Many of the coactivities were directed at the development of Pilipino American studies, advocating for the inclusion of relevant education that reflected the historical and cultural perspectives of Pilipino Americans and the recruitment and hiring of bilingual and bicultural personnel. Accordingly, within the framework of the campus community connection (3Cs) we/I played the "mentor/role model" in leadership development and training. Easily forgotten and even taken for granted, the "role models" inspire, catalyze, lead, and make things happen—at times in the forefront and other times in the background. Activists and advocates, they establish the contacts and attract others to join in the spirit of *bayanihan*—collective efforts—for worthy community causes. In the 1970s, the impact of the role models was felt far and wide: locally, regionally, and nationally. They created a basis for some noteworthy united fronts, building coalitions and making use of their own resources (self-help) and "piggy back-ing" on regional/national conferences held by mainstream organizations.

1980s: Responding to the Retrenchment

If the 1970s were a decade of promise, the 1980s were a time of retreat, retrenchment, and curtailment tied to the social, political, and ideological climate of conservatism. It was characterized by the chipping away and dismantling of minority programs on campus and in the community. There was the false and misleading assumption that the problems of racism, poverty, and education had been resolved and that minorities and people of color had gained enough and no longer needed assistance. Funds for poverty programs decreased, affirmative action and minority scholarships diminished, ethnic studies were curtailed almost to a halt, and the list goes on.

As the priorities of the 1980s shifted, so did the push and significance of social action and the activism of community organizing. Deeply affected, some of us scram-bled for whatever jobs were to be had and joined unemployment lines with the nagging feeling of betrayal and being left out in the cold. However, the spirit, the dreams for social change, and the visions continued, perhaps at a slower pace, but still daring to move on and push for the efforts already started. By the middle of the 1980s, con-cerned Pilipino Americans and new faces renewed their spirit to organize the confer-ence "Pilipino Americans: Facing Up to Our Challenges," held in Wilmington, California. The issues and concerns included problems associated with youth and their growing up, the elderly, the new immigrants, the college students, and community or-ganizing. The spirited conference ended with a list of recommendations.[8]

Barriers to Organizing

The workshop on community organizing resolved that the community, which is now deluged with hundreds of organizations, *must* organize, proactively, and face the so-cioeconomic problems faced by youth, the elderly, and immigrants. Understandably, organizing is a difficult but a challenging task in a community that has overcome mis-takes and failures because of unresolved and conflicting agendas, uncompromising "personalities," and the negative side of *pakikisama* and other related cultural prac-tices by Pilipinos. Deeply rooted in aged traditions and culture of the MA-I people based on such codes as the *Maragtas* and *Kalantiaw, pakikisama* is neatly intertwined with the basic and encompassing value *bayanihan* (collective spirit of togetherness). Values are practiced within the circles of loyalties—first, serving and protecting the immediate family circle; second, the extended family of relatives; third, the *compadre* and *comadre* circle (Spanish influence), and finally, the outer circle, neighbors, and community residents of the *barangay* (village/neighborhood).

The misuse of *pakikisama* is further complicated when it is operationalized by someone or a group who supports or promotes a person, a group, or a cause based on a particular loyalty regardless of a predictable negative outcome. In an attempt to explain the Pilipino values—conflicts and dilemmas—writers make reference to the Pilipino's "desire for smooth interpersonal relations" (SIR) in conjunction with such related values as *utang na loob* (debt of gratitude or obligation), *amor propio* (being extra nice and self-esteem), *hiya* (shame and face saving), and *bahalana* (fatalism) attitudes and behaviors.[9]

Other barriers to organizing include the more than eighty-seven languages or dialects; although Tagalog is the official language, Pilipinos prefer to speak what is familiar and, when appropriate, sharply shift to the popular use of "Taglish," a mixture of Tagalog and English. Non-Pilipinos find this amusingly smart. If the values and cultural traditions are in conflict with each other, so are the American values of individualism, assertiveness, and outright competition affecting the organizing processes. Moreover, there is the long-term negative impact of foreign domination and colonization—over 350 years of Spanish rule; almost 100 years by the United States; 3 years by the English, and 4 years by the Japanese. As a result, the colonization, oppression, and exploitation transformed the Pilipino psyche, emotional makeup, and behavior, typically described by sociologists, historians, and writers as "colonial mentality," "crab mentality," and *ningas cogon* (easy to ignite, quick to disintegrate, or no follow-through). These kept the Pilipino disunited and slow to progress and engendered low self-esteem. During the workshop, community organizing and development were recognized as efforts to identify problems, needs, and solutions, however limited, short-sighted, or short lived. To the questions of how efficient previous attempts have been, who was organizing, and what are the basic knowledge base and experiences, the recommendations and answers to the questions were as follows:

Very few social workers are focusing on Pilipino concerns, and fewer still are trained community organizers;

A handful of organizers must deal with a wide range of ethnic and regional perspectives, do routine and patch-up jobs, and they disappear or burn out rapidly;

The efforts of the non-Pilipino professionals and volunteers serving the community need to be coordinated.

Some proactive recommendations included these:

- A need to establish services with accountability, credibility, and primary responsibility to the community;
- Pilipino Americans must organize by building linkages and bridges with other ethnic communities, accepting differences, and recognizing commonalities and approaches to organizing.

In response to the question of barriers to effective community organizing, the participants acknowledged these:

- Regionalism and diversity based on geography/languages and place of birth in the Philippines;

- Ego pride, social status consciousness; individual quests for power, praise seeking rather than promoting collective community power;
- Inability to identify and capture resources and political, social, economic, and educational information;
- Lack of communication and linkage among leaders, which allows self-interest to supersede community efforts;
- Stereotype of a divided community and disunity among groups: the various groups of seniors, students, immigrants, professionals, and the American born versus the Philippine born.

"In a very negative way, the 'colonial mentality' and 'crab mentality' have been identified as the core of the problem around organizing. They came about as a result of centuries of colonization, by Spain, America, and Japan, and through exploitation and suppression that created self-depreciation and disharmonious relationships among the people, between regions, and in the leadership hierarchy. The colonial mentality disregarded the historical relevance of ethnicity and pride, and devalued traditional cultures and history," the report concluded.

Qualities of an Organizer

In view of the difficult tasks in organizing, a good organizer should have several critical qualities to organize successfully. In no particular order, the report enumerated the following:

- Recognize cultural and individual differences, minimizing their impact and emphasizing similarities;
- Tolerance, sensitivity, and an open mind, to allow for better communication;
- An ability to cope with fragmentation and frustration and confidently pursue objectives despite obstacles and disappointments;
- Be a motivator, listener; be proactive and creative;
- Personal knowledge and familiarity of issues; understanding and learning the history and roots of the problems or the group;
- Taking the initiative to develop a person-to-person approach to constituency building.

Other items in the report include sustaining and maintaining interest in the organizing process and recommendations for the participants, as action-oriented challenges after the conference. Some significant recommendations are as follows:

- Roundtable discussions to create common goals and objectives;
- Issues and problems should be brought to a body where ideas and changes can occur, based on self-determination, consensus, and democratic process;
- Outreach to other organizations and other ethnic groups;

- A working definition of community organizing should be developed and long-range goals established;
- A political force and new leaders should be developed.

It is worth noting that following the 1985 conference, two politically oriented organizations were established—Republican and Democratic in affiliation—which were active in local, statewide, and national partisan politics. Successes and failures of these groups have not been assessed.

If there are community organizing skills and experiences to be learned and if there are groups of significance to be studied, researchers and students should look into some local and national organizations—some of which are fraternal associations, historical societies, youth groups in San Francisco and Los Angeles, medical and nurses associations, and veterans groups. These groups have gone through some ups and downs in their organizational formation and development, according to media reports and through the Pilipino "bamboo telegraph," *tsismis* (gossips).

Further studies should focus on the role of Pilipinos in labor/union organizing (such as Larry Itliong and Phil Vera Cruz, Pilipino Organizing Committee) activities of the farmers, later to be known as the United Farm Workers; the Alaskan fisheries (Wards Cove case); and the union organizing in the cities where there are many Pilipino Americans. Similarly, there are related areas to explore: organizing efforts and dynamics in related nonprofit groups; the church/clergy community; and informal networks: "Bagoong Connection," *kapihan* (coffee meetings) and "breakfast meetings" and college and university student groups and movements.

Future Challenges

The future of community organizing in the Pilipino American community and the involvement of Pilipino Americans in the process are more than just a concept. As long as problems and issues confront the elderly, youth, women, the physically challenged, the undocumented, the at-risks or the healthy, and the victims of wars—the Amerasian (Pilipino) children and the veterans of World War II—community organizing will be a relevant strategy toward a healthier and stronger society. What then are the challenges?

- For the Schools of Social Work, Council of Social Work Education, and undergraduate schools to fully address the community organizing needs; do research, gather data, and develop a basic knowledge base that reflects community needs; and recruit, support, and challenge students to be COs;
- For the mainstream social work agencies and the community-based agencies to utilize creatively the experiences and expertise of the few Pilipino American organizers as consultants, volunteers, and mentors;
- For the schools and community-based organizations (CBOs) to develop and implement a basic curriculum (campus community connection) with the following content:

1. Pilipino Americans: from colonials to immigrants to citizens; experiences in racism, civil rights, cultural pluralism, and acculturation processes; conflicts and confrontation; Pilipino values versus American, finding the balance;
2. Contemporary problems: community, family, individual; micro and macro levels; strength, contributors, resources, community networks, and related organizations;
3. Profile of the community: waves and patterns of immigrations, the Sacada "brawn power" workers; the military "brawn stewards and cabin boys," the "professional brain drain"; and the martial law "political exiles and refugees"; impact of colonization by Spain, the United States, Japan; the MA-I people and culture and history; and the demographic and socioeconomic characteristics and related data.

• For the schools, organizations, students, and practitioners to operationalize the "paradigm shift" and incorporate in theory, knowledge, and practice such concepts as multiculturalism, bilingual and bicultural competency, and ethnicity and identity empowerment of the community through justice, peace, self-determination; and civil rights.

Readings and references should be supplemented with anecdotes by guest speakers and lecturers to speak on current issues and subjects that are of historical importance to the Pilipino American community and in the Philippines.

Community Organizing Activities in the Community

In some parts of California, the documented series of serious problems sparked some positive actions from the Pilipino American mainstream communities. Agency surveys, university studies, and anecdotal newspaper articles presented the extent of the problems and exploded the "model minority myth." Indeed there are deep-rooted problems impacting on individuals, families, and the community. These problems are heavily interrelated with the economic downturn and employee layoffs as well as subtle racism, anger, and backlashes directed against the legal and illegal immigrants and newcomers. The 1980s and 1990s can be characterized as decades of cutbacks of services and negative legislation; state and national targeting of social services, welfare, educational and health services, legal and illegal immigrants; and antiaffirmative action campaigns directed against women and minorities.

Meanwhile, in the Pilipino American community, be it in the rural or urban areas, the intense problems include the elderly and the Pilipino World War II veterans who did not obtain their equity benefits; women; teen suicide and pregnancy; school dropouts, youth violence, and gang activities; abuse of alcohol, drugs, and tobacco by some youth and elderly people; the startling growth of HIV/AIDS; physical and mental health; unemployment and poverty, and more.

Responding to these problems, some concerned individuals and agency staff have intensified their community organizing and delivery of services. Grassroot organizers and professionals, challenging community denials, came together and responded to the problems the best they knew how—self-determined and self-directed, utilizing their resources, along with their search for continuing funding. Some organizing efforts are worth noting:

- In San Jose, in the summer of 1992, the Filipino Youth Coalition, a grassroots and youth-oriented program, came "together to help foster pride within the County of Santa Clara and particularly in the Filipino Community... with the dream to build for our future, an active program that provides ongoing projects that foster the heritage of Filipinos." After two years of providing limited services and funded primarily by the youth, parents, and some organizations, city funding became available and sustained the financial support. One program of FYC is Project Peace (Pilipino Educational and Community Experience) whose goal is to "stem gang activity through the formation of culturally sensitive support groups, academic/career planning, and crisis intervention programs strategically located at Mt. Pleasant, Silver Creek, and Independence High Schools, as well as in Ocala and Morrill Middle Schools."[10]
- In the summer of 1996, FYC became the lead agency for a collaborative and coalition building conference, held at San Jose for seven youth-serving agencies. The Filipino Youth Providers Service Conference was the beginning of an organizing effort "to build and strengthen the community" and was cosponsored by the City of San Jose Parks, Recreation, and Neighborhood Services. Representation came from the Filipino Youth Coalition of San Jose Search to Involve Pilipino Americans of Los Angeles, Filipinos for Affirmative Action of Oakland, Filipino American Social Services of Vallejo, West Bay Filipino Multi-Services Corporation of San Francisco, Union of Pan Asian Communities and PASACAT of San Diego, and Filipino Bayanihan Resource Center of Daly City.[11]
- In Vallejo, Solano County, by 1992, the Filipino Social Services of Solano County Inc. started out of a partnership coalition project with the City of Vallejo's Fighting Back Partnership, addressing issues of drugs and alcohol abuse. The program strove to be culturally sensitive and inclusive of all various subgroups within the Pilipino community. From a status of a task force, FASS enriched its objectives toward the youth, as a multi-service center serving seniors and immigrants, and as a community resource. The Youth Internship Project, run and administered by the youth, propelled youth to organize and mobilize as a result of a youth-oriented survey that revealed the extent of youth problems—alcohol and drug abuse, sexual activity and pregnancy, youth violence and gangs, and generational gaps among families. Further, FASS organized and developed services like parenting classes; career conference; youth and parents dialogue, *Mag Usap Tayo* (Let's Talk), *Magkaisa Tayo* (Being One and United), and Youth to Youth Conference; the seniors' nutrition program; and immigration assistance. FASS is supported by

Solano/Napa Agency on the Aging and various consultants and individuals from the community.[12]

• In Oakland, for the past twenty-three years, the Filipinos for Affirmative Action have organized around rights of immigrants and minorities, employment of new-comers, reunification of families, education, and related social services. In the forefront of social justice and advocacy for civil rights, FAA is active in coalitions like the East Bay Asian Consortium, the Coalition for Immigrant and Refugee Rights, Filipinos Against Proposition 187, Filipino Civil Rights Advocates, (FILCRA), Filipino Youth Services Coalition, Asian Youth Services Network, Youth/Violence Prevention Coalition, Asian Law-Caucus, Immigration Clinic, Filipino Veterans WW II Support Network, and more. Among its credible organizing efforts are Recovery for East Bay Asian Youth (REBAY), working "with youth and their families to increase resiliency and protective factors to reduce the likelihood of alcohol, tobacco, and other drug use... youth experience multiple stresses such as family unemployment and underemployment, language and cultural barriers, racism, violence in their families or neighborhoods; and inter-generational conflicts which increase risks of dropping out of school, teen pregnancy, gang involvement, and substance abuse." In addition, FAA's program includes Girls Development Project in Union City middle schools, targeting at-risk youth with academic and behavioral problems; prevention alternatives focus on HIV/AIDS education, martial arts, basketball, weight training, field trips, peer support group discussions, and individual counseling. In short, FAA, with its multiple funding, seeks "to serve the most needy through our employment and immigration services... to maintain stability in immigrant families by helping youth weather the many challenges placed before them... to mobilize the Filipino community into a broader coalition of activists in defense of the many civil rights that are in jeopardy."[13]

• SIPA (Search to Involve Pilipino Americans), a Los Angeles community-based organization, was established in the early 1970s in response to issues facing youth. In the recent past, additional community needs challenged SIPA to diversify and expand its services—enhancing the quality of life of Pilipino Americans by providing resources, services, and advocating for community issues. SIPA offers an array of services, such as individual, group, and parent counseling; educational assistance; cultural and recreational programs; promoting healthier lifestyles through health education and preventive services that are linguistically and culturally appropriate; playing an active role in the development of neighborhood services, housing, community gardens, historical murals, and strong advocacy and networking activities with other human services in Los Angeles County; leadership training for youth and statewide networking and organizing.[14]

• In San Diego, through the Union of Pan Asian Communities (UPAC), an agency serving various Asian, Pacific, and Southeast Asian groups, organizing efforts evolved around documented problems impacting on Pilipino Americans. These include *gangs*—the fastest growing and highest rate of suspects who have committed murders and aggravated assaults in the API community (San Diego Police); *alcohol, tobacco* and other *drugs* (ATOD)—20 percent of Filipino youth enrolled in San Diego Unified School District have ridden in a car driven by someone who has been drinking alcohol and 57 percent tried smoking cigarettes; *suicide*—15.6 percent, as reported in a 1993 study by CDC/SDUSD, have seriously contemplated suicide, with 23 percent attempting it, compared to national data of 8 percent attempted (CBS News, 9/26/96); live births by teen mothers have the highest rate in San Diego according to the San Diego County Department of Health Services, 1994. Statewide information from the Vital Statistics of California, 1990, confirms this observation that Pilipino mothers have the highest birthrate among Asian and Pacific Islander teenagers.[15]

• In San Francisco, the West Bay Pilipino Multi-Service Corporation, an agency that started in the early 1970s, began its work around the Mission District, south of Market, focusing on similar problems identified in other areas. West Bay's organizing and networking efforts centered on individual and community services for youth, the elderly, the new immigrants, HIV/AIDS, housing development, extensive interethnic relationships in the San Francisco area, and linguistic prevention and education on ATOD.[16]

In conclusion, it is very apparent that the Pilipino American community and population will dramatically expand, and in the process of transition and Americanization, their lives will be affected by social, labor, economic, political, civil rights, health, and welfare issues. If the indicators are correct there are unending and unfinished agendas, challenges, and opportunities for community organizing. In such a state of affairs, necessity dictates the need to train and develop responsive and proactive community organizers, social workers, advocates, and policy makers and to join hands to deliver direct services, organize strategies, evaluate the processes and products, research the experience, and support worthwhile causes.

Notes

1. The term *Pilipino American* is used rather than "Filipino American" because it is related to the ethnic consciousness that emerged in the 1960s and 1970s during the civil rights movement. The spelling *Pilipino* is associated with ethnic pride and the discovery of ethnic roots and heritage, like the terms *black, chicano,* and *Asian.* Activists further asserted that this spelling should be used because there was no "F" in the alphabets/languages of the MA-I people before Spain colonized the islands.

2. United Way, *Needs Assessment on the Asian Pacific Islander Communities* (Los Angeles, 1988).

3. Asian American/Health Forum, Inc., "Population Projections for API" (San Francisco, April 1989).

4. Asian Week, "Asian Pacifics in America" (San Francisco: Grant Printing House, August 1991).

5. Bill Tamayo, "Legal and Civil Rights Issues in 2020: Civil Rights Policy," *The State of Asian Pacific America,* LEAP Asian Pacific American Public Policy Institute and UCLA Asian American Studies Center, Leadership Education for Asian Pacifics, 1993.

6. *Los Angeles Times,* "Land of Language," July 5, 1993, Sec. E.

7. Walter LaFeber, *The New Empire: An Interpretation of American Expansion, 1860–1989* (Ithaca: Cornell University Press, 1963).

8. PANA, "Facing Up to Our Challenges," Los Angeles, March 1985.

9. Pal Hunt et al., *Sociology in the Philippine Setting* (Quezon City, Philippines: Phoenix Publishing House, 1971).

10. *Filipino Youth Coalition.* [Brochure]. 1658 E. Capital Expressway, #568, San Jose, CA 95121.

11. Filipino Youth Providers Service Conference Program, July 17–19, 1996, San Jose State University.

12. Fighting Back Partnership, "Filipino Task Force's Youth Survey on Alcohol, Drugs, Sex, Gangs and Family," and Filipino American Social Services, Income Brochure, 505 Santa Clara St., Vallejo, CA 91590.

13. Filipinos for Affirmative Action, "Annual Report, July 1, 1994–June 30, 1995" and Brochure, 310 8th St., Suite 308, Oakland, CA 94607.

14. SIPA, brochures and related information. 3200-A W. Temple St., Los Angeles, CA 90026.

15. Union of Pan Asian Communities, brochures and related articles, 1031 25th Street, San Diego, CA 92102.

16. West Bay Pilipino Multi-Service Corporation, brochure and related articles, 965 Mission St., Suite 500, San Francisco, CA 94103

Suggested Readings

Barrugh, Herbert, Robert W. Gardner, and Michael I. Levin. *Asian Pacific Islanders in the U.S.* New York: Russell Sage, 1993.

Boradus, Emory S. "Anti-Pilipino Race Riots." In *Letters in Exile: An Introductory Reader in the History of Pilipinos in America,* pp. 51–62. Los Angeles: Asian American Studies Center, 1976.

Buaken, Manuel. *I Have Lived with the American People.* Caldwell, Idaho: Caxton, 1948.

Bulosan, Carlos, *America Is in the Heart.* Seattle: University of Washington Press, 1947.

Clifford, Sister Mary Dorita. "The Hawaiian Sugar Planters' Association and Filipino Exclusion." In *Letters in Exile,* pp. 74–89.

Corpuz, Onofre D. *The Philippines.* Englewood Cliffs, N.J.: Prentice-Hall, 1965.

Friend, Theodore. *Between Two Empires: The Ordeal of the Philippines, 1926–1946.* New Haven: Yale University Press, 1965.

Gall, Susan B., and Timothy L., eds. *Statistical Record of Asian Americans.* Detroit: Gale Research, 1993.

Lasker, Bruno. *Filipino Immigration to the Continental U.S. and Hawaii.* Chicago: University of Chicago Press, 1993.

McWilliams, Carey. *Brothers under the Skin,* rev. ed. Boston: Little, Brown, 1946. *Factories in the Field.* Boston: Little, Brown, 1940.

Melendy, H. Brett. "California's Discrimination Against Pilipinos." In *Letters in Exile,* pp. 35–43.

Morales, Royal F. Makibaka: *The Pilipino American Struggle.* Los Angeles: Mountainview, 1974.

Poole, Fred, and Vanzi, Max. *Revolution in the Philippines: The U.S. in a Hall of Cracked Mirrors.* New York: McGraw-Hill, 1984.

10

Living in the U.S.A.: Central American Immigrant Communities in the United States

CARLOS B. CÓRDOVA

Central American Migrations to the United States

Central Americans have a long-standing tradition of migrating to the United States that dates back more than a century. Central Americans have migrated to the United States as a result of political and economic factors that have affected their countries throughout the years. Economic and political instability have created the right conditions for Central Americans to migrate to this country. Significant numbers of early immigrants arrived in the United States during the 1930s and 1940s and resettled in San Francisco, Los Angeles, Houston, and New Orleans, escaping their failing economies, political persecution, and the lack of personal freedoms.

These immigrants, as active members of social migration networks, helped establish the social and economic foundations in the Latin American immigrant communities that would benefit the future generations of Central Americans who would later arrive in the United States. It is important to note that Central Americans relied mostly on family networks rather than ethnic, neighborhood, village, or national migration networks during the early migrations to the United States. Furthermore, many of these immigrants were members of the urban middle classes and had relatively high levels of education. Many were intellectuals, teachers, labor organizers, political dissidents, or exiled military officers who were not in agreement with their Central American governments.

A few decades later, during the 1960s, Central American immigration to the United States significantly increased as a result of the new policies of the Immigration Act of 1965, which created immigrant quotas to countries that historically had not been included in U.S. immigration policies. The 1965 law encouraged professionals and skilled laborers to migrate to the United States and permitted the resettlement of numerous young working-class and middle-class Central American families. Many U.S. cities had well-established Latin American immigrant communities that attracted Central Americans to their neighborhoods. Newcomers resettled in the Latin American neighborhoods because of the existing social networks, familiar cultural traditions, and support systems that were maintained by the Latin American immigrants residing in those communities. The new Central American arrivals further developed the economic, social, and cultural structures of the Latin American ethnic communities, networks, and economic enclaves in San Francisco, Los Angeles, Houston, New York, New Jersey, New Orleans, and Washington, D.C. The impact of the new immigrants to the already established Latin American communities was clearly discernible during the late 1960s and early 1970s.

The influx of Central American immigrants to this country increased at an extremely rapid pace in the late 1970s and early 1980s. Presently, Central America ranks as the second Latin American region contributing legal and undocumented migrations to the United States. Before the 1970s, most Central American immigrants arrived with legal immigration status as permanent residents or with student visas. The U.S. Bureau of the Census has reported that the total number of legal immigrants from Central America counted in the 1990 census was 1,323,830 persons. Of the total figures only 277,731 were U.S. born; 1,046,099 were foreign born individuals. According to census data, 59,737 arrived in the United States prior to 1965, 256,149 arrived between 1965 and 1979, and 730,213 arrived between 1980 and 1990.[1]

In the 1980s the migration patterns changed because of the sociopolitical and economic conditions prevailing in the Central American region, which resulted in large numbers of Salvadorans, Guatemalans, and Nicaraguans entering the United States without legal documentation or as political asylum applicants. The pre-1979 migrations were mostly economic in nature; the post-1979 migrations were generated by the economic and political realities faced by the nations in the region.[2, 3, 4]

Demographic Characteristics of 1970–1994 Central American Immigrants to the United States

The Latino population in the United States increased to more than 22.4 million people in 1990, showing a 53 percent increase since the 1980 census. The fastest growing population is Central and South Americans who reportedly add up to 2,359,432 persons. The 1990 census demographic count of the Central American populations appears to be a low estimate as they do not include an accurate enumeration of the undocumented population residing in the United States.[5]

The exact demographic figures of legal and undocumented Central American immigrants are not currently available. The demographic statistics calculated by the Immigration and Naturalization Service (INS) estimates that there are well over 2 million Central Americans living in this country. These figures do not appear to reflect an accurate account because the majority of Central Americans in the post-1979 migration movements entered the country as undocumented workers or as political asylum seekers and were not included in most of the demographic surveys conducted by U.S. governmental agencies.[2] While the author was conducting field research among Central American immigrants, many families commented that they had not filled out the census questionnaires or any official-looking documents. Some of the reasons given included the fact that even though they had legal immigration status, they did not understand the significance and importance of the census and were apprehensive and fearful about having any type of interaction with the INS or any other governmental agencies.[3]

Sociopolitical and economic crises are the most important determinant factors for the contemporary Central American migrations to the United States. Guatemala, El Salvador, and Nicaragua have been affected by armed insurgency against the established sociopolitical systems. Since 1980, more than 200,000 people have been assassinated by right wing paramilitary groups, death squads, and the armed forces in El Salvador and Guatemala. During this time of war and persecution the most common targets for assassination were labor leaders, Indian leaders, intellectuals, community organizers, Catholic priests, lay preachers, catechizers, agricultural workers, and students.[2] The Sandinista revolution against the Anastasio Somoza dictatorship in the late 1970s and the Contra war in the 1980s claimed an additional 200,000 victims in Nicaragua.

It is important to consider the entire spectrum of cultural, social, and political factors in an analysis of the demographic makeup and social organization of Central American communities in the United States. One should not attempt to generalize the demographic, political, or socioeconomic characteristics of this population because of the complex nature of Central American communities and their migration determinants. It is imperative to look at the sociopolitical conditions of the various countries to avoid creating stereotypes or generalized characterizations of the different Central American nationalities. Central American communities have divergent political ideologies ranging from conservative right wing views to orthodox Marxist orientations. A community in a specific geographical location may manifest a wide diversity of political views such as in the case of San Francisco or in Los Angeles. On the other hand, the Central American immigrant community may hold a more unified political ideology, as is the case in Miami. It is possible to observe more similarities across socioeconomic class status rather than in national identity issues among the different Central American populations. The fact remains that large numbers of individuals of various

Central American origins presently living in the United States come from middle- or working-class backgrounds. They include teachers, high school and university students, secretaries, accountants, homemakers, domestic workers, office workers, and skilled factory workers in their countries. In the 1980s, large numbers of rural agricultural workers arrived in the United States escaping political persecution, forced relocation, or the unsafe political climate in their native rural communities.

Central American Migration Patterns to the United States

At least three different migration patterns have over time been followed by Central American immigrant populations as they resettled in the United States:

1. The first pattern is followed by urban dwellers relocating in urban centers in the United States. It is expected that individuals accustomed to city life will make every possible attempt to relocate in an urban environment in order to take advantage of the opportunities available in U.S. cities. These individuals have higher levels of education and possess some of the skills necessary to be incorporated successfully into U.S. society. The Central American communities in San Francisco and Los Angeles are examples of this migration.
2. The second pattern is observable in rural populations relocating in U.S. urban communities. These populations have lower levels of education and quite often are not well prepared to be incorporated successfully into the U.S. urban environment. These situations may be observable in Houston, Washington, D.C., and Los Angeles.
3. The third pattern is followed by rural dwellers relocating in U.S. rural areas and continuing to work as agricultural laborers in the United States. This pattern is commonly observed in the large agricultural fields in California and Florida.

Guatemalans

The history of Guatemalan migrations to the United States has not been fully analyzed and documented by social scientists. Guatemalans began to arrive in the United States following the 1954 military coup that overthrew the democratically elected government of Jacobo Arbenz. After the coup, many individuals were exiled or fled the country to escape political persecution, and they resettled mostly in California. This migration was characterized by an urban middle-class population made up of intellectuals, political activists, union leaders, and university students.

According to the 1990 census, the legal Guatemalan immigrant population in the United States prior to 1965 was only 6,608 persons. Between 1965 and 1979, the Guatemalan population rose to 60,500, and between the period of 1980 to 1990, Guatemalan demographic figures in the United States increased to 148,888 persons. The 1990 census also states that 52,783 U.S.-born persons were of Guatemalan national origin.[1]

During the early 1980s, numerous Mayan communities were systematically destroyed as part of an anti-insurgency strategic plan of action on the part of the Guatemalan military government. Their entire populations were involuntarily relocated in strategic villages known as Development Poles, or they were forced to migrate to Mexico and the United States as a result of the repression and campaigns of terror carried out by the armed forces. The refugees were subjected to government military actions that resulted in the massacres of the elderly, women, and children, who make up the vast majority of the refugee population.[2, 3, 6, 7]

In rural areas in the U.S. Southwest, the Central American population is composed mostly of indigenous rural people who made a living from traditional agriculture in Central America. The Mayan indigenous culture is governed by the rhythm of the corn agriculture and the seasons, and people prefer rural over urban lifestyles. Large numbers of Guatemalan Mayan immigrants are unskilled young males with low educational backgrounds, employed as seasonal migrant workers in the agricultural farms throughout the sun belt states. Numerous Guatemalan Mayans work in the agricultural fields of Florida, Texas, Arizona, Oregon, Washington state, and California.

The situation of Guatemalan Mayan people in the United States is difficult because they hold non-Western cultural values and are often monolingual, speaking only in the Mayan languages. The majority of Guatemalans working in Florida are Kanjobal-speaking people and originate from the town of San Miguel Acatlan, which is located in the northern province of Huehuetenango. Mayan people have encountered major cultural problems that disrupted their culture and religion and forced the discontinuation of their rituals and cultural traditions related to the cultivation of corn. The Mayan refugees in Florida work in the harvesting of the citrus fields and no longer engage in the cycle of corn agriculture.[8]

The following case illustrates the complexity of the Mayan acculturation experience in this country as it took place in San Francisco, California. A young Mayan couple had a serious run-in with the local authorities when their neighbors noticed the young teenage girl was pregnant. The neighbors reported the young man to the police and to social services, and he was arrested and accused of child molestation. They spent more than six months in a legal battle to get married and to keep their child, and as soon as the man was released from custody they fled California and resettled in Florida. They could not understand why the authorities would interfere in their own personal affairs. It is common practice in Mayan communities for a man in his mid-20s to marry a young teenage girl. The common belief is that a man at that age will be more experienced and would have saved enough money to support a family. This cultural practice is not accepted at all in the United States.[9]

In U.S. urban centers, the majority of Guatemalans are of urban backgrounds and originate from middle- and working-class backgrounds in Guatemala. This population is mostly Mestizo, Ladinos, or Spanish speaking and has higher levels of education and is more skilled and better prepared to cope in U.S. culture and society than the Mayans. Nevertheless, Mayans are also found in some of the larger metropolitan centers such as Los Angeles, Dallas, Houston, and San Francisco. The 1990 census estimated that 268,779 persons of Guatemalan origin resided in the United States; 52,783 were born in the United States and 215,996 were foreign born.[1] The Immigration and Naturalization Service also estimated that by October 1992, there were at least 121,000 undocumented Guatemalans in the United States.[10]

Salvadorans

The Salvadoran immigrant population in the United States is not a homogeneous social group. They come from different socioeconomic and cultural backgrounds and hold diverse political ideologies. In the 1970s, members of the ruling classes could foresee the developing political crisis, and many of them left El Salvador and resettled in Florida and California. They already had established economic, cultural, and political ties in the United States. For decades, the Salvadoran upper class had taken their fortunes out of Central America and deposited them in U.S. banks. Many were educated in U.S. universities, and their socioeconomic status, educational background, bilingual skills, and legal residency status or U.S. citizenship helped them to readily adjust to their new life. This phenomenon of upper-class migrations is characteristic of Latin American revolutions as it was observable in the case of Cuba and Nicaragua.

On the other hand, the large numbers of Salvadoran immigrants arriving in the United States after 1979 came without legal immigration status and originate from middle- and lower-class backgrounds, many of them lacking the economic and social support available to upper-class Salvadorans. A significant number of them do not have the educational, occupational, and language skills needed to succeed. The working-class populations throughout the various Central American countries have strong similarities in their social and cultural experiences and have very little in common with the upper-class social and cultural experiences.

As in the case of Guatemalan immigrants, the majority of Salvadorans left their country to escape the civil war and to search for personal safety and a new life. Salvadoran society has been severely affected by a long history of political corruption, and the impact of the civil war has been multidimensional. The judicial system does not offer protection to civilians, and threats and intimidation prevent justice and freedom from existing in El Salvador.[2] Many Central American immigrants bring with them those fears and the residual effects of living in a society severely impacted by a climate of terror. They project those fears to their social experiences while living in this country and are extremely apprehensive of interacting with governmental agencies and the authorities.

Since the early 1980s Salvadorans make up the largest of all of the Central American groups in the United States, but exact demographic figures are not available because of the undocumented immigration status of a large percentage of this population. The Bureau of the Census estimated the Salvadoran population living in the United States in 1990 to be over 565,081 people, of which 106,405 were U.S. born and 458,676 were foreign born.[1] Furthermore, the 1995 Immigration and Naturalization

Service reports place the number of undocumented Salvadorans at 298,000 persons living in the United States without legal immigration documentation. Salvadorans rank second in the numbers of undocumented persons in the United States surpassed only by the undocumented Mexican population.[10]

These new immigrants arrived in the United States as a result of already established ethnic and family networks such as in the case of San Francisco, Los Angeles, Houston, New Jersey, Chicago, New York, and Washington, D.C. Migrations to the United States are a social process that is mediated by long-standing family, friendship, ethnic, hometown, and community ties that facilitate moving and ease the immigrant's integration into the new environment.

Nicaraguans

The Nicaraguan migrations to the United States began in the 1930s and were characterized by a flow of people escaping persecution and repression from the Somoza government. Just as in the case of other politically motivated migrations, this population was composed of middle-class individuals, professionals, intellectuals, university students, labor organizers, and political dissidents. Many of these Nicaraguan exiles settled in New York, New Orleans, San Francisco, and Los Angeles.

During the 1940s Nicaraguans entered the United States in search of economic opportunities, but many of these individuals eventually returned to their country after World War II to become part of a new rising entrepreneurial class. During the 1960s, the Nicaraguan population in the United States was the largest of all of the Central American national groups. As the political turmoil in the 1970s escalated to armed conflict, many Nicaraguans sought refuge in the United States. After the fall of the Somoza government and the Sandinista victory, many of the original immigrants from the 1930s and 1940s or their descendants returned to live in Nicaragua.

During this same period of time, other Nicaraguans associated with the former government arrived in the United States. Some of the first Nicaraguans to arrive during the early 1980s were members of the upper class that fled Nicaragua because of their ties with the former Somoza dictatorship and their political disagreements with the Sandinista government. Some were businessmen who had direct economic ties to Somoza and his government; others were former members of the National Guard who escaped from the Sandinista army. The majority of these Nicaraguans resettled in Florida and California and brought with them their wealth and their conservative political ideology. During the mid-1980s, Nicaraguan immigrants were working-class youth who left their country to escape the Contra War and the military draft.

According to the 1990 census, 202,658 persons of Nicaraguan origin were residing in the United States; of that total figure 38,363 were native born and 164,295 were foreign born. In addition, the 1990 census states that 12,127 Nicaraguans arrived in this country prior to 1965; 30,118 arrived between 1965 and 1979, and 122,050 Nicaraguans arrived between 1980 and 1990.[1] According to Immigration and Naturalization Service data, it estimated that in October 1992 at least 76,000 undocumented Nicaraguans were living in the United States.[10]

Hondurans and Costa Ricans

There is an extreme scarcity of academic studies of the Honduran and Costa Rican immigrant communities in the United States because their populations are not very large. The majority of Hondurans reside on the U.S. East Coast from Florida to New York. Their social and cultural experience has not been studied in depth. One can assume that not many Costa Ricans live in the United States or have left their country because of a long history of political stability and democratic traditions in that Central American country. The 1990 census estimates that 131,066 Hondurans resided in the United States; 30,076 were U.S. born and 100,990 were foreign born. The Census Bureau also estimated that 57,223 Costa Ricans were in the United States; 17,785 were U.S. born and 39,438 were foreign born.[1]

The Structure of Central American Communities in the United States

Central Americans arrive in U.S. metropolitan centers following already established ethnic and family networks. Newcomers use ethnic or family contacts to secure employment, housing, or to meet any immediate needs. Once the person is settled and able to save money, other relatives begin to arrive. After a few years of living in Latin American neighborhoods, many Central American immigrants adapt socially to the new environment and acquire the necessary employment skills and education to participate fully in the mainstream economic life. Many relocate in other ethnically mixed neighborhoods or suburban cities. Others take advantage of economic opportunities and develop business enterprises in Latin American neighborhoods and utilize the immigrant labor force to maximize their profits.

In an ethnic enclave the new immigrant becomes familiarized with a new social environment as it provides the proper mechanisms and institutions to gradually introduce new arrivals to U.S. society. Latin American enclaves maintain the culture, language, religion, foods, and traditional festivities. Concrete features illustrate the clear distinctions between an ethnic enclave and ethnic immigrant communities. As a rule, immigrants initially relocate in ethnic communities while developing a few small business enterprises to meet local consumption demands. However, ethnic neighborhoods lack the sophisticated economic structure and the extensive division of labor of the enclave.[11] The Central American enclaves in San Francisco, Los Angeles, Washington, D.C., and Houston, among others, demonstrate a well-diversified economic base and division of labor.

The economic structure of the enclave provides for bilingual professional services to the community. The ethnic enclave allows the immigrant to receive legal, educational, immigration, medical, dental, accounting, income tax consulting, counseling, employment training and referral, and food services. This sector is made up not only of immigrants, but also of first- and second-generation Central Americans and Latin Americans providing professional services. Other bilingual non-Latinos and mainstream professionals and merchants also provide services in Spanish within the enclave.

The enclave provides familiar settings by allowing the development of regional associations that support the immigrant with cultural, social, and recreational activities. Regional and hometown associations as well as the enclave provide new immigrants with support structures and resources that develop cultural identification, security, and a sense of belonging in the host society. Regional associations allow the preservation of cultural traditions and the retention of a strong cultural and national identification as a Central American. Many regional associations are named after towns, cities, states, or regions where the immigrant populations originate in Central America. Some organizations are affiliated with religious societies, sports clubs, artistic or cultural organizations, or social service organizations as they exist in Central America. Some of the most popular regional associations are identified with soccer or baseball clubs that participate in Latin American or mainstream sports leagues. These associations have well-structured organizations and large memberships. Their members pay dues and usually rent a small place as a recreation center. Other regional associations are dedicated to religious worship to a patron saint or a special Catholic deity. Such are the examples in the Nicaraguan community with groups dedicated to the worship of Our Lady of the Conception, *La Purísima,* or Saint Dominic, *Santo Domingo.* Salvadorans have religious associations dedicated to El Salvador del Mundo.

The study of Central American enclaves and the immigrant's social interaction in the community may be analyzed under the neo-Gemeinschaft model developed by Rivera and Erlich.[12] This model is based on Toennies's concepts of Gemeinschaft, or community where the primary relationships are conducted and involve intimacy and privacy; and Gesselschaft, or society, which represents the individual's public life or the pursuance of secondary relationships for utilitarian and survival reasons.[13] Rivera and Erlich expanded Toennies's model to explain the formation and interaction dynamics of ethnic groups in this country. Ethnic enclaves develop as subgroups within society as a result of an antagonistic social environment in which the members of the immigrant or minority group are not totally functional in the mainstream society and thus become victims of discrimination and economic exploitation.

According to this framework, the immigrants will develop secondary relationships only at the societal level (Gesselschaft) where the individual experiences discrimination as a result of racial, cultural, and linguistic differences. Primary relationships (Gemeinschaft) are restricted to members of the same national or ethnic group. This model is also applicable to analysis of the religious views and preferences of Central American immigrants because they often attend religious services in Spanish in their own ethnic neighborhoods. This is an important fact to consider because the church is one of the primary social institutions in the life of an immigrant or refugee, and it is often regarded by them to be the most important institution besides the family.

The Emergence of Political Power and Influence in Central American Communities

The socioeconomic and political diversity observed in Central American communities plays an important role in preventing cohesion and empowerment for its members; thus these communities end up having limited political power and influence within the U.S. political structure. The Central American communities often are divided on issues related to national identity and region of origin, political affiliations in Central America and the United States, ethnicity, religion, and socioeconomic status. These divisions do not allow the necessary social cohesion needed to transform this population into a strong political body that will be able to seek viable political solutions to the problems and realities they encounter in this society. There is a need to develop responsible and accountable political and social activists within the Central American community in order to confront critically the wide range of problems they face in this country.

Another drawback to empowerment in Central American communities is the common belief on the part of immigrants that their stay of residence in the United States will be temporary. Therefore, immigrants become isolated and neglect to participate in political affairs at the community, municipal, state, or national levels. Unless individuals have some degree of political sophistication, many Central Americans have demonstrated apathy toward U.S. political and social issues. Over the years, community activists attempted to persuade Latin American immigrants to become U.S. citizens and to register to vote. These efforts were fruitless because large numbers of Latin Americans believed if they became U.S. citizens, it was a betrayal to their national identity and citizenship. This situation has begun to change rapidly since the passage of Proposition 187 in California and strong anti-immigrant currents affecting the United States since the early 1990s. The passage of the welfare reform bill and the new immigration legislation by the federal government has motivated thousands of Central Americans and other Latinos to apply for U.S. citizenship in order to retain their social service benefits while living in the United States. For the first time in decades, community activism and political empowerment is taking root in Latino communities as a response to immigrant bashing and anti-Latino legislation being passed at the national and local levels.

Central American community organizations have attempted to achieve political power in the past. Some organizations were closely associated with political parties or organizations in Central America. Casa El Salvador, Casa Nicaragua, and Guatemalan organizations have close ties with Central American popular revolutionary movements. In California, the popular revolutionary groups were successful in their actions against U.S. policies in Central America. Their success was based on the fact that they did not limit their activities to only within the Latin American communities. They reached out to the mainstream and created multiethnic coalitions by working closely with international solidarity coalitions and networks such as CISPES, Amnesty International, or the Emergency Response Network. Their main objectives were to deal with issues that directly affected the Central American region, but did not place their main emphasis on the empowerment efforts within the local communities.

On the other hand, other organizations such as the Coalition for Immigrant and Refugee Rights and Services have worked within the local community structure to advocate for immigrant issues, especially for abuses against immigrant women. Their efforts have been very successful in organizing within the local immigrant community by creating bridges between different immigrant communities.

The Paulo Freire and the Liberation Theology Models of Community Empowerment

The Freire method of community empowerment is based on the pedagogical and organizational strategies that bring about critical consciousness in individuals and the community. Paulo Freire's methodology has been widely used in Latin America in conjunction with the Theology of Liberation by the Catholic-based communities in the empowerment of political activists, union leaders, lay preachers, campesinos, and students. Freire's methodology teaches basic literacy skills to adults while providing the students with basic notions of political awareness to develop praxis and community social action. On the other hand, the Theology of Liberation has provided a new analysis of the teachings of the Gospel that focuses on bringing positive changes to the experiences of the poor in Latin America.

These pedagogical strategies have been implemented by base community organizations and educational centers in the United States while teaching English language skills to Spanish monolinguals. Freire's pedagogy introduces basic concepts of social and political awareness in language lessons as the means of empowering new immigrants. In San Francisco, the Mission Reading Clinic, Project Literacy, and the High School Step to College Program at San Francisco State University have achieved great successes in their educational efforts while utilizing the critical education methodology.

Other successful organizations include the refugee self-help committees located in various U.S. cities such as San Francisco, Los Angeles, New York, and Washington, D.C., among others that have been successful in the implementation of these methodologies. Three refugee organizations have been effective in the internal affairs of the Central American while representing the refugees in the mainstream society and local political structures: (1) the Comité de Refugiados Centro Americanos (CRECE), which provides refugees with social services, (2) the Central American Refugee Center (CARECEN), the legal and immigration services and advocacy agency of the refugee organizations in Washington, D.C., Houston, San Francisco, and Los Angeles, and (3) El Rescate in Los Angeles.

In these organizations, the refugees themselves work together to empower other refugees. They are designed following the organizational models of Paulo Freire's Critical Consciousness and the Central American Catholic Base Communities as organized under the Theology of Liberation model. Because of their organizational structure, history, philosophy, and empowerment efforts, these community groups are recognized to represent the leadership in the Central American refugee community. They address issues affecting the social experiences and cultural adaptation of Guatemalan and Salvadoran immigrants and refugees.

CRECE has provided the refugee community with basic survival services such as food and clothes distribution, emergency housing, medical services, job referrals, cultural survival skills, and employment skills development workshops. They provide educational information to the mainstream communities by making presentations at schools, universities, churches, and home meetings where they give testimonies of their experiences in Central America. CRECE is an active advocate of refugee rights in Central America and is also actively involved in the repopulation of refugees in El Salvador.

CARECEN provides legal representation to refugees in political asylum hearings, gives health referral services, trains health promoters, and produces literature for the Central American refugee community. In the mid-1980s and early 1990s, CARECEN played an important role in the formation of the Central American National Network (CARNET), which included thirty-eight refugee agencies and grassroots organizations in the United States. CARECEN and CRECE have demonstrated a strong commitment to empowering the Central American community. The development of local leadership is an important priority in their selection and training of low-income refugees who work as refugee rights promoters and refugee advocates. The promoters provide services to the refugee community, speak in public forums, and monitor and attempt to impact legislation affecting the Central American refugee community at the municipal, state, and national levels. Their achievements have included the declaration of cities of refuge in which local governments and law enforcement agencies would not cooperate in Immigration and Naturalization Service raids against undocumented workers. Unfortunately, in San Francisco as well as in other municipalities, City of Sanctuary ordinances have been repealed because of legislation passed by the municipal and state governments which declared the ordinances illegal.

These organizations work closely with religious organizations, the network of churches associated with the Sanctuary movement, Catholic Charities, the Baptist Ministries, and the Quakers, among others. They receive funds and direct services from religious organizations and private foundations. One successful model can be seen in the work done by St. Peter's Church in the heart of San Francisco's Mission District. Led by the efforts of refugees working side by side with the local pastor, they have created a Central American refugee program that provides a wide variety of services including a long-term shelter for homeless men, mental health counseling, rights advocacy, day laborer advocacy, cultural support, and language classes to the Mayan population in the area.

What Needs to Be Done in the Near Future

The Need for More Research Studies

Further theoretical and practical research studies are necessary to fully comprehend and resolve the acculturation issues faced by Central American immigrants in the United States. The specific areas in need of a greater scope of examination are legal, medical, psychological, educational, professional, and occupational skills, and re-training, nutrition, counseling, and religious issues affecting this population. There is a need for studies in the major metropolitan and rural centers where the Central American populations are resettling. Mainstream professionals, researchers, and religious organizations must develop critical awareness and cultural competency to address effectively the needs of Central Americans in the United States.

Institutions of higher education must implement broad curricular offerings across the various disciplines addressing the cultural, socioeconomic, and historical realities that address the basic needs of this rapidly growing population. In cities with high numbers of Central Americans, universities must include specific curricular offerings and training programs for students enrolled in undergraduate and graduate studies. Course offerings must be developed to bring to light a critical understanding of the ethnic, cultural, economic, religious, and sociopolitical backgrounds of Central Americans residing in their geographical areas.

A number of recent studies have attempted to explain why Latin American immigrants are leaving the Catholic religion and converting to Protestantism. They show interesting findings that could help in organizing with Central American communities. These studies analyze the immigrant's expectations of the church, the role of the priests, and the nature and structure of religious services.[14, 15, 16] Marin and Gamba[14] find of particular significance the high degree of dissatisfaction with U.S. Catholicism expressed by recent Latin American immigrants. Furthermore, they found that the lower the levels of acculturation to the U.S. culture, the higher the levels of dissatisfaction.

Protestant ministers take very seriously their role as missionaries by actively walking and targeting the Latino barrios and ethnic immigrant communities. They also place a high degree of importance in their work among the youth by taking on challenging issues such as drug abuse, gang violence, and education among young Latin American immigrants. In most cases, these ministers who are recruited from the ranks of the local populations are fluent in Spanish and competent to understand the immigrant's cultural experience. Protestant churches provide a feeling of family and community and are sensitive to the immigrant's cultural experiences.[15]

The Need for Immigration Changes

Under the present-day anti-immigrant climate, their undocumented immigration status is the most serious problem faced by the majority of Central Americans in this country. There is a great urgency to modify the governmental policies and practices at the macro level in order to have a positive impact in the economic, social, and cultural experience of this population. Extensive work must be done to stop the wave of anti-immigrant attitudes and violence that has escalated during the past few years. Many government officials are engaging in immigrant bashing to blame immigrants for the ills of our society while ignoring numerous studies which indicate that immigrants do not depress the local economies but stimulate growth and stability.

The American Civil Liberties Union and the United Nations High Commission on Refugees have declared their position that Salvadorans and Guatemalans in the United States are prima facie refugees and should not be deported or forced to return to their countries of origin. Temporary refuge and extended voluntary departure status has been granted to Salvadorans but not to Guatemalans as an attempt to solve this complex problem. It must be noted that extended voluntary departure has been granted in the past to other refugee populations.

Central American activists and refugees strongly believe that when individuals escaping the terror and political violence of the civil war arrive in this country, the U.S. government has a legal and moral obligation to treat them in a humane manner consistent with U.S. and international laws. If Central Americans were granted refugee status or political asylum, their most difficult acculturation problem would be resolved, thus resulting in their gradual adaptation and incorporation into U.S. society. The immigration status of these individuals prevents their adaptation and incorporation into U.S. society and culture. Undocumented Central Americans have a difficult time finding employment because of their immigration status. This creates an underclass of workers who can find subminimum wage employment only in the ethnic enclave, the domestic, and secondary labor sectors.

The Need for Counseling Services

It is important to reframe immigrants' perceptions regarding counseling and social services. In Latin America, the extended family and the church provide economic, emotional, spiritual, and social support to individuals. Family cohesion and support are strong, providing security and stability to the individual and the community. Social services are seen as charity in the traditional Central American culture, and to receive charity is not considered a positive communal action. People must work to make a living and only the lazy or disabled are expected to receive charity. This attitude may create complications for them in the United States. For instance, individuals may not seek medical help until an illness or problem becomes a serious, life-threatening emergency. It is a common belief that if an able-bodied individual cannot afford to pay for a medical service, then one seeks home remedies or assistance from family or friends but not from the government or the church.

It is essential to inform undocumented Central Americans of available social services. They must know their legal rights as well as the legal implications of their undocumented status. Although there are community agencies providing information and referral services, organizations need budget increases to provide more efficient services. Financial support is needed to expand available facilities and services and effectively train their professional staff. There is a need to develop culturally sensitive counseling and social services at low cost or free of charge that provide support to Central Americans in their relocation and acculturation experiences. At the micro level, community organizers must offer classes or workshops that provide cultural, social, and political awareness as well as survival skills. Workshops must include an orientation to U.S. cultural, legal, and social systems to ensure understanding and familiarity with societal dynamics of the United States.

Basic cultural differences must be explained to newcomers to develop a clear understanding of the host society. It is important for the newcomer to acquire understanding and competency about the cultural attitudes, values, and laws of the United States. For example, concepts of time and punctuality are themes to discuss with newly arrived immigrants. In Central America, the pace of life is slower and punctuality is not considered as important as it is in this country. Individuals need to be acquainted with proper procedures and expected behavior such as scheduling, canceling appointments, and punctuality when they cannot attend interviews or meetings.

Other important subjects for community organizers and school professionals to discuss with recently arrived immigrants are the values, attitudes, and laws related to child-rearing practices and child abuse. It is common in Central American culture to discipline children using corporal punishments such as spanking or belting a child even in public situations. What is accepted behavior in Central America, however, might be child abuse in this country. In Central American culture it is expected for a parent to discipline a child with punishments that may include spanking, belting, or forcing a child to kneel on the floor for prolonged periods of time. If a parent does not punish a child during an expected situation, people might feel the parents are too permissive and are allowing the children to run their lives. In the United States, corporal punishment is not a widely accepted child-rearing practice. Spanking a child on the buttocks may be accepted but only in extreme situations.

A high incidence of child abuse by undocumented Central Americans is reported by community agencies, clinics, hospitals, and schools. Parents must be aware of the different values, attitudes, and laws dealing with child rearing to prevent any legal problems for the family. It is imperative to develop cultural awareness, competency, and sensitivity on the part of school administrators and teachers, community organizers, doctors, and other professionals who frequently interact and treat Central Americans. A problem was brought to the author's attention by a high school counselor in San Francisco when a Salvadoran father had belted a young teen student on the legs. The child showed bruises from the punishment, and the school administrators called the father to a meeting to discuss the problem. The father was upset at the school administrators for threatening to report him to the authorities for child abuse. In anger, the father told the principal that if he was expected not to discipline the child in the traditional ways, then the child would be the responsibility of the school officials and they would have to assume the cost of bringing up the son. There are also instances in which the children begin to threaten to report the parents to the authorities for child abuse. This situation creates discord within the family because the parents see their traditional roles challenged by what they consider disrespectful children.

The majority of family problems encountered by this population arise from the conflicts between the values and cultural systems held in U.S. society and the contrasting nature of Central American values and traditions. Children and adolescents, especially girls, are given more rights and privileges in this country. When teenagers begin to date, problems may arise as a result of interethnic or interracial prejudices, freedom to go out with friends, and sexual attitudes and practices. The cultural values held in this society are considerably different from the traditional family values held in Central American society. The author encountered one case of a Salvadoran family in which their young teenage daughter started to date a young African American man. When the young woman became pregnant, the father was deeply disturbed because of his racial prejudices, to the point that the young woman was cast out of the family, and for a period of more than three years, the father refused to see her or talk to her. It was not until the family received counseling and became critically aware of ethnic issues in this country that the father dropped his racist attitudes and the young couple were accepted into the family. The process took a great deal of intervention on the part of community activists, teachers, and friends who were close to the family.

Problems often develop in the family, resulting in intergenerational conflict between the parents and their children. Conflicts develop when children and adolescents find part-time employment to meet the family's financial responsibilities. Emotional problems are created for the father because of the disruption of the traditional image of the father as the financial provider for the family. Problems may arise because the young usually acculturate faster than the older adults. They learn English at a more rapid pace than the adult family members. Children are used as interpreters assuming more responsibilities for the family. When the parents interact with the mainstream society, the children serve as interpreters for the family business affairs that include interactions with the utility companies, school officials, landlords, and so on. These interpreting responsibilities empower the children, placing them in a bargaining situation with the parents. Children begin to negotiate with parents for privileges as well as for access to more material things they desire for their social activities.

Educational Needs

Language acquisition is an important process of the acculturation experiences faced by Central American immigrants in the United States. Mastering the English language is necessary to improve the socioeconomic and cultural experience of recently arrived immigrants. Besides giving cultural awareness of the host society in the basic English language curriculum, educational programs must include counseling for newcomers. Also it is important to implement empowerment pedagogies such those of Freire's critical education to develop social and political awareness on the part of newcomers.

Professionals, university professors, and teachers encounter serious obstacles because they cannot find employment in their areas of expertise. Many professionals experience downward social mobility and are often employed in menial occupations that generate frustrations and emotional and psychological problems. It is difficult for attorneys, architects, or professors to earn a living as dishwashers, janitors, or babysitters. Their high expectations of the opportunities available in the United States and the disappointment of not fulfilling their expectations creates a high degree of stress.

Occupational retraining programs are needed for such individuals. Professionals need to find employment in fields related to their areas of expertise and should receive academic counseling and training to prepare them for accreditation by the appropriate professional qualifying boards. The development of English language courses designed for professionals is needed so they can pass the accreditation examinations to practice their professions.

Medical and Mental Health Care Needs

Many of the medical and health services to immigrants and especially those offered to the undocumented are currently being threatened by anti-immigrant hysteria. Legislators have sponsored the passage of restrictions that would not allow undocumented persons or their U.S.-born children to receive any type of medical services. If such legislation is passed, the immigrant health crisis will escalate to serious epidemic conditions.

The Central American population in the United States is in great need of culturally sensitive health-care services. It has special needs in the areas of health and nutrition. Recent immigrants suffer from a variety of tropical diseases such as parasites, gastroenteritis, malnutrition, tuberculosis, and high mortality rates. Further academic research is needed on the incidence of psychosocial trauma and post traumatic stress disorders (PTSD) in Central Americans. Until recently only a small number of social workers, psychologists, and psychiatrists had studied the problem, and more scientific and psychological studies need to be conducted to understand and develop successful treatment for individuals affected by the various forms of psychosocial trauma and PTSD.

Many Central Americans are not familiar with Western mental health concepts and psychological treatment. It is common belief in Central America that healthy and sane individuals do not need the services of psychologists and that only the mentally ill do. The incidence of mental health problems such as psychosocial trauma, post traumatic stress disorder, alcoholism, and abuse of pharmaceutical drugs is reportedly high among Central American immigrants. Central Americans suffer psychological and physiological stresses created by the civil war and their relocation experiences. These stresses are categorized as various forms of psychosocial trauma by Latin American psychologists.[17]

Psychological stresses common to political refugees are also manifested in Central Americans. Individuals may suffer from post traumatic stress disorder (PTSD) related to the environment of violence and the effects of the civil war. They are reported to suffer anxiety and acute depression, which may result in hospitalization and intensive psychiatric treatment. Individuals or their relatives who were victims of political violence in Central America often manifest various forms of psychological problems upon their arrival and settlement in the United States. Torture victims suffer from PTSD symptoms exhibited as severe depression, guilt, nightmares, hyperalertness, insomnia, suicidal tendencies, and withdrawal. Psychiatric evaluations of Central Americans conducted by refugee centers in the San Francisco Bay Area have concluded that a significantly large number of their clients suffer from psychosocial trauma and PTSD. Reports documenting the impact of psychological disorders on the immigrants and their families suggest that marital and family relationships are negatively affected by such mental health problems. Conflicts, depression, alcohol and drug abuse, frustration, domestic violence, separation, and divorce are the recurring consequences.

At the macro level, the medical profession has the moral and social obligation to develop competency on the cultural perspectives of health and disease as believed by the Central American population. Psychologists, psychiatrists, doctors, nurses, and hospital staff need to understand the traditional healing concepts and methodologies used by Central Americans to effectively treat the medical and mental health problems of this population. Workshops and curricular offerings need to be developed by universities, hospitals, and clinics to develop in their professionals a critical awareness of the socioeconomic, political, and cultural backgrounds of undocumented Central Americans.

Culture-bound diseases in Central Americans patients are often reported by doctors in hospitals and clinics. Many illnesses are perceived to be of supernatural or magical origins. Patients usually do not respond to Western medical methodologies unless they undergo the necessary rituals or take remedies as determined by the traditional cultural beliefs in Central America. In California, efforts are being made to develop effective methodologies and programs to treat Central American patients in hospitals and community agencies. Because of the high incidence of torture cases reported on recent Central American immigrants and refugees, a national coalition of medical and mental health professionals and organizations was created to treat survivors of torture. Increased efforts need to provide adequate treatment to individuals who have suffered psychological and physical torture.[18]

Employment Needs

Employment is a major issue concerning the social adaptation and economic stability of Central American immigrants in the United States. Employment opportunities closely depend on the immigration status of the participants, a situation that forces the majority of undocumented individuals to find employment in the ethnic enclave, in the secondary labor sector, or in domestic labor.

Working conditions in the enclave appear to be more acceptable to newcomers and undocumented workers because cash wages are often paid. Cash payments minimize the fears of disclosing a person's immigration status to strangers who do not ask for necessary documentation needed to work as required by the Immigration Reform and Control Act of 1986 (IRCA; i.e., a social security number or an alien registration card).

Conclusion

The spectrum of problems faced by Central Americans may dishearten many church leaders and community organizers in the United States. Their challenges and responsibilities are many and range from the development of a body of knowledge and understanding around immigration issues, educational concern, housing, and the broad dynamics of acculturation. Added to these responsibilities are the cultural sensitivity and critical awareness required for successful community action.

Because of a scarcity of literature on organizing with Central Americans, community and religious organizers must modify and adapt existing methods of practice and strategies. Social action models, with the exception of the Sanctuary Movement, the Paulo Freire literacy model, and the Theology of Liberation model applied in the Catholic base communities, are the least favored because of the attention drawn to the people involved in the process. They usually bring a negative outcome as police or immigration officials become aware of the individuals and their possible undocumented immigration status. Furthermore, because many Central Americans live marginally in our society, they have a strong reluctance to engage in this level of social change and advocacy. Traditionally, the poor and disenfranchised tend to be conservative in nature and are reluctant to engage in direct confrontation tactics.

Community and economic development models are more acceptable and effective in working with Central Americans. They are more status quo in their orientations and offer more real material gains like employment, housing, and the development of an economic exchange market that may exist parallel to the traditional mainstream market systems. The utilization of Paulo Freire's methods for developing critical awareness and empowerment are especially relevant in organizing with Central Americans because they do not posit false expectations, emphasizing very real material and educational rewards. Furthermore, many Central American immigrants are already familiar with Freire's methods, as they were implemented in the Central American Catholic base communities. These challenges are obvious; the strategies have to be determined on a day-by-day basis as we work with and learn to develop a critical understanding of the communities.

Notes

1. U.S. Bureau of the Census, 1990 Census of Population and Housing, Special Summary Tape File 3, Persons of Hispanic Origin in the United States, (Washington, D.C.), Pep 1994.

2. American Civil Liberties Union. *Salvadorans in the United States: The Case for Extended Voluntary Departure.* National Immigration and Alien Rights Project, Report No. 1. (Washington, D.C., April 1984).

3. Camarda, R. *Forced to Move: Salvadoran Refugees in Honduras* (San Francisco, CA: Solidarity Publications, 1985).

4. Córdova, C. B. "Undocumented Salvadorans in the San Francisco Bay Area: Migration and Adaptation Dynamics." *Journal of La Raza Studies,* 1(1), 9–37 (Fall 1987).

5. Córdova, C. B., and del Pinal, J. *Latinos: Diverse Populations in a Multicultural Society* (Washington, D.C.: National Association of Hispanic Publishers, January 1996).

6. Manz, B. *Refugees of a Hidden War: The Aftermath of Counterinsurgency in Guatemala* (Albany: State University of New York Press, 1988).

7. Amnesty International. *Annual Report* (Washington, D.C., 1983).

8. A. F. Burns. *Maya in Exile: Guatemalans in Florida* (Philadelphia: Temple University Press, 1993).

9. This case was documented while the author served on the board of directors of the Father Moriarty Central American Refugee Center in San Francisco, California, 1982–1985.

10. Immigration and Naturalization Service. World Wide Web Page. (http://.www.us-doj.gov/ins/publications) Immigration to the US in FY1995. Table 7.

11. Portes, Alejandro, and Bach, Robert L. *Latin Journey: Cuban and Mexican Immigrants in the United States* (Berkeley: University of California Press, 1985).

12. Rivera, Felix G., and Erlich, John L. "Neo-Gemeinschaft Minority Communities in the United States: Implications for Community Organizing." *Community Development Journal,* 16(3) (October 1981): 189–200.

13. Toennies, F. "Gemeinschaft and Gesselschaft," in Talcott Parsons et al., eds. *Theories of Society* (New York: Free Press, 1961), 1–191.

14. Marin, Gerardo, and Gamba, Raymond. *Expectations and Experiences of Hispanic Catholics and Converts to Protestant Churches.* (San Francisco: University of San Francisco, Social Psychology Laboratory, Hispanic Studies, February 1990).

15. Deck, A. F. "Fundamentalism and the Hispanic Catholic." *America* (January 25,1985).

16. Vilar, J. J. D. "The Success of the Sects Among Hispanics in the United States." *America* (February 25, 1989).

17. Martín-Baró, Ignacio. "Political Violence and War as Causes of Psychosocial Trauma in El Salvador." *Journal of La Raza Studies,* 2 (1) (Summer/Fall 1989), 5–15.

18. Cordova, C. B., *Migration and Acculturation Dynamics of Undocumented Salvadorans in the San Francisco Bay Area.* Doctoral dissertation (University of San Francisco, 1986).

References

Burgos, E. *I . . . Rigoberta Menchu* (New York: Schocken Books, 1984).
Carmack, R. M. (Ed.). *Harvest of Violence: The Maya Indians and the Guatemalan Crisis* (Norman: University of Oklahoma Press, 1988).

Chinchilla, N., Hamilton, N., and Loucky, J. "Central Americans in Los Angeles: An Immigrant Community in Transition." In J. Moore, and R. Pinderhughes (Eds.), *In the Barrios: Latinos and the Underclass Debate* (New York: Russell Sage Foundation, 1993).

Córdova, C. B. "The Mission District: The Ethnic Diversity of the Latin American Enclave in San Francisco, California." *Journal of La Raza Studies,* 2 (1) (Summer/Fall 1989), 21–32.

Córdova, C. B. "The Social, Cultural and Religious Experiences of Central American Immigrants in the United States." In A. M. Pineda and R. Schreiter (Eds.), *Dialogue Rejoined: Theology and Ministry in the United States Hispanic Reality* (Collegeville, Minn.: Liturgical Press, 1995).

Deck, A. F. "Proselytism and Hispanic Catholics: How Long Can We Cry Wolf." *America* (December 10, 1988).

Deck, A. F. *The Second Wave: Hispanic Ministry and the Evangelization of Cultures* (New York: Paulist Press, 1989).

Freire, Paulo. *Pedagogy of the Oppressed* (New York: Seabury Press, 1970).

——. *Education for Critical Consciousness* (New York: Seabury Press, 1973).

Greeley, A. M. "Defection Among Hispanics." *America* (July 30, 1988).

Hamilton, N., and Chinchilla, N. (Eds.). *Central Americans in California: Transnational Communities, Economies and Cultures: Conference Proceedings* (Los Angeles: Center for Multiethnic and Transnational Studies, University of Southern California, 1996).

Mahler, S. *American Dreaming: Immigrant Life on the Margins* (Princeton, N.J.: Princeton University Press, 1995).

Melville, Margarita B. "Hispanics: Race, Class or Ethnicity." *The Journal of Ethnic Studies,* 16(1) (1988), 67–84.

Montes Mozo, S., and Garcia Vasquez, J. J. *Salvadoran Migration to the United States: An Exploratory Study.* Hemispheric Migration Project, Center for Immigration Policy and Refugee Assistance (Washington, D.C.: Georgetown University, 1988).

Muller, T., and Espenshade, T. with Manson, D., de la Puente, M., Goldberg, M., and Sanchez, J. *The Fourth Wave: California's Newest Immigrants* (Washington, D.C.: The Urban Institute Press, 1985).

National Lawyers Guild. *Immigration Law and Defense* (New York: Clark Boardman Company, 1981).

Pineda, A. M., and R. Schreiter (Eds.). *Dialogue Rejoined: Theology and Ministry in the United States Hispanic Reality* (Collegeville, Minn.: Lithurgical Press, 1995).

Portes, A., and Rumbaut, R. G. *Immigrant America: A Portrait* (Berkeley: University of California Press, 1990).

Suarez-Orozco, M. *Central American Refugees and U.S. High Schools* (Stanford: Stanford University Press, 1989).

United Nations Human Rights Commission. *Report on the Situation of Human Rights in El Salvador* (Washington, D.C.: Author, 1983).

11

Southeast Asians
in the United States:
Accelerated and
Balanced Integration

VU-DUC VUONG

April 1975 marked the end of American military involvement in Cambodia, Laos, and Vietnam, and at the same time opened a new chapter in the ongoing saga of immigration to the United States: the Southeast Asian wave.* By the end of 1995, twenty years later, nearly 1.5 million Southeast Asians have migrated to the United States, both as refugees and as immigrants. The Southeast Asian diaspora in the United States is thus the largest one in the world and, thanks to the resources and circumstances in this country, potentially the most influential one as well. This chapter briefly profiles this community, raises some of the critical issues for the turn-of-the-century period, and advances a strategy that can enable it to achieve its full potential in the twenty-first century.

*For the purpose of this chapter, *Southeast Asian* refers to refugees and immigrants from three countries only: Cambodia, Laos, and Vietnam. It is accurate when used in the context of the refugee status because currently the United States recognizes no refugees from any other Southeast Asian country. The author concedes that the term is less accurate in a more general sense, although still preferable to the term *Indochinese,* a vestige from the French colonial days. The use of *Southeast Asian* is also a vehicle to unite and organize the three nationalities by emphasizing the common bonds and circumstances of people who are now in similar situations but who had much to disagree about in their respective pasts.

Southeast Asians in the United States: A Profile

When the Phnom Penh and Saigon regimes fell to the communists in April 1975, only a few thousand Southeast Asians were living in the United States. Most were students in American universities and the rest were diplomats, bureaucrats serving in the United States, or military personnel in training. Virtually overnight the United States admitted over 130,000 refugees, mostly from Vietnam, to these shores. (See Table 11.1 on pages 204–205.) This earliest group was dispersed throughout the country, from Duluth to New Orleans, from Maine to Hawaii, in a deliberate policy of minimizing the impact on local communities and of accelerating, ideally, the assimilation process.

During the next three years, 1976 to 1978, refugee outflow from the three countries dwindled down to a trickle, to about 37,000. More than half came from Laos alone because relatively few left Vietnam or Cambodia. In Cambodia, it was then the reign of the Khmer Rouge that massacred at least one million of the people, including the majority of the professional and educated class. In Vietnam, the incarceration of tens of thousands of former public servants and officers of the overthrown regime and the initial, somewhat hopeful wait-and-see attitude among many who did not escape in 1975 accounted for the reduced outflow of refugees.

By the end of 1978, and during 1979, two major events in Southeast Asia unleashed another exodus from that region. In the South, Vietnam invaded Cambodia, overthrew the Khmer Rouge, ended the genocide, and set up a new Cambodian government under its protection. As Vietnamese tanks rolled into Phnom Penh, they awakened and unchained a population that the three and a half years of Khmer Rouge atrocities had rendered incapacitated; hundreds of thousands of liberated surviving Cambodians poured across the borders into Thailand or Vietnam, and the principal Cambodian wave of refugees began.

To the North, tensions between China and Vietnam, which were close allies during the war against the United States, led to the harassment of the Chinese population in Vietnam and open warfare along the border. Anti-Chinese policies in Vietnam caused a massive, unprecedented exodus of "boat people" from Vietnam that included both Chinese ethnics and Vietnamese who had given up on hope for a better Vietnam.

A third prong of refugee movement occurred in Laos; hundreds of thousands of Laotians, predominantly of the Hmong, Iu Mien, and Khmu hill tribes, crossed over into Thailand, and hundreds of thousands of new refugees out of Vietnam braved high seas in their minuscule boats to reach Thailand, Malaysia, Indonesia, the Philippines, and Hong Kong. During the four-year period from 1979 to 1992, the United States alone admitted well over 400,000 refugees from Southeast Asia. The refugees who made it to a country of asylum during this period were often referred to as the "second wave" of Southeast Asian refugees.

Since 1983, the number of Southeast Asians admitted to the United States as refugees has leveled off and hovers between 35,000 and 50,000 annually. Most of the refugees admitted were among those who escaped from their homeland and waited in a refugee camp in a third country; as they were accepted for resettlement, other fellow refugees continued to leave and took their place in the camps. In addition, an increasing number of refugees were admitted and flown out of Vietnam by plane under the auspices of the Orderly Departure Program established in the wake of the boat people exodus in 1979. Toward the end of the 1980s, the characteristics of Southeast Asians admitted to the United States changed again: starting in 1989, this country at long last formally accepted Amerasian children and their current families as refugees and at the same time welcomed, on humanitarian grounds, military personnel and other government officials of the South Vietnam regime who had been incarcerated after the war ended in 1975.

Also in 1989, the United Nations, the United States, Vietnam, and other countries of asylum in Southeast Asia reached a "Comprehensive Action Plan" (or CAP), both to discourage more refugees from leaving and to expedite the disposition of status of those already in camps, thus allowing the countries of asylum to close these camps. By the end of 1996, Thailand, Malaysia, and Indonesia had closed all their refugee camps, either by resettlement or repatriation; only about 15,000 refugees remained in Hong Kong and about 1,600 in the Philippines. Hong Kong planned to repatriate most of the remaining refugees back to Vietnam by the time it reverted back to China on July 1, 1997; and the Philippines granted temporary resettlement opportunities to those who wanted to stay in that country.

In terms of status, most Southeast Asians were admitted as refugees during the first decade of the resettlement effort (1975–1985), but in the second decade, a growing proportion were admitted as immigrants, often sponsored by their relatives already in the United States. Both refugees and immigrants were allowed to seek work immediately, but only refugees were eligible for government assistance, from English and vocational classes to welfare benefits, disability support, and medical care.

After residing in the United States for one year, a refugee became eligible for permanent residence status, and four years later, he or she was allowed to petition for citizenship. An immigrant is admitted as a permanent resident upon arrival, receives a "green card" (permanent resident status), and at the end of a five-year waiting period can also petition for naturalization. It was estimated that by the end of 1995, more than half of all Southeast Asians in the United States had become citizens. In 1996, as Congress and the administration adopted new measures aimed at curbing immigration and cutting social spending by not only reducing benefits but also limiting such reduced benefits primarily to citizens only, the Southeast Asian community, like other predominantly immigrant groups, scrambled once again to gain citizenship status.

In terms of procedures, most Southeast Asian refugees and immigrants arrived in the United States in one of two ways: a few directly from the home country such as under the auspices of the Orderly Departure Program (ODP), and the majority through a selection process in refugee camps throughout Asia. ODP essentially was an escape valve for people who had reason to leave Vietnam (persecution of some sort, or sponsorship by a family member already resettled, for instance) and who had been accepted for resettlement by another country to leave Vietnam legally and safely. The procedure

TABLE 11.1 Refugee Admission to the United States, 1975–1995

As of June 30, 1996

FIRST ASYLUM	JUNE, 1996 POPULATION	ARRIVALS SINCE 4/75	*Reductions since 4/75*					RPC TRANSFERS U.S. CASELOAD
			TO U.S.	TO OTHER COUNTRIES	VOLUNTARY REPATRIATION	RELO-CATION	OTHER	
Hong Kong	16,766	222,876	53,008	76,188	52,894	5	5,159	16,393
Macau	0	7,678	2,427	3,966	0	0	576	868
Indonesia—Khmer	302	1,915	0	50	1,601	0	15	15
Indonesia—Vietnamese	3,500	126,203	45,230	47,381	9,122	0	264	20,382
Malaysia	124	258,768	91,414	107,264	9,197	1	552	48,963
Philippines	2,246	54,137	11,572	25,822	2,329	0	47	16,091
Singapore	5	35,271	5,732	21,127	104	1	10	7,831
Japan	0	4,228	3,069	5,497	262	0	1	354
Korea	0	401	8	361	0	0	2	135
Taiwan	0	38	2	41	0	0	1	20
Other	0	40,857	3,313	28,718	0	0	14	1,017
Thailand—Khmer	0	250,983	50,479	79,201	13,167	41,172	472	97,198
Thailand—Highlanders	5,115	184,588	54,425	22,434	13,192	0	3,817	69,050
Thailand—Lao	1,047	195,795	72,266	49,594	10,688	1,000	3,377	51,053
Thailand—Vietnamese	3,764	162,144	39,198	50,880	13,151	0	550	55,578
TOTAL FIRST ASYLUM:	32,869	1,545,882	432,143	518,524	125,707	42,179	14,857	384,948
RPCS								
Bataan—Khmer	0	3,958	4,562	0	0	0	0	0
Bataan—Highlanders	0	2	82	0	0	0	0	0
Bataan—Lao	0	10,400	11,464	0	0	0	1	0
Bataan—Vietnamese	0	43,434	47,321	1,979	0	12	1	0
Bataan—ODP	330	0	0	0	0	0	0	0
Bataan—Prior to FY '87	0	166,790	158,905	5,087	0	0	138	0
SUBTOTAL Bataan/Philippines	330	224,584	222,334	7,066	0	12	140	0
SUBTOTAL Galang/Indonesia	0	55,501	50,651	4,669	0	0	146	0

	From Bangkok	From RPCs	IVs	NIVs	AmCits	Parolees		CUMULATIVE TO U.S. Through June 1996
Phanat Nikhom—Khmer	0	3,192	3,792	7	0	0	15	0
Phanat Nikhom—Highlanders	0	58,928	60,271	7	0	0	1,810	358
Phanat Nikhom—Lao	0	9,746	10,405	0	0	0	44	0
Phanat Nikhom—Vietnamese	0	3,402	2,240	0	0	0	21	0
Phanat Nikhom—Prior to FY '87	0	24,200	21,518	0	0	0	0	181
SUBTOTAL Phanat/Thailand	0	99,468	98,226	14	0	0	1,890	539
TOTAL RPCS:	330	379,553	371,211	11,749	0	0	1,902	825
VN Direct to U.S. in 1975	0	124,547	123,003	0	1,547	0	0	0
Other to U.S. in 1975	0	12,000	12,000	0	0	0	0	0
VN to China in 1977–79	0	263,000	0	263,000	0	0	0	0
GRAND TOTAL FIRST ASYLUM/RPCS:	33,199	1,945,429	938,357	793,273	127,254	44,081	15,682	384,948

----Fiscal Year 1996----

ODP	Refugees		IVs	Non-Refugees		Parolees	CUMULATIVE TO U.S. Through June 1996
	From Bangkok	From RPCs		NIVs	AmCits		
Family Reunification	727	–	6,129	400	–	1	186,829
Former USG Employees	18	–	22	–	–	8	4,567
Others	21	–	–	–	–	–	25,860
AmerAsian Children	–	–	170	–	–	–	20,706
AmerAsian Relatives	8	–	440	–	–	–	57,950
Former Political Prisoners	3,076	–	–	–	–	–	32,958
FPP Relatives	9,029	–	–	–	–	–	121,538
TOTAL ODP:	12,879	0	6,761	400	0	9	450,408

Source: U.S. Department of State.

Refugee Reports, U.S. Committee for Refugees, a project of the American Council for Nationalities Services (Nashville, Tenn.: 1996) required two authorizations: from the Vietnamese side, authorization to leave, and from the recipient country, authorization to immigrate. It was therefore very susceptible to political caprices on either side, and indeed ODP was often delayed, scaled down, or simply held hostage by one side or the other during the first ten years of operation following the 1979 agreement. Nevertheless, ODP provided safe passage for well over 100,000 Vietnamese during that period. ODP remained a much more humane and sensible alternative to clandestine escapes on land or by boat.

For the vast majority of Southeast Asians, however, clandestine escape was the only available means. In general, Laotians and Cambodians crossed the Thai border and the Vietnamese left by boat to a country of asylum. By the end of the federal fiscal year 1995, well over two million Southeast Asian refugees had reached a country of first asylum. The number of people who perished during these flights will never be known with any level of certainty; they disappeared in the jungles or at sea.

First asylum countries provided shelter and basic needs with funds from the United Nations and contributions from other developed nations. Under the best of circumstances, which almost never happened, refugee camps in these countries epitomized the welfare state that can cause debilitating dependence if continued too long. More frequently, however, most governments resorted to mistreatment of refugees as a way to discourage more from coming. Thus, in 1981, for example, Thailand "pushed back" Cambodian refugees across the border into a mine field; in 1983 Hong Kong established the "closed camp" system, a jail-like facility with little service beyond subsistence and no opportunity for resettlement elsewhere; in 1988, Thailand, Malaysia, and Indonesia pushed boats back out to sea often at imminent risk to the refugees; in 1989, the Comprehensive Action Plan provided for "screening" of eligible refugees in camps, thus creating additional opportunities for capricious and unfair treatment; and in more recent years, countries around Southeast Asia simply repatriated refugees back to Vietnam or Laos and closed the refugee camps. As of December 1996, all camps in Thailand, Malaysia, and Indonesia had been closed and refugees in those camps repatriated to Vietnam; only two countries still housed refugees: the Philippines where the intervention of the Catholic church obtained a temporary relief for some 1,600 refugees, and Hong Kong where the remaining 15,000 or so refugees were expected to be sent back by the time the People's Republic of China took over that territory in July 1997.

Of the over two million who made it to a country of first asylum, most were able to petition a third country to accept them as refugees. The potential recipient country set up interviews and from that point on, procedures varied from country to country as to eligibility criteria and preparation for resettlement. The United States, for example, sent admissible refugees to one of the three refugee processing centers for some cultural orientation and some rudimentary English instruction before sending them to this country for resettlement. Overall, the developed world has admitted nearly two million refugees worldwide with Australia, Canada, China, France, and Germany as major resettlement countries after the United States.

Similarities and Differences

Numbers and circumstances aside, Southeast Asians refugees in the United States make up a most varied community in virtually every aspect. Beyond the mere fact that they come from three different countries, thus speaking at least three different languages, Laos and Vietnam also contain linguistic minorities. The Hmong and Iu Mien, two primary hill tribes resettled in the United States, speak two different languages, from each other and from the mainstream "low land" Lao language. In Vietnam, overall a highly literate country with a literacy rate of about 85 percent, a number of Chinese ethnics still cannot read or write Vietnamese. In each country, there are sufficient numbers of adult illiterates in their own language, making English instruction a far more challenging task.

Their respective pasts also vary greatly. Cambodians have suffered the most—physically as well as psychologically—under the genocidal Khmer Rouge. It is safe to say that no Cambodian family, from the royal down to the poorest, was left untouched by tragedy during that brief but most brutal reign. Before the war, however, Cambodian life was easy, with ample food and a leisurely lifestyle. Many believe that the Khmer (another name for Cambodia) Empire peaked in the twelfth century as illustrated by its sophisticated waterworks and celebrated temples of Angkhor Wat. The Khmer empire, in its heyday, encompassed today's South Vietnam and the eastern part of Thailand.

Vietnam had been at war almost constantly since the 1930s, first against the French, then against the Japanese, then the Americans, and most recently against the Chinese and the Khmer Rouge, and almost always against each other. Instead of a genocide, Vietnam suffered a half century of steady hemorrhaging of its best and brightest youths.

Even Laos, though not completely embroiled in the recent wars, was not spared from the fighting. During the American phase of the Vietnam War, Laos provided cover for the Ho Chi Minh Trail, a major supply route, and the Hmong tribesmen were recruited, paid, and trained by the CIA (Central Intelligence Agency) to assist the American war effort.

Vietnam was the most urbanized of the three countries, although agriculture remains the backbone of all of them. Constant warfare in Vietnam had driven many people from the countryside to cities in search of some measure of security and jobs. In 1954, when the country was divided in two, nearly one million northerners moved south, and the majority of them were resettled on the outskirts of major towns. In Laos and Cambodia, by contrast, a more agricultural way of life prevailed until very near the end of the war. Thus people were still able to live on their lands and the hill tribes were still able to practice slash-and-burn farming.

Education levels also vary greatly. At the risk of gross generalization, it can be said that the great majority of Vietnamese were literate in their own language, having received some form of formal education. More recent surveys and estimates, as noted earlier, place the literacy rate in Vietnam at about 85 percent. This high literacy rate derives from two major factors: for centuries, education has been the esteemed vehicle out of poverty and the Vietnamese language, in modern times, had adopted a Roman alphabet that greatly simplified learning. The proportion goes down in Cambodia, and even further down in Laos, where some hill tribes did not have a written language until a few decades ago. Urbanization would most likely have played a role as well, at least to the extent that one would have to rely more on literacy to function in an urban setting.

The predominant—and in a sense unifying—religion in all three countries was Buddhism. Only in Vietnam was there a significant minority of Catholics and Protestants. Because Buddhism is not a highly structured religion, such as Christianity, Islam, or Judaism, most people keep their faith and beliefs to themselves rather than displaying them with outward or public practices and observations.

Because of the protracted war and the presence of several million Americans supporting the war effort, many Vietnamese had ties to the defeated regime as government officials, armed forces personnel, or support personnel for the Americans. Likewise, the Hmong in Laos who fought alongside the Americans during the war found themselves in the same situation. In Cambodia, unfortunately, most of the former government officials, the educated class, and the trained professionals were decimated by Pol Pot's Khmer Rouge.

After 1975, instead of a blood bath that many had feared, the communist regimes in Laos and Vietnam incarcerated the people from the "old regime" in re-education camps where they were usually put to hard labor during the day, indoctrinated at night, kept isolated from their families except for an annual or occasional visits, fed at subsistence levels, and generally mentally tortured. These people—estimated at about 100,000 in Vietnam—would qualify as political refugees under both UN and U.S. standards. But it took until September 1989 for the United States and Vietnam to agree on their fate. By this time, most had been released from re-education camps but were not allowed back into normal life; they were denied job opportunities and food rations. The United States agreed to accelerate these refugees' and their families' resettlement in the United States while Vietnam agreed to let them go.

Another vestige of the war with an even more direct link to the United States was the Amerasians, literally the common children of Vietnam and the United States. Estimated at between 7,000 and 15,000, these are the children that American servicemen fathered while serving in Vietnam and, in most cases, abandoned after returning home. The children, although most are now adults, and their mothers and often their siblings survived as best they could in a society that, for the most part, refused to accept them. After 1975, they also became the living reminders of the defeated enemy.

Congress passed a bill in 1982 giving preference to the admission of these children and their families, but it took until 1989 for them to begin to arrive in any significant numbers. They too are an integral part of the Southeast Asian community in the United States, and perhaps particularly in the United States where they can function as natural bridges.

Demographically, Southeast Asians in the United States are a comparatively young group with more than half of its population under 25 years old. By definition, the first generation of refugees and immigrants are survivors, and most have to start from scratch once they arrive in the United States. Consequently it comes as no surprise to anyone that they are motivated to work hard, to save, and to invest in their children. But the aging process is inevitable, and persons in their prime back in 1975 begin to take their place as "elders" in the community while the "children" of yesterday become young professionals and budding leaders.

By the same token, as the generations diverge, and their respective experiences of resettlement differ increasingly from one another, the gap between the "parents" and "children" generations also take on more defining characteristics. First and foremost of these differences is the war experience; the parent generation, who in 1996 would range in age from 45 to 70, grew up and made its mark in the war. Their children, generally under 30, had little taste of war and were educated primarily in the United States or at least in a postwar Southeast Asia. It is only logical, even inevitable for some, that many of the parent generation still look toward the past, toward their own youth, to what they had lost, to what could have been. Some even still dream of going back and retaking what they consider as "their" country and "their" government. Their children, however, who grew up in this country, who were exposed to the dynamics of democracy in this nation, and who, especially now, have the necessary training to engage fully in American life, look in the opposite direction: the future. To this generation, America is their future and the arena where they can excel. Vietnam, Laos, or Cambodia are in the backs of their minds, and perhaps many would like to find out more about these lands, even help them a little, but they are not connected by blood or by a defining experience anymore, as their parents are. The war, to them, is no more than a historical event, affecting their lives but not deciding for them who they should be and how they should behave.

In terms of permanent settlement, the initial policy of dispersal failed. Southeast Asians came from a tropical climate, so after the first snowy winter on the East Coast or in the upper Midwest, many refugee families packed up once again and headed to the South or West, following the sunshine. Equally important, the overwhelming need for community support—including the availability of familiar foodstuffs, customs, languages—drove Southeast Asians to California in particular where the already firmly established Asian American community welcomed them with open arms and provided immediate support. For the Vietnamese in particular, the explosive growth of the Silicon Valley in the 1970s and 1980s provided the biggest job opportunity for newcomers, unmatched by any government programs. By 1990, fully half of all Southeast Asians, including the majority of Hmong and Cambodians, were living in highly concentrated regions in the Golden State: Orange County and Los Angeles County to the South, the Bay Area to the North, and all along the Central Valley. Other states with substantial Southeast Asian populations include Washington, Texas, Minnesota, New York, and Massachusetts. With such a variety of backgrounds and differences in circumstances, it follows that the needs in the Southeast

Asian community are equally varied, and the next section focuses on some of the more critical ones.

Southeast Asians in the United States: Critical Issues

Issues that are of critical importance to Southeast Asians in America in the 1990s and beyond can be roughly separated into two categories: Issues particular to Southeast Asians, or adaptation issues, and those they share with other populations in this country, or maintenance issues. To be sure, the categories are only conceptualizing tools; they are neither mutually exclusive nor are they exhaustive.

Issues specific to Southeast Asians range from the obvious ones like language, acculturation, and employment to the more subtle ones like overcoming the traumas and regaining a sense of stability, of security, and of order, to name a few. The English language is a barrier for virtually all Southeast Asians who did not go to grade school in the United States. To the extent that one overcomes that barrier, by learning and practicing, the issue recedes. However, for many adult Southeast Asians, effective mastery of English remains an elusive goal. The chance of becoming fluent in English becomes even more unattainable for the small segment of the population who did not have any formal education, thus lacking even the fundamental building blocks of learning. Moreover, there are levels of fluency appropriate for different lines of work or positions in society; the level that enables a shopkeeper or a key-punch operator to function often is not adequate for a loan officer or a software engineer. It becomes therefore an almost unending process of self-improvement if one wants to progress and move up.

But far more intractable than the language issue is acculturation, in the sense that one not only understands what surrounds him or her, but also that one can take part and function well in that environment. In this context, newcomers essentially must be able to build their own support networks and to be at ease enough in whatever circumstances, from lunch counter to the board room, from the ball park to the church pew, to be able to function effectively.

If language is the prerequisite for basic communication, the social skills are the prerequisites of acculturation. Sometimes, these are just basic, elementary skills such as the ability to strike up new friendships, to express displeasures, to make oneself heard, to cite a few examples. But at times these skills can also be quite sophisticated and complex, such as playing the corporate culture and dynamics to one's own advantage, or competing openly, successfully, in the electoral process.

By this standard, Southeast Asians still have a long way to go before achieving acculturation. Witness a few situations. In schools, many Southeast Asian students do excel academically, but often glossed over is the fact that many of the same students are quite isolated from the rest of the student body, unable to cross over the invisible walls that separate them from the others. Many only socialize with fellow Southeast Asians. When does a support network become a crutch? How does a student balance his or her need for a secured identity and the need to participate fully in school activities, to build up new friendships that will carry them into their future?

In the workplace, few Southeast Asians have developed lasting, trusting friendships with their coworkers. Although many have managed to move up to skilled professional levels, it is still rare for Southeast Asian professionals to function as effectively in social settings as in their respective assigned duties or to perform public duties as easily as their secluded tasks.

At first glance, it may seem irrelevant. The type of "as long as I can do my job well, it will be recognized" mentality still prevails. Unfortunately, recognition seldom comes automatically, and in the workplace, racial stereotypes and outright prejudice are still a fact of life. Thus the deadly combination of corporate discrimination against minorities in general, on the one hand, and the newcomers' own inability to build allies, on the other, can and does lead to untold numbers of blocked career paths in the Asian and Southeast Asian communities. In the electronic industry Asians provide a disproportionate range of skills, from engineering and design to assembly and shipping, yet get very few leadership, decision-making positions. Their frustration has led to a very high incidence of job switches and the growth of small, privately owned firms. Many realized they could not win the corporate battle and opted for independence and more risk where they could exercise both skills and leadership.

In the political arena, Asians contribute a disproportionately high amount of money to candidates, yet very few get political appointments and fewer still get their issues seriously considered. As for elected positions, they are still few. For Southeast Asians, the situation is even bleaker; they are still well outside of the arena. By the end of 1996, there was still only one lonely Vietnamese American elected official in the United States, Councilman Tony Lam in the city of Westminster, California. There were talks and attempts at organizing Vietnamese and other Southeast Asian PACs (political action committees) in areas of high concentration of Southeast Asians; however, not one group has proved to be either effective or even lasting, while increasingly Southeast Asian leaders, professionals, and businesspeople look toward their homelands as lands of opportunities. It is therefore a long and difficult road ahead before Southeast Asians, and to a lesser extent other minorities, can truly achieve full acculturation, full integration.

In addition to language and acculturation, Southeast Asians in America also face many other collective and individual road blocks. On the collective side, the lack of a democratic tradition in all three countries becomes an impediment to efforts at organizing the community in the United States. From the lack of basic practices such as a tradition of open debate, open disagreement without becoming enemies, to more fundamental dynamics such as a peaceful, honorable way to retire the old leadership to make room for a new one, Southeast Asians often are unable to tolerate different points of view that can move the community forward.

Compounding the lack of a democratic tradition is the half century of warfare, of clandestine operation, of deceit and betrayal, and of corruption and incompetence that make many Southeast Asians unable to function in the broad daylight of public scrutiny. And without public scrutiny and debate, allegiance and loyalty by necessity are based on factors other than the intellectual or moral correctness of the cause. To this day, Southeast Asians, and Vietnamese in particular, tend to take things or people as serious only if they have a few layers of secrecy about them.

The protracted war left another legacy: distrust of one another and the facility with which one labels one's enemy. Factionalism and the "us versus them" mentality might have been necessary and useful to protect war secrets; in an open, democratic society they greatly hinder the efforts to integrate and build bridges with other people, including with former enemies. During colonial times, many people lost their lives after having been fingered as "collaborators" with the French or as "communists." Never mind if the proof was unconvincing or that many others also lost their lives on the mere suspicion of being a resistance fighter. Today, being labeled as " communist" carries the same stigma and danger. Unfortunately, the tradition is alive and well in the United States and at times still practiced with gusto, at least within the Vietnamese community.

In the last twenty years, for instance, one can count at least three major efforts to organize the Vietnamese community nationally: first was the resistance movement in the early 1980s to raise funds, train an army, and retake the country from the communists; then came in the mid-1980s the foundation of the Vietnamese Congress to gain a national voice for the Viet-American community in the public arena; and most recently in the early 1990s, funded Vietnamese agencies formed a national network to support each other and to advocate on issues affecting the community.

The first movement, started by military officers at a time when the wounds were still fresh and most refugees still hoped one day to return to their former status, played skillfully on these sentiments and was a very successful fund-raising campaign for several years. With those funds, what the resistance movement provided was not an army trained to retake Vietnam but mostly misuse of funds and public bickerings among its leaders. The Vietnamese public grew tired of it, ended its financial support for the most part, and by the early 1990s, the resistance movement was but a hollow shell, with some moneymaking projects and a few propaganda organs.

The Vietnamese Congress, organized primarily by former government officials of the South Vietnamese Republic and typically based around Washington, D.C., aimed at unifying the Vietnamese voice in the United States, setting the Viet-American agenda for advocacy, and influencing the policy of the United States toward Vietnam. The leadership of the Congress, mostly older men who thought their former positions in the government still commanded respect and loyalty and who were by and large both inefficient and removed from the average working Vietnamese, proved to be no more adept at organizing than their former South Vietnamese government at governing. There are still national conventions and elections every two years, always in the summer in Washington, D.C., but the key leadership positions rotate strictly among the Vietnamese older men from inside the mental Beltway.

The third effort, NAVASA (National Association of Vietnamese American Service Agencies), was founded in 1993 by two key agencies in the field for some time: the Indochinese Resource Action Center (now SEARAC, for Southeast Asian), an advocacy group in Washington, D.C., and the Center for Southeast Asian Refugee Resettlement (now SEA Community Center), a grassroots direct service agency in the Bay Area. After the failure of the other two efforts, NAVASA's goal was much more modest: to gather people already active in community services together for a national network that is both democratic and action oriented. In its third year, NAVASA member agencies spent the better part of the year maneuvering to oust one of the founders, SEACC, from the board of directors because this agency openly promotes bridge building between the United States and Vietnam, its former enemy. The other founder, SEARAC, already has pulled out of the coalition and devoted some of its direct services to assist returning refugees in Vietnam. As of the end of 1996, some of the NAVASA board was still plotting a change in the bylaws to expel SEACC from the board at its next meeting. The future for NAVASA looked equally bleak.

Such are the vestiges and legacies of the half-a-century war in Vietnam. The most difficult challenges, once again, are not the ones from outside, but rather those from inside of each person. Perhaps it will take a few more generations of breathing liberty, of speaking the truth, and of operating in the broad daylight of democracy before Southeast Asians in America can leave this sad legacy behind.

On the individual side, let us first consider the issues that were caused by circumstances. The most obvious one is the assault on one's status, sense of dignity, sense of security, and the ability—however limited—to control one's own life and destiny. Becoming a refugee is, by definition, to lose everything: job, status, wealth, friends, even family members. Some may be replaceable, some are not, and as refugees, people know they will carry these physical and emotional scars for the rest of their lives. But they lost more than wealth and loved ones; they lost something deep inside themselves: the security and the ability to control their own lives to some extent. During the escape, they were at the mercy of traffickers, of pirates, of bandits, of troops from several governments, and these people acted swiftly and often mercilessly. In camps, they were at the mercy of the soldiers who ran the camps and at the mercy of the United Nations, which fed, clothed, and took care of them. When applying to a resettlement country, they were completely at the mercy of immigration officers. At any point in the many steps along the way, there were no reconsiderations, no appeals. It is this sense of hopelessness that they must overcome, and the only way to achieve this goal is to regain some sense that they are back in control of their own lives and, if nothing else, that they have finally found a place where they belong.

Depending on the specifics of the escape and conditions in camps, some Southeast Asians may have to recover from survivor's guilt; from atrocities inflicted on them, on their families, or merely witnessed; from rape, robbery, and beatings; and from starvation. And the list goes on. It will be a long time, if ever, before these refugees will not jump at the sound of a car backfiring, before some of them will forget the rapes and beatings suffered, or for that matter, that some of them will accept that earthquakes are only natural phenomena and not the expression of some supernatural discontent.

The same traumas of escape, and the ability to escape itself, often cause other types of dysfunctions within families as well. Many families are divided and separated;

many children are separated from their parents and must fend for themselves. Although separation is usually a burden, sometimes even being reunited causes other tensions no less serious; one of the spouses, for instance, has moved on with life beyond the moment they were separated and the mutual expectations are no longer valid. How can they restore harmony, mutual respect, and love? How can they avoid dwelling on the past traumas and avoid becoming bitter or paranoid?

Even under the best of circumstances—a rare, painless escape and resettlement, for example—external changes in the new society can cause serious disruptions in the family life of most refugees. Spousal roles often have to be readjusted where life requires two or more breadwinners instead of one. Difficulties in understanding, helping, and controlling one's own children can lead to abuse, bitterness, or breakup. Disparity between children's potential and parents' expectations can easily lead to alienation.

Southeast Asians also have their share of other generic problems, literally from the cradle to the grave. As is the case with many poor people, prenatal and neonatal care is not yet widely practiced. Many preventable diseases, particularly those associated with diet and lifestyle, still continue unabated and some such as heart disease and cancer are increasing.

As children grow older, many parents still lack adequate understanding of how the school system works to supervise and help their children. By the teenage years, many parents—and young people—have difficulty coping with the bewildering youth culture in this society, and sometimes their reactions range from excessive control to virtual neglect.

On the other end of the age spectrum, the romanticized myth of the Asian extended family begins to break down as well. Older Southeast Asians, even when they live with their children, are increasingly isolated: few can learn a new language, few can afford to drive, very few can find employment even if they are very motivated to work. During the daytime, when the adult children go to work and the grandchildren are at school, many elderly are virtual prisoners in their own home, unable even to answer the phone or the door. Where there are preschool-age grandchildren, often grandparents become built-in babysitters without pay. In the worst scenario, they may even be abused, mentally if not physically, and are often neglected by their own children.

It follows that among the Southeast Asian elderly population, depression is rampant, due in part to such external conditions and in part to their own sense of loss, of uselessness, of isolation, and of frustration. Sadly, they are often given perfunctory respect and symbolic filial duty. But, throughout the whole country, there are fewer than half a dozen programs specifically designed to assist the Southeast Asian elderly.

For women, the newfound freedom, educational opportunities, and economic potential—all liberating and empowering—can also become cause for family dysfunction and for personal dilemma. How would a Hmong girl, barely into puberty, resist the family pressures and traditions to be married, in order to finish high school? How to reconcile the need of a college graduate, who is still single, to live on her own with her parents' wish for her to live at home until marriage? How would a successful career woman switch from her assertive, logical attitude at work to the deferential behavior expected of her at home?

Juveniles fare no better. Many are lost between the two worlds. At home and in the community, they no longer have the complete command of the native language, customs, and culture, and often are looked at as having lost their roots. At school and in society at large, they may be able to communicate but without fully understanding the social context, the cultural implications, or the peer dynamics. In effect, they are neither here nor there, and they want to be in both places. The dropout rate among Southeast Asian students is increasing steadily, and more and more youths tangle with the law, from truancy to drugs, from car theft to robbery, and even murder. Even those who stay in school and are good students often find it a continuing personal trauma to maintain an apparent balance between the two worlds.

In this context, despite the outward signs of success in academia, in business, and soon, one hopes, in politics as well, the Southeast Asian community in the United States still has to overcome barrier after barrier, to resolve conflict after conflict, and to devise new strategies for this new environment.

A Strategy for Accelerated and Balanced Integration

After two decades of working with refugees from Southeast Asia, one can now conclude that it is possible for newcomers in the last part of the twentieth century to join the American mainstream much faster and much more effectively while still keeping a balanced identity. As one can readily see, this is a marked departure from the traditional "Americanization"—or what used to be erroneously called the "melting pot"—of immigrants and refugees, where normally the first generation stays out of the mainstream, labors hard, and invests in the second generation, who joins the professional ranks, and by the third generation, one becomes a monolingual, monocultural, homogenized "American."

It is now possible—and indeed indispensable and preferable—on the one hand to collapse the two- to three-generation process into one while on the other hand to develop a new model of a truly pluralistic "American," fit for the age of global economy and human cooperation. It is possible to expedite the integration process because circumstances have changed drastically in the last half of this century.

First and foremost among these changes are the achievements of the civil rights and related movements. Equal protection under the law and equal opportunity for all people regardless of race and sex open up whole new vistas that used to be off limits to newly arrived immigrants. Better housing, better employment, and better educational opportunities, in turn, promote a sense of belonging and dignity among the newcomers.

The second major change is the revised immigration law itself. The 1965 changes in the Immigration and Naturalization Act are still unrecognized as an important milestone in the development of American society. It abolished the racist Asian exclusion and the inherently self-perpetuating formula of admitting immigrants according to the existing percentage of each ethnic group in the country. It replaced those policies with the comparatively more egalitarian admission quotas: a maximum of 20,000 people per country per year under a ceiling of 180,000 per year for the Western Hemisphere and another 180,000 per year for the rest of the world. Beginning in 1968, when this law took effect, the United States as a society underwent a radical change in its demographic complexion. Only very preliminary data are beginning to trickle in and included among these is a faster integration of newcomers.

The third major change lies in the domestic and global economies. From the 1960s through the 1980s, the United States lost its predominance abroad while at home the economy shifted noticeably from production to service industries and new technologies developed at breakneck speed. Thus newcomers are no longer confined to a few labor-intensive sectors; because of the changes and their own education, they find themselves excelling in technological fields. It does not take much skill to deduce that a first-generation immigrant today, who happens to be an engineer in Silicon Valley or a medical researcher, would look at the United States—and at the same time be perceived by the rest of society—very differently from his or her counterparts of a couple of generations ago who toiled in fish houses, steel mills, or laundries.

These changes have not been easy and consistent; rather, the changes have taken place in spite of racism, exploitation, and sexual harassment of refugees. But, because of these major changes, Southeast Asians have more avenues within which to develop their potential.

The United States must evolve into a truly pluralistic society, and in this context, recently arrived refugees and immigrants—who happen to be more brown skinned than any other pigment, reflecting the world we live in—serve both as the catalyst and the vehicle toward this goal in the twenty-first century. One cannot repress a sense of wonder about the profound human instinct for improvement as well as about the momentous events of the five-year period from 1989 to 1995. Through these roller-coaster years we witnessed the Soviet withdrawal from Afghanistan; the Vietnamese withdrawal from Cambodia; the United States cutting off the Nicaraguan Contras, then invading Panama to impose its order; the euphoria of the Peking spring followed by the June massacre and the aftermath of repression; recognition of Tibet's struggle for independence; the Prague civilized revolution; the taking down of the Berlin Wall in Germany, the bloody and swift retribution in Rumania; the breakup of the Soviet empire and other subsequent social and political unrest within Russia; the almost universal acceptance of democracy; and so much more. The human race seems determined to redeem itself from the brink of self-annihilation and to make the world into a better place.

The basic needs for human happiness and dignity can be reduced to two simple components: food and freedom. The common threads running through virtually all people's movements in the last half century, from independent struggles to civil rights marches, from Tiananmen Square to Tibet, from Rhodesia to Rumania, from Pretoria to Prague, from Nicaragua to Sri Lanka, from the Baltic to Burma, from boat people to migrant workers, from Seoul to San Salvador, are either basic physical well-being or a sense of freedom, thus dignity, and often both. Food means not just a full stomach but also a sense of security about tomorrow, opportunities to improve one's economic situation, and a reasonable belief that one's children will live in an even better world. Freedom, likewise, prescribes not only individual liberty but also a democratic society, respect for human rights, and a process where citizens effect changes. In a real sense, people no longer live by bread alone, they also want to determine their lives, and collectively with others, their futures.

In this context of global evolution and interdependence, no country can afford to be an island or can mandate deference from the rest of the world. Rather, we depend on each other for materials, for markets, for the environment, for peace, and for travel, among other things. Conversely, successes or disasters in any part of the world can be instantly felt on a global scale. Witness, for example, Chernobyl, the Brazilian rain forest, Tiananmen Square, the Berlin Wall, elections in South Africa, or the peace efforts in the Middle East.

The United States, consequently, has to learn to deal with the rest of the world not as a commander but as a partner, more powerful to be sure, but inherently equal. The popularity of the English language, rock music, and blue jeans notwithstanding, the United States can no longer dictate the political regimes or the terms of trade as it used to do until very recently. Rather, it has to market its products, negotiate its terms like everyone else, and respect other people's self-determination. In other words, the United States has to persuade rather than prescribe, convince rather than conquer, and therefore, to be successful its people must be able to communicate with its partners. This is precisely where the melting pot model of assimilation must be discarded and replaced by a balanced integration approach. This delicate balance functions at least at two levels: between the old and the American cultures and among the three key aspects of modern life: social, economic, and political.

Certain portions of the Southeast Asian community, most notably in the San Francisco Bay Area, have deliberately adopted this model of accelerated and balanced integration. Field-tested for only a little over a decade, it is evidently still too early to render a verdict on its validity and usefulness. However, based on the early results, one may draw some preliminary conclusions. At the very least, this chapter can serve both as an interim report from the field by a community development practitioner as well as a restatement of the strategy. By necessity and in fairness to other practitioners who pursue alternative models, I must narrow the scope of this strategy to the work and ongoing experience I lead at the Southeast Asian Community Center, until August 1996 known as the Center for Southeast Asian Refugee Resettlement (the Center, or CSEARR).

Balanced Integration: A Case Study—
The Southeast Asian Community Center

Started in 1975 and incorporated in San Francisco, California, as a social service agency assisting newly arrived refugees, CSEARR has evolved over the years and expanded its services to meet the needs of a growing and diversified constituency. By 1985, CSEARR operated throughout the San Francisco Bay Area with offices in four adjacent counties, providing a nearly comprehensive spectrum of services, from greetings at airports when refugees first land to making business loans to help them start their own business enterprise. In between, the center teaches English, finds jobs, upgrades skills, translates, counsels, helps people become citizens, and generally troubleshoots on any issues involving refugees or Southeast Asians.

It was established as a community-based organization (CBO), a nonprofit corporation, and it continues to be led, managed, and staffed predominantly by former Southeast Asian refugees. Each year during the period prior to 1990, the center served approximately 10,000 clients with a staff of sixty. Three-quarters of the staff come to this country as refugees; in this sense we spring forth from the community, we empathize with the people we serve, and we understand and anticipate community needs.

As a community-based agency, the center's mission, philosophy, and ultimate goal is to integrate and empower the Southeast Asian community in the United States. The single guiding principle running through all of CSEARR's services and activities is the empowerment of the people it serves.

The center teaches English so newcomers can function in this society. It offers vocational training and employment services so fellow refugees can get back on their own feet financially. It provides a wide range of social services—from orientation to earthquake preparedness, from the reduction of smoking to AIDS prevention—so its served communities, young and old, male and female, can keep their bearings in this bewildering environment. It facilitates citizenship naturalization and voter registration so its fellow citizens can begin to regain some control of their own lives. It provides to business both technical assistance and small business loans so pioneer entrepreneurs can lay a solid economic foundation for themselves and the community. At the same time, the center also facilitates the maintenance of former languages and cultures so these new Americans and their children retain their roots, their identity, and their dignity as complete human beings.

We want both integration and identity for several reasons. First and more practical, being an ethnic minority with distinct skin tone and facial features, there is simply no way for Southeast Asians to become white Anglo-Saxons as the melting pot would like. We can accommodate and acculturate, but we can never assimilate. Second, the United States has changed and is well on its way to becoming a truly pluralistic society. Thus the ability to retain one's culture and language is fast becoming a source of pride rather than a cause for embarrassment. Third, it is an advantage for the United States—economically, politically, and diplomatically, to mention just a few areas—to have citizens who are multilingual and multicultural. Having statespersons, professionals, scientists, businesspeople, and artists who are fluent not only in English but also in another language is a definite asset for this country in dealing with the rest of the world. And lastly, it is the right thing to do.

To reach this balance of integration and identity, we at the Southeast Asian Community Center pursue a three-pronged strategy: social services, economic and community development, and political participation. Essentially a social service agency, we also know that the center is only as stable and effective as the community is influential, thus this strategy.

Although social services are the fundamental requirement every community organization has to provide to its members, those same services are effective and lasting only if buttressed by a certain amount of political and economic weight. On the other hand, pure economic or political power, without ties to community services, runs the risk of losing its proper perspective and often ends up chasing power for its own sake. And naturally, political power does not exist in a vacuum without economic power, either as cause or effect, or both.

Firmly rooted in this strategy, the center has provided consistent quality and innovative social services to fellow Southeast Asians since 1975 and will continue to do so in the future. It has facilitated the establishment and development of over 800 small businesses owned and operated by Southeast Asians. It has formed a revolving loan fund to help nearly 100 businesses that have no access to standard capital. It has encouraged community people to become citizens, to register to vote and actually to vote, and increasingly to run for offices as well. Concurrently, it has hosted candidates' forums without endorsements and used communications media to educate the community on issues of importance. These economic and nonpartisan political activities will continue in the foreseeable future.

The social, economic, and political integration is thus only one side of the equation: to enable Southeast Asians in the United States to function effectively in this society. The other side of the equation—maintaining the former language, culture, identity—enables the same people to live happily and with dignity; they preserve the past to help maintain them for the future. As a by-product, the United States also benefits from their linguistic and cultural abilities; they enable this country to become a more effective power in the Pacific Basin if it can use these talents well.

As we enter the last three years of the millenium, no one among us is immune from the effects of the revolutionary changes taking place all around this planet, and few of us can remain unmoved by these events. It is hardly an overstatement any more to claim that all of us are taking some part in these momentous events and that we are, in effect, shaping a new human dynamic for the next century. These are heady days; a little scary, but full of hope.

It is in this context of global change that the very small Southeast Asian community in the United States intends to make its modest contribution to human development by replacing the melting pot assimilation model with a new strategy of accelerated and balanced integration. This model is applicable obviously to fellow ethnic minorities in the United States; in the global context of increasing ethnic identity, pride, and blurring of national boundaries, this model can be of use to all ethnic groups everywhere. Before 1989, such a strategy was deemed excessively optimistic, if not altogether unrealistic. In light of the ongoing fundamental changes in the way we think and behave, anyone who can live in only one culture and function in only one environment will be a person with a disability. An accelerated and balanced integration—not just by the minority community but also by the majority population of society—has become the best vehicle to brave the new world. This, in the end, is what community organizing is all about.

12

Community Development and Restoration: A Perspective and Case Study

ANTONIA PANTOJA AND WILHELMINA PERRY

Community development work in poor communities can no longer attend only to the problems of social need. The problems that beset these communities relate directly to their lack of access to capital and credit, legitimate employment opportunities, and essential physical resources (housing, health care, financial institutions) that improve the quality of life.

To interpret the need in any form other than economic is to continue engaging in paradigmatic frameworks that attribute poverty to moral or personal failure. No matter how sophisticated the analysis, even when cloaked in an understanding of minority status and economic exclusion, moral and personal themes continue to dominate the prevailing social policies and the development of social programs. Welfare reform, without access to economic opportunities and resources, comprise policies that continue to victimize and blame the poor.

Our work in Cubuy and Lomas, Puerto Rico, was undertaken with a strong foundation of the values and work methodology of our profession, but we also bring a political and economic analysis to our understanding of dysfunctional communities. When we began our work in community development practice in 1986, only a few functioning entities existed in the minority communities. Those that existed were well established and had functioned successfully from the days of the war on poverty. Today, community economic development corporations exist in both rural and urban areas throughout the United States, South and Central America, and Europe. The National Congress of Community Economic Development Corporations, based in Washington, D.C., boasts over two hundred members worldwide. In the National Conference of Business Incubators, the numbers of community-based economic development entities represent a significant percentage as compared to its beginning membership. The entrance of highly competent professionals from the world of finance into the field of community work has brought to community boards and community residents the knowledge of how economics works. Community organizations are sitting side by side in neighborhood, national, and world conferences to plan strategies for rebuilding their communities. They are learning how their monies can be used to build capital funds for development and how accumulated funds from union pensions, equity investors, and lending institutions can assist them in creating low-income housing, new industries, and neighborhood, and financial lending and saving institutions. At this time large intermediary institutions such as the Local Initative Support Corporation (LISC), Housing Assistance Council (HAC), and many others function to gain access to these funds through grants and loans to community organizations.

When we review the literature of the 1960s relating to community economic development in minority communities, two major perspectives emerge: (1) those who favored black capitalism as an integrated component of mainstream capitalism, and (2) those who favored a complete rejection of capitalism, advocating a separatist perspective and the creation of an alternative and parallel economic system based on principles of nationalism. Today, the dichotomy of the two positions no longer exists. The techniques and principles of financial acquisition are now fully at the disposal of low-income community residents. The fundamental question, nonetheless, remains: money and credit access toward what goals and values, and guided by whom?

Social work professionals, on the front line of community work, have to become knowledgeable about the economic processes that convert natural and human resources into the goods and services that can create business development and employment opportunities, equity capital funds, and physical infrastructure development. Although we may not be able to do all the work needed, we remain a profession vital to the processes of development, and the challenge is before us. After ten years of functioning, Producir, Inc. has become a fully developed and internationally recognized rural community economic development corporation. Its philosophy and model of work has been presented in Cuba, Colombia, South America, and throughout the United States. Invitations have been received from foundations in Colombia and Chile. Producir work with our community farmers has been highlighted in a special CNN documentary, *Field of Dreams* (1996).

The basic philosophy and objectives of the corporation have not changed, but the model of work has been altered. Our work now focuses exclusively on economic development activities, and our organizational structure and staffing reflect the changes necessary to sustain this direction. Social welfare–related programs that were initially developed by Producir in support of the economic development component have now been delegated to newly organized community entities or remain only as they support the major functions of our work. For example, a college preparation program for high school youth offers community service and work preparation as aspects of an effort to augment the future professional base of employees to sustain Producir's economic development work. A program of community health education activities provides a direct service for residents in a community where no medical care is available, but the community outreach also serves as an educational and promotional activity to direct residents to the new health facility that is being constructed by Producir. Producir no longer engages in vocational or continuing education activities. These programs are now administered by a privately operated vocational training institute. Producir works closely with the institute's administration to plan classes, recruit students, and ensure that the mission and values of community economic development are an integral part of the curriculum. All cultural programs, services to senior citizens, and family social services are undertaken by resident corporations that have received startup funds and technical assistance from Producir.

Our major activities currently focus on our work with local merchants who occupy rental locations in Producir's new business incubator, a 10,000-square-foot central facility, constructed, owned, and operated by the corporation. The business owners-residents of the facility, Plaza Taina, are strongly active partners in its management and promotion. A second major activity is our work with local growers. A worker-owner corporation of local residents produces, markets, and distributes hydroponically grown vegetables to local food chains. As a continuing member of the corporation, Producir provides technical assistance, access for farmers to a research and demonstration laboratory, and access to startup loans. Major economic development projects under construction are a community health facility and twenty units of low-income housing. Producir has been required to undertake all the necessary work to bring these projects to reality: locate funds, combining funds from several sources, develop and monitor the design processes, engage and supervise the construction and program responsibilities related to the projects, monitor the flow of cash, maintain fiscal records for accountability auditing, and maintain ongoing relationships with our residents to keep them informed and participating in our work.

The work of Producir continues to be sustained by monies from local and federal governments, private industry, foundations, and private donations. Sustaining funds for our basic operational budget continues to be a challenge. We share this situation with many other community economic development corporations that can actively attract construction funds in significant amounts, but these funds do not generally pay for administrative costs. To fulfill our commitments and philosophy for self-sufficiency, all of our projects must generate income that becomes unrestricted funds for Producir's operating budget. In 1996, Producir created four subsidiary for-profit corporations to purchase and retain four buildings in the metropolitan housing market that are primarily rented by low-income persons. A subsidiary of Producir owns and oversees the management of the 918 rental units. An "oversight fee" paid to the owners by the Department of Housing is allowing Producir to acquire unrestricted funds to build a trust fund that will bring a degree of financial stability to the corporation (see Figure 12.1 on page 224).

What Is Community? Definition

Community as Geographic Locale

In early January 1985, we arrived at our farm in Cubuy. Living in the hills and on a farm was entirely foreign to both of us. We quickly learned that two women living alone would need some help with the heavy work. John Luis, a young man in the area, was a member of a crew of handymen that helped us out. As custom requires, he became like a family member rather than simply a "stateside" handyman. He was unemployed and his prospects for a job were dismal. We began to involve him informally in sessions on entrepreneurship skills. Eventually, he asked whether his friends and family members could join him in these sessions. Before we could proceed to accept his suggestion, John Luis explained that we had to talk with his family and the parents of other youths who would be coming. We visited homes to introduce ourselves and explain the purpose of the youth sessions. Before long, the sessions expanded to formal Saturday morning meetings with eight of his relatives and friends.

Word spread around the small village that two "American" teachers from California had come to live in the area and that they were teaching the children. Within a week, John Luis brought a verbal invitation for us to present ourselves at a meeting of the local association. Not knowing what to expect, we arrived at the meeting fully equipped, carrying documentation as to who we were. We were seated in a small room opposite eight older gentlemen and one woman who never spoke throughout the meeting. The men were dressed in the true "jibaro" style. They wore sparkling clean and ironed "guayaberas." We introduced ourselves and they asked why we had come to their village. We spoke for several hours. At the end, fully satisfied, the association asked us to work with the entire community in solving its serious unemployment problem. We told the association that we needed a planning and action committee. They named a committee, immediately including some of those present and others whom they could notify. Our work began that night. Every Thursday evening we met to plan and create a model for action. As a result of our work, Producir, Inc., an economic and community development corporation, was legally incorporated in June 1986.

The two barrios are connected by custom, history, language, church affiliation, and family relationships. In spite of hardships, people wish to remain in the area. Our distance from the municipality (thirty minutes by car) binds us together as residents to handle and solve problems that we must face together, such as electricity blackouts, the shutoff of water, lack of public transportation, difficult and ill-kept

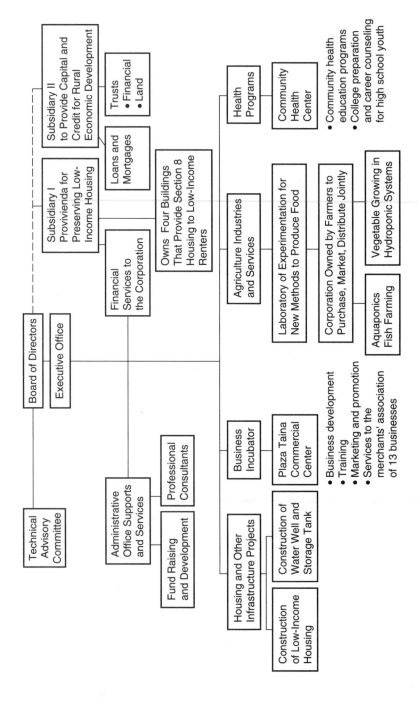

FIGURE 12.1   Producir, Inc. Model of Work (February, 1997)

roads, flooding caused by continuous rain, and lack of all the basic services that one takes for granted in an urban area.

A second type of community can be a group of people who have no physical location that they own or inhabit but are bound together by historical and/or contemporary circumstances; racial, religious, or national origins; and who share a common set of values, mutual expectations, and aspirations. In this typology of community there are many groups we consider reflective of the cultural pluralism movement. Among these groups are communities of ethnic groupings, homosexuals, women, seniors, the physically impaired, environmentalists, religious groups, and so on. Most of our work has been done in locality-based communities, and we will proceed from this information base. However, we maintain that our model of community development also has usefulness for emerging communities of special interests.

Many traditional sociologists, writers, and social observers will say that communities no longer exist. They characterize communities as inventions of primitive and prehistoric people. We are even taught that a desire to belong to a community is an outdated need not entertained by sophisticated people who are socially or physically mobile. They arrived at this conclusion by noting the following conditions:

- Neighborhoods (geographic entities) are no longer intact because modern people come and go, meeting their needs in different institutions of the total society.
- The community functions of mutual support, social control, socialization, and defense that were once met in local neighborhoods are now met for all people by the state through commonly shared and supported government agencies.
- Work, as the basic economic function that once held people together, is now performed wherever it is best for the production process and the market, and companies no longer feel it is necessary to be located where the workers live.

These statements serve three purposes: (1) they postulate the idea that the human person is an island unto herself or himself and that this condition of "aloneness" is the natural and preferred state; (2) they deny and negate the tenacity of the human community and the inventiveness of people to sustain themselves within social groupings that meet their needs; and (3) they promote the destructiveness of human communities by devaluing all forms that do not meet some traditional norm.

Why is it necessary to destroy the realities of communities and even to deny the concept of community? By doing so a process is set in motion that separates the individual from his or her group and standards of behavior, expectations, and support systems. Each person is rendered vulnerable and weak, and each person becomes a potential employee left to negotiate his or her own "contracts" in the marketplace. Each person who is not a member of the dominant group of the society becomes a potential absorber of the products and behavior of an "idealized" dominant culture. The processes that are the prerequisites and reasons for destroying the community are also the foundations for securing our society's inequitable functioning.

In a political environment, where individuals are constantly being disconnected from their communities, the dominant group in our society retains control. No equally strong community group or coalition of smaller communities ever effectively challenges its power base.[1]

Community: Model for Analysis

Over time, we have developed a model for analyzing community to provide an organized way of approaching community development work. We found it necessary to proceed in this way because we found in our work with learners that they held unexpressed ideas that communities were created by metaphysical processes, or they had never intellectually examined the origin of community. Their knowledge base of anthropology and sociology had been so completely fragmented or discarded that learners who were members of oppressed communities were not able to understand and accept that their people had originally made communities and had the power, capacities, and right to continuously search and re-create more perfect forms for their well-being and meeting their basic needs (see Figure 12.2).

Once learners acquired an understanding and acceptance of the right and need for change, it became necessary to have a guide (road map) by which analysis and action could occur within some rational, orderly, and sequential series of steps by which community restoration/development could occur.

Using a multidisciplinary knowledge base for our work, we have organized a coherent explanation as to how and why the human group invented community. Based on a perspective of the human person that is multidimensional, the model helps the community worker to understand how people, who are the creators of communities, can reconstruct them again and again when changes are required and/or desired for the continuing survival of the group. Our working model relates each human need to a system of institutions that were invented by people to fulfill their needs in a collective human system, that is, the community.

In our model of community development/restoration (of which parts are presented in this chapter) the most crucial and essential function of community is the function of production, distribution, and consumption.[2] This function is performed by a series of institutions related to human work that form the economic system of a community. Without this function and the systems that perform it, the human group cannot adequately survive.

Other functions of community were invented by humans to satisfy other needs and to support the economic function. These functions include the following:

- *The socialization function,* to teach the members of the community the accumulated knowledge (the science and technology, the history of the group, the language to communicate, the norms, rules and customs).
- *The social control function,* to create rules, laws, accepted behavior, and the punishments or rewards for violating or accepting these standards and the institutions that would create, enforce, and reward.

Dimensions:

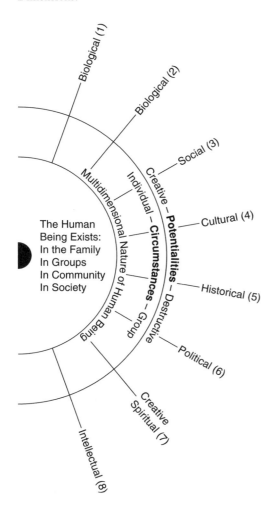

Basic Needs:

1. Food, water, shelter, cloth-ing, medicine, exercise, rest, recreation, work tools, ma-chines, sexual expression
2. Love, belonging, identity
3. To exist in groups and pat-terns of relationships, to lo-cate oneself in relation to others, to form groups and associations, to get help from others in time of emergency
4. To express ideas in symbols (language, art); to celebrate life in ceremonies, rituals, and festivals; to establish norms, values, and customs
5. To tell and record the deeds of the group and of individu-als; to study the past to eval-uate the present events
6. To use power to control, to attack, to defend, to protect, to create order through rules, laws, organizing systems
7. To depict the past, the present, and the future through pictorial forms, color, sound, words, acting, movement; to explain that which is not known
8. To find explanations, inter-connecting the nature of things: the environment, the elements, nature, and natural phenomena; to develop knowledge to control the el-ements of nature; to investi-gate and experiment

FIGURE 12.2   Nature of the Human Being: Her/His Dimensions and the Needs These Create

- *The social placement function,* to institute associations, groupings, and ceremo-nies that would help each member of the group to accept it and find a position in it, and to be accepted and be given recognition by the group.
- *The function of mutual support,* to develop an array of institutions and relation-ships that would ensure that each member of the group would be assisted and provided for in times and circumstances of emergency or extreme need.

- *The function of defense,* to create a manner through which the group and its members would be protected against attack and dangers from within the group and from outside the group.
- *The function of communication,* including mobility and expression, to create a common language and symbols (verbal, written, pictorial, and expression through sound), to create methods of moving in space, and methods of expression of ideas and expressions of the senses.

These functions and the institutions that perform them vary from one human community to another according to geographical, historical, cultural, and other circumstances that surround the particular group (see Table 12.1).

Communities Becoming Dysfunctional: Forces at Work

We do not believe that minority communities want to live in slums with dilapidated housing and drug-infested schools. People suffer these conditions because they become powerless and unable to correct the situations that destroy their well-being. We believe that our communities have been abandoned by the institutions to whom we have relinquished control for community services. Our children are not educated by the public schools. Our housing is inadequate or nonexistent. The police do not protect our neighborhoods. The churches in our neighborhoods preach and talk to one another. The public welfare services operate as instruments to define and promote morality and behavior. With all these circumstances, the tenacity and perseverance of the human community is clearly demonstrated in the retaining of their language, their families, their culture, the secure and enduring social affiliations, and mutual support systems.

We maintain that people who live in rural and urban communities function with kinship bonds, communication networks, and communal relationships. These are the functions that the larger society allows to exist or does not destroy in processes of institutional controls or cultural domination (internal neocolonialism). Dysfunctional internal processes are precipitated by the destruction of the "economizing function" that is primary and central to a community's stability. Once this function is destroyed, all other supportive functions become severely impaired or deteriorated. Without the right to work, to be productive, there can be no legitimate roles. Community members are rendered economically impotent and dependent with some subsequently internalizing this dependency and abandoning their rights and privileges to be in charge of their own communities.

Throughout history, all communities have developed the functions of community that we have discussed above. However, some communities have emphasized one function over another. We do not know why some communities expand, become aggressive, and use their power and technology to conquer and absorb others. It is as if the function of defense had been viciously twisted and turned into attack. Various

TABLE 12.1   List of Human Needs and the Systems and Institutions That Function to Satisfy Them

Dimension	Need	Systems of Institutions	Functions
Biological	• Food • Shelter • Water • Tools/Machines • Clothing • Medicine • Rest & Recreation	• Economic Systems	Production Distribution Consumption (Work—convert resources into goods & services)
Social Psychological Cultural	• Medicine • Sexual expression for pleasure and recreation • Patterns of relationships Verbal & nonverbal language	• Family System • Education System • Religious System • Linguistic System	Socialization Communication
Political	• Using controlling/destructive potentialities of power • Need for protection from inside and outside forces that would destroy, capture assets, resourc- es, people	• The State/Nation • Government System • Family System • Religious System • Judicial/Penal System • Legislative System • Police • Military System • Family System	Social Control Defense
Historical Cultural Psychological	• Tell and retell events and acts of heroic figures • Provide a way of locating one- self in a social context • Need for identity and belonging	• Civic Participation System • Historical Societies • Museum Associations • Clubs, Civic Organiza- tions • Social Organizations	Social Integration
Creative Imaginative	• Record in symbolic and actual language life of group • Need to explain that which is not immediately known • Need to depict the world as it was, as it is, as it would be using common symbols and the senses	• Folk object festivals • Art disciplines • Religious institutions • Philosophical schools of thinking	
Intellectual	• Desire to find explanations, relationships, connections, answers about nature of things, events, environment and its elements • Use of knowledge to control the elements of nature	• Education System • Scientific & Technolog- ical System • Philosophical System	Socialization
Social Psychological Cultural	• Help to individual or group when established functions go wrong	• Social Welfare System • Religious System • Family System • Friends • Neighbors	Mutual Support

explanations can be found in literature and in the writings of other disciplines. To our knowledge, there is no empirical data to explain these activities. Therefore, we use world history and analysis as the basic sources for our understanding.

Historically, some human communities have attacked other communities to use their economic productivity, their territory and natural resources, their scientific and technological knowledge, or the labor-power of their people. Over time, through aggressive activities of conquest and annexation, these communities become nations with great accumulated wealth, large landed territory, slaves, armies, and low-paid workers. These nations acquire colonies to provide raw natural resources and to provide potential customers to purchase finished manufactured and processed goods and products. Members of the conquered and colonized communities have been brought into the metropolises of the great aggressive nation-empires to become part of the large numbers of unknowing and low-paid workers. These imported groups become the impoverished internal colonies that suffer great social problems.

Today and within the context of our national sphere, these destructive forces are institutionalized and sanctioned, not only through public policies, but through traditions, customs, and values taught in school to the general population. Minority group communities are denied their rights, access to information, and knowledge. They are denied access to protection of the law by denying them participation in the political processes that govern the country.

The dynamics and mechanisms of destruction are now less direct and obvious. Because they are covert, they are more difficult to identify. Their impact is so insidious that the victims are blamed for their own situation and, ultimately, they learn to blame themselves. We are at a time in the history of our minority communities when racial oppression, political and economic disenfranchisement, withdrawal of basic social supports and services, and internal crime threaten to destroy completely any solidifying ties that hold people together in the ghettos and barrios of the United States. The threat also applies to any solidarity that existed among different groups of disenfranchised and oppressed peoples. We know, however, that no matter how destroyed a community may appear to be, some members are willing to rebuild their lives and the life of their community to obtain a better situation for themselves and their families.

It is around these desires and expectations that community development and community restoration take root. In the United States during the 1960s and 1970s, as people grew in consciousness of the forces of destruction described above, they began to analyze how their communities become destroyed. It is within this analysis and learning that members acquired "conscientization" and that community building and development must take place.

The work of community development must begin with the worker and the community asking these questions:

• What functions of the community have been destroyed?
• Which are still functional and which are dysfunctional?

- What are the forces at work that destroy the community?
- What are the destructive forces emanating from the colonizing process?
- What are the destructive forces that are set in motion in the total society to keep colonized members of the community in a state of oppression?
- What are the forces that keep community members subjugated and colonized and in a state of subjugation and oppression?

Once these realities are understood, the rebuilding process can begin on solid ground.

What Makes an Effective Community Development Worker?

In our model of community development, no particular profession or discipline has a monopoly on the capacity to prepare people for the work. A community development worker can be a priest, an artist, a human service professional, a social worker, a planner, or an environmentalist, among others, but all these persons must share a philosophy, a political perspective, knowledge, and methodology for working with people. We do not think that one can be fully prepared in a formal educational institution because we do not believe the dominant society's institutions prepare people to value cultural differences—the ultimate desirability of a truly pluralistic society—nor are students taught to examine, analyze, and challenge the society's practices of inequality. We believe education in a formal institution so partializes and fragments knowledge that it is impossible to acquire the necessary conceptual lenses to approach the holistic work that community development requires.

The worker, as a member of the community, must bring enormous energy and personal resources that can be sustained only if she or he has a deep and unswerving commitment to eliminating circumstances of economic oppression and social injustice. The decision to work in community brings one face to face with the inconsistencies of our country's professed values and democratic principles and the actual practices of institutionalized inequality and injustice. It is frequently impossible to institutionalize the desired changes or the gains accomplished. The business of oppression and racism does not go away, and social change efforts can often be characterized as "one step forward, two steps back, and so forth."

Ultimately, in community development work, it is the members of that community who will decide who is with them and who is not. They choose whom they will work with and whom they want to work with them. Community residents make these choices based on their gut reactions, their ideological views of people, and the demonstrated and informed results of their work together.

"Conscientization" is an important process in our model of work. It means that the community development workers must bring a political perspective, knowledge, and skill that community members may not initially possess. This being the case, the community development worker must face the task with willingness and conviction to allow her or his knowledge, access, influence, and resources to be used by and in behalf of the community. This permits that the work will proceed on relationships based on equal rights. The partnership will result in services, resources, knowledge, skills, and increased rights becoming available to community members. What characteristics make for an effective community development worker and how does effectiveness come about? Obviously there is no litmus test that can be applied. Table 12.2 on pages 234–235 illustrates the knowledge base, skills, characteristics, and values that we consider necessary for an effective community development worker.

What Is Community Development and Restoration?[3]

New communities are constantly being created and existing communities are being adapted to survive in a changing, frequently hostile, environment. In the United States, people move in and out of several communities to meet multiple needs. Investments and affiliations vary, based on the needs being met, but most people still consider that they have a "home-base community." In fact, human beings have lived in communities throughout history because the human person cannot survive alone. We invented community because we need community.

People need each other to sustain activities that support life and ensure full development of the group and each of its members. Accumulated knowledge, from biology, sociology, psychology, history, the sciences of government and political relations and economics, to knowledge of art and religion, attests to and explains the fact that the human species survives, even though more powerful and physically better equipped forms of life have disappeared. This survival into full development can be traced to the human being's capacity to think (remember, analyze, synthesize, and integrate). Human groupings have used these capacities to provide for the basic needs of the group and its members using the human resources and resources of the environment in different ways according to the natural circumstances in which they find themselves. These differences are called culture.

In our community development restoration activities, we are intervening in an environment that has become destructive to people, and we are acting to influence, direct, and reshape energies, values, and work efforts toward a more desired functioning. We use community development/restoration with a specific meaning. It has philosophy, a definition of goals and products. It also has a methodology consistent with the philosophy and an evaluatory process from the beginning to the end.

We emphasize development to reinforce the participatory and educational goals involved in community work. Community development, as we define it, rests heavily on a series of developmental processes, but the tangible, concrete end-product goals are equally significant, and development/restoration cannot take place unless process and product goals are equally valued and operationalized. Community development requires timely realized products that have both short- and long-term accomplishments and impact. We are talking about products and outcomes that include worker/owner business ventures, cooperatives owned by the community members, cultural activities, and celebrations reinforcing and securing the group's history and values, and social service delivery systems cooperatively or collectively owned by community members.

In our definition, community development/restoration is the work with people through which members of an economically dependent and politically disenfranchised community accept to work together with the following purposes:

1. To understand the forces and processes that have made them and keep them in their state of poverty and dependency.
2. To mobilize and organize their internal strength, as represented in political awareness, a plan of action based on information, knowledge, skills, and financial resources.
3. To eradicate from individuals and from group culture the mythology that makes them participants in their own dependency and powerlessness.
4. To act in restoring or developing new functions that a community performs for the well-being of its members—starting with the economizing function.

Development involves people working in a process of understanding, acquiring skills and knowledge, and learning how to use new information that can change the circumstances of their lives. By development, we mean:

• A process of education that allows people to analyze and understand forces that create and sustain the integrity and conditions of exclusion for persons such as themselves.
• A process of education by which people come to know they possess strength, knowledge, and skills; they can access, value, and utilize their individual and collective resources as they can be integrated into community development goals.
• A process of education in which people are learning how their activities, values, fears, and behaviors allow them to be victimized.
• A process by which community members learn to defend themselves against forces, inside and outside their community, that would deny them their rights, resources, and privileges.

What Is Community Restoration and Development? Major Processes

We are presenting the model of practice included in this chapter as the guide for our current work. Through continuing practice and study, we expect to develop it to its fullest potential. The project and its work are done within the context of activities of a movement in which symbols, myth, campaign, and slogans are significant in involving people to secure their emotional investment as well as their commitments.

TABLE 12.2 What Characteristics Make for an Effective Community Development Worker?

Basic Formal and Preparatory Experiences	Basic Prerequisites, Philosophical and Political Worldviews	Basic Characteristics and Skill Base	Knowledge Base
• No particular prior profession and/or educational experience is required. • Positive experiences in which the person experiences herself/himself as a member of a community. • Direct experiences with discriminatory circumstances and/or practices of being excluded because of one's membership in a particular group. • A member (by birth and/or acceptance) of the community in which work is to be undertaken.	Believe that: • The human person should be viewed as a multidimensional person with multiple needs emanating from this nature. • People do not choose to live or survive alone. • The human community is an invention of people to meet current and changing human needs. • Culture groups differ in their environmental context and adaptation to environment, and it is around these adaptations and choices that cultures are made. • Intolerance for injustice and commitment to equal opportunities and access.	• Planning and management skills. • Communication skills. • Problem-solving skills. • Analytical and conceptual skills. • Flexibility. • Investigative and evaluative skills. • Creativity and inventiveness. • Curiosity and an exploratory approach to problem solving. • Self-confidence and integration as a person. • Ability to recognize, mobilize, and integrate resources within a work effort.	A working conceptual base that allows for an acceptance and willingness to use knowledge holistically from these areas: • Definitions, functions, and origins of community (anthropology). • Social systems functioning (organizational theory). • Basics of economic anthropology. • Political science (theories of community power, use of power in political arenas, origins, functions, processes of social policy, analyzing social and group interaction policy arenas). • Social change theories, strategies, community organizing models (social work). • Leadership development theories.

- Sufficient skills in working with people who have gained knowledge, confidence in their interactional skills and their abilities to understand and influence others.

- Sufficient skills in working with people to have understanding and appreciation of others, their personal differences, cultural context, and behaviors as members of groups and communities.

- Physical strength and endurance to work hard and long hours.

- Human persons cannot realize maximum productivity and fulfillment living alone and/or isolated from relationships with others.

- Human groups that identify themselves as communities have the right to define their needs and create/control the systems necessary to meet these needs.

- The human community is made dysfunctional when its needs are controlled from the outside.

- A community that may appear to be in the process of dysfunction has the desire and internal capabilities for restoration/redevelopment processes.

- Ability to work, within time constraints, to realize product and process goals.

- Ability to learn, acquire new knowledge, integrate, change and adapt to new ideas and information.

- Specific skills as may be required by particular program activities such as fund raising, entrepreneurial, business development.

- Patience and respect for a truly democratic way of working with others.

- One must become a continuous learner with an appreciation of the fact that learning can come from many sources.

- Perspectives on racism, feminism, and agism.

- Traditional and radical analysis of the development of the United States, particularly U.S. history as it relates to its colonies, internal and external.

- Definitions, manifestations, and uses of culture.

- Definitions and perspectives on cultural pluralism.

- Origins of language and relationship of language to culture.

- Comparative philosophies and definitions of the human person.

- Basic concepts and principles of logic and community.

- Sociology of knowledge.

- Perspectives on "creative education" and analytical thinking.

- Theories of role performance, social and group interaction.

We present the model in three phases and use our work in Producir, Inc., Cubuy and Lomas, Puerto Rico, to demonstrate our philosophy, principles, and methods of work. Figure 12.3 represents the community development model as it is operationalized in Producir, Inc. Each of the four organizational components was developed with the community functional areas in mind. Although each organizational component may carry aspects of all seven functions, each has a primary function.

- Phase I: Contract-making between community development worker and community.
- Phase II: Development of political awareness and the decolonization process within the action planning body.
- Phase III: Activities of community development/community restoration within the total community (see Table 12.3 on page 238).

Phase I: Contract-Making

This phase involves the introduction of the community development worker to the community. We prefer that the worker be a member of the community where the work is to take place. In our case, we are residents. In the case of students of the Graduate School,[4] all learners were residents who had to receive approval and endorsement from a community agency for themselves and the basic idea for an educational plan.

The important consideration is that the community development worker must have an invitation and an endorsement for the work to be done. The worker must be accepted as a member of the community with a compatible base of experiences, values, and affiliations. As a member of the community, he or she must have the freedom to work with residents who may be challenging the legitimacy of the existing power arrangements. The worker's decision to work in the community must be legitimized by (1) residents who suffer some problem that they wish to change, and (2) a group that makes a commitment for comprehensive work that will require their time and energies.

Community development work cannot be undertaken by agencies controlled by outside entities or heavily funded by government. Examples of these are: agencies heavily staffed by professionals whose commitments and interests are outside the area; agencies whose missions are rooted in social welfare programs; and agencies whose personnel or past activities/accomplishments are questioned by residents.

Once a decision is made by a worker and a community group to begin working together, it is necessary to have direct and clear discussions about the mutual responsibilities and expectations. At this time, decisions are made regarding objectives, organizational base, legal considerations, funding sources, manner of working, representative nature for the working group, accountability, and communication with the community.

Board of Directors

Friends of *Producir*

Objectives: (1) provide fiscal, secretarial, and office support to the corporation, (2) assist business operations in developing systems for fiscal, documentation, reporting, monitoring, and analysis, (3) undertake quality control, record keeping, and communications.

Fiscal Systems and Office Services

Board of Community Savings and Credit Cooperative

Community Savings and Credit Cooperative

Objectives

1. Stimulate value of collective capital accumulation among residents.
2. Create capital base using local funds.
3. Identify, mobilize, and utilize outside financial resources to augment capital base.
4. Organize other cooperative departments to meet community needs.

Business Incubator

Objectives

1. Stimulate entrepreneurial activities.
2. Identify and mobilize the use of human and natural resources for economizing activities.
3. Develop and organize an array of support resources for items 1 and 2.
4. Offer direct services for new and/or existing business activities that would create jobs; develop and implement an overall economic development plan for the area.
5. Policy advocacy.

Center for Creativity and Invention

Objectives

1. Strengthen sense of community and direct toward goals of production.
2. Mobilize all segments of community for self-help programs and activities.
3. Identify, recognize, and celebrate aspects of history, culture, language, and values.
4. Organize and assist residents to develop programs and services in expressed areas of need/desire.
5. Policy advocacy.

Functions

Production/Distribution/Consumption

Working Committees	Program	Special Projects	Program
• Education • Loan • Supervision	• Education for residents. • Education for member services: savings, loans, and other financial operations. • Create cooperative businesses that would meet community needs and create jobs.	• Development of local multiuse center • Association of growers • Young adults entrepreneurship	• Training/education for growers in hydroponics; new technologies. • Entrepreneurial programs for youth. • Business development programs/services using existing and/or new skills of residents. • Research/demonstration/resources mobilization (personnel, financial) around new ideas. • Feasibility and marketing surveys. • Loan packaging.

Functions

Socialization, social control, defense, mutual support, communication, and social integration

Special Projects	Services to Residents
• Institute for the family and the child (child care family services) • Youth rural leadership program • Newspaper • Oral history project • Christmas festival • Library • Senior project • Graduate student training • Special community education projects	• Community education organizing. • Program development with local groups. • Dissemination of information. • Community surveys. • Celebration of culture, history, values, and customs.

FIGURE 12.3   Community Development Model for Poducir, Inc.

TABLE 12.3   Major Phases in Community Development Work

	Phase I	Phase II	Phase III
OBJECTIVE AND MAJOR EMPHASES	*Contract-Making* • Have worker and community introduction; establish agreements for work together; form an action group (a committee or a corporation) • Establish consent; roles of mutuality; defining work mission and goals; expectations for products and outcomes	*Developing Political Awareness* • Secure the organizing body • Prepare a planning action committee for work to be undertaken • Assess the scope and parameters of work and make a plan of work • Legitimize activity in community • Refine and initiate a plan of work • Resource development • Collect information from inside/outside community	*Community Development Activities* • Implement a plan of action with goals and products • Organize and establish community participation beyond initial core group • Add other resources to extend the core group activity • Legitimize entity • Provide services and activities • Creation of new production and distribution ventures in cooperative modes • Establish or reopen service, cultural, educational, artistic institutions
PARTICIPANTS	• Community • Community development worker • Community group to undertake project	• Analysis of information circumstances re: community • Community	• Establish business entities through their delegates • Community through multiple strategies of services, board membership, community activities, task groups
MAJOR ACTIVITIES	• Community meetings for education and information • Identification and meeting with leadership	• Community development worker • Outside resources • Legally established entity for sponsoring work	• Community development worker • Community sponsoring entity • Other entities providing resources • New businesses open and producing • Services and activities
SOME BASIC PRODUCTS/ OUTCOMES	• Identifying members of a committee or corporation composed of community members • Preparing profiles of community from census data • Agreement to work together with a philosophy that works • Clearly stated objectives and products to be pursued • Statistical profile of community	• Community meetings for education and information • Data collection and analysis • Resource development • Communicating with community and establishing processes • Augmenting initial core with personnel, others • Assessment and analysis of functions of the community • A model for work and action • An action body informed and ready to involve others in implementing plan	• Community meetings for education and information • Board and sector planning committees, meetings, and projects • Resource development • Institution building and leadership development • A number of cooperative and worker/owner businesses • New buildings, housing, businesses, services, and recreation • Specific products and goals as indicated in action plan • Community mobilized and in action through multiple strategies to realize goals and objectives as planned

Phase II: Development of Political Awareness (Phases II and III May Occur Concurrently)

No work can be expected to be lasting or continued by community members unless they have grown in awareness and understanding, adopting additional skills of analyzing, planning, acting, and evaluating; secured a working relationship among themselves; and tested themselves and grown in understanding, commitment, and operationalizing the mission, goals, and objectives for the work.

In the case of Producir, this phase took almost a year of weekly and ongoing meetings with a core group of ten persons selected by the local social and civic association, and it still continues with board members, personnel, and residents. Meetings were held with us and with others who handled information, content, or skill areas. During this time, the group was also engaged in activities such as writing bylaws and articles of incorporation; obtaining legal incorporation and tax-exempt status, developmental and organizational structure; acquiring an office; securing a first grant; program planning; visiting government agencies; gaining friends and supporters; fighting takeovers by a larger established entity; hiring personnel; establishing program and service priorities; and developing a process for expanding the planning/action base by adding members to the board.

The development of political awareness involves the acquisition of various types of information and content that are internalized and applied in concrete activities and for concrete goals:

- Information from residents through community surveys, available from census data, municipal data, other surveys, and local leadership, and information that allows them to analyze the situation of their community.
- A community profile of resources, institutions, services, businesses, leadership base, organization groups, needs, deficiencies, and discussions that allow for an understanding of the social stratifications within and outside the community.
- Governmental planning and economic policies regarding the area (intentions, projections, plans, uses) and beyond that have consequences for the area and allow for controls over residents.
- Basic content and conceptual lenses for the community development work (definitions, origins, nature of community, nature of social problems, nature of power, concepts of leadership, systems theory, social policy formulation, nature of human person, and belief systems about people).
- Basic skill learning—planning, fund raising, data gathering, policy development and analysis, budgeting, grantsmanship, public presentation, analysis of information, and communication skills.
- The emphasis in this phase is always on the acquisition of information and skills; its analysis and decision making regarding the use of the information for policy, programs, and activities, and decisions regarding the methods to be used. In this process, analysis of information and experiences is constant for members to learn the difference between reality, gossip, and hearsay, individual experiences

as contrasted with group experiences, prior indoctrinations in contrast to newly acquired information; and community development goals in contrast to the development of social service programs and activities.

This phase must culminate with the community development worker's engaging the core group in deciding whether they wish to continue in this activity. Do they have the disposition, interest, time, and energy? Can they hold themselves accountable to the community? Do they view themselves and their lives as intimately connected to the well-being of the community? Can they risk and/or protect the interest of their community?

Phase III: Activities of Community Development and Community Restoration within the Total Community

This is the phase that has major characteristics of need assessment; augmenting the core base to include personnel and others; program planning/development; resource mobilization; setting in place the evaluating and feedback mechanism; securing the philosophy and methodology through the system; community organizing and educating for participation in the work; providing services and activities to residents; and legitimizing the entity and integrating new persons (personnel, consultants, residents, community groups).

In this model, Phase III is continuing and has no end as one usually sees in organizing models. Since the worker is a member of the community, there is no traditional exit process for her or him and there is no final transfer of power/control/authority from a professional worker to a community group. The central role of the worker is constantly shifting as new leadership constantly emerges through board membership, personnel, and neighborhood and/or community committees that assume different responsibilities for sustaining the philosophy and implementing the owner-worker work plans. New organizations, businesses, and worker-owner ventures and cooperatives are developed by residents. The board of the entity is expanding and changing with representation from various segments of the community. Because communities change, the activities of the work will change. Since the processes of destruction and deterioration are constants, the work of community development must be continuous.

After ten years of action in direct service in the practice of community economic development activities in a low-income rural community of Puerto Rico, we have worked with community residents and professionals of all disciplines as, together, Producir has planned and implemented strategies to improve the quality of life by making resources and opportunities for services and wealth accessible to residents. We have witnessed the field of community development change dramatically from an area of social service delivery to a highly technical one requiring knowledge of areas such as urban planning, housing, financing, economic development, financial planning, and the packaging and implementation of financial strategies from various funding sources (foundations, private and public sectors, utility companies, banks and other financial institutions, and financial and business intermediaries). In the process, we have learned and expanded our own knowledge, skills, conceptual frameworks, and practice skills to remain as the facilitators and monitors of a development process that ensures that values of community and human development are understood, respected, and implemented.

Today in a field where many professionals practice, it is our belief that the profession of social work has abandoned the lead position that it once had in community development in favor of new professionals who bring a broader conceptual and knowledge base to analyzing and acting upon the circumstances impinging on low-income communities. Our reticence to enter the field of economic and community development can be understood in terms of the high priority given by the profession to the learning of clinical individual practice skills. Many of us working in the area of community economic development are making significant contributions as conceptualizers of the intervention strategies, the actors who facilitate the integration of multidisciplinary teams of workers, and the practitioners able to give guidance to the aspects of the community development model that relate to the mobilizing and education of residents to participate in the activities most vital to changing the realities of their lives. We can no longer claim any unique specialty in this area of work. We have only remained viable and effective in the larger context because we have moved beyond the traditional limits of our own profession. If we value, and we do after all these years of experience, the values, understanding of process, human development and resident participation, we have before us the opportunity to enrich our educational institutions and expand our field practices to provide students interested in the field of community development the opportunity to enter and remain effective in the partnerships of new professional work teams that are defining and shaping the future opportunities for low-income communities.

Notes

1. This point of view was developed in the 1950s, when progressive social scientists renewed the concept of community and analyzed the circumstances under which a community can be destroyed (Joyce Lardner, Charles Hampden-Turner, Robert Blauner, Thomas Gosset, Franz Fanon, Albert Memmi, and others).

2. We wish to acknowledge the writings of Ronald Warren, *The Community in America;* Melville Herskovitz, *Economic Anthropology;* Frederick Engels, *The Origin of the Family, Private Property and the State,* with an Introduction by Eleanor Burke Leacock, among others, for assisting us in organizing our ideas on functions of community. These writings are listed in the references that follow.

3. We have added the concept of restoration to community development to recognize that, even under the most destroyed circumstances, many functions continue to exist.

4. Drs. Pantoja and Perry established a Graduate School for Community Development, in San Diego, California, that existed from 1974 to 1983.

References

Peter L. Berger and Thomas Lockman, *The Social Reconstruction of Reality* (Garden City, NY: Doubleday, 1966).

Robert Blauner, *Racial Oppression in America* (New York: Harper & Row, 1982).

John C. Boger and Judith W. Wegner, *Race, Poverty and American Cities* (Durham: University of North Carolina Press, 1993).

Frederick Engels, *The Origin of the Family, Private Property and the State,* Eleanor Burke Leacock, ed. (New York: International, 1972).

Paulo Freire, *Pedogogy of the Oppressed* (New York: Seabury Press, 1970).

Thomas S. Gossett, *RACE: The History of an Idea in America* (New York: Schocken Books, 1971).

Charles Hampden-Turner, *From Poverty to Dignity* (Garden City, NY: Anchor Press/Doubleday, 1975).

Jacquetta Hawkes and Sir Leonard Woolley, *History of Mankind, Cultural and Scientific Development, Vol. 1, Prehistory and the Beginnings of Civilization* (New York: Harper & Row, Publishers for UNESCO, 1963).

Melville J. Herskovitz, *Economic Anthropology, The Economic Life of Primitive Peoples* (New York: W. W. Norton, 1952).

Inter-American Development Bank, *Community Development Theory and Practice* (Mexico City, Round Table, Inter-American Development Bank, 1966).

Kim Klein, *Fundraising for Social Change,* 3rd ed. (Inverness, Calif.: Chardon Press, 1995).

Thomas S. Kuhn, *The Structure of Scientific Revolutions,* 2nd ed. (Chicago: University of Chicago Press, 1970).

Joyce A. Lardner, *The Death of White Sociology* (New York: Vintage Books, A Division of Random House, 1972).

Peter Medoff and Holly Sklar, *Streets of Hope* (Boston: South End Press, 1994).

Albert Memmi, *The Colonizer and the Colonized* (Boston: Beacon Press, 1967).

Albert Memmi, *The Dominated Man* (Boston: Beacon Press, 1971).

Michael Novak, *The Rise of the Unmeltable Ethnics* (New York: Macmillan, 1972).

Jose Ortega y Gasset, *The Revolt of the Masses* (New York: W. W. Norton, 1957).

Antonia Pantoja, Wilhelmina Perry, and Barbara Blourock, "Towards the Development of Theory: Cultural Pluralism Redefined," *Journal of Sociology and Social Welfare, 4* (September 1976), 125–146.

David Ricci, *Community Power and Democratic Theory* (New York: Random House, 1971).

Walter Rodney, *How Europe Underdeveloped Africa,* rev. ed. (Washington, D.C.: Howard University Press, 1981).

William K. Tabb, *The Political Economy of the Black Ghetto* (New York: W. W. Norton, 1970).

Ronald L. Warren, *The Community in America,* 2nd ed. (Chicago: Rand McNally, 1972).

Richard Weisskoff, *Factories and Food Stamps, The Puerto Rico Model of Development* (Baltimore: Johns Hopkins University Press, 1985).

13

Epilogue: The Twenty-First Century—Promise or Illusion?

FELIX G. RIVERA AND JOHN L. ERLICH

This chapter began with a reference to the Civil War in the last edition. We made the analogy that there is still a war going on in our streets—a war of poverty, racist violence, and cultural chauvinism in its most corrosive forms. The politically advantageous welfare reform legislation is another manifestation of how the powerful prey on the poor and disenfranchised by robbing communities of color of their legal immigration and welfare rights. We have two choices: we can ignore the problem and proceed with business as usual, or we can up the ante and take the war to the politicians, racists, and hate mongers with a passion not seen in our communities for years. Yes, we have reasons to be pessimistic, but we also have reasons to be optimistic. Can the downward spiral continue? Perhaps. Perhaps not. But for now, the statistics are daunting. In the April 1997 issue of *The Nation,* U.S. Senator Paul Wellstone from Minnesota wrote:

> Poor people are increasingly hemmed into poor neighborhoods, with everything that entails: poor schools, crime, violence, lack of accessible jobs and all the rest. The number of people living in concentrations of poverty (in neighborhoods of more than 40 percent poverty) went up by 75 percent from 1970 to 1980 and then doubled between 1980 and 1990. More than 10 million Americans (that constitutes about 4 million poor families) now

243

live in very-high-poverty neighborhoods. Minorities are poorer than the rest of Americans: 29.3 percent of African-Americans and 30.3 percent of Hispanics were classified as poor in 1995. Female-headed households are even poorer. 44.6 percent of the children who live in such families were poor in 1994, and almost half of all children who are poor live in female-headed households.[1]

There are signs of increased outrage throughout the country; there is more and more organizing going on. We no longer have the luxury of "safe" community organizing and less threatening social work practice in general.

The Continued Urban Centralization of Problems: Persisting Racial Inequality

Despite slow expansion in the suburbs, smaller towns, and rural areas, it is no accident that the changing and emerging communities described by our authors are largely an urban phenomenon. The inner cities within the inner cities continue to offer shelter to new arrivals mainly because of housing costs, employment possibilities, and ethnic support structures. It is these neo-*gemeinschaft* pockets that have been victimized by dramatically increasing poverty rates.[2] Census data demonstrates this long-term pattern in urban ghettos and barrios.[3] There was a 59 percent rise in poverty between 1969 and 1982, from 8 to 12.7 million. Poor inner-city African Americans increased by 74 percent, from 3.1 million in 1969 to 5.4 million in 1982.

Those people of color who have managed to escape the inner cities since the 1960s have been more than replaced by a wide variety of immigrant and migrant populations—refugees from China, Hong Kong, and Taiwan; those escaping political and economic oppression in South and Central America; Native Americans seeking employment off reservations; and the like. This "crystallization" of the underclass is supported by the secondary labor market and its underpaid service occupations and other menial employment.[4] Massey has also shown that, indeed, a majority of the most recent immigrants and refugees tend to come from Latin America and Asian countries.[5] Direct connections between home countries and inner cities are supported by bridges to family or group economic and social ties.

The economies of these Little Havanas, Manilas, and Hong Kongs help support the growth of inequality in the United States. Race is and continues to be the main determinant of inequality. Whites continue to be overrepresented in white-collar jobs. They are almost twice as likely as African Americans (1.71 times) and Latinos (1.97 times) to hold these kinds of jobs. Forty-seven percent of African Americans and 43 percent of Latinos work in the service sector, compared with only 27 percent of the white community.[6]

The research by Tienda also suggests the growing evidence of poverty among people of color.[7] She identifies three general conditions for the exclusion of people of color from the labor market: (1) limited access to education, (2) the role played by ascription (discrediting by blaming) as a method of placement that triggers racism and exclusion from participation in political, social, and economic systems, and (3) uneven distribution of opportunities for social advancement.

Education continues to be both a strength and weakness for communities of color. When compared to students from foreign countries, American students fare poorly. The Asian community has the largest number of students of color in higher education. This has created a backlash among universities, who wish to stem the tide of such large concentrations of Asian students. This was a major cause of the passing of California's Proposition 209, which attempts to make university admissions a "color blind" process.

Differences and Similarities

Differences in culture, language, economic, political, and social histories, and the disparate ways the communities of color see their agendas for the future present a picture of diversity. This section of the epilogue addresses the similarities and differences of the communities. The information is not intended to be used to ensure entry into communities or as "correct" organizing rhetoric but rather as a place for *beginning* to understand communities of color from a social change perspective. It would be presumptuous to assume that a thorough understanding of any culture can be garnered from a single exposition or book chapter.

We have adopted Teresa A. Sullivan's multipurpose model of distinctive populations and subpopulations as a design for their discussion.[8] Sullivan identified race, language of choice, time of arrival in the United States, national origin, and minority status as the most important variables affecting a group's identity with their attendant implications for community organizing.

Race.   Although the concept of race is useful in the discussion of different skin characteristics (African American, Asian, etc.), it does not endure in a more analytical look at these communities. For example, within the African American communities are all gradations of skin tone, from the darkest to the lightest color differentiation. An outsider looking at that community could find no easy skin-color label. The African American community does not have any unique surnames that can be used for purposes of identification. Many names that have descended through the years were given by masters during slavery. The phenomenon of taking Muslim names is an added variable that must be assessed, for it lends another important dimension to the identifiable characteristics of the group. The confusion this causes in those unaware may prove embarrassing, for there is a potential problem for mistaking one group for another by surname alone.

The issue of color as an indicator of race in the Asian community is further complicated by distinctive physiological characteristics. Again, the uninitiated may fail to distinguish among Japanese Americans, Chinese Americans, Pilipino Americans, Vietnamese, Cambodians, and Laotians. However, to members of those distinct culturally different groups, the uniquenesses are readily apparent. It is dangerous to think of the Asian community as monolithic. The chapter on the Southeast Asians, for example, addressed the problems faced by numerous ethnic enclaves within Vietnam, Cambodia, and Laos. Add skin hue to the picture, and we can see that there are too many differences to permit an assessment by race alone.

Native Americans are also difficult to identify by racial characteristics alone. Some have been mistaken for Latinos, some for Asians, and some for whites. Most Native Americans have "white" names, unless they, like many African Americans, go back to their tribal or ancestral names.

The Latino community presents an even more complex phenomenon. Because of Spanish colonization, the slave trade from Africa, and the mingling of Indian and Moorish blood, racial characteristics are not easily discerned. Add to this confusion the immigration in the nineteenth and twentieth centuries of Europeans to Latin America, and the problem becomes even more complicated. And if these racial characteristics were not confusing enough, we can add Asian racial features to many segments of the population. The Japanese Peruvian elected to the presidency of Peru, Alberto Fujimori, is an excellent example of this. Differences among the Latino population range from black to the fairest of individuals. Further complicating this reality is the use of surnames that may reflect Irish, German, Spanish, Italian, Chinese, or Japanese ancestry. The resulting racial mixture has led to some exotic names in an attempt to classify them, such as mulatto, mestizo, coyote, zambaiqo, lobno, chamiso, morisco, café con leche, and castizo.[9] In an attempt to unify the various Latin American racial groups, Vasconcelos identifies Latin Americans as belonging to "La Raza Cósmica."[10] Thus, despite national differences, language and cultural ethos serve to bind Latin Americans into one cosmic identity. However, when asked who they are, they do not answer "Latino." Rather, their answers reflect their cultural nationalism. They say they are "Cubano," "Chicano," "Salvadoreño," or Puerto Rican, even if they were born in New York or Los Angeles.

To summarize, community organizers must not lump cultural and ethnic groups by skin color alone. There are more differences than similarities when we address the issue of race. All too often organizers work from a stereotype of what they have been socialized to believe is a "typical" individual of color. That stereotype would soon be challenged when they met an African Cuban American whose last name is O'Reardon!

Language of Choice.   Another significant variable is language. This identifying characteristic was relatively simple until the heavy migrations from Southeast Asia began: communities of color generally spoke English or some variation, or else they spoke Spanish or some variation of it. However, as the model we presented in Chapter 1 indicates, the primary and secondary levels of intensity of contact make speaking in the communities' native language a must. The Southeast Asian community presents new and unique challenges to organizers; the many languages represented in this community are a challenge, even to individuals from that cultural group who have been somewhat removed from the community and have lost fluency in the language. As we also mentioned in Chapter 1, organizers must be sensitive to the dialect or parallel language spoken in that inner city. Some of the nuances of language may be class specific, thereby possibly offending someone from another class, or, what is accepted parlance in one community may be insulting or derogatory in another community with another group speaking the same language but coming from a different country. In sum, it behooves organizers to be aware of the language levels, nuances, idiomatic expressions, and accepted slang. Organizers using the accepted mode of speaking will be welcomed allies.

Time of Arrival in What Is Now the United States.   Time of entry into the United States is significant for both historical and strategic purposes. The implications of time of arrival are germane to issues of pride and self-esteem, citizenship, and of turf and proprietorship. Organizers need to understand the dynamics of time of arrival—both historical and contemporary—so as to better analyze the ethos and sense of community shared by specific communities of color and subgroups within that community.

Native Americans were in the United States long before white people arrived with their "Manifest Destiny." Most Indians lost everything, thereby making them total victims of an external oppressive force. The resultant loss of self-esteem is still experienced today as described in the chapter by Edwards and Egbert-Edwards. Organizers cannot join in the struggle with Native Americans without being sensitive to the issues surrounding their lost and current lands.

The Spanish influence on this country has also been significant. Mexicans living in the United States have felt a sense of proprietorship—many still believe white people are living illegally on their lands. The heavy influx of Latinos from Cuba and Central America in the last twenty years has caused a backlash in the dominant society; border crossings have become armed camps, and the Immigration and Naturalization Service has taken on an air of control beyond the mandate of its office. The backlash has been responsible, in part, for the demise of bilingual programs and schools of ethnic studies across the country. Families have been split up by the new immigration laws.

The Cuban experience has been markedly different; as political refugees, they have been victimized by the earlier refugees in places like Dade County, Florida. The 1980 Mariel immigrants received harsh treatment at the hands of the non-Hispanic population as well as some of the conservative Cuban Americans. The fact that many of these new arrivals were Afro-Cuban, male, and young cannot be ignored, for it has played a significant role in the racism and xenophobia they have experienced.

The Puerto Rican experience, as discussed by Morales in his chapter, is unique. Being part of a commonwealth has given Puerto Ricans citizenship, which permits them to move back and forth between the mainland and the island. Much of their rancor toward the United States has to do with what they see as preferential treatment toward many Cubans and Central Americans because their political refugee status has permitted these groups to obtain social services much more readily than the Puerto Ricans. Another difference is that Puerto Ricans, while experiencing a diaspora that began in the 1940s, are still being treated as second-class citizens decades after their arrival in the United States, whereas more recent arrivals have not had to put up with the intensity and length of discrimination suffered by them.

The Asian community's time of arrival in the United States also evokes strong feelings about preferential treatment of one group over another. The classic example, of course, was discussed by Murase in his chapter on the Japanese American experience in this country. Although the Japanese made their presence known after the Chinese immigrated to the West Coast, it was the Japanese Americans who were put in concentration camps during World War II, not the Chinese. This has led to deep resentment within both communities. Similarly, the Vietnamese friends of the U.S. government were given preferential treatment in resettlement and social services, again causing resentment in other Asian communities. However, the "boat people" have been victims of gross racism because they were not part of the preferred group and also because these newer arrivals were poor and therefore largely without connections.

The African American experience has been well documented. African Americans arrived in this country in the 1600s and have been treated as second-class citizens ever since. Their struggles for liberation and self-esteem have been embittered when they see new arrivals being given preferential treatment. The reparation settlements for the Japanese American community have come under attack by some African Americans; their position is that their experience of slavery for hundreds of years also makes them eligible for some kind of reparation.

Organizers cannot get involved with a community without knowing its history within the United States and the implications of that history for organizing strategies. The similarities and differences of the various communities' experiences are deeply ingrained in the degrees of their wishing to belong to the mainstream. The longer a group has been present in this country, the more reliance organizers can place on broader values, a sense of place and history, and the roles these groups can and should play within that continuum. The more recent arrivals require more education about those values and systems and an understanding of the double oppression they frequently experience—from inside their communities and outside. The implication of not having citizenship is critical. Experience has shown that people without citizenship are much more reluctant to involve themselves in a public struggle; they are more accepting of the injustices around them. And if that group entered the United States without papers, then it is safe to assume that their fears, negative self-esteem, and unwillingness to involve themselves in a struggle for self-determination and social justice will be greater than those of the other "documented" communities.

National Origin.   National origin is an important variable because, as we have stated several times, organizers cannot lump all Asians, Latin Americans, or African Americans into one monolithic group, assuming their oppressions are generally similar. Each country has its unique culture, history, political ethos, art forms, and social makeup. For example, one cannot assume that all Central Americans are the same. In comparing the neighboring countries of Costa Rica and Nicaragua, Harrison has pointed out a multitude of differences that one must recognize and respect.[11]

Asian communities with differing national origins have different languages, cultures, and social systems. Some of the histories of these countries have been intertwined since World War II with distrust and even hatred that have abated but little. Similarly, the Native American nations usually share English as a common language, but their tribal customs, languages, and traditions are unique, and successful organizers must get to know these differences.

Citizenship has not helped the quality of life experienced by African Americans and Puerto Ricans, who are born citizens of the United States. Their continued oppression and exploitation were well documented by Devore and Morales in their respective chapters. A brief observation is in order, however. Many individuals within these communities believe that programs benefiting other communities of color should be available to them—political refugee services, for example.

Minority Status.   The confusion between minority and ethnic status has not been resolved by social scientists, planners, or politicians. Traditional definitions of minorities as meaning "fewer than" is no longer valid in such large and diverse states as California, whose population will be over 50 percent people of color by the year 2000. Part of the problem with the term is that it has taken on a definition convenient for those interested in labeling communities of color as second-class citizens. To identify a group as belonging to an "ethnic" group means the community has specific uniqueness—culturally and often linguistically—that removes from it the stigma of being "second class" and places it with many mainstream groups in the country. Thus Italian, Irish, Jewish, and Polish neighborhoods are seen as "ethnic," whereas Chinese, Vietnamese, Nicaraguan, and other communities of color are perceived as "minority" neighborhoods. What distinguishes one from the other? What about African American communities? Those communities of recent arrivals are more "ethnically pure" vis-á-vis the traditional variables of culture and language. Yet the role played by *color* and *racial* differences feeds into the racist views of people who have low toleration for diversity.

This racism and xenophobia continue to be manifested in the media. Thus during the Gulf War all individuals who looked "Arab-like" were accused of being Iraqis and victimized by these stereotypes. Foreign accents, unfortunately, are tolerated only if they are western European in origin.

Imagine the reactions of people of color experiencing the racism and xenophobia of the United States for the first time. Latinos, if they are Afro-Cuban, Afro–Puerto Rican, or Mexicans or Central Americans of Indian descent, will not have favorable experiences. Similarly, white Puerto Ricans or other Latinos, who have never perceived themselves as minorities within their countries, are shocked when they come to the United States and are victimized by a society intolerant of their accents. What is especially difficult for organizers to understand about the Latino experience, for example, is the awareness that, notwithstanding the similar experiences of racism and exploitation, not all Latinos identify as minorities. Some are given that status; others are not.[12]

Cambodians, Vietnamese, Chinese, and other Asian groups continue to be perceived as minorities rather than ethnic groups. Nevertheless, whatever the perceptions of the dominant society, white Americans treat groups that have been the majority in their countries as second-class citizens in the United States. Consequences for these groups' treatment of ethnic subgroups from their own country should not be ignored.

The implications of minority status perceptions require that organizers be sensitive to the ethos, and possible stigma, shared by the community, especially with recent arrivals. The education that must take place hinges on the notion that these communities must be made to feel like "subjects" rather than "objects"; they must be aided to believe they can effect meaningful changes in their lives and for their communities. They must be helped to develop a sense of empowerment that leads to action.

An Agenda for the Twenty-First Century

When asked, communities of color are clear on what they need: jobs, housing, child care, economic revival of inner cities, better health and welfare systems, fair immigration laws, and education. What is less clear, however, are the strategies and tactics deemed most efficacious in achieving these goals.

Although the perceived needs of communities may be similar, some of their cultural and sociopolitical experiences have led to differences in the ways they have perceived their situations and ways to alleviate those problems. Political attitudes range from the extreme right to the extreme left. Some cultural nuances discourage public behavior, and other groups are hampered because so many of their communities are monolingual in languages other than English. Recent arrivals, especially the undocumented, are often reluctant to engage in self-help activities that may thrust them into the public arena. Further complications are presented by the generational differences found in these communities. With these caveats in mind, we will discuss strategies and tactics that seem the most viable. Based on the conditions described throughout this book, we have identified coalition building, increasing the communities' power base through political and legislative reform, working toward ending racism in all its manifestations, nurturing the growth of true cultural pluralism, using the Internet, and implications for social work.

Coalition Building

If disenfranchised communities are to be heard they need to join together, identify common concerns and issues, and present a united front to the world outside. Communities also need advocates, brokers, and leaders who are able to hold together diverse interests, agendas, and strategies for change.

The problem in coalition building arises when we try to identify the cadre responsible for forming the coalition and issues of self-determination within communities and their impact on coalitions. Historically, coalitions have had difficulty staying together, even when the group was homogeneous. Working with communities of color involves so many problems and so many generational, race, ethnic, and sociopolitical issues that keeping a coalition together seems almost impossible. Added to these problems are concerns over short- versus long-term issues.

Dluhy has identified some of the organizing principles of coalitions as consisting of the following: bread-and-butter, consciousness raising, networking, preassociation, prefederation, and presocial movement.[13] Depending on the rationale for forming the group, there are then structural, political, ideological, resource, staff, membership recruitment, and communications issues that need to be resolved. Thus organizers interested in forming and working with coalitions must be aware of the dynamics and difficulties in working with them at the various task levels. Given the nature of fear and caution in many communities of color, the process is always difficult.

To say that coalitions are best served with single, winnable, issues is too simple; the many concerns intrinsic to communities of color are such that isolating single issues around which to organize is too limiting. This may be the prudent way to organize, but experience has shown that when organizers are working with their communities, it is difficult to maintain a single focus at the expense of other concerns.

Roles for European American Organizers

Should white people work with communities of color through coalitions? As we pointed out in the introduction to the book, there have been instances in the history of social change in which organizers from outside the community have played specific and successful roles in bringing about meaningful change. What is different today, however, are the dynamics of the inner cities with their racial and ethnic representation. We need to refer to our Organizer's Contact Intensity and Influence model from Chapter 1. The organizer needs to determine the level of coalition building at which he or she is functioning. Simply stated, it is foolish for an organizer not from the community—racially, linguistically, or culturally—to attempt to gain its confidence and trust. The organizer will have that many strikes against her or him to start with. However, we are aware that there are always exceptions to the preference stated here. This is particularly the case in circumstances where the coalition includes white organizations or multicultural organizations (which include whites). In sum, the coalition-building task has to be undertaken within the unique context presented by the organizing challenge. Communities of color cannot afford to ignore progressive members of the dominant society; they have been with us for centuries, and their expertise and connections need to be encouraged and nurtured by our communities.

Politics and Legislative Reform

The 1990s have presented challenges to communities of color comparable to those of the civil rights drives of the 1960s. The steady erosion of civil rights since the Reagan administration has been swift and thorough. President George Bush's veto of the 1990 Civil Rights Act does not augur well for the years ahead. Moreover, the appointment of conservatives to the Supreme Court presents a challenge to communities of color for the next twenty-five years. Organizers working within these communities need to develop a shared vision of the struggles ahead and set limits to compromises that lead to partial victories. The unfulfilled (and fulfilled) Clinton agenda presents little new hope.

The gross distortion of societal resources into the hands of relatively few (and overwhelming white) people makes something of a mockery of often-repeated commitments to multiculturalism. It is no wonder that communities of color distrust political systems to provide them with their fair share of dollars when the top 1 percent of the population owns 48 percent of the country's financial wealth, and the bottom 80 percent owns but 6 percent.[12] In this long-standing pattern, from 1977 to 1987 for example, the top 10 percent saw its income rise by 24.4 percent while the bottom 10 percent saw its income fall by 10.5 percent. No amount of rhetoric about voluntarism can obscure the fact that the 1997 tax changes expand this inequity.

Racism

Communities of color must get together to fight for an end to racism, experienced by them from both outside the community and from other communities of color. Kenji Murase, in his chapter on Japanese Americans, warns against "exceptionalism": the white community defines a particular community of color as a model minority because it embraces the values of the white middle class. What follows, of course, is the conclusion that the other communities of color are lacking because they have a deficit that does not make them exceptional.

Finally, we caution against the malignancy of intracommunity racism. Several of our authors have addressed this sad dilemma. Organizers need to be prepared to deal with it, especially organizers from a different cultural and racial group who have gained the confidence of groups other than their own. According to Tienda,

> *The looming question for the 1990s revolves around the course of political participation of minority groups, and the viability of rainbow coalitions to provide economic and social concessions to minority constituencies, as well as protecting the gains achieved during the 1960s and early 1970s. But, in defining and striving for collective economic and social goals through "rainbow" political strategies, it is important to recognize that growing divisions within and between groups, with their deep class and regional underpinnings, almost certainly will undermine the formulation of collective*

minority agendas designed to improve the economic position of all people of color.[7]

The Uses of the Internet for Social Change

More and more, the Internet is becoming a valuable tool for community organizing. The information it contains may be useful for all segments of the organizing process, from fact finding to communicating with others across the country. Schwartz commented,

> *An Internet Activities Support Center would be a place where any citizen group in a community could turn to get help in accessing the Internet— including securing an Internet account, learning how to use software, training in Web page development—whatever they require on a one-stop shopping basis.*[14]

While the Internet may be regarded as rather academic and elitist, it is now ironically perceived as one of the more democratic forms of communication. No longer is it necessary to own a computer to take advantage of the Internet. Schools and libraries now make access to the Internet relatively easy and affordable. Web pages can be created with a modicum of skill and resources.

Social Work

How might social work respond more effectively to the challenges presented by communities of color and those wanting to work in them? The trends that have clearly emerged in the 1990s point to what many consider a sellout of the original mandates of the profession. Specht has taken a critical position against those who, he believes, have made an about-face from the original mission of the profession.[15] Specht points out the surveys by the National Association of Social Workers showing that 75 to 80 percent of U.S. social workers are committed to psychotherapy as a major form of intervention. He makes a passionate plea for social workers to get involved in building strong communities.

A research study published in *Social Work* underscores Specht's concerns. In answering the question "Is social work racist?" McMahon and Allen-Meares point out the disturbing trends in the social work literature from the 1980s.[6]

> *Social work, by adopting an individualistic approach, tends to blame the victim while ignoring the ecological perspective and person-in-environment configuration. It gives lip service to fighting conditions of poverty, institutional practices that perpetuate racism, and other conditions external to the individual.*

Writing about how social work deals with people of color, the authors state:

> [T]he surveyed literature, by adopting a generally individualistic approach, ignores societal conditions and the ecological perspective. Taken as a whole, as a decade's reflection on social work practice with minorities, the literature can be categorized as naive and superficial. It can devalue minority values by urging or expecting minority clients to accept and assimilate the social and family values of the majority society. [And] [s]ocial workers, therefore, must be more than sensitive or aware; they must be antiracist if there is not going to be a breach between their ideals and reality. Being antiracist implies transformative action to remove the conditions that oppress people. There is no neutral position. Not to take a stand is a political statement in itself because it reinforces the present institutional racism. Antiracist social work means both helping people reflect on their situation so that they can understand the oppressive system they are in and working with them to change it. It means a shift in practice to social activism and social change by working for racial equality and social justice.

Are schools of social work (and others who prepare students for the human services) responsible for offering training to those who want to work in these communities? We believe they are. Either they are, or the rhetoric of support for diversity, equality, and social justice needs to be made consistent with what is offered. Otherwise, to maintain the rhetoric without the community involvement is to perpetuate a fraud, a fraud born of promises all too often in the past honored by avoiding and sidestepping issues that bring the academic program into conflict with universities, powerful welfare programs, institutions, or governmental bodies.

For social work—educational programs and local units of the National Association of Social Workers—this means actively and aggressively recruiting students of color, building appropriate support structures so these students can be retained, and finding the scholarships, paid field work, and loan funding that will make it possible for these students to survive economically. Without a strong base of economic support, the commitment to diversity and community organization is mostly hot air. Indeed, social work's pretentious language without action to support it makes a caricature of what we say we believe and undermines our recruitment of minority students who truly want to serve their communities.

At the same time, much can be done to support research, especially ethnographically sound research, in communities of color. There is little reason why our assistance cannot be put at the service of ethnic enclaves as it has been put at the service of welfare departments, mental health agencies, and public schools.

The curricula of schools of social work can be greatly enriched by the documented experiences of both established and emerging communities of color. Indeed, this should be regarded as a marvelous opportunity for the growth and development of what we know about people of color, but in this case clearly adjusted to take account of local—state, city, and neighborhood—conditions.

The issue of multicultural education in schools of social work needs to be addressed. It is imperative that the curriculum be sensitive to the inclusion of materials on communities of color. Even though the Council on Social Work Education has an accreditation standard that requires such material in the curriculum, some schools of social work have made the material—watered down at best—an elective course. We believe the material must be taught in a required course, but also that it should be disseminated throughout the curriculum. In that way students will learn about communities of color from a total social work perspective, clearly needed in a society that is reluctant to pay attention to understanding and working with communities of color.

Given the limitations of the job market for organizers and community developers, academic programs need to reflect better not only full-time roles for organizers, but part-time (or "own time") opportunities as well. However, such efforts are no substitute or excuse for not vigorously seeking to develop employment opportunities for students of color (and white students) who want to help empower emerging and changing communities of color. An unscientific, but fairly comprehensive survey of a national sample of schools of social work suggests that such efforts on any major scale are virtually nonexistent. Surely, this arena has room for a great deal of work.

There is also a sense, as noted by a number of our authors, that many people of color continue to feel their interests are the last attended to, regardless of the economic situation. As one young Latino put it, "Upturn or downturn, somehow it's never our turn." The political conservatism that has extended from the 1980s into the late 1990s suggests an extension of a celebration of "diversity" with a lot of rhetoric, modest high-visibility programs (filled with "photo opportunities"), and very limited medium- and long-term financial commitments. Given the budgetary constraints that now appear likely to extend into the twenty-first century, especially in light of deficit reduction and health care and welfare reforms, this resource problem is not going to take care of itself. It would appear, then, that one part of the social work commitment to the maintenance of efforts in minority communities will involve working with those communities (and other local organizations, like the Urban League) to secure public and private external funding.

Certainly there will be roles for white people in these funding efforts. There will be, just as certainly, roles for white people in a variety of activities described in this book. However, white organizers must resist the tendency to slip, slide, or be pushed into inappropriate leadership roles, especially because they feel they can "do it better" or "do it more quickly." They must also resist the all-too-human temptation to allow their feelings to be hurt (and thus withdraw from the field of action) if they are regarded with suspicion or their commitment to a particular group of color seems denigrated. There are no "Friend of Minorities of Color" stripes to be won and then kept forever.

For organizers of color and white organizers, there will be no quick fix or easy answers. Coalitions may need to form, devolve, and come together again. But the rapid changes occurring in communities across the country demand sustained vigilance if anything approaching full advantage of the opportunities to back social work's posturing with action is to be taken.

Conclusion

The chapters of this book may be regarded as a challenge, an agenda for community organizers with a commitment to working with communities of color. Issues and problems have been identified, along with change experiences, and the strategies and tactics that may bring about meaningful change in the future.

Disenfranchised, abandoned, and underserved communities of color need organizers with an abiding commitment to helping these communities establish and reestablish dignity and opportunity. In this era of developing information superhighways, perhaps what is most urgently needed is a new vision, or a sense of new visions. If empowerment is to have any real meaning beyond rhetoric, communities of color must be supported in building and controlling their own visions of the future and be aided in the difficult struggle to realize those visions. But the challenge this represents should not be regarded as merely a local or regional phenomenon. As many of our authors have pointed out, the role and power of the United States in the world will be influenced by the nation's treatment of communities of color. These larger connections must not be neglected in a world where ancestral homes of people of color are becoming increasingly close to our everyday lives. This continuity can be actively supported to sustain a sense of pride and belonging or neglected and further contribute to a sense of discrimination and loss. If the promise of diversity is ever to become a reality, it must embrace a future in which participation in social change can lead toward empowerment and power, justice and self-respect.

Much has been said and written about building a bridge to the twenty-first century. If the power and prestige of the United States within an ever smaller geopolitical world is to be seen as equitable for all, then it behooves those in power to realize that their success in the new century will depend in part on how they treat communities of color. The price of continued neglect, no matter how benign, will be very high for us all.

Notes

1. Wellstone, Paul, "If Poverty Is the Question..." *The Nation* (April 14, 1997), p. 15.

2. U.S. Bureau of the Census, *Current Population Reports,* Series P-60, "Characteristics of the Population Below the Poverty Level, 1982" (Washington, D.C.: Government Printing Office, 1984).

3. Rivera, F. G., and Erlich, J. L., "Neogemeinschaft Minority Communities: Implications for Community Organization in the United States," *Community Development Journal,* 16 (October 1981): 189–200.

4. Wilson, William J., *The Truly Disadvantaged* (Chicago: University of Chicago Press, 1987).

5. Massey, D. S., "Dimensions of the New Immigration to the United States and the Prospects for Assimilation," *Annual Review of Sociology,* 7 (1981): 57–85.

6. McMahon, Anthony, and Allen-Meares, Paula, "Is Social Work Racist? A Content Analysis of Recent Literature," *Social Work* 37, no. 6 (November 1992): 533–539.

7. Tienda, Marta, "Race, Ethnicity and the Portrait on Inequality: Approaching the 1990s," *Sociological Spectrum,* 9 (1989): 23–52.

8. Sullivan, Teresa A. "A Democratic Portrait," in Pastora San Juan Cafferty and William C. McCready (eds.), *Hispanics in the United States: A New Social Agenda* (New Brunswick, NJ: Transaction Books, 1965).

9. Morner, Magnus, *La Mezcla de Razas en la Historia de America Latina* (Buenos Aires: Paidos, 1969). Translated by Jorge Piatigorsky as *Race Mixture in the History of Latin America* (London: Little, Brown, 1974).

10. Vasconcelos, José, *La Raza Cósmica,* 4th ed. (Mexico: Espasa-Calpe Mexicana, S. A., 1976).

11. Harrison, Lawrence E., *Underdevelopment Is a State of Mind* (Cambridge: Center for International Affairs, Harvard University & University Press of America, 1985).

12. Gary Wills, "A Tale of Two Cities," The New York Review of Books, October 3, 1996.

13. Dluhy, J. Milan, with the assistance of Sanford L. Kravitz, *Building Coalitions in the Human Services* (Newbury Park, CA: Sage, 1990), p. 25.

14. Schwartz, Edward, *Net Activism: How Citizens Use the Internet* (Sebastopol, CA: O'Reilly, 1996), p. 181.

15. Specht, Harry, *Unfaithful Angeles: How Social Work Abandoned Its Mission* (New York: Free Press, 1994).

Appendix

Nuts and Bolts of Effective Actions

ACTIONS: A group of people confronting a target with a list of demands for institutional change.

NUTS AND BOLTS OF ACTIONS

A. PREPARATION

1. Demands—specific, immediate, timely, winnable, and builds organization.
2. Target—person with the power to meet demands.
3. Research—gather intelligence on issues/handles, key players.
4. Reconnaissance/scouting—staging, route, doors, target's office, obstacles.
5. Media plan—before, during, after.
6. Plan agenda—spokesperson, confront target, testimonial, demands, timing.
7. Recruit members and supporters to attend. Have something for everyone to do.

B. DURING

1. Briefing—review of the plan for everyone.
2. Gather at staging area.
3. Receptionist—ask or walk by.
4. Security—ignore, divert, deceive, or other.
5. Confront target—letter/list of demands, yes or no sign, etc.
6. Leave with answers and victory!

CONTINGENCIES

1. Receptionist

   • Do you have an appointment?
   • Target is out of the office.
   • Target is too busy or in the middle of an important meeting.
   • Target will be out in a few minutes.

2. Security

   • Threatens to call the police.
   • Police actually come.
   • Police threaten arrest.

3. Responses from target

   • Meet with three representatives.
   • Answer tomorrow.
   • Why didn't you set up an appointment?
   • Makes new offer that sounds good.
   • Attacks organizer.

4. Power enhancers

C. AFTER

   1. Debrief immediately.
   2. Letter to target to get commitment in writing.
   3. Follow-up.

Organizing Strategy Chart

Goals	Organizational Considerations	Constituents	Target	Potential Allies	Potential Opponents	Tactics
1) List the long-term goals of your campaign 2) List the intermediate goals of your campaign. What constitutes a victory? What are your demands? How will your campaign: •Win concrete improvements in people's lives? •Give people a sense of their own power? •Alter the relations of power? 3) What are the short-term or partial victories you can win as steps toward your long-term goal?	1) List the resources that your organization brings to the campaign. Include: money, staff, facilities, reputation, media, etc. •What is the budget, including in-kind contributions, for this campaign? 2) List the specific ways in which you want your organization to be strengthened by this campaign. Fill in numbers for each: •Expand leadership group. •Increase experience of existing leadership. •Build membership base. •Expand into new constituencies. •Raise more money. 3. List the internal obstacles or problems to solve.	1) Who are the people most directly affected by the problem who can be recruited to become members of your organization? •What are their interests in this issue? •What do they gain if we win? •What risks are they taking? •Who do we have active in our organization? •What power do they have over the target? •What new communities do we want to do outreach to?	1) Primary targets: A target is always a person. It is never an institution or elected body. •Who has the power to give you what you want? •What power do you have over them? 2) Secondary targets: •Who has power over the primary target? •What power do you have over them?	1) Who cares about your issue enough to join in or help your organization? •What are their interests in the issue? •What power do they have over the target?	1) Who are your opponents? •What will your victory cost them? •What will they do/spend to fight you? •How strong are they? •How can you appeal to their self-interest? •How can you win them over to your side or at least keep them from fighting you?	*A specific activity, usually among a set of activities, that moves an organization toward its goals.* 1) For each target, list the tactics that each constituent group can best use to make its power felt. Tactics must be: •In context •Flexible and creative •Directed at a specific target •Make sense to the membership •Backed up by a specific form of power Tactics include: •Media events •Actions for information and demands •Public hearings •Strikes •Voter registration and voter education •Lawsuits •Accountability sessions •Elections •Negotiations

Campaigns

June 11, 1996
by Gary Delgado
Center for Third World Organizing

1. What are organizing campaigns?

Organizing campaigns are large-scale activities focusing on a specific issue and de-fining and exploiting that issue to benefit both individual people and their organization.

2. Why do a campaign? (generally)

a. *Common experience* provides people with a sense of their potential collective strength.

b. *Direct action* upsets and disrupts the dominant forces of everyday life and per-mits people to see the potential for different ways for the society to be orga-nized and their roles in that new or different society.

c. It develops a *concrete framework* from which people can collectively analyze their situation.

d. It is a forum for the *development of leadership* and a front on which soldiers become initiated into battle.

e. If well done, it can *win concessions* that will strengthen the hand of the orga-nization and redefine the organization's "power potential."

f. It can redefine and *expand your community* (people to be organized).

3. Characteristics of a campaign

a. *Clear time frame*—There are advantages to both short- and long term cam-paigns. Successful short campaigns build a group's sense of immediate but they may also give people a false sense of the way things work. Longer cam-paigns (six months to a year) are harder to sustain interest in and tend to cause organizer and member to burn out. Many times, however, they provide many more opportunities for development of in-depth analysis and leadership. The most important aspect of defining the campaign's time frame is laying out in-cremental steps for evaluation so that people can feel some sense of progress or movement even if they haven't reached their ultimate objective.

b. *Clear target or enemy*—The campaign should be clearly focused against some-one who has the power either to grant the organization's demands or to success-fully pressure those who do. The target may change during the campaign, but the campaign should always aim at specific people rather than amorphous bu-reaucracies or institutions.

c. *Definitive issues*—A campaign must be defined in a way that automatically suggests the solution. Vague "problems" cannot be the focus of a successful organizing campaign. For example, it is not possible to organize around "un-employment." It may be possible to organize around getting 100 jobs for com-munity residents at a construction site.

  d. *Definitive constituency*—Although you may be organizing in a specific geographic area, your issue will redefine the constituency that will be most active
  in the campaign. For instance, if you're organizing around school issues, parents with school-age children will probably be the driving force in the campaign. If the issue is rent control, renters will probably be more active than
  homeowners. It is important to note that even though people may be in the same
  general socioeconomic category, their interests on specific issues may vary. It
  will be the organizer's job to work with people to define the issue so that it
  appeals to the broadest possible constituency without compromising the integrity of the campaign.

  e. *Conflict and polarization*—A primary purpose of an organizing campaign is
  to educate people. Part of that education is to help people in the organized
  group see the similarities in their situations. Another part is to help them have
  a collective presence in dealing with their opponents so that they can understand the nature of the political and economic system. For example, all parents
  have a legal right to see their children's school records. However, when an individual requests access to the records, the request is frequently denied and
  they are humiliated for even asking. Getting parents to demand access to the
  records as a group and in person does two things: it builds their sense of collective strength and it clearly defines and de-legitimizes the function of the
  education bureaucrats.

4. Role of the organizer and leadership
  a. To understand as many dimensions of the problem as possible.
  b. To see how with an individual you can develop an approach from inside their
  experience.
  c. Validation of people's ideas.
  d. Develops trust between themselves and members of the organization.
  e. Tries to "nurture" and develop new leadership.

Questions to Ask in Planning a Campaign

June 11, 1996

1. UNDERSTANDING THE ISSUE
  • What is the problem we are trying to solve?
  • What is the root cause(s)?
  • What could we demand that would change the situation?

  Remember good issues criteria.
  • What is the political context of this problem?
  • Has this happened before? Where?
  • Has anyone else worked on this issue in other parts of the country?

- Who are the front-line decision makers?
- How would this issue fit into our group's long-range goals to redistribute power and resources?
- For whom and for what is the group being organized?
- How will this campaign build your organization and membership?

2. DEFINING GOALS

Goals are the things you want to accomplish through your campaign. Campaign goals specifically are called *demands;* your demands should be specific, clear, and get to the root(s) of the problem.

We have different levels of goals—immediate, medium, and long term. Each goal is like a step on a ladder, all finally leading to your big victory. Fighting for each goal as a piece of the campaign will give a chance to evaluate and for people to win some things on their way to the big one so they don't get discouraged. Each goal is a portion of the solution and the basis for your group's demands.

3. RESEARCH FOR HANDLES

A handle is a legal, moral, political, or economic point that shows why your position on the issue is the correct one. It helps your group get sympathy while showing how your target is lying, cheating, ignoring you, or just not doing his/her job. Campaign research is like detective work, not like school work—you are looking especially for things your organization can use to win its case.

4. CONSTITUENCY

- Who is most directly affected by this problem?
- Who do we have active in our organization?
- Who do we want to reach out to so they will join our organization?
- What is our history with those groups of people?
- What is their interest in this issue?
- How will we find, talk to, involve them in the organization?

5. ALLIES

- Who else has an interest in this issue and why?
- How could they help us win?
- What is our relationship with them—what do we stand to lose?
- How can we keep control of our campaign?
- Would this combination of people work well together or get bogged down in coalitions politics?

6. OPPONENTS

- Who is likely to oppose our efforts?
- What is their self-interest?
- How can we win them to our side or at least keep them quiet?

7. RESOURCES
- Money.
- Staff.
- Active members.
- Experience of leadership.
- Anger of your membership.
- Strength to disrupt the system.
- Ability to influence decision makers.
- Contacts with media.
- Alliances that could lead to other resources.

8. IDENTIFY TARGET(S)
- Who has the power to give us what we want?
- What structures does the target hide behind?
- Who can influence that person?
- Will the target go along or resist us?
- Where are the target's soft spots?
- What is the target's self-interest?
- Where do we find the target?

9. TACTICS
••• FUN •••
- Based on the resources you have or can get.
- Always in experience of your members, but also stepping up difficulty.
- Fresh and new so they don't get boring.
- Always out of the experience of your target.
- Opportunities for your membership to practice.
- Involves new people.
- Shows your power.
- Draws the target out.
- Keeps continual pressure on.
- Leads to your peak tactic.
- Fun and exciting to watch (for the media).

10. TIMELINE
- Plan around community schedules—weather, elections, start and end of school, holidays, etc.
- Plan around organizational schedule—vacations, other activities.
- Plan in 6–10 week chunks, or whatever your members can stick it out for.

11. ENDING A CAMPAIGN
If you win, there are several options:
- How can you publicize your victory?
- How can you use your victory to recruit members?
- Build your reputation, raise money?

If you lose, there are several options, too:
- Admit defeat and regroup for a different attack.
- Put the issue on the back burner and get to work on something else.
- File a lawsuit: this effectively takes the campaign out of your hands gracefully, puts it on the back burner, but doesn't completely admit defeat.

12. EVALUATION

Each tactic should have a purpose, and each step should have an evaluation. Here are some questions to ask:
- Did we meet our goals for the issue?
- Did we increase our membership?
- Were we successful at mobilizing and making the most of our supporters?
- Did we build the image of our organization that we wanted?
- How did the target try to divide or defeat us?
- Were we successful at countering the target's tactics?
- Did we stick to our strategy?

Doorknocking

June 10, 1996

Doorknocking Defined

Doorknocking is a give-and-take process of:

• *LISTENING*	"The kids haven't anywhere to play," may mean the issue is a park
• *PERSUADING*	"Of course, one person alone can't fight these big utilities, but if we have a group . . ." and
• *ASKING*	"Will you join? Will you come to the first meeting?"

Much must be accomplished in the span of only several minutes.

(Community Organizing Handbook #1 published by The Institute, 1976)

Doorknocking Sequence

1. Getting in the door...
- Introduce yourself and the organization and explain why you're at their door.
- Ask to come in to talk to them about problems in their neighborhood.

2. Breaking the ice...
- After sitting down, repeat your name and organization.
- Get their name, confirm address, get phone number; Write it down.
- Glance around. Ask or acknowledge something you observe.
- Ask them how long they've lived in the area/if they know their neighbors.

3. What makes them tick...
- Ask what they think are the major problems in their neighborhood.
- Ask if they would like to do something about these problems.
- Explain that the organization brings people together to work on issues such as those the members decide are a priority.

4. Ask a person to join...
- Explain the issue that members are working on. Ask if they support the issue.
- Explain what membership means. Use props (i.e., membership card).
- Ask the person if they would like to join others in their neighborhood in fighting these issues. Name other people on the block who joined.
- Ask them to become a member. Collect dues. Issue card.

5. Increase the commitment...
- Invite them to the next meeting or action.
- Ask for names of neighbors that may also want to join.
- Ask them to do something for the organization (doorknock neighbors, host housemeeting, volunteer in office).
- Congratulate, thank, flatter, acknowledge.

Doorknocking "What Ifs" and Tips

What if...	Then...
• **The television is on...**	Ask to turn it off or down.
• **A person is silent...**	Ask open-ended questions that require more than yes/no answers.
• **A person is too busy to talk to you...**	Tell them you will not take up a lot of their time (5 min.) or...ask them when is a better time to come back.
• **They ask a question you can't answer...**	Be honest, say you don't know, and tell them you will find out and let them know (call them back or visit them again!).

Tips

• **Don't hear no...**	Hesitation does not mean NO; give more information or ask more questions.
• **Get a yes or a no...**	Different ways so that they get a clear yes or no.
• **What to take...**	Flyers, doorknocking cards, membership cards, pencil, pen.
• **Be yourself...**	Keep an open mind, be friendly, be honest, make eye contact, HAVE FUN!!

Types of Power over Decision Maker

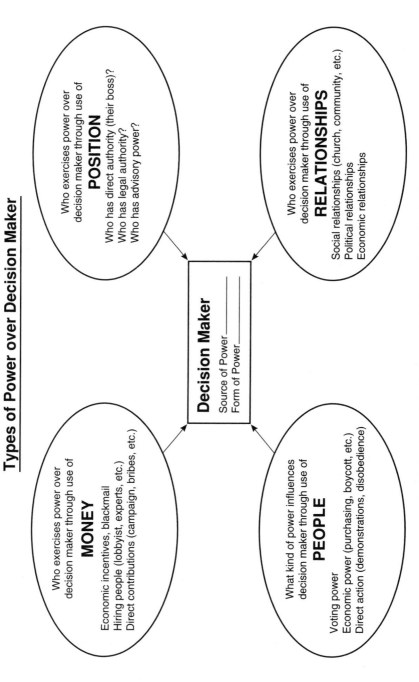

POSITION

Who exercises power over decision maker through use of

Who has direct authority (their boss)?
Who has legal authority?
Who has advisory power?

RELATIONSHIPS

Who exercises power over decision maker through use of

Social relationships (church, community, etc.)
Political relationships
Economic relationships

MONEY

Who exercises power over decision maker through use of

Economic incentives, blackmail
Hiring people (lobbyist, experts, etc.)
Direct contributions (campaign, bribes, etc.)

PEOPLE

What kind of power influences decision maker through use of

Voting power
Economic power (purchasing, boycott, etc.)
Direct action (demonstrations, disobedience)

Decision Maker
Source of Power_____
Form of Power_____

Chart Courtesy of The Environmental & Economic Justice Project

Developing Power Analysis of Communities, Constituencies, and Issues

June 10, 1996

Step 1: Identifying Major Forces and/or Players in Key Arenas

- Social power structures (religious/community institutions, organizations, individuals)
- Economic structures (businesses, industries, financial institutions)
- Political structures (formal government, private associations)

Step 2: Researching and Developing Profiles

- What information do we need to know?
- How do we go about getting it?

Step 3: Developing and Analyzing Power Analysis

- Who are the key forces?
- How is power being exercised?
- How can we build our power?
- How can we exercise it in the most effective way?

Chart Courtesy of The Environmental & Economic Justice Project

Developing a Profile of the Target/Decision Maker

June 10, 1996

1. What power does the decision maker have to meet your goal/demands? By what authority?
2. What is the decision maker's background and history?
3. What is the decision maker's position on your issue/goal? Why?
4. What is the decision maker's self-interest?
5. What is the decision maker's history on the issue?
6. Who is the decision maker's boss?
7. What/who is the decision maker's base of support?
8. Who are the decision maker's allies?
9. Who are the decision maker's opponents/enemies?
10. What other social forces influence the decision maker?

Power Analysis Case Study Form

Case Study for: _____ Location: _____

1. What is the ***problem*** you are trying to solve? _____
_____

2. Who is the ***cause*** of the problem? How/why? _____
_____

3. What is your ***long-term goal*** (solution to the problem)? _____
_____

4. What are your ***specific demands*** (incremental steps/victories toward the long-
term goal)?

   1. _____
   2. _____
   3. _____
   4. _____

5. Who is the ***decision maker*** who can meet your goal and/or demands? _____
_____

   • What is the decision maker's official title/job? _____
_____

   • What is the decision maker's position on the problem? Why? _____
_____
_____

   • What is the decision maker's power to meet your goals/demands? _____
_____

6. Who are the ***key opponents***?

Opponent 1: _____

   • What is their self-interest? _____

   • What kinds of power do they have?

      1. _____
      2. _____
      3. _____

- What are the key ways in which they influence and/or exercise power on the decision maker?

    1. _____

    2. _____

    3. _____

Opponent 2: _____

- What is their self-interest? _____

- What kinds of power do they have?

    1. _____

    2. _____

    3. _____

- What are the key ways in which they influence and/or exercise power over the decision maker?

    1. _____

    2. _____

    3. _____

Other Opponents:

Opponent	How they exercise power over decision maker
1.	
2.	
3.	

7. Who is the primary *organization* leading the fight? _____

_____

- Who is the organization's primary constituency (the main group of people involved)? _____

- How many people can the organization mobilize into action? _____

- What kinds of power does the organization have?

_____

_____

How has/does/can the organization exercise power over the decision maker?

- _____

- _____

- _____

8. Who are the key *allies* involved in the fight?

Ally	Primary Constituency	Kinds of power they bring to the battle
1.		
2.		
3.		

9. What kinds of *activities/actions* have you engaged in to get the decision maker to meet your demands and long-term goal?

- _____
- _____
- _____
- _____

Glossary of Selected Organizing Terms

Action   Collective activity that brings people with a common problem in direct confrontation with an individual who has the power or influence to solve the problem by meeting the demands of the group. Types of actions include going to where the targeted individual works, lives, hangs out, or worships, also known as "group field trips" or simply "paying a little visit"; and accountability sessions where the targeted individual is invited to a meeting to answer to a large group of angry people.

Alliance   Long-term relationship of two or more organizations built on a shared vision, politics, and action around a common set of issues.

Campaign   Set of collective activities planned and executed over a defined period of time whose purpose is to mobilize the support and resources necessary to win a victory for the organization.

Coalition   Short-term relationship of two or more organizations around a single issue or single common interest.

Constituency   Grouping of people whose self-interest would be served if they supported your organization or campaign.

Doorknocking   Technique of membership recruitment that relies on brief visits to people's homes, door to door.

Empowerment   Will and capacity to have control over the social, political, and economic forces that affect one's life.

Fund-raising   Asking for money to support organizing activities.

Goal   Broad statement that describes what a person or group wants to do and how they want to do it.

Handle   Legal, moral, political, or economic fact that stands in contrast to the position taken by the oppressors. It shows your position is fair, just, and legal and exposes a weakness of the opposition waiting to be exploited.

Holistic   Perceiving a thing or situation in its totality, rather than its parts.

Issue   Description of a problem that suggests its solution.

Leader   Member of an organization who demonstrates the ability to take initiative in analyzing problems and thinking through solutions, the loyalty and trust of other members in the organization (followers), and the commitment to be actively involved in the planning and execution of the campaigns.

Membership Organization   An organization that charges membership dues and works to achieve the goals of the membership.

Mission   Purpose for an organization's existence.

Objective   Specific statement that describes steps to achieving a goal that are timely, measurable, and quantifiable.

Problem   Something that people would like to see changed.

Research   Finding out information that will help you expose weaknesses in the positions taken by the opposition or information about the target, such as where they work, whom they know, and so on. Also known as *reconnaissance* or *intelligence gathering.*

Service Organization   An organization that provides a social service for people in the community and depends on community support, foundations, and so on, to survive.

Strategy   Overall plan to destabilize the position of the target that gives direction and focus to other elements of the campaign.

Target   Individual with the power to grant the organization its demands.

Task   The daily work (minute by minute) that must be engaged in to carry out an activity.

Value   The principles and ideals that tell the individual what is right and what is wrong, acceptable, or unacceptable.

Vision   An ideal state based on one's values that the person strives to bring into existence. A dream of what could be, rather than what is.

Index